In the Name of Love

Reading
WOMEN
Writing

a series edited by
Shari Benstock and Celeste Schenck

Reading Women Writing is dedicated to furthering international feminist debate. The series publishes books on all aspects of feminist theory and textual practice. *Reading Women Writing* especially welcomes books that address cultures, histories, and experiences beyond first-world academic boundaries. A full list of titles in the series appears at the end of this book.

IN THE
Name of Love

WOMEN, MASOCHISM,
AND THE GOTHIC

Michelle A. Massé

Cornell University Press

ITHACA AND LONDON

First published 1992 by Cornell University Press.

International Standard Book Number 0-8014-2616-2 (cloth)
International Standard Book Number 0-8014-9918-6 (paper)
Library of Congress Catalog Card Number 91-55552

Printed in the United States of America

*Librarians: Library of Congress cataloging information appears on the last page of
the book.*

⊗ The paper in this book meets the minimum requirements of the
American National Standard for Information Sciences—Permanence
of Paper for Printed Library Materials, ANSI Z39.48-1984.

To my parents,
Annette and Lucien Massé,
and in memory of my brother,
Lenard Massé, 1956–1977

Contents

Acknowledgments

This book has been a part of my personal and professional life for several years and accordingly is to no small degree a record of others' generosity.

I extend my loving thanks to Clarice Chauvin and Louise Soldani, who, in their very different ways, exemplified for an often obdurate undergraduate what it meant to be a teacher, a scholar, and a feminist. Roger Henkle, Claire Rosenfield, Robert Scholes, and Mark Spilka helped me to grapple with the theory of the novel as a graduate student. In patiently responding to my dissertation, "Narcissism and the Bildungsroman," Roger, Bob, and Mark helped me to articulate further the issues of genre, gender, and psychoanalysis that inform this study. Without Roger's care and enthusiasm, I might never have begun a dissertation, and, since those awkward years, he and Bob have been an unfailing source of friendship, support, and advice.

Roger has died since this book was accepted for publication. I grieve the loss of a dear friend and colleague but, in this context, am most aware of my debt as a student. I selfishly wish that Roger could have seen this book in print but know that in some crucial ways its appearance would have made little difference to him. Roger's wholehearted commitment to his many students was never based on the possibility that we might go on to become "somebodies": he always thought we already were. That commitment is a part of his legacy, one handed on to generations of new students because of Roger's generosity to their teachers.

Both Roger and Bob wrote an inordinate number of recommendations for grants with good humor and enthusiasm, as did Gale Carrithers, Jan Cohn, Anna Nardo, and James Olney. My gratitude for the indispensable gift of time they helped to give me is joined with my thanks to the National Endowment for the Humanities, the Newberry Library, the Monticello Foundation, and Louisiana State University's Council on Research.

Meticulous work—and astute commentary above and beyond the call of duty—by Scott Nelson (citations), Donna Perrault (index), and Mary Wyer (copyediting) helped this project make the transition from manuscript to book, as did suggestions from Bernhard Kendler, Carol Betsch, and Helene Maddux of Cornell University Press. I am also indebted to Margaret Atwood for permission to reprint quotations from her novel *Lady Oracle* (© 1976), to Gloria Naylor for permission to reprint quotations from her novel *Linden Hills* (© 1985), and to the University of Chicago Press for permission to use, as Chapter 1, a version of my article that appeared in *Signs: Journal of Women in Culture and Society* 15 (Summer 1989): 679–709.

Several colleagues who read this book in whole or in part have influenced my thinking about its focus and direction as well as specific critical issues. I am grateful to James Catano, John Fischer, Devon Hodges, Claudia Johnson, Deborah Kaplan, Neil Lazarus, and the evaluators of the manuscript for their time and critical acumen. In addition, I thank the students who forced me to clarify my discussion of psychoanalysis, feminism, and the Gothic, and who added their own insights to my understanding. Anna Nardo and Robin Roberts read each chapter in progress, and often in several versions. They have my gratitude for helping to keep this project on schedule, for numerous editorial and critical recommendations, and for their unstinting support.

Elmer Blistein, Ruth Oppenheim, and Keith and Rosmarie Waldrop contributed early and continuing encouragement. While I planned and wrote this book, Keith and Rosmarie, Viet Lazarus, and my sisters, Doris Massé and Rochelle White, gave me a limitless supply of warm praise, stern reminders, sympathy, and humor for which no acknowledgment is quite adequate.

My final acknowledgment is to James Catano for an incalculable combination of all of the above. Jim read drafts, listened to me, left me alone at other times, responded with aplomb to jokes about "Husbands and Horrors," and gave loving support to often contradictory demands. As critic, friend, and spouse, he has my thanks and my love.

MICHELLE A. MASSÉ

Baton Rouge, Louisiana

In the Name of Love

Introduction

As this project developed, two questions appeared regularly whenever I discussed the intersections of the Gothic novel, masochism, and feminism: "So—*are* they (the novels, the characters, women) masochistic?" and "Why *do* feminists still use Freud?" Posed with varying degrees of perspicacity and concern, these questions have forced me to clarify my own assumptions. To a large extent, this book is my response.

Interestingly, no one doubted that the Gothic novel was the appropriate genre through which to investigate masochism. My own interest in how specific psychoanalytic issues help to shape certain genres led me to focus on the Gothic precisely *because* it is a critical commonplace that the genre is "about" suffering women whose painful initiations provide some vague pleasure for women authors, characters, and readers. Any truism so widely accepted about what is often termed "female Gothic" decidedly called for a closer look.

At the same time, I was intrigued by the relationship between the genre's uncertain critical status (except in its sublime manifestations), its identification as a woman's genre, and its status as a mass-culture phenomenon that has endured for three centuries.[1] Major "mainstream" women authors from Charlotte Brontë and Jane Austen to

[1]Indeed, I discern what seems to be an inverse relationship between popularity of the genre and critical attention when I consider the critical genealogy of note 3 together with Janice Radway's excellent account of publication history. The Gothic flourished in the 1950s, enormously successful mass-market paperback lines began in 1960, and enthusiasm waned only about 1974 (*Reading the Romance* 31–33). The dearth of critical work from 1950–1970 thus coincides with the genre's period of greatest production and popularity, and the revival of critical interest in the 1980s intersects with falling sales.

Alice Walker and Margaret Atwood have written Gothic novels, but somehow the genre's critical stock never goes up. Indeed, individual authors may even be devalued by their work in a genre often assumed to be for adolescent girls or the not-terribly-intelligent. Boundaries between characters (was it Emily? Ellena? Catherine?) and even between authors blur and merge as all become exchangeable and typical Gothic women.[2]

To account for what these authors see where traditional critical theory often shows only a blank page, I consider formal characteristics of the Gothic—frequently predictable characters, the Ur-plot of separation from the known, exposure to horror, alliance of horror and romance plot, and often conservative resolution—as examples of the involuntary repetition Freud associates with the uncanny. What, however, is the source and goal of this repetition? Traditional analyses, which rely heavily upon women's supposed pleasure in pain, often reply "masochism." That tautological reply only underscores the term's significance, though, insofar as masochism is understood as the innate donnée of femininity.

I too see masochism at the center of the Gothic. On one level, then, my answer to that first question is simply yes: the Gothic novel is indeed "about" masochism. But that "yes" must be followed by crucial modifications that have to do both with society's role in the construction of masochism and with the widely differing functions of masochism for Gothic protagonists. The novels' central concern with masochism does not mean that characters (or women) are masochistic, although many are. Instead, my premise is that what characters in these novels represent, whether through repudiation, doubt, or celebration, is the cultural, psychoanalytic, and fictional expectation that they should be masochistic if they are "normal" women.

I understand masochism not as some monolithic term of textual diagnosis but as its own story within the history both of psychoanalysis and of the individual. Thus, throughout this book, I discuss masochism and the Gothic as mutually illuminative explications of women's pain. Psychoanalysis helps us to understand the Gothic's emphasis upon masochism as a key issue in feminine identity. In its

---

[2]A strange instance of this merging, particularly given the book's thesis, occurs in Pierre Macherey's *A Theory of Literary Production*. In his brief discussion of what he calls the "mystery" or Gothic novel and its two simultaneous movements of establishing and dispelling mystery (34), he addresses the issue of Ann Radcliffe's status in relation to her popularity. The text he uses as an example is, as he startlingly and casually notes, probably "not written by Mrs. Radcliffe but is a forgery" (28).

turn, however, the Gothic glosses the often mysterious plots of psychoanalysis and culture, plots that erase the process of the masochist's formation in order to point insistently at the happy ending ideology promises. Both the Gothic and psychoanalysis stage what Freud calls the beating fantasy, in which a spectator watches someone being hurt by a dominant other. Each narrative often simultaneously avows that the spectacle was just make-believe *and* that the spectator should leave her bystander's role to become a participant.

Here and throughout this project, I want to emphasize that the intertwining of love and pain is not natural and does not originate in the self: women are taught masochism through fiction and culture, and masochism's causes are external and real. Critics of the sublime school often find that a woman's suffering "stands for" something else. As a feminist, I do not entertain this hypothesis or find it entertaining. When a woman is hurt, as she is throughout the Gothic, the damage is not originally self-imposed: we must acknowledge that someone else strikes the first blow. At the same time, however, I want to emphasize not just what is done to women but what they then *do* about it. Feminism, which insists that we cannot look away from the body or face of a woman in pain, demands its own reconsideration of the narratives psychoanalysis and fiction offer. This book is a part of that ongoing reconsideration.

Masochism is the end result of a long and varyingly successful cultural training. This training leaves its traces upon individual characters and upon the Gothic itself, which broods upon its originating trauma, the denial of autonomy or separation for women, throughout the centuries. Women's schooling in masochism, the turning inward of active drives, seems to naturalize that denial and makes it appear to spring from within rather than without. Insofar as a Gothic protagonist internalizes these lessons, she sees her trials as unique to herself and avoids systemic inquiry about the source of her suffering. She carefully monitors herself, finds her virtue in her renunciation, and teaches other women to do so as well.

The Gothic, then, is a pointed reminder of cultural amnesia in its insistent representation of the *process* through which a woman becomes a masochist and assigns subjectivity to another. And, as long as the trauma that gives rise to masochism remains—as long as Western culture's gender arrangements persist—the Gothic will endure. Girls who, seeking recognition and love, learn to forget or deny that they also wanted independence and agency, grow up to become women who are Gothic heroines. The ideology of romance insists that there never was any pain or renunciation, that the suffering they experience is really the love and recognition for which they long or at least its prelude.[3]

This pattern structures every Gothic novel. Every Gothic heroine knows, consciously or not, Edmund Burke's dictum: "We submit to what we admire, but we love what submits to us" ("Inquiry" 132). And all have been taught to want love, in whatever guise, above all else. What does differ in the novels, however, is the representation of masochism's function for protagonists. Many characters submit for love; few come to love submission. Some texts identify and resist masochism's intangible, ubiquitous pattern; some highlight its use as a strategy for survival; some, few vestiges of self remaining in their protagonists, internalize and replicate the dynamics of oppression.

---

[3]Criticism of the Gothic shows its own distinct generations, as well as the near-death of the critical line from 1950 to 1970. The first generation, what Judith Wilt might call the "great old ones" (12), dates from about 1920 to 1950. The conventions of the Gothic are often the occasion for much scholarly wit, and the Gothic heroine proves a tempting straw woman, seldom considered as much more than another convention. The primary interest is in the Gothic as a by-blow of the sublime and a progenitor of Romanticism. In addition, the genre is usually firmly defined historically, spanning some sixty to eighty years that begin with Horace Walpole's *The Castle of Otranto* (1765) and ending with Charles Robert Maturin's *Melmoth the Wanderer* (1820) or the Brontës (1848). The most influential definers of the genre in that generation are: Ernest A. Baker (*The Novel of Sentiment and the Gothic Romance*, 1934), Edith Birkhead (*The Tale of Terror*, 1921), James R. Foster (*History of the Pre-Romantic Novel in England*, 1949), Alice M. Killen (*Le roman terrifiant*, 1923), Mario Praz (*The Romantic Agony*, 1933), Eino Railo (*The Haunted Castle*, 1927), Dorothy Scarborough (*The Supernatural in Modern English Fiction*, 1917), Montague Summers (*The Gothic Quest*, 1938), and Devendra P. Varma (*The Gothic Flame*, 1957).

With the exception of Varma's 1957 study, there are no major studies of the Gothic for a twenty-year period. The 1970s show a small second generation struggling to reestablish the line and an increasing willingness of critics to consider the Gothic as a genre important in its own right: Brendan Hennessey (*The Gothic Novel*, 1978), Coral Ann Howells (*Love, Mystery, and Misery*, 1978), Robert Kiely (*The Romantic Novel in England*, 1972), and Elizabeth MacAndrew (*The Gothic Tradition in Fiction*, 1979).

The 1980s show a much enlarged, primarily female generation of critics and a resurgence of interest in the genre and, for the first time, in its female protagonists, an interest supported by work in feminist theory, popular culture (including film), and cultural theory. With few exceptions (such as Elizabeth Napier's book, the tone and approach of which is singularly akin to that of the first generation), the current scholarship displays a rare analytic vitality as it broadens the generic and historical scope of the Gothic and reconsiders its central issues. See, for example: Margaret L. Carter (*Specter or Delusion?* 1987), William Patrick Day (*In the Circles of Fear and Desire*, 1985), Eugenia C. DeLamotte (*Perils of the Night*, 1989), Kate Ferguson Ellis (*The Contested Castle*, 1989), Louis Gross (*Redefining the American Gothic*, 1989), George E. Haggerty (*Gothic Fiction/Gothic Form*, 1989), Annie LeBrun (*Les châteaux de la subversion*, 1982), Elizabeth Napier (*The Failure of Gothic*, 1987), David Punter (*The Literature of Terror*, 1980), Bette Roberts (*The Gothic Romance*, 1980), Eve Kosofsky Sedgwick (*The Coherence of Gothic Conventions*, 1980), S. L. Varnado (*Haunted Presence*, 1987), Joseph Wiesenfarth (*Gothic Manners and the Classic English Novel*, 1988), and Judith Wilt (*Ghosts of the Gothic*, 1980).

My focus in this book is on how and why women incorporate the expectations of their world so that they eventually hurt themselves as others once hurt them. To this end, I explore the ways in and degree to which individual characters recognize their constraints and struggle to achieve what mobility, voice, and vision they can in a world of other- and self-imposed limitation. Their goal is modest, but it is one, I think, that carries radical implications for all women.

Clearly, I cannot dismiss masochism as some patriarchal canard (dearly as I would love to do so). Nor can I claim that, within the Gothic novel, women consistently subvert masochistic expectations, triumphantly overcome them, or exist solely as victims, mute witnesses to domination. There are novels that warrant each interpretation, but no single one is true for all novels, and each has its own problems. To be only a victim is to have no self and to cede the absolute power of the victimizer; to overcome domination entirely suggests that one can entirely escape the constraints of a given culture and upbringing without becoming a dominator in turn; to subvert can run the risk of idealizing the margins while the center remains unchanged.

The day when women, minorities, and the working class can achieve what Freud describes as the goal of analysis—"common unhappiness"—is, in my mind, a utopian moment to which I look forward. Until that time, however, we must consider the forms of *un*common unhappiness, such as masochism, that inform women's experience and their fiction and recognize the individual psychodrama (and the insistence that it remain that) as part of a larger cultural production of discipline and punishment. Women do not merely reflect but help to shape that system: insofar as they internalize its values, they potentially remain victims or accomplices.

In trying to understand how that internalization happens, I find no mode of analysis so useful as psychoanalysis. The role of the unconscious, ego formation, and the vicissitudes of instinctual development, as set forth by Freud, are an indispensable part of my own thinking as a feminist literary critic. Like most feminists, I reserve a large fund of skepticism and disagreement for many of Freud's statements on gender and sex,[4] even when making what allowance I can for a representation of things as they are, rather than things as they should be, for a culture, period, and biography not my own. None-

[handwritten margin note: radical fem. no biol. basis for gender dif.]

---

[4]Throughout this book, I use "sex" (female or male) to refer to biological identity and "gender" (feminine or masculine) to designate the behaviors or attributes a society deems appropriate for one's biological sex. The first is, except in rare instances, fixed, while the second is not.

theless, I credit a good many of Freud's observations in regard to masochism, as Chapters 2 and 3 demonstrate, while often doubting his interpretation of what they mean.

By drawing this distinction, I am also drawing attention to "Freud" as a system of thought that can itself be analyzed and deemphasizing the gargantuan Father of feminist nightmare. We are not Freud's daughters. Whether we envision him as the benevolent, all-knowing patriarch with whom we seek merger or the glowering Blakean Nobodaddy from whom we flee, we construct (with a good deal of cultural help, mind you) a dangerous fantasy of paternal omnipotence. That fantasy must not become any part of feminist reality. (And my admonition here is to myself as much as to my audience.)

Dreams can beget reality, as they so often do in the Gothic, but they can also begin responsibility—that of women for their own psyches and bodies. Freud's voice cannot but be heard (and often loudly, as in this project), yet psychoanalysis is no monologue. There have always been other voices that help to create another reality for women. Karen Horney, Clara Thompson, Paula Caplan, Jessica Benjamin, and Louise Kaplan are some of those voices in this book. By insisting on masochism's reality *and* its construction, they point the way to a reconstruction where no woman will "naturally" take pleasure in pain nor assume that "of course" dominance is a part of love.

My response, then, to the second question posed me—"Why *do* feminists still use Freud?"—is that we cannot afford not to. Resistance (that dread term) to psychoanalysis by some feminists and non-feminists is a way of asserting individualism and integrity of identity: "no one and nothing 'made' me" (in any of the verb's multiple senses). Yet, unless we work at understanding how the structures of domination we most loathe in our world are a part of ourselves also, we risk replicating them even in our denial and resistance. Our will, reason, and intellect can identify what we see "out there"; they are not enough to change it as long as, to paraphrase Pogo's immortal words, we are (or may become) the enemy.

Masochism at first seems a lonely business: a woman hurts herself for her own obscure pleasures. The goal of the supposed masochistic woman, within both the Gothic and psychoanalysis, however, is to find a partner to help her with her task. Furthermore, both in the beating fantasy and in the Gothic's own themes and audience, there is an ambivalent third party, the spectator. I have organized this project so that we, spectators also, can view the Gothic masochist from each of these perspectives. To do so, I have begun the book with a fiction-based discussion of two issues central to Gothic masochism, repetition and trauma. These concepts and a working definition of the Gothic help us to make sense of the psychoanalytic construction of masochism in the section that follows (Chapters 2 and 3). I then use psychoanalysis's most fully developed story about masochism, the beating fantasy, to consider the function of that pattern in several novels (Chapters 4 through 6). In concluding, I consider several texts that map paths away from the Gothic masochism that originally seems to provide no exit.

In Chapter 1, I argue that we must consider "normal" feminine development as a form of culturally induced trauma and the Gothic novel its repetition. That repetition is not generated by masochistic pleasure but instead, like the response to other forms of trauma, is an attempt at mastery and a revised reality principle. In order to examine this process at work, I focus on elements of repetition within fictional texts and on a particular generic repetition that I call marital Gothic: texts that begin, rather than end, with marriage, in which the husband becomes the revenant of the very horror his presence was supposed to banish. I chose "The Yellow Wallpaper" as the focal text for obvious thematic and structural reasons.

radical [handwritten annotation in margin]

In Chapters 2 and 3, I analyze a particular masochistic drama and its implications within psychoanalysis: the beating fantasy, a drama shaped by trauma and characterized by repetition as emphatically as is the Gothic's. That fantasy is, as I view it, both a representation and a critical examination of masochism. Freud supposes three stages to the beating fantasy, and these stages, I argue, shape psychoanalysis's own narrative. In the first, the subject imagines that "my father is beating a child"; in the second (repressed) that "my father is beating me"; in the third, conscious formulation, a spectator sees that "a child is being beaten."

Chapter 2 presents the beating drama, in which a woman is the spectator of cruelty, as the playing out on a psychoanalytic stage of the complexities of the voyeur's relationship to wrongful authority (sadism) and victimization (masochism). The woman spectator practices a covert form of the active instincts for vision, knowledge, and action which the masculine beater displays so aggressively. At the same time, she remains distanced from the beater/beaten dyad, in which she watches the representation of "normal," passively acquiescent femininity. As Charles Maturin notes of an execution in *Melmoth the Wanderer*, however, the too-easy separation of spectacle and spectator is chimerical. "The drama of terror has the irresistible power of converting its audience into its victims" (257); conversely, one can only assume that the victim would dearly prefer to play the role of spectator or even executioner.

My particular focus in Chapter 3 is upon psychoanalysis's own story of how development affects the turning inward (repression) or outward (sublimation) of instinct for women and how those women, like Gothic heroines, sometimes manage to use culture's yoking of masochism and romance to assert identity and to influence those around them. In addition, Chapter 3 further develops the examination in Chapter 2 of the fluidity of the beating drama's three roles in psychoanalysis and of the function of voyeurism for the spectator/protagonist. What we see is that her frequently commented-on immobility and passivity, even if mandated by external causes, nonetheless enable her to observe and learn a good deal about the laws that govern her world, just as the Gothic protagonist may gradually come to understand her own.

In Chapters 4 through 6, I analyze three texts that illuminate the ways in which the beating drama works both for and against the Gothic heroine in fiction. Each novel makes clear, albeit in very different contexts, that the role of spectator is liminal and rarely remains a permanent position. It is a way for the protagonist to protect the self, but also to know what position she will next assume. In order to consider the protagonists' varying final identifications with the beaten, the beater, or the spectator, I use the pattern suggested by Freud's "A Child Is Being Beaten."

The first text analyzed in this section, Pauline Réage's *Story of O*, represents the most extreme and self-abnegating identification with the victim. In the second, Daphne du Maurier's *Rebecca*, the nameless protagonist becomes a participant through identification with the "beater," her husband Max. Jane Eyre, like du Maurier's protagonist, easily recognizes her own identification with the beaten and, like the other woman, is for a time taken by the possibility that she can repudiate the role through identification with her mate. Finally, however, Jane renounces the either/or decision of being beater or beaten, master or slave. In addition, she modifies the role of spectator. Brontë's resolution is provisional and guarded, but it may well defer, if not prevent, the reappearance of the Gothic. In all three novels, the protagonists' spectating is what allows them to question the dyads of lover/beloved, sadist/masochist, and the ties that bind.

The texts I consider in Chapter 7, ranging from Atwood's *Lady Oracle* to Gloria Naylor's *Linden Hills*, outline some of the strategies through which individual characters begin to recognize the Gothic as systemic abuse rather than an individual love story, wryly acknowledge repetition as set in motion by themselves, not others, or refuse the Gothic's premise of domination. The Gothic's repeated, excruciatingly detailed representation of how women come to interweave love and pain helps us to understand how we too might awaken some day from the Gothic nightmare that is our own as well as our culture's.

1

Things That Go Bump in the Night: Husbands, Horrors, and Repetition

Traditional accounts of Gothic plots are familiar enough. The Ur-plot is a terror-inflected variant of Richardsonian courtship narrative in which an unprotected young woman in an isolated setting uncovers a sinister secret.[1] After repeated trials and persecutions, one of two possible outcomes usually follows: the master of the house is discovered as the evil source of her tribulations and is vanquished by the poor-but-honest (and inevitably later revealed as noble) young man, who marries the woman; the master of the house, apparently the source of evil, is revealed to be more sinned against than sinning, and he marries the woman. Strangely enough, in both scenarios the narrative is shaped by the mystery the male presents and not by the drama of the supposed protagonist, the Gothic heroine.

In traditional psychological readings, we nonetheless focus on the repressed desire of the heroine as the key that opens the text and reconstructs her character. Culturally prohibited from speaking of passion, unable to move toward the object of desire, the heroine remains the passive center of the novel and of the female adolescent's erotic dream. The phantasmagoric horrors that bombard her are the natural companions of repression, the price she must pay for her transgression—desire—even when it is only obliquely acknowledged and represented. By being a perennially passive victim, she remains a "good girl," never entirely aware of her own sexual longings. We then understand her repeated ordeals as peculiarly female pleasures, testa-

---

[1] See Leslie Fiedler's *Love and Death in the American Novel* (63–66, 74–88) and Praz's *Romantic Agony* (97–102) for early and influential arguments on Clarissa as a Gothic archetype. See also Frances L. Restuccia's "Female Gothic Writing" for a critique of Fiedler's gender assumptions.

ment to the masochism Freud calls "an expression of the feminine nature" ("Economic Problem of Masochism" 161). These painful pleasures thus become foreplay to the fulfillment that marriage promises at the novel's end, when pleasure principle gives way gracefully to reality principle.

This familiar reading, in which marriage's heterosexual genitality is revealed as the reality principle before which the problematic pleasures of the female body yield, only succeeds in rescreening the uncanny for us just as the novels themselves often do by their final unveilings. By light of day and end of novel, the heroine's nightmare visions supposedly disappear, cured by the *medicina libidinis* offered in the conservative and comic resolution. Our repression-based analyses thus construct a reassuring critical fiction in which most of the heroine's fears are not "real," while those that are will be erased by the transition from unjust to just authority, by the move from father's house to husband's. By localizing anxiety—in fear of mother, self, older generations, homophobia, gender archetypes, or, most simply, genital sexuality[2]—we forge our own escape from the Gothic labyrinth by restricting its area and thus affirming our desire for a just and rational "real" world where horror cannot appear. In this transition from supposed pleasure principle to reality principle, however, the voice of the heroine as speaking subject is also erased, lost in the epithalamium of the fictional closure. In the "real" world of the frame, the woman can exist only in relation to another—usually as a daughter in the beginning, a bride at the end. Insofar as we credit the shift as progress, we rewrite the Gothic and assure its repetition.

I here want to reconsider the erased, retrospectively trivialized heroine's text and the trauma and repetition that give it shape. Repetition compulsion shapes individual texts, the genre's propagation of new

[2]See, respectively: Tania Modleski, *Loving with a Vengeance*; Claire Kahane, "The Gothic Mirror"; Ellen Moers, "Female Gothic" and "Traveling Heroinism" in *Literary Women*; Wilt's *Ghosts of the Gothic*; Sedgwick's *The Coherence of Gothic Conventions* and *Between Men*; Day's *In the Circles of Fear and Desire*. In her introduction to *The Female Gothic*, Juliann Fleenor convincingly argues that in what Robert Hume terms horror-Gothic, "horror of the self, of female physiology, is closely tied to the patriarchal paradigm" (7) as well as to conflict with the mother. Although all the authors cited point out the heroine's internalization of the principal conflict stressed, it must be emphasized that establishing a dialectical opposition between protagonist and a localized source of conflict is a risky business, often producing a forced synthesis that echoes the texts' own sanguine erasure of difference. I agree that self, mother, father, heterosexuality, and homosexuality are indeed sources of often simultaneous conflict, but all point, in the best Gothic tradition, to something more ominous, the refusal of the heroine's existence as subject. It is precisely the impossibility of full closure or resolution that generates new texts, despite our desire for transcendent third terms that resolve specific conflicts.

texts, and the genre's relationship with culture. My argument is that repetition in the Gothic functions as it does for certain other traumas: the reactivation of trauma is an attempt to recognize, not relish, the incredible and unspeakable that nonetheless happened. If we situate the source of horror or trauma in the "real" world of "rightful" authority that frames early narratives such as Ann Radcliffe's *The Mysteries of Udolpho*, the structural and thematic repetition of the novel's body moves beyond the pleasure principle. The originating trauma that prompts such repetition is the prohibition of female autonomy in the Gothic, in the families that people it, and in the society that reads it.[3] History, both individual and societal, is the nightmare from which the protagonist cannot awaken and whose inexorable logic must be followed.

To develop this argument, I examine repetition and its functions on three connected levels. The first, psychoanalysis, provides a methodology. Like criticism of the Gothic, however, psychoanalysis usually aligns itself with the ideology of that closing "real" world, no matter how briefly pointed to. I want to offer a corrective reading of the texts—and of our psychoanalytic and critical assumptions—by reconsidering the issues of trauma and repetition. Those issues will frame discussion of a particular variant that I call "marital Gothic," a later form of the genre where the husband is present at the beginning rather than the end of the story and "repeats" the role of the father. Studying the trope of the husband allows us to consider how and why the figure who was supposed to lay horror to rest has himself become the avatar of horror who strips voice, movement, property, and identity itself from the heroine. The last area of investigation

---

[3]Although reader response criticism is beyond the scope of this project, I suspect that the predominantly female audience's repetitive Gothic reading addresses the same needs and problems as those we see in the heroines: covert acknowledgment that "love" is often synonymous with the disavowal of identity and an attempt to deal with that knowledge by repetition. Bruno Bettelheim's comments in *The Uses of Enchantment* are to the point here. He argues that the child reader's sense of helplessness is mirrored by the violent and frightening material of the tales, as is the need for reassurance that even the weakest can and do survive. The child's need to listen to or read the same tale again and again underscores the use of repetition in gaining mastery. For particularly useful discussions of Gothic reading, see Norman Holland and Leona Sherman, "Gothic Possibilities"; Kay Mussell, "'But Why Do They Read Those Things?'"; Mary Poovey, "The Proper Lady," in *The Proper Lady and the Woman Writer;* and Janice Radway, *Reading the Romance.* Several studies particularly consider the function of romance reading in relation to gender and class to refute the perception that, as Alison Light puts it, "romance readers (with the exception of a few up-front intellectuals) are either masochistic or inherently stupid" ("'Returning to Manderley'" 8). See also Leslie Rabine's "Romance in the Age of Electronics" and Lillian Robinson's "On Reading Trash," in her *Sex, Class, and Culture.*

focuses on a single well-known text, Charlotte Perkins Gilman's "The Yellow Wallpaper," which unites and explicates the concerns outlined here through its use of formal and structural repetition. In the end, what we find is that Freud's uncanny is uncovered as not just the familiar but the familial, and the horror from which the heroine cannot escape is the limitation of her identity to a mirror for the self-representations of father and husband. Furthermore, the overdetermined repetition of this dilemma within individual narratives and in the Gothic genre marks a persistent and active attempt by authors, their characters, and readers to rework the feminine social contract.

Trauma and Repetition Compulsion

In "Souls," a contemporary story by Joanna Russ, the wise Abbess Radegunde understands that repetition, like regression, can be in the service of the ego. She is asked if the Christian god can cure a raped nun who keeps reliving her experience like one of Charcot's showcase hysterics. "'No,' said the Abbess. 'Only by undoing the past. And that is the one thing He never does, it seems. She is in Hell now and must go back there many times before she can forget'" (32). Transgression, regression, repetition—the stuff of analysis itself and of the Gothic—are here, as well as the problem of what constitutes the "cure" that returns one to the world in which atrocity happens. This reenactment of a single traumatic episode is uncanny to those around the nun, an impression doubtless heightened by her resemblance to the inhuman as she mechanically relives one set of actions temporally, linguistically, and kinetically. Within the Gothic, the trauma is less obvious, so that the eerie repetition of incident, character, structure, and of the formula itself becomes more puzzling the longer we view seemingly static heroines experiencing ordeal after ordeal. Little pleasure principle and still less *jouissance* are evident. But as Freud also reminds us in "The 'Uncanny,'" repetition compulsion is formidable, "a compulsion powerful enough to overrule the pleasure principle, lending to certain aspects of the mind their daemonic character" (238).[4]

[4]Peter Brooks's *Reading for the Plot* includes excellent discussions of repetition and fiction, particularly in "Freud's Masterplot" and "Repetition, Repression, and Return." Brooks argues that "plot itself is working-through" (140)—a statement I would modify by the more conditional "can be." As his discussion of plot's "tumescence," "arousal," "discharge," and "terminal quiescence" indicates, however, he sees both repetition and plot, with their persistent search for origins and ends, as death-driven. Furthermore, Brooks's articulation and applications are of a still-masculine "masterplot." Marianne Hirsch's *The Mother/Daughter Plot*, insightfully suggests that other economies structure the feminine plots she explicates.

In his work on war and other traumatic neuroses, Freud was forced to reappraise the relation between repetition and pleasure. Just as "children repeat unpleasurable experiences for the additional reason that they can master a powerful impression far more thoroughly by being active than they could by merely experiencing it passively," so the victim repeats trauma until it can be incorporated in present time as felt experience (*Beyond the Pleasure Principle* 35).[5] Freud acknowledges that in such repetition, the symptom is a witnessing, a possible prelude to the establishment of pleasure principle and of (a revised) reality principle. The compulsion to repeat trauma is the patient's "way of remembering," a force that can be allied to therapy itself, and "impossible to classify as wish-fulfilments" ("Remembering" 150, "Remarks" 117–18, *Beyond the Pleasure Principle* 32). Such patients share for a time what Mario Praz characterizes as the lot of the Romantic: "a universe [of] suffering and pain" (144). According to Freud, it is emphatically "not in the service of" pleasure principle that their dreams "lead them back with such regularity to the situation in which the trauma occurred. We may assume, rather, that dreams are here helping to carry out another task, which must be accomplished before the dominance of the pleasure principle can even begin. These dreams are endeavouring to master the stimulus retrospectively, by developing *the anxiety whose omission was the cause of the traumatic neurosis*" (*Beyond the Pleasure Principle* 32; emphasis added).[6] Here and elsewhere (e.g., "Fixation to Trauma" 275), Freud refers to "the task" the patient must complete, the task whose immediate goal is the development of an appropriate anxiety to cope with real danger. Freud's emphasis on activity, omitted anxiety, and the need for mastery immediately casts a new light on the particular dream that is the Gothic.

Freud assumes a predisposition to trauma in the omission of anxiety. The victims of martial and marital trauma often share a trust in abstract qualities that they believe inform and interpret experience. The victim of war trauma frequently credits patriotism and heroism as organizing rubrics; the heroine of marital Gothic invests her faith in love and duty. Both find their ideals to have little efficacy in dealing with their experiences. Each then relives trauma in an attempt to revise reality principle and to establish pleasure principle. The crucial

[5]See also Marie Balmary's comments on this point in *Psychoanalyzing Psychoanalysis* (41); Gilbert J. Rose's study, *Trauma and Mastery in Life and Art*; and Richard B. Ulman and Doris Brothers's *The Shattered Self*, which discusses repetition in relation to post-traumatic stress disorder.

[6]For further observations, see "Fixation to Traumas" 273–85.

differences lie in the repetition and duration of the traumatic event and in social recognition of the injury. The victim of shell shock will not always awaken to the sound of actual bombs, nor will contemporary society deny the validity of the trauma. The atrocity will not always be present, although its past existence must be incorporated by the victim. In contrast, the heroine of marital Gothic will always reawaken to the still-present actuality of her trauma, because the gender expectations that deny her identity are woven into the very fabric of her culture, which perpetuates her trauma while denying its existence.[7]

When we thus extend our consideration of what we are willing to recognize as trauma, we begin to see a revised analysis of the Gothic in which the stimulus, suppression of identity, exists not only in the past but also in the present and in the implied future of the narrative, when the heroine "wakes" from a dream of trauma to find it represented in the real world. The iteration assures that the dreaming and waking cycle will be repeated yet again; the source of trauma, after all, remains unchanged. Although we usually think of trauma as a specific incident with exterior causation, it can also be a situation that endures over time, shaping individual identity and ways of dealing with the environment.[8] Nowhere is this more obvious than in

[7]Freud's early *Studies on Hysteria* (coauthored with Josef Breuer), in which he states emphatically that *"hysterics suffer mainly from reminiscences"* (7), offers intriguing comments on links between hysteria and trauma, the construction of trauma over time, and its link to social suppression. These insights remain largely undeveloped or repudiated in later work on women, just as the seduction theory shifted its emphasis from what might have been done to a child to the child's own role in an Oedipal drama. In the early text, Freud argues for "the concept of traumatic hysteria" (5), brought about not by a single precipitating event but "a group of provoking causes [that] exercise a traumatic effect by summation and . . . belong together in so far as they are in part components of a single story of suffering" (6). These *"successions* of *partial* traumas and *concatenations* of pathogenic trains of thought" (288) may be split from consciousness and thus *"denied the normal wearing-away processes by means of abreaction and reproduction"* (11). The patient's "psychical state" is one explanation for the missing response; the "nature of the trauma," when "social circumstances made a reaction impossible" (10) is the suggestive second possibility.

[8]Michael Balint's discussion of trauma in *The Basic Fault* clarifies the importance of this idea: "The trauma itself, of course, is not necessarily a single event; on the contrary, usually it amounts to a situation of some duration caused by a painful misunderstanding—lack of 'fit'—between the individual and his environment. . . ."

"Thus it comes about that the individual is made to adopt his own method for coping with the trauma, a method hit upon in his despair or thrown at him by some ununderstanding adult who may be a well-wisher, or just indifferent, negligent, or even careless or hostile. As I have just said, the individual's further development will then be either prescribed or, at any rate limited, by this method which, though helpful in certain respects, is invariably costly and, above all, alien. Still, it will be incorporated in his ego structure—as his basic fault—and anything beyond or contrary to these methods will strike him as a frightening and more or less impossible proposition" (82).

gender expectations, and nowhere is the trauma of those expectations more fully presented than in the Gothic. What Lillian Robinson
calls "culturally induced fantasies" (131) are not the flight and per-
secution of the main plot, but the frame's sanguine assurances that
the danger is over. As it closes, the Gothic novel lulls the heroine into
repeating the omission of anxiety. And it does so for significant ideological reasons, reasons very like those we see evidenced in Freud's
most famous analysis of a hysteric, Dora.[9]

The comparison of Dora and the Gothic heroine gives us a startling,
if partial, plot similarity. A young girl who dotes on her father is much
impressed by her early reading about love. She is somewhat interested in a man, but is repelled when he reveals a sinister side to his
character. She attempts to flee, but time and again finds herself in an
isolated setting with him. She locks herself in a room, but the key is
taken from her; she tries to get help by telling someone what has
happened to her, but she is told she imagined her danger. Her mother
is herself helpless, and the one woman she thought she could trust
betrays her. She suspects a dark secret in her family that curses each
generation and that would explain much of what has happened to
her. She refuses to do what her parents want and is brought, not to a
cell to contemplate her sins and the virtues of obedience, but to Freud
to analyze her own desire as precipitant for her story.

What is significant here is the stance from which analysis proceeds.
In listening to the story of an eighteen-year-old who has been pursued by the husband of her father's mistress since she was fourteen,
Freud aligns himself with the world of male homosocial exchange that
reduces Dora to a bargaining chip. In his own narrative, he acknowledges that her father wants her to agree to Herr K.'s advances so that
his affair with Frau K. is not disturbed, and he cedes that Dora is
probably right when she suspects that both she and her mother have
been infected in some way by her father's syphilis. In passing, he
notes a depressing array of couples: the idolized aunt in an unhappy
marriage who dies of a mysterious wasting disease; the mother and
Frau K., whose husbands complain they "get nothing" (*Fragment of an
Analysis* 26) from them (although Dora's mother has certainly gotten
something from her husband); the governesses who are seduced and
abandoned. Nonetheless, Freud's proposed closure of this plot is that
Dora marry Herr K.—a shocking suggestion unless we realize that
the reality Freud and Gothic endings prefer repeats a social construction of gender that they have a stake in preserving.

[9]For an excellent collection of recent appraisals, see Charles Bernheimer and Claire
Kahane, eds., *In Dora's Case*.

The sins of the father are decidedly visited upon the children here, but what sets Freud's teeth on edge is not Dora's victimization but her refusal to accept that it is her fault. The idea that prevailing social ideology can be trauma to the woman whom it affects is beyond his ken.[10] Though he recognizes the injustices of Dora's father, he—as father, man, and analyst—can only urge the restoration of "rightful" authority, embodied in a husband. Although Freud sees Dora reenacting her relation to her father in her responses to Herr K. and to himself, his analysis remains rooted in the assumptions of patriarchy. He does not notice the ways in which his dealings with Dora replicate those of father and lover. From his conservative stance, resistance to father, would-be lover, and analyst can only be deplored as a further aberration and ascribed in later notes to a basic lesbian tendency.

At the time of finishing the history, however, he is more sanguine after hearing of her marriage, and he suggests a predictable and happy ending in his last words. "Just as the first dream represented her turning away from the man she loved to her father—that is to say, her flight from life into disease—so the second dream announced that she was about to tear herself free from her father and had been reclaimed once more by the realities of life" (122). The cliché-ridden language that closes Dora's case history and announces her later marriage is striking in its overtones of (analytic) sinning, redemption, and closure, as well as in the equivalency of "life" and Herr K., "realities" and her husband.

Herr K. and Dora's eventual husband are separated syntactically and conceptually from her father in this passage, and yet the decisive progression from Herr K. and love, through father and disease, to husband and reality is subtly undercut. There will be no repetition, the text implies, unless it is caused by Dora herself, but the redundancy of "reclaimed once more" and its move from active to passive voice suggest a propellant other than Dora. So too the interpolation of "father" as usual first term sets in motion a continuing cycle of seduction: from father to Herr K., from father to Freud, from father to husband. . . . As Freud elsewhere notes, symptoms "represent not only the repressed but also the repressing force which had a share in their origin" ("Resistance and Repression" 301).[11] The earliest and

---

[10]Freud's earlier scope is more generous, as notes 7 and 11 indicate.

[11]The political implications of Freud's dictum are evident in Balmary's extension: "The dominated carries out the repressed of the dominant" (35). Freud is again far more explicit about the influence of the dominant parent upon the child's neurosis in early work. In a December 6, 1896 letter, he clearly outlines a startling genealogy of paternal perversion begetting hysteria as resistance: "It seems to me more and more that the essential point of hysteria is that it is a result of perversion on the part of the

most convenient name for the dominant or repressing force is "the father," but we err if we stop with that localized signifier for the forces that collectively bring about the muteness of Dora and the paralysis of the enclosed Gothic heroine.[12] Their passivity is overdetermined, engendered not only by some single representative of authority but also by larger social institutions that reproduce themselves by what Nancy Chodorow calls "legitimating ideologies" to "create expectations in people about what is normal and appropriate and how they should act" (35).

The heroines of the Gothic, inculcated by education, religion, and bourgeois familial values, have the same expectations as those around them for what is normal. Their social contract tenders their passivity and disavowal of public power in exchange for the love that will let them reign in the interpersonal and domestic sphere. Courtship is the heroines' first adult testing of that pact and marriage the second. Yet, like Dora, they are surrounded by couples who testify to the transaction's failure. What *is* gives the lie to what they are told *should be*, and they are haunted by the discrepancy. Freud identifies the uncanny with such revenants, which are "in reality nothing new or alien, but something which is familiar and old-established in the mind and which has become alienated from it only through the process of repression," something "known of old and long familiar" ("'The Uncanny'" 241, 220). The father is the daughter's familiar, promising power through love if she maintains the self-abnegation that is her part of the bargain. Yet he or his surrogate is only a representative for the deep structure of patriarchal exchange systems.

The Gothic plot is thus not an "escape" from the real world but a repetition and exploration of the traumatic denial of identity found there. Both the nightmare stasis of the protagonists and the all-enveloping power of the antagonists are extensions of social ideology and real-world experience. The silence, immobility, and enclosure of the heroines mark their internalization of repression as well as the power of the repressing force. Indeed, their frequently commented-

---

seducer; and that heredity is seduction by the father. Thus a change occurs between the generations:—

> 1st generation: Perversion
> 2nd generation: Hysteria. . . .

Thus hysteria is in fact not repudiated *sexuality* but rather repudiated *perversion*" (*Origins* 179–80).

[12]In *The Daughter's Seduction*, Jane Gallop comments on the catch-22 of homological and heterosexual desire between daughter and father (41). See also her chapter "Keys to Dora," which gives a convincing reading of how Dora's case exacerbated Freud's own sense of powerlessness.

on passivity, lack of differentiation, and lack of development through experience only emphasize this point. As Joanna Russ notes, "The Heroine's suffering is the principal action of the story *because it is the only action she can perform*."[13] Each attempt at escape only brings her again to something that cannot be evaded or exorcized by her efforts.

Her suffering, its causes, and its results test the benefits of being a "good girl." Returning to benign reality, earning a husband, and erasing horror are the wages promised for virtuous passivity at novel's end. The momentum created by the repetition of ordeals within individual works overcomes the ending, however. The ending's reassurances have specious weight when balanced against the body's mass of suffering: there is a surplus of anxiety still unaccounted for by "reality." We thus have to shift our critical focus from the "faults" of the heroine that are implied by an analytic language of masochism and repressed desire. By looking instead at the encapsulating social systems that engender repeated trauma, we gain a new understanding of the structure and function of the Gothic dream.

The boundaries between Gothic and real clearly are not as fixed as we once thought.[14] In addressing horror's existence in the real world, much recent feminist criticism also points to the need for and appropriateness of a revised psychoanalytic model. Margaret Homans rightly comments that "the coming true of a dream, the discovery in the object world of what was at one time purely subjective, is actually more frightening than the subjective experience itself" (267). Eve Sedgwick succinctly characterizes this fear, the same one described at the beginning of Henry James's *The Turn of the Screw*: "To wake from a dream and *find it true*" (*Coherence of Gothic* 28). Tania Modleski and Sybil Vincent explicitly connect the pursuit and ordeals of Gothic plot to social realities. For Vincent, the genre "permits us to experiment,

---

[13]Joanna Russ, "Somebody's Trying to Kill Me and I Think It's My Husband: The Modern Gothic," Fleenor 50. In the same collection, this issue is underscored by the comments of Ann Ronald ("Terror-Gothic") and Cynthia Griffin Wolff ("The Radcliffean Gothic Model"). Ronald, noticing how Emily remains untouched by her ordeals in *The Mysteries of Udolpho*, concludes: "So experience really is no experience at all" (181). Wolff identifies the business of Radcliffe's heroines as "to experience difficulty, not to get out of it" (211). The not-unusual exasperation evinced by both emphasizes that the genre does not in fact function well as "escape" literature.

[14]Alice Walker's disagreement with "gothic" as an appropriate description for *The Third Life of Grange Copeland*—"a grave book in which the characters see the world as almost entirely menacing"—is predicated on the idea that the genre excludes reality. She agrees with Welty who, "in explaining why she rebels against being labeled 'gothic,' says that to her 'gothic' conjures up the supernatural, and that she feels what she writes has 'something to do with real life'" (*In Search of Our Mothers' Gardens* 263). With the revised analysis I predicate here, much of Walker's work and that of other modern authors reenters the Gothic realm.

to play at terror, to become familiar with it and recognize it as a fact of life" (157). Modleski also emphasizes that the "facts of life" are not limited to genital sexuality: "The Gothic has been used to drive home the 'core of truth' in feminine paranoid fears and to connect the social with the psychological, the personal with the political" (*Loving* 83). The home, Freud's *heimlich*, is both starting point and destination, the house of the father repeated in the house of the husband—the house the heroine thought was supposed to be her own.

Marital Gothic

The Gothic genre can be viewed historically as a serial writ large. Part 1, the earliest form of the genre, concerns itself with courtship and closes with a wedding, the restoration of order, and the return of reality. Horace Walpole's *The Castle of Otranto* (1765) and Radcliffe's *The Mysteries of Udolpho* (1794) and *The Italian* (1797) are the best-known examples of such texts. Part 2, a variant beginning in the nineteenth century, takes up the story where Part 1 left off. Marital Gothic begins with, or shortly after, a marriage—the same marriage that provided a sacramental expulsion of horror in Part 1. Perfect love supposedly has cast out fear, and perfect trust in another has led to the omission of anxiety discussed above as an antecedent of trauma and repetition compulsion. Yet horror returns in the new home of the couple, conjured up by renewed denial of the heroine's identity and autonomy. The marriage that she thought would give her voice (because she would be listened to), movement (because her status would be that of an adult), and not just a room of her own but a house, proves to have none of these attributes. The husband who was originally defined by his opposition to the unjust father figure slowly merges with that figure. The heroine again finds herself mute, paralyzed, enclosed, and she must harrow the Gothic in an attempt to deal with that reality through repetition.

The protagonist's options for escape are confined to those the environment and her own internalization of its codes permit. Her protest is restricted to what her self-knowledge allows to be voiced and what those around her can hear and understand. Literal difficulties with speaking to others in the texts are echoed, as Sedgwick states, by "the difficulty the story has in getting itself told," "accompanied by a kind of despair about any direct use of language" (*Coherence* 13, 14). If what Sedgwick identifies as the main themes of the Gothic, the unspeakable and live burial (4–5), cannot be named, they must be acted out in a mimed display of horror.

Courtship Gothic's representations of marriage and of the protagonist's chance of choosing her own mate necessarily precede and illuminate spousal relationships in marital Gothic. Two stories, one recent and one from the early nineteenth century, together help us to define the significance of marriage in the Gothic. In Alice Walker's contemporary "Roselily," the discrepancy between the hope for independent identity and the threat of further cooption in marriage is graphically inscribed by the alternating presentation of ceremonial service and narrative commentary on the page.

> *let him speak*
> Her husband would free her. A romantic hush. Proposal. Promises. A new life! Respectable, reclaimed, renewed. Free! . . .
> *or forever hold*
> She does not even know if she loves him. . . . She thinks she loves the effort he will make to redo her into what he truly wants. His love of her makes her completely conscious of how unloved she was before. . . . It seems to her that he [the preacher] has always been standing in front of her, barring her way.
> *his peace*
> Her husband's hand is like the clasp of an iron gate. (7–8)

The passage plays with the dangers of being "reclaimed," like Dora, by someone who knows you "better than you know yourself." The hesitation of "she thinks," the repetition of "love," and the possible fatuity of Roselily's expectations are pitched against the ominous overtones of ceremony and narration. "Or forever hold," "redo her into what he truly wants," "barring," "iron gate," and the ugly pun of "his peace" promise the equation the collection's title makes: *In Love and Trouble*. The preacher who represents tradition and bars her way is ostensibly opposed to the husband, but the husband is yoked to that tradition at the end of the ceremony by the same metaphor. The husband who will remold her, forever hold her, and whose loving clasp will be like a gate closing off all exit is a Gothic husband.

The most trenchant fictional analysis I know of this Gothic discrepancy between the romantic ideology of marriage and its praxis is made in Charles Brockden Brown's "Carwin the Biloquist." Ludloe, discoursing to his protégé, Carwin, on how to get ahead in the world, tells him that he can easily gain a substantial income, home, servants, and furniture. Intrigued, Carwin wants to know what he has to do to earn such a bonanza. Ludloe replies:

"Nothing. It may seem strange that, in accepting the absolute controul [sic] of so much property, you subject yourself to no conditions; that no claims of gratitude or service will accrue; but the wonder is greater still. The law equitably enough fetters the gift with no restraints, with respect to you that receive it; but not so with regard to the unhappy being who bestows it. That being must part, not only with property but liberty. . . .

The attachment and obedience of this being will be chiefly evident in one thing. Its duty will consist in conforming, in every instance, to your will. All the powers of this being are to be devoted to your happiness. . . . Your slave is a woman; and the bond, which transfers her property and person to you, is . . . marriage." (289)

In Ludloe's dispassionate description, wedding vows proclaim no expansion of identity for the woman, but a reduction to "it" and "property" that needs husbanding. His commentary is obviously and dramatically at odds with how marriage is presented to the heroine during the courtship period. These heroines are well schooled in deference to authority before any lover whispers promises of undying devotion, however. They often have seen the proof of Ludloe's statement in their own families' relations. Love, reinforced by duty, is the tortured bond between what they see and what they are told to believe. In the prototypical *The Castle of Otranto*, Hippolita gently chides Isabella and Matilda when they venture to complain about Manfred's wanting to divorce Hippolita, to marry Isabella, and to marry off Matilda. "'It is not ours to make elections for ourselves; Heaven, our fathers, and our husbands must decide for us (81)' "[15] This trinity of authority is united even when the husband at first seems to offer a new dispensation. As the citations from Walpole and Brown suggest, love means giving for the heroine: person, property, attention, deference, devotion, and identity. Any hesitation, doubt, question, or criticism about rightful authority marks what the heroine is taught to consider *her* failure. If the heroine has incorporated what society tells her is properly feminine, has eschewed the self-determination Hippolita frowns on for women, has repressed the contradictory evidence of her mother's own life, then her only response to the uses and abuses of authority is to increase her passivity. In patient Griselda or Hippolita fashion, she must find her identity in the refusal to revolt, in the willingness to "prove" her love by undergoing

[15]Hippolita's message is still heard, according to Miriam Darce Frenier's study of Harlequin romances published between 1970 and 1982. Wives' loving patience will change the "sardonic, cruel, distant, and strange" behavior of husbands. Whether their marriages are forced or voluntary, "if wives behaved like battered women, they would obtain and keep good marriages" (57).

harsher trials. When these stereotypical ideals are embraced, the failure to earn love is understood as the heroine's failure for not giving enough. What is demanded in the transaction is never called into question. Indeed, narrative sympathy often remains with the perpetrator of trauma, not its victim.

When heroines choose suitors independently in Gothics with comic resolution, all suffering is forgiven and forgotten in the restoration of social order. The suitors' nobility of heart is usually discovered to be matched by nobility of pedigree, and the happy couple are fondly clasped to the now-approving paternal bosom. In fact, the most tyrannical of fathers sometimes show a grudging admiration for the young male upstarts before the revelation is made, and accord is often complete afterward. The younger male's challenge of the *senex iratus* still acknowledges the older male's social power, while the heroine's resistance undermines its basis in the family. Even when the younger and older males struggle in standard Oedipal ways, the social ties uniting them prove stronger than those connecting any of them to women. In *Otranto*, for example, as in Dora's case history, there is a very lively trade in women. To ratify various alliances, Frederic is offered Matilda, and Manfred Isabella. The exchange does not stop with the older generation offering their daughters to each other, however; Theodore is also offered both women to consolidate blood lines, property, and the bonds among the men.

What is missing in these homosocial swaps is the heroine as subject rather than commodity. Matilda's and Isabella's admiration of Theodore is extraneous in deciding to whom they will be given. The affinity between husband and father is most glaring in cautionary tales where the heroine moves past admiration to elopement, from passivity to activity. The interests of older and younger male generations consolidate to eliminate such a threat. Two particularly interesting examples, Anne of Swansea's "The Unknown! or the Knight of the Blood-Red Plume" and William Ainsworth's "The Spectre Bride," are structurally, thematically, and ideologically similar. In both, young women of unimpeachable virtue fall in love with mysterious strangers who appear at their fathers' castles, and who are attracted to them precisely because of their virtue. Paternal authority is threatened in each: the father of Ainsworth's Clotilda dies after a visit from the stranger; Swansea's Erilda recoils in horror after her swain suggests patricide. Both heroines nonetheless elope, albeit with impeccable motives. When Clotilda's suitor Byronically laments his role as an outcast, she reassures him like any good girl faced with the pain of the man she loves: "'You are unhappy, love, and your poor Clotilda shall stay to succour you. Think not I can abandon you in your misfortunes. No! I will wander with thee through the wide world, and be thy servant, thy slave, if thou wilt have it so'" (Ainsworth 365). Erilda's suitor has to urge on her the same renunciation Clotilda so dutifully embraces as a token of love, but both spouses-to-be gain the benefits, as Ludloe promised Carwin.

In the confusion of flight from a forced marriage, Erilda mistakenly stabs her father and has the same revelation as Clotilda in elopement: both lovers are demons. Erilda's incubus thoughtfully counsels her on her offense before stabbing her with a trident and pitching her in the sea. "'You are lost to Heaven—you scrupled to commit an immediate murder, yet planned a lingering death for the parent who had nurtured you—you would not stab, but preferred planting daggers in your father's bosom. Murderess! . . . reflect on his daughter's infamy'" (Anne of Swansea 258–59). Clotilda's fiancé throws her off a precipice, but "her last parting glance was cast in kindness on his face," while he bellows, "'not mine is the crime!'" (Ainsworth 370). Each woman dies a slow death after her fall, a death as luridly embellished as that of Matthew Lewis's Ambrosio in *The Monk*, and each is damned eternally for her flouting of patriarchal strictures.

Two points stand out here. The first is the women's clear adherence to the code of Gothic virtue. They knowingly commit no violation: they obediently place the desire and suffering of an other above their own, but it is now their suitors' wills that they follow instead of their fathers'. Their punishment for this normal transfer, undertaken for the love supposedly sanctioned by the Gothic, highlights the structure of patriarchy that underlies the ideology of romance. The women's resistance is not the usual abnegation that pleads only for veto power on potential mates or for a life in the convent. Both do agree to flee their fathers' houses, although their common motive is to spare their lovers pain as much as to seek their own pleasure. Yet even Clotilda's mild recognition that "for the first time she regretted that she was yet at home" (Ainsworth 362) nonetheless points to a major infraction of filial obligation. Still, neither suspects the diabolical identity of her husband-to-be, and certainly neither gets pleasure, power, or profit from the discovery, as Ambrosio does for a time from his connection with the demoness Matilda in *The Monk*. The second striking oddity is the demons' revulsion and indignation at what the women have done: denied the law of the father. Swansea's demon explicitly states that it is Erilda's transgression of her father's will, rather than the stabbing, that damns her. According to the authority of hell, heaven, fathers, and husbands, it is unquestionably Clotilda and Erilda who have sinned, not the father who demands of Erilda, "'If you value my affection, Morven must be your future lord; if not, your father is lost to you for ever'" (Anne of Swansea 249). The internal logic of these stories suggests that self-determined marriages can be nothing but demonic pacts and the death of fathers: whatever happens to the heroine is fit punishment for her presumption.

For heroines trained to find their identity in the love of fathers and husbands, a threat like that of Erilda's father undermines the foundations of personality. Erilda's resistance is unusual, even though her suitor functions as a transitional object to whom she transfers her allegiance. Such a transference is helped by society's qualified acknowledgment that daughters should become wives, but for the wife who then wakens to horror in marriage there is little recourse. The heroine who believes she has escaped courtship Gothic's economy of loss finds herself with no apparent capital of her own in marital Gothic. She must cleave to her husband. Some valorize their own pain because it allows the spouse to feel whole; many, as mentioned above, discipline themselves to become that desired: all testify, by word or action, to Gothic marriage as a *mise en abîme* of horror. In Walker's contemporary *The Third Life of Grange Copeland*, for example, Margaret marries no demon, but her expectation of ecstasy, freedom, and love is as decisively denied as it was for earlier heroines. "Misery had wakened her, and he had not needed to tell her she had married not into ecstasy, but into dread. Not into freedom, but into bondage; not into perpetual love, but into deepening despair. And he had not needed to tell her who was behind their misery . . . for someone, *something* did stand behind his cruelty to her (he made himself believe)" (176). The husband's need, like that of Grange, to believe himself justified in his actions has dire consequences for the wife in marital Gothic.

The demon's self-exculpating "It's not my fault!" is a litany within marital Gothic that is projected as the heroine's presumed culpability. The ground of the Gothic is littered with wounded and dead wives whose husbands assure them that their injuries are self-inflicted, caused by some larger force, or negligible because of the husbands' own pain. While love means endless giving for the heroine, for the husband love means never having to say he's sorry. In William Beckford's "The Nymph of the Fountain," Conrad is told by a servant that his wife of many years is a sorceress. "It cost his heart a hard struggle before he could determine the fate of the supposed sorceress" (172): without speaking to her about the charges, he leaves orders that she be boiled in her bath. Mr. Lunt, in Hugh Walpole's "Mrs. Lunt," is aggrieved by his wife's haunting him: "'If I killed her, she deserved it; she was never a good wife to me, not from the first; she shouldn't have irritated me as she did—she knew what my temper was'" (141).

Throughout the Gothic, husbands' beliefs in their own entitlement lead to wives' physical and psychological destruction as they fail to merge their identities entirely with their husbands'. Leigh Hunt's Otto suffers from the same sense of unfairness as Mr. Lunt after his wife's death because it "was a relief to him" to have her "patience" absorb his anger ("A Tale" 355–56). Everard, in Elizabeth von Armin's *Vera*, demands minute and entire devotion to his needs. Indignant at Vera, his first wife, for thoughtlessly falling from a window after fifteen years of marriage, he rejoices at the docility of his young second wife, Lucy. When her aunt warns him that, if he continues his suffocating expectations, "'it won't be anything like fifteen years this time,'" he is livid at what he projects as the presumption of all women, who "invariably started by thinking they could do as they liked with him" (311, 316).[16]

Menacing husbands who terrorize and eventually kill wives also try to make their own desires the center of two lives in Edith Wharton's "The Lady's Maid's Bell" and "Kerfol." The latter story plays grimly with covert and overt motives. The husband's "great love" is defined by his great jealousy and his immuring his young wife in a country estate. She weeps because she has "nothing in life to call her own. But that was a natural enough feeling in a wife attached to her husband; and certainly it must have been a great grief to Yves de Cornault that she bore no son" (89). The smooth assumptions of "natural" and "certainly," the ironic shift in emphasis to his grief and her failure, and the subtle asymmetry of relations here are juxtaposed to the Gothic barbarity with which he strangles each dog she owns and lays it on her bed when he suspects her of dalliance.

In each of these stories, the husband's actions are wholly explicable in his own mind, and often those of others, because he believes that his wife should be a narcissistic extension of himself rather than a discrete personality. Such a stance allows him to excuse himself and accuse her when his claims are not filled. Law and religion endorse his belief. In "Kerfol," the jury that tries Anne de Cornault for the death of her husband (the dogs' ghosts kill him) cannot comprehend

---

[16]Perhaps the strangest instance of this sense of masculine entitlement is found in Helen R. Hull's "The Clay-Shuttered Door." Killed in an automobile accident because her husband insists upon driving drunk, Thalia Corson remains animate to host dinner parties until he closes an important merger, held to earth by his "fear and self-desire" (225).

her unhappiness. What to her is a life of desolation and constant threat is to them a spoiled wife and a few dead dogs. They cannot hear her tale of trauma when it involves acts of commission, and those of omission simply do not exist for them. "It was true that her husband seldom spoke harshly to her; but there were days when he did not speak at all. It was true that he had never struck or threatened her; but he kept her like a prisoner at Kerfol" (93). Because of her rank, Anne is not executed but "handed over to the keeping of her husband's family, who shut her up in the keep of Kerfol, where she is said to have died many years later, a harmless madwoman" (101). "Keeping" a wife calls for stern measures; Anne's madness, like that of many another heroine, is finally the only escape route she has.

In all the stories discussed here as marital Gothic, women want to believe that they will be loved and honored as the language of courtships and weddings avows. Being a wife promises the freedom denied a daughter by increasing access to a larger world and tradition. What these women discover, however, is what Virginia Woolf experiences in a very different setting in "A Room of One's Own": "how unpleasant it is to be locked out; and . . . how it is worse perhaps to be locked in" (24). Ordinarily "dead" metaphor lives in her essay and in marital Gothic. Using the same words as the narrator of "The Yellow Wallpaper," Woolf can only wonder "What was one to do?" (8). Within or from their locked rooms, what these women have to say makes no sense to those around them. Their discourse is exclusively "other," incomprehensible to the hegemonic grammar of male authority that only recognizes voices echoing masculine desire.

One last instance of marital Gothic by Wharton, "Mr. Jones," elegantly highlights the silence, immobility, and enclosure that define the perfect wife and the perfect victim in marital Gothic. The frame is set in the twentieth century. Lady Jane Lynke inherits an ancestral house, but she finds that visitors are not welcome, that there are rooms she isn't allowed into, and that her life is becoming more and more confined through the strictures of the always unseen majordomo, Mr. Jones. Lady Jane tries to find the elusive Mr. Jones and also investigates the history of a sad-faced, unidentified ancestress. She collects this history piecemeal, over the strong objections of her housekeeper, who answers directly to Mr. Jones. She discovers that the husband of her subject is Peregrine Vincent Theobald Lynke. In vivid contrast to this extravagance of names, the woman he married in 1817 is identified on their tombstone as "Also His Wife." The story Lady Jane assembles reveals a literally mute and deaf wife married for her property and then sequestered. A piteous and eloquent letter epitomizes the plea of the heroine in marital Gothic to have her voice heard and her existence acknowledged.

> "My dear Lord, Acknowledging as I ever do the burden of the sad impediment which denies me the happiness of being more frequently in your company, I yet fail to conceive how anything in my state obliges that close seclusion in which Mr. Jones persists—and by your express orders, so he declares—in confining me. Surely, my lord, had you found it possible to spend more time with me since the day of our marriage, you would yourself have seen it to be unnecessary to put this restraint upon me. It is true, alas, that my unhappy infirmity denies me the happiness to speak with you, or to hear the accents of the voice I should love above all others could it but reach me; but, my dear husband, I would have you consider that my mind is in no way affected by this obstacle, but goes out to you, as my heart does, in a perpetual eagerness of attention, and that to sit in this great house alone, day after day, month after month, deprived of your company, and debarred also from any intercourse but that of the servants you have chosen to put about me, is a fate more cruel than I deserve and more painful than I can bear."
> (192–93)

"Also His Wife" lives in constant receptivity, "a perpetual eagerness of attention." Her needs for communication, movement, and space— for the marks of identity—are compressed to an austere minimum, and still she asks too much. She acknowledges infirmity and impediment because of her literal muteness, but also to reassure Lynke that she poses no threat. Still, she is too noisy in her demands. Seclusion, restraint, deprivation, and exclusion from all communication are her punishment.

Like other heroines of marital Gothic, "Also His Wife" trustingly has omitted anxiety for love's sake. She must learn it in her plot, although no pleasure principle follows here: trauma is the organizing principle of her existence. In this story, as in others, the suppression of voice and identity is replicated in individual biography and persists historically as well. Lady Jane, heiress and author, is herself curbed by the ghost of Mr. Jones, whose delegated authority is nonetheless powerful enough to endure for a century. Within this political unconscious, it is more necessary to repress sex than class.[17] And, as long as

---

[17]The story provides a neat hierarchical ranking. Mr. Jones embodies tradition through male authority and the delegated class authority of his master; the combination allows him to restrict Lady Jane, despite her rank. Mrs. Clemm, the housekeeper, has the authority of neither class nor sex: Mr. Jones kills her, rather than Lady Jane, for disobeying his orders.

the heroine's painfully learned anxiety remains entangled with what she and her husband are taught is love in the real world, there is no way she can consciously articulate her plight or end it.

"The Yellow Wallpaper"

In Charlotte Perkins Gilman's "The Yellow Wallpaper," set in turn-of-the-century America, the narrator, like "Also His Wife," has no name. To her physician-husband John, she is "darling," "little goose," and "little girl"; to herself she is an "I" articulated only with difficulty (21, 15, 23). I have chosen this much-discussed text as an example precisely because its familiarity lets the *unheimlich* of psychoanalysis emerge more clearly.[18] Omission of anxiety, trauma, reenactment of trauma, and attempted resolution shape the protagonist's clandestinely composed narrative so that her story exemplifies the central issues of authority in marital Gothic. Brought to the country for a summer rest-cure from her work, writing, she tentatively and unsuccessfully tries to achieve voice and mobility in her marriage. John—and through him society—cannot hear her protest against the unthinking placidity into which she is being trained, and she gradually displaces her sense of suppression and restriction to the women she sees imprisoned by the yellow wallpaper.

The narrator knows that something is wrong with the way she feels and the way she is living. It is John who insists that nothing can be wrong with her that more food, more sleep, and less stimulation will not cure. She is brought consequently to what she describes as "ancestral halls," "a hereditary estate," "a haunted house" (9) and, like the protagonists of "Kerfol" and "Mr. Jones," frequently left alone while her husband goes about his business. The house, cut off from all outside communication, is nonetheless a microcosm of social existence. What is expected of the narrator is clearly indicated by the new baby whom she seldom sees, and Jennie, the sister-in-law who is "a perfect and enthusiastic housekeeper" (17), unlike the narrator. The

[18]For insightful discussions of the protagonist's "reading," see Annette Kolodny's "A Map for Rereading" and Judith Fetterley's "Reading about Reading." For readings that focus particularly upon feminine discourse or the "writing" of what Paula A. Treichler calls the narrative's "impossible form" (73), see Treichler's "Escaping the Sentence," as well as the thoughtful responses by Karen Ford, Carol Thomas Neely, and Treichler herself, and Richard Feldstein's "Reader, Text, and Ambiguous Referentiality in 'The Yellow Wall-Paper.'" In "Feminist Criticism, 'The Yellow Wallpaper,' and the Politics of Color in America," Susan S. Lanser makes a persuasive, original case for the reproduction and repression of racism in the text and in white feminist analysis.

most powerful influence is exerted by John, of course, who is adamant in his insistence that she trust in him, that she recognize her own perceptions as "fancies," and that she improve her self-control and discipline accordingly. Her anxiety is symptomatic of the traumatic denial of identity; all her environment can suggest is the omission of that anxiety for love's sake. She can only re-present the trauma because what reality principle shows her is that *no* pleasure principle is possible in John's world. Like Dora, she is supposed to believe that the fault is her own.

Despite the narrator's uneasiness at the effects of her vegetative existence, John insists that all will be—*is*—well if she will only accept his analysis of her condition. If she will only trust in him as husband and doctor, she need have no anxiety. "'Can you not trust me as a physician?'" (24). "'I am a doctor, dear, and I know'" (23). John's "knowing," which is grounded in the "real" world of gender expectations and hierarchy, is at odds with the protagonist's "knowing" that something is badly awry in the relation between her world and John's. Although the speaker is excruciatingly aware of the two worlds, John sees only one, in which she must conform for the sake of others. He urges her to "take care of myself for his sake" (22), and, when she hesitatingly suggests that only her bodily health is improving, he vehemently repudiates any implied mental illness and places her a sorry third in his scheme of values. "'My darling,' said he, 'I beg of you, for my sake and for our child's sake, as well as for your own, that you will never for one instant let that idea enter your mind!'" (24).

According to John, only by exercising greater self-control can the protagonist act as she properly ought—for others—and rid herself of her chimerical anxiety. When she suggests that her "sensitivity" is "due to this nervous condition," John is quick to refute the possibility that there might be any reason for her perceptions: "But John says if I feel so, I shall neglect proper self-control" (11). The speaker knows that her misery can only be seen as a self-indulgent dereliction of "my duty" (14). Originating in her own unhappiness with the roles assigned to her, it can have no validity in John's schema, where the only parts cast for her are wife and mother. "John does not know how much I really suffer. He knows there is no *reason* to suffer, and that satisfies him" (14). The speaker's suffering disappears—or is supposed to—in the light of John's rationalism. It remains her own fault insofar as she uses her "imaginative power and habit of story-making" (15) and does not use her "will and good sense to check the tendency" (16). Because neither John nor society will alter gender

expectations, the onus is on the protagonist to change her expectations. "He says no one but myself can help me out of it, that I must
use my will and self-control and not let any silly fancies run away
with me" (22).

John can see no logical reason for her depression; therefore, she
cannot be depressed. The protagonist's acceptance of the daily regimen he prescribes leaves him unable to perceive her mental retreat.
As she continues to withdraw to the only autonomy possible to her,
John continues to maintain that she is "improving" because she
sleeps all day, eats well, and speaks less and less. When she cries, it is
privately, even if "most of the time" (19), and what to her is a frightening loss of energy is to him an encouraging placidity. He presumes
her confirmation of his wise diagnosis: "'You know the place is doing
you good'"; "'You really are better, dear, whether you see it or not'"
(15, 23). When the narrator stops all resistance and becomes "more
quiet" because she has something "to expect, to look forward to, to
watch" in the drama of the woman imprisoned in the wallpaper, his
course of treatment has succeeded entirely, and "John is so pleased to
see me improve!" (27). The narrator has become an exemplar of
Gothic passivity to any spectator. What this text demonstrates beautifully, however, is the strenuous activity of working through that is
the unseen counterpart of her seeming stasis.

The narrator cannot alter John's logical cosmogony; she can only
absent herself from it psychically while physically embracing its precepts on what she should be. Her powerlessness in the face of John's
authority as husband and doctor is overwhelming. His decrees are
endorsed by her brother, representative of paternal power, and by the
medical system, which sanctions husbandly authority as completely
here as the legal system does in "Kerfol." There is no escaping the
confines of John's diagnostic rubric.

> If a physician of high standing, and one's own husband, assures
> friends and relatives that there is really nothing the matter with one but
> temporary nervous depression—a slight hysterical tendency—what is
> one to do?
> My brother is also a physician, and also of high standing, and he says
> the same thing. (10)

John's suggestion (threat?) that she might be sent to Weir Mitchell, the
alienist, in the fall, only underscores the unanimous and far-reaching
accord of domestic and medical authority. A friend "who was in his
hands once" tells her "he is just like John and my brother, only more

so!" (19). It is not surprising that the metaphor chosen for the suffocating wallpaper is that "it sticketh closer than a brother" (17).

John's infantilizing treatment of the protagonist denies her adult identity. The dimunitives he uses to address her, like the room he chooses for her, are childish, but become ominous when imposed on an adult. Both communication and mobility are taken away from her "for her own good," and the net effect is rather like *Gaslight* with the husband "meaning well." The protagonist wants a room that opens on the piazza, but "John would not hear of it" (12). The isolated room he prefers may have been nursery or asylum, and it shows the ambiguous jointure of children and infantilized women with its bolted-down bedstead, barred windows, rings on the wall, and gated stairway. Her movement is further restricted by the "schedule prescription" John has worked out for each hour of her day, which requires her sleeping after each meal and "resting" between those times. There is no room for deviation within John's plan: "He is very careful and loving, and hardly lets me stir without special direction" (12). She cannot reach out for contact, and neither can anyone reach in. When she asks for company because "It is so discouraging not to have any advice and companionship about my work, . . . he says he would as soon put fireworks in my pillow-case as to let me have those stimulating people about now" (16). John, like Conrad in William Beckford's "The Nymph of the Fountain," is able to pronounce sentence and go to town; the protagonist has no such recourse. She cannot stir from her "haunted house," and can move very little within it, like the women she eventually sees trying to escape the bars of the wallpaper.

Writing, which would allow interior journeys, is also forbidden, and we must assume that this is in large part because it is "unnatural" articulation for a woman. Jennie, that exemplar of domesticity, suspects its dangers: "I verily believe she thinks it is the writing which made me sick!" (18). John "hates to have me write a word," but is willing to "read to me till it tired my head" (13, 21). Writing is seditiously independent and active; dutifully listening to John's voice is appropriately wifely and passive.

The protagonist is discouraged from any willful use of voice in writing or speech—from any assertion of herself as a subject with the potential power to alter her social world. At different points, she asks for another room, to repaper the room in which they do stay, to have or make visits, to move back to town early, and to have her schedule changed. Although "response" and "spouse" are etymologically related, they have no connection in John's practice. In each request,

John hears only an attempt to question his judgment, and he refuses her. Granting one petition would establish an inappropriate precedent and rebalancing of power. "He said that after the wall-paper was changed it would be the heavy bedstead, and then the barred windows, and then that gate at the head of the stairs, and so on" (14). One of the few times he "agrees" with her, his trivialization and dismissal of her belief that she is getting no better are chilling in their obtuseness. "'Bless her little heart!' said he with a big hug, 'she shall be as sick as she pleases!'" (24). All told, then, the severity and duration of the narrator's trauma in this text is unquestionable. Her environment systematically strips away any vestigial autonomy, resists change, and limits her identity to a functional aspect of John's.

The lack of response and recognition demonstrated by John's infantilizing tone and his use of the third person assures the narrator's use of repetition to identify and master her predicament. Repetition structures her narrative locally and globally, and is further accentuated by her account's febrile and chattily superficial tone and diction. The story's form and content thus precisely mirror the protagonist's psychological movement as she repeats what cannot be borne or believed. The impact of local repetition marks the text from the first, when "what is one to do?" appears three times in the first two pages (10). The most conspicuous verbal marker is the perennial "John says" or "he says." What originally seems like docile echolalia indicating the narrator's wholesale incorporation of John's views assumes remarkable flexibility of intonation in the course of the story, however, and eventually functions as a covert and ironic commentary on any subsequent statement. This particular tag allows the speaker to avoid direct confrontation or rebuttal and yet express her own view by implicit opposition.

Much of the local repetition, which is sensory and related to the wallpaper, also works as an oblique commentary—a corrective to the stimulation refused the narrator, and a concretization of the intangible forces that repress her. The paper itself occasions olfactory, visual, tactile, and kinetic repetition that is a grotesque exaggeration of and rebellion against the monotonous schedule of her days. Its sulfurous smell is as ubiquitous and invisible as the cultural codes that surround her: the "subtlest, most enduring odor I ever met" (29). The physicality of her contact with the wallpaper increases as the story continues. She begins by only looking at the paper again and again to see if she can trace its pattern and hence its organizing principle. Later, she maps it with her hands, and, finally, she copies the movements of the women she sees by crawling around the room. Her obsessive repetition of someone's—possibly another woman's—earlier compulsion explains the "smooch" on the paper. "I wonder how it was done and who did it, and what they did it for. Round and round and round—round and round and round—it makes me dizzy!" (29). Like the whirling of Hoffmann's Nathanael in "The Sandman" or the automaton-like actions of the raped nun in Russ's "Souls," the circularity of the protagonist's movement and voice records the loss of all connection with the outer world and, in this case, a dreadfully ironic miming of what that world wanted.

The most prominent repetition in the story's structure is the frequent and abrupt transition from individual voice to distanced, "rational" discourse. On the local level, statements that are non sequiturs yoke together disparate elements in one sentence to create a new logic and causality. On the global level, the narrator's frightening and futile consideration of her circumstances precipitates shifts to "safe" topics: the house, its rooms, and its paper. The sharp alternation between the two emphasizes their mutual incompatibility in John's world until, by story's end, the protagonist merges them by entering the realm of the yellow wallpaper.

Local non sequiturs are introduced in a mild form at the very beginning of the story, when the protagonist is musing on the mystery of their rented house. "John laughs at me, of course, but one expects that in marriage" (9). The personal declarative, "John laughs at me," is oriented by the conjunction "but" to gender expectations and distanced by the universal "one." The yoking is not complete, however, and the two clauses remain jarringly discrepant, with no further commentary to bridge the gap between them. The discordance is increased when, shortly after, we are told that "John is a physician, and *perhaps* . . . *perhaps* that is one reason I do not get well faster" (9–10). There is no room in John's philosophy for such a nonsensical sentence, and the protagonist's emphasis indicates her own hesitation at the linking. As readers, we form the chain of signification that brings together ideolect and communal language, feminine speaking subject and masculine hegemonic discourse. By the time the speaker notes that "it is so hard to talk with John about my case, because he is so wise, and because he loves me so" (23), we are able to translate both dialects. The narrator's "case" really is incommunicable because of John's gender-inflected ideology of wisdom and love that makes his own voice (and that of other males) the only one he can hear. John's system is impermeable, but the wallpaper may be comprehensible, may allow her a measure of expression and self-determination: "I had no intention of telling him it [her "improvement"] was *because* of the wall-paper" (28).

She displaces what cannot be fathomed or consciously said about her role as wife and mother to the house and the wallpaper. At a certain pitch of intensity, she ostensibly moves away from talking about herself to discussion of safe, inanimate objects, and this repeated transition organizes the story globally. "John says the very worst thing I can do is to think about my condition, and I confess it always makes me feel bad. So I will let it alone and talk about the house" (10–11). This rhythmic structure of alternating topics exemplifies her need to deal with the denial of identity she finds in marital Gothic. The repetition of trauma is denied and then re-presented vividly in the wallpaper's puzzlingly systematic bars. "I wish I could get well faster. But I must not think about that. This paper looks to me . . ." (16). Her seemingly decisive change of focus here and elsewhere, further emphasized by paragraph breaks in the original, nonetheless yokes the two topics in the same way as her use of conjunctions on the sentence level. These repetitions—like the thematic ones that unite husband, brother, medical and social authority—allow her to present symptomatically the forces that repress her, as do the economical allusions to the Gothic genre provided by setting and plot.

Like so many heroines of the Gothic, the protagonist cannot alter the environment that traumatizes her. Her attempts to modify it by increasing her independence of voice and movement are fruitless. Instead, she recreates and relives her situation via the wallpaper, still holding to the letter of the law on what it means to be a good girl and a good wife. She does not act against others ("I thought seriously of burning the house" [29]) or herself ("To jump out of the window would be admirable exercise" [34]), because steps like that are "improper and might be misconstrued" (35). Instead, she immerses herself in her madness, achieving a dreadful freedom by doing for herself what John has hitherto done to her. Within a system that only she can understand, she gains autonomy and power.

The narrator can now guard herself in a way that was impossible when she half-believed in the omission of anxiety for love's sake. The "real" world can only offer her renewed trauma. Her revision of reality principle is necessarily radical: she creates an alternative world in which pleasure is possible and John's "loving" authority can be questioned. "I have found out another funny thing, but I shan't tell it this time! It does not do to trust people too much" (31). When John asks "professional questions" of her and Jennie, she exults in his inability to understand what has happened, and for the first time explicitly discounts his wisdom. He "pretended to be very loving and kind. As if I couldn't see through him!" (32). By carrying out John's strictures to the edge of doom, she retaliates and assures response. She says, "I want to astonish him" (34), and she does. Finally identified with the woman in the wallpaper, and the only one to comprehend that identification, she can jovially reciprocate his dimunitives by calling him "young man" (35). When she locks herself in the room so that she can crawl in freedom, John is for the first time silenced "for a few moments" (36).

> Then he said—very quietly indeed, "Open the door, my darling!"
> "I can't," said I. "The key is down by the front door under a plantain leaf!"
> And then I said it again, several times, very gently and slowly, and said it so often that he had to go and see. (36)

John must now pay attention to her statements and himself be schooled in repetition. By embracing the horror that was thrust upon her previously, the protagonist finally achieves a sadly limited and ironic autonomy. John will still decide what happens to her physical self, but she has taken her psychic self out of his reach. Through repetition, she has learned that she will never have voice or identity in John's world. She has ended the appearance of horror by refusing to return to the reality of marital Gothic.

The impasse of Gilman's narrator between individual insight and unchanging social codes is one faced by all Gothic heroines. The web of authority that constructs their social reality is first perceptible to most in family relationships, but they discover it to be finely and inextricably linked to religious, legal, medical and educational systems as well. All reverberate when any one point is touched and, needless to say, no neat sweeping away is possible. The wedding ceremony is supposed to clean the house of paternal authority, but it instead ushers in the husband as an avatar of the father. The heroine is restricted by laws to which she is subject, but according to which she can be no subject. She must somehow solve a cultural conundrum that offers the right to exist socially in return for the disavowal of autonomous identity. Insofar as the heroine's identity is bound by what she has been told of love and duty, the Gothic plot can only be symptomatic: the endless recollection and repetition of a trauma that remains unknown to her while its effects shape her life. When there is a working through or resolution, however, the heroine begins to see her own plight as explicable and no longer unique. This new consciousness—basically, the awareness of gender expectations—cannot in itself end the traumatic prohibition of identity. Thus, individual insight is crucial but inadequate to resolve the Gothic plot. To end repetition, the heroine must resituate herself in relation to authority—no easy task, as heroine after heroine attests.

A key detail omitted from the previous discussion—the wallpaper itself—is a fit emblem for the cipher of gender authority. The narrator believes that there must be a logical "principle" or "laws" (20) determining the pattern of the paper, because there are supposed to be rules for such things, just as there must be comprehensible reasons for gender expectations. Yet, what she sees are curves and angles that "plunge off at outrageous angles, destroy themselves in unheard of contradictions" (13), although she suspects that "the interminable grotesques seem to form around a common centre" (20). She is determined to find that "common centre," to know the principle by which it multiplies itself and generates sub-patterns. "I *will* follow that pointless pattern to some sort of a conclusion" (19). Just as the structures of authority in *The Castle of Otranto*, "Kerfol," and "Mr. Jones" remain inaccessible to their protagonists, so too the paper's laws resist her analysis. "You think you have mastered it, but just as you get well underway in following, it turns a back-somersault and there you are. It slaps you in the face, knocks you down, and tramples upon you. It is like a bad dream" (25). The paper, unlikely concretization of authority's horror though it is, is inescapable and aggressive when challenged. It is old and has endured over time: "I get positively angry with the impertinence of it and the everlastingness" (16). Others have been subjected to it and angered by its overpowering ubiquity, and she worries about its effect being repeated over generations, just as Lady Jane realizes that her restrictions are the same as those that limited her nameless predecessor a century ago.

The narrator's repeated study of the paper's controlling patterns lets her see what the cultural codes embedded in this story and all Gothics also reveal: a trapped woman. Indistinct at first, "the faint figure behind seemed to shake the pattern, just as if she wanted to get out" (23). The figure and the bars restraining her become more sharply formed in time, although "subdued" and "quiet" in certain lights, when the pattern "keeps her so still" (26). At first it seems that the women who try to escape only become dead witnesses to hopelessness.

Sometimes I think there are a great many women behind, and some-times only one, and she crawls around fast, and her crawling shakes it all over. . . .

And she is all the time trying to climb through. But nobody could climb through that pattern—it strangles so; I think that is why it has so many heads.

They get through, and then the pattern strangles them off and turns them upside down, and makes their eyes white!

If those heads were covered or taken off it would not be half so bad. (30)

The protagonist inverts the loving and entire acceptance of au-thoritarian strictures that Hippolita and others proclaim. Better de-capitation, an honest separation of body and head, than being one of the living dead. Through her repetition, she gains enough understand-ing of the pattern to know that some escape is possible, and her identity and interests merge with the woman behind the bars. "I pulled and she shook, I shook and she pulled, and before morning we had peeled off yards of that paper" (32). Here, at last, is reciprocity.

By entering the world of the yellow wallpaper, the speaker has improved her lot through the mutated freedom that lets her creep an everlasting round by day and be again locked up at night. Her "es-cape" is obviously partial, destructive, and deeply ironic, even if we credit her present-tense narrative as a testament of survival. It is nonetheless escape to the only freedom available to her, and it func-tions as a scathing indictment of authority in the outside world. While other Gothic protagonists struggle to deal with their prohibited iden-tity, this speaker has recognized her dilemma, measured the scope allowed to her, and disabused herself of belief in the benevolent intention behind those limits. Clearly aware of trauma and able to identify its source in the ideology of authority, she has entered a cognate world in which she can move and speak. The narrator suc-ceeds in what every protagonist of marital Gothic desires: her exis-tence as a autonomous subject has been recognized. She has spoken, if only once, and been heard.

The Gothic heroine's story is not simply one of self-awareness in which the burden is the individual's alone, however: it necessarily implicates and indicts the culture that refuses her voice. Her anxiety is grounded in a real and present danger, and her repetition actively attempts resolution. Her resistance to authority—finally, to her own victimization—is extraordinarily complicated by its seemingly ubiq-uitous manifestations and by her own continuing relationships to her culture. What action *can* follow recognition? Dora gives notice and walks out the door; others register their protest by joining the dubious martyrs' list of the dead and the mad that simultaneously inscribes opposition to and the ruling power of hegemony. What finally does lay Gothic horror to rest is the refusal of masculinist authority as the only reality to which one can turn and return.

2

"A Woman is Being Beaten"
and Its Vicissitudes

The Gothic novel is a peep show of terror. Distanced—and, of course, safe—in our role as observers, we watch the protagonist's repeated trials by experience and think ourselves dispassionate and immune. The protagonist also often begins by assuming that she is only a witness to the events in which she soon finds herself a partici- pant. The bond between spectator and spectacle is far more intimate, however, as the narrator of Isak Dinesen's "The Deluge at Nor- derney" dryly affirms: "It is doubtful whether any spectacle can be enjoyed in the same way by those people who may, after all, run a risk of becoming part of it and by those who are by circumstance entirely cut off from any such possibility. . . . In the same way it is unlikely that even the most pious old lady would attend the trial and burning of a witch with quite the untroubled mind of the male au- dience around the stake" (21). Every female reader of the Gothic is such a spectator, whether or not she acknowledges her uncomfort- able affinity with the victim and her own risk. The aunts, mothers, and older women whose stories the protagonist thinks can never be her own might themselves sadly recognize her familiar plot as it develops before them and remember when they too thought that they would be exceptions, untouched spectators of Gothic relationships.

The role of spectator seems to promise protection. Minimally, you are safe for the duration of the spectacle: you know at least that it's not you who is burning at the stake this go-round. What the spectator learns at the pageant of horror may also prevent her from becoming a victim later. The vantage point of spectator can also, of course, en- courage the belief that one's self could never be the victim. Standing apart from the event viewed, the watcher may come to believe herself uninvolved and even privileged by dint of her vantage point. As Freud emphasizes, the urges to look and to know—what he terms the scopophilic and epistemophilic instincts—are closely related to one another and to sadism. To look, then, can be to know, to be privy to the forbidden knowledge that means power. This knowledge is sometimes denied, sometimes reluctantly acknowledged, and sometimes embraced, but each protagonist of the Gothic must, in her role as voyeur, come to terms with it in order to deal with her own suffering and that of others.

In the last chapter, I explored how repetition compulsion can be a way to overcome trauma. Some characters do not survive recognition of the gap between experience and gender ideology: their testaments to the destructive contradictions of culture are their madness and deaths. Without joining the cult-of-dead-women fan club, we can nonetheless honor the representation of an anguished integrity. Other characters, like Hippolita in Walpole's *The Castle of Otranto*, replicate oppression as they blindly and unwittingly repeat their own trauma. Thus, culture's traumatic denial of women's identities can be either disavowed or recognized through repetition. Julia Kristeva claims: "The literary narrative that utters the workings of repetition must necessarily become . . . a narrative of the infamous" (24). The Gothic is such a narrative and its infamous scandal is a suffering woman.

In this chapter and the next, I want to consider the psychoanalytic presentation of that most "natural" female instinct, masochism, and how it, like repetition compulsion, can move toward death or life, erasure or recognition of subjectivity. My argument is that masochism too can further individual psychic survival when pressed into the service of a besieged ego. This is not to valorize the depreciated pole of the psychoanalytic and cultural dichotomies, masochism/sadism, passive/active, but to question the very interpretative splitting process that leaches initiative, volition, and activity from the masochist. Key psychoanalytic issues related to masochism—its function in maintaining identity, scopophilia, beating fantasies, and the development of active and passive instincts—will frame and direct our understanding of the Gothic's central concerns. The urge to look, for example, so evident both in Gothic heroines and in patients as they try to decipher the secrets of others, at first seems a mode of knowledge readily available to all. Yet looking and being looked at are finely monitored and expressed instincts, as we will see in the common beating fantasy. Furthermore, what appears within the field of vision—in this case, the beating fantasy—may well be a commentary upon specific kinds of knowledge the spectator has gained through experience. Behaviors that at first seem masochistically passive display a startling amount of initiative on the part of women who need to know what they and others are doing in a Gothic spectacle.

This chapter emphasizes Freud's construction of "normal" femininity and masculinity through the specific focus of the beating fantasy. In order to investigate the biases of that construction and its implications for female development, in Chapter 3 I place "A Child Is Being Beaten" in the context of other essays that discuss the crucial significance of the active drives and their centrality to the anal stage. The beating fantasy can then be understood as not only the persistent representation of subordination in which "a child is being beaten" but also as part of an analytic strategy that situates "normal" feminine passivity—a reluctance to look, know, or act aggressively—in a pre-Oedipal period. The girl's active drives, rechanneled through passive, inward-turning routes, will pave the way for the masochistic, exhibitionist woman who is supposed to be blind to the forbidden knowledge that shapes her life.

Masochism in the Service of the Ego

Masochism, like repetition compulsion, can be a psychic strategy that makes the best of a bad business, that insists on wresting identity and self-affirmation from the biased social contract that traumatizes women. Within the silent and immobile enclosure of the Gothic heroine, the traditional analytic confines of the woman patient, or the "good" housewife's culturally mandated domestic setting, strange and subtle renegotiations can take place. For example, masochism's embarrassing "pleasure in pain" shades easily into altruism's noble self-sacrifice, so prized socially. A woman who is recognized and valued for her service to others may well find in her self-abnegation a stable core of identity and, even if she sometimes longs for wider fields of activity, rest content. In other instances, a woman may look coolly at the pact her world offers her, and reject it with every power at her disposal.

Just as recollection and repetition do not always lead to working through, then, neither does masochism represent simply a capitulation to or resistance against the cultural trauma that denies a woman's identity. It may point to either. It also marks the compromised ground of a large and disturbing group: those who recognize in a limited fashion the discrepancy between what they see and what they are told to believe and who then direct their energies toward "passing" within the system that oppresses them. Their strategy is not simply that of the survivor. They fully incorporate and perpetuate the cultural split that enables hierarchy. What they resent is not the system that subordinates them, but their own exclusion from its upper reaches. Thus, when possible, they will use their understanding of the Gothic world to achieve what power they can within it. At its worst, this "use" is not subversion or resistance, but complicity. Ironically, their partial uncovering of culture's gender duplicity helps to preserve and strengthen hierarchy's structure.[1]

Trauma is not a proof of individual merit in life or fiction. Women's identities are articulated through their responses, which cover a spectrum of possibilities, and not solely through the event. Several basic but difficult corollaries follow the central truth of women's Gothic trauma and the masochism that so often accompanies it: being oppressed does not make one a de facto nice person; entirely identifying oneself as a victim (as distinct from knowing that victimization is a truth but not one's whole identity) has manifold problems; the abused may in turn replicate their own trauma and become abusers. Thus, for many of the group described above who try to succeed in a Gothic world, the aim is not to deny or resist the self-destructive aims of gender ideology but to close the gap between self and dominant other, individual expectation and social reality, by full merger. What I am suggesting here is emphatically not the infamous "willing victim": the aggressor remains responsible. Indeed, such victims' embrace and attempted manipulation of patriarchal rigidity may argue that they are the most psychically damaged characters. Their victimization can erode what we usually like to consider an essential core of identity. Such a victim will identify with her oppressor and this deterioration of ego then affects her dealings with others.

The valence and use of masochism can also vary. Masochism, as Ann Greif reminds us, is a "reification of early trauma in which pain becomes associated with pleasure in all its forms, from sexual pleasure to romantic love" (3). Masochism is a sensitive node that registers the paradoxical relations between women and culture brought about by that early and continuing trauma; it is, as Clara Thompson maintains, "a form of adaptation to an unsatisfactory and circumscribed life" ("Cultural Pressures in the Psychology of Women" 133).[2]

---

[1] Foucault's analysis of the deployment of power is very much to the point here. See particularly *The History of Sexuality. Vol. I: An Introduction* and *Discipline and Punish*.
[2] As Paula J. Caplan argues in *The Myth of Women's Masochism*, "A misogynist society

In traditional analytic nomenclature, masochism on the one hand acknowledges the infliction of genuine pain; on the other, it insists that the woman is responsible for soliciting her own suffering. The agency of the dominator is erased, and we focus on the obscure and puzzlingly passive desires of the woman. In corrective readings, the dominator's power is emphasized, and we recognize the masochist as a victim. In both cases, however, the woman is absence—much like the Gothic heroine whose mystery so often centers on the dominating presence of the manor lord. Other corrective readings that recast the masochist as the "real" dominator err in simply reversing, rather than addressing, the basic dichotomy.[3]

In discussing masochism, I do not want to emphasize what is done *to* the women without also examining what they are *doing*—the ways in which they use masochism as a strategy to create and maintain identity, not solely as a sad acknowledgment of absence. In trying to avoid either/or options of active/passive, agent/victim, I am arguing against a polarization that simply switches who's on top (but always assumes that one must be) and in favor of a mutual and deeply problematic regulation through which both sadist and masochist define self and other. Jacqueline Rose's skepticism about binary analysis is to the point here: "Perhaps for women it is of particular importance that we find a language which allows us to recognise our part in intolerable structures—but in a way which renders us neither the

---

has created a myriad of situations that make women unhappy. And then that same society uses the myth of women's masochism to blame the women themselves for their misery" (22). Robert Robertiello also identifies social causation as the source of women's masochism rather than inherent biological or psychological factors. And, as Elizabeth A. Waites argues in "Female Masochism and the Enforced Restriction of Choices," labeling the result of enforced restriction masochistic "is at best an evasion of determining factors and at worst a naive excuse for cruelty" (539). In the same issue of *Victimology*, see also Lenore Walker's classic essay upon masochism as a learned behavior, "Battered Women and Learned Helplessness." In *Bound by Love*, Lucy Gilbert and Paula Webster present a compelling analysis of how both parents, acting as social agents, teach daughters submission. Natalie Shainess's *Sweet Suffering*, in contrast, displays a disturbing readiness to displace social agency by naming as masochism all pain inflicted upon women, even in instances as extreme as date rape (7).

[3]The literature of sadomasochism shows the same ac/dc switching, as Gertrud Lenzer demonstrates in her analysis of Sacher-Masoch and German writings of the 1930s, in which women's inferior, masochistic status easily transmutes into her all-powerful domination. As William Blake suggests in the endless reversals of "The Mental Traveller," such reversals leave the basic dichotomy unchanged.

She lives upon his shrieks & cries,
And she grows young as he grows old.

Till he becomes a bleeding youth,
And she becomes a Virgin bright;
Then he rends up his Manacles
And binds her down for his delight. (19–24)

pure victims nor the sole agents of our distress" (*Sexuality* 14).[4] *In the Name of Love*, like the Gothic novel itself and much contemporary feminist work in criticism and in psychoanalysis, is part of the search for such a language.

Just as we err in our frequent desire to sort characters or patients into "pure victims" or "sole agents," so too we can be misled by the tempting dichotomy of external/internal causation. Masochism, the learned behavior of the oppressed, cannot be cheerfully or easily sloughed off even should such a utopian opportunity present itself. It is a basic coping strategy to defend the ego, one internalized by oppressed women and others: modification is slow and itself painful, as it is for any such strategy. The key dilemma here, as Jessica Benjamin emphasizes, is in understanding the purposes of that internalization: "The individual tries to achieve freedom through slavery, release through submission to control. Once we understand submission to be the *desire* of the dominated as well as their helpless fate, we may hope to answer the central question, How is domination anchored in the hearts of those who submit to it?" (*The Bonds of Love* 52). Given oppression as a premise, masochism can work to create and preserve a coherent self, to control repetition of trauma, and to regulate others as well as the self.

The greatest incentive for masochism is stated with wry brevity by a patient: "'I guess if you're a victim, you're never alone'" (Montgomery 34). Someone is always there for the masochist, even if only as mental representation. At the same time, however, masochism emphasizes the self as discrete from others through the distance between masochist and sadist, a distance bridged only by pain. Masochism, as James Sacksteder points out, can serve as the precarious center of a functioning and stable identity. "A masochistic identity is a type of negative identity, which, however costly and pathological, nonetheless represents for some individuals their best possible effort at creating and maintaining a separate and autonomous sense of self, one that salvages for them a modicum of satisfaction, security, and self-esteem and thereby staves off tugs toward identity diffusion, psychotic regression, and/or suicide" ("Thoughts on the Positive Value of a Negative Identity" 106).[5] What at first seems solely an indication of

---

[4]Kristeva also emphasizes the permeability and friability of the boundaries between subject/object/abject. See particularly her chapters "Approaching Abjection" (1–31) and "From Filth to Defilement" (56–89). As Teresa de Lauretis points out in a different context, feminist thinking that is "contained within the frame of a conceptual opposition that is 'always already' inscribed . . . will tend to reproduce [patriarchy]" (1–2).

[5]Greif adds to the point in her "Historical Synthesis": "The masochistically disordered person lives in an experiential world of misery, humiliation, and anxiety, pri-

loss and grotesque heterosexual adaptation is also a mechanism that assures continuity for the ego. The repetition of masochism is not simply a gendered death-drive but the individual's fight for life and a future.

The young girl's relations with both parents show the same double movement toward unity and toward separation. Neither parent—nor their numerous social surrogates—is solely accountable for the masochist. The girl whose nascent autonomy is persistently discouraged finds approval and recognition only through her loving tractability. If she must choose between loss of love and loss of autonomy she will choose, as Paula Caplan maintains in *The Myth of Women's Masochism*, to keep the love that mirrors and affirms her existence (79). In doing so, she imitates her mother. But, as Benjamin argues, she is also effecting her transition from the too-close mother to the father who represents difference and autonomy in stereotypical contemporary child-rearing. Her later, dominant lover will mirror both relations and "actually provides a dual solution, containment *and* excitement, the holding environment and the road to freedom—the joint features of both the ideal mother and father" (120). Thus, even within the confines of masochism, the girl simultaneously seeks security *and* freedom, and will continue to do so as best she can. The seeming passivity of masochism disappears the more we consider: its passivity is primarily that of means, while its end remains the activity refused the girl by her culture. By repeating this traumatic prohibition, she achieves self-control and potentially masters trauma, as Robert Stoller makes clear in *Sexual Excitement*: "Masochism is a technique of control, first discovered in childhood following trauma, the onslaught of the unexpected. The child believes it can prevent further trauma by re-enacting the original trauma. Then, as master of the script, he is no longer a victim; he can decide for himself when to suffer pain rather than having it strike without warning. Or, when we have more of the hidden text, we can see masochism as an attack ('suffering is my revenge')" (125).[6]

---

marily constituted for self-protection against harsh emotional and interpersonal realities that threaten the self with painful fragmentation" (2). For an early and influential analysis of masochism as self-preservation, see Esther Menaker's study, *Masochism and the Emergent Ego*, particularly "Masochism" (52–67).

[6]Angela Carter says of Sade's Justine: "If her suffering itself becomes a kind of mastery, it is a masochistic mastery over herself" (*The Sadeian Woman and the Ideology of Pornography* 50). As she continues to point out, however, mastery of oneself that prohibits stopping the suffering of others or rebellion against one's oppressors is sadly limited. I would argue that a large part of the social function of masochism is precisely to keep women's energies engaged in this self-monitoring.

Masochistic fantasy—or the Gothic novel—allows the spectator to move from what Stoller calls "unprotected trauma" to a place where she "controls the action herself" (106). Stoller's discussion of masochistic fantasy is particularly useful here in dealing with why a woman might persistently image her own humiliation or that of others when no external coercion is at first obvious. Fantasy keeps "the details of the earlier traumas and frustrations embedded in the fantasy, to allow an endless repetition that reverses trauma to triumph" (30). While on the one hand masochistic fantasy asserts its similarity to earlier trauma, on the other it stresses its differences, differences evident in what Stoller talks about as the "scripts" of fantasy.

What is evident is that the most dedicated masochist in practice or fantasy has "no *compulsion* to repeat pain and self-destruction, only the wily wish, the compulsion *not* to repeat suffering" (123).[7] The masochist offers her own fantasy to ward off a worse dream or reality. By presenting herself as spectacle, she asserts that she always/already has paid enough. By casting herself as the spectator of sado/masochistic fantasy, she ambiguously signals her distance from the story and characters she so tenaciously represents.[8] In both cases, however, she has no doubt but that someone must suffer, and there is an admixture of pleasure in the spectacle. For by producing the script of the beating fantasy or a Gothic plot, the script writer works to assure her own agency. Furthermore, even the figure whose position is most troublingly passive, the beaten, is recognized and perhaps even valued by dint of her very suffering. She too achieves her own form of agency and object relations via pain: her passivity may control others; her conspicuous and silent suffering can shout an accusation at her

[7]Stoller continues here and in his later work to distinguish these instances from the exact repetition of traumatic neuroses. See also Louise Kaplan's *Female Perversions*, which draws upon Stoller's concepts of script and masquerade to construct a compelling gender-based analysis of perversion.

[8]In Carole Maso's *Ghost Dance*, this quandary is beautifully presented in the final sado-masochistic meeting between Vanessa and her lover Jack. The scene's status as fantasy or reality remains unclear (as does the very existence of Jack), so that his statements as he binds, blindfolds, and beats her may be taunt, challenge, or sorrowful admonishment. He insists that he too is a victim and that it is she who controls the scenario, who "'want[s] to be the victim forever.'" He demands that she "'picture yourself free'" and repeatedly enjoins "'Fight back,'" "'Save yourself.'" When she asks for his help, he scoffs at her naiveté. "'How can you possibly believe that a man, a stranger really, can come in here and rescue you—help you—save you?' He laughed. 'Don't buy into it, Vanessa. It is the myth of the oppressor'" (189–91). If the scene is "real," Jack's comments are a cruel mockery of Vanessa's helplessness (and a chilling representation of how seemingly idyllic relationships can change without warning); if it is fantasy, Vanessa's self-punishment tightens the bonds between the erotic and the masochistic as a socially endorsed relationship.

tormentors; her abuse may even be used to justify her own later abusing of others. In Emily Brontë's *Wuthering Heights*, for example, the once-meek Isabella demonstrates all of these when she goads Heathcliff to draw blood before her escape; crossing her own masochistic threshold enables the restoration of aggression, pleasure, and agency. "'I experienced pleasure in being able to exasperate him: the sense of pleasure woke my sense of self-preservation'" (143). Catherine Clément sketches some of the manifold possibilities in her discussion of the sorceress and the hysteric in "The Guilty One" section of *The Newly Born Woman*. "These women, to escape the misfortune of their economic and familial exploitation, chose to suffer spectacularly before an audience of men: it is an attack of spectacle, a crisis of suffering. And the attack is also a festival, a celebration of their guilt used as a weapon, a story of seduction" (10). This "guilt used as a weapon" points to the ambiguities of external and internal in relation to masochism: the guilt acknowledges an external law as well as some internalization of its strictures, and its transformation to weapon shows abject passivity wielded for active retaliation.

The masochist attempts to bypass what Benjamin calls "the core conflict between assertion and recognition" (31) by demanding that others recognize and love her precisely for her *non*assertion. Her silent suffering becomes her claim to fame. In two separate case histories, masochistic boys imagine almost entirely identical scenes in which the whole school is assembled for the presentation of awards to "'the most outstanding boy who had been treated badly'" (Marie B. Singer, "Fantasies of a Borderline Patient" 334)[9] "'We have never had another boy who has gone through so much'" (Jack Novick and Kerry Kelly Novick, "Beating Fantasies in Children" 241).[10] Girls demonstrate the same ambitious competition in passive endurance. The early admiration of Joan Foster, the protagonist of Margaret Atwood's *Lady Oracle*, for Moira Shearer in *The Red Shoes* foreshadows Joan's future career as a Gothic novelist. "I adored her: not only did she have red hair and an entrancing pair of red satin slippers to match, she also had beautiful costumes, and she suffered more than anyone" (87).[11] Joan's teary enthusiasm for those who suffer beautifully and

[9]Albert, seen between the ages of ten and seventeen, is particularly interesting because, like Freud's Gothic-writing patient, Anna Freud, he recasts his fantasies as written narrative, "The Adventures of Bob and Albert."

[10]The Novicks also comment that boys' final stages in beating fantasies often involve affirmation of their "status as special."

[11]Edward Joseph suggests in a case reference that a daughter who learns to transform "ideas of suffering into a positive attribute" from her mother may then compete with her mother in masochism (45–46).

best is part of her training in femininity. Her appreciation and applause exonerate and exalt the noble victim. Stoller, describing how humiliation leads to pleasure in the fantasies of Belle, also points out that it is not the pain but its reward, being recognized by admiring hosts, that prompts pleasure. "First, what is happening to the girl in the story is not taking place in reality. Second, there is another audience present but not in the script: the decent people of the world, God and his heavenly host, all the laws of morality and goodness in the universe—a throng of understanding and sympathetic observers who recognize her suffering and know she is finer than her tormentors. Despite appearances, the odds are stacked for her" (*Sexual Excitement* 72).[12] That throng of observers witnesses a bravura performance and, through its response, asserts that the masochist not only exists but is exceptional.

The masochist, then, can rework her enforced helplessness and pain so that, at least in fantasy, she gets the present she was promised for being a "good girl": recognition and love.[13] Furthermore, she can achieve a form of active agency through her masochism, in which she controls, accuses, or hurts others. Ann Barr Snitow's observation about romance and pornography is also true for the masochist's fantasy: all bear witness to "a universal infant desire for complete, immediate gratification, to rule the world out of the very core of passive helplessness" ("Mass Market Romance" 154). The sadist learns that he must get out there and demand his gratification; gender roles teach the masochist that her influence over others will continue to be through her helplessness. The strategies available to her are nonetheless what Ethel Person identifies as "a power maneuver, one expressed in the 'passive' voice." By pleasing the beloved, she makes herself "indispensable" and seeks to "bind the beloved to [her]

[12]In *Good-Bye Heathcliff*, Frenier attests to the dangers of this strategy: "even as I was—and behaved like—a battered wife, I knew a kind of 'reverse benefit,' the power of the victim wife-mother, that has been ignored in most feminist studies. Hence, my ironic concession that if patriarchy had remained 'benevolent,' I would probably have never revolted against it" (2).

[13]This reworking can also be attempted in life, albeit usually less successfully. One extraordinary account of such a transformation is *The Diaries of Hannah Cullwick, Victorian Maidservant*. Cullwick, subordinated by class and sex, is encouraged by an upper-class "reformer," Arthur Munby, to seek the heaviest and dirtiest jobs available; she also wears chains under her clothes, licks his boots, calls him "Massa," and appears before him filthy or with blacking on her face as often as possible. (After an eighteen-year courtship, they marry.) He urges her to find her self-worth and pride in the lowliness of her jobs. Astonishingly, she does. Her journals, which record her back-breaking and humiliating activities, also bear witness to the strength of the drive for recognition and self-respect, however unlikely the means.

through guilt" (*Dreams of Love* 175–76). Even in the most hackneyed of fantasies, the conclusion, like Scherezade's, is the triumph of the threatened woman, who gains control not only despite but through the terms of her subordination. Often, then, "what appears to be pain-dependent behavior turns out to be a vehicle of power for the weak" ("Some New Observations" 254).

The masochist's suffering, first imposed upon her and then embraced, can accuse the other without any overt sign of revolt and without a word being spoken. As Bernhard Berliner epigrammatically declares, "Suffering is the weapon of the weak and unloved."[14] The severity and duration of the masochist's suffering can be a way of insisting "I am *not* doing this to myself," of pointing a finger at her shadowy tormentor. By insisting upon the other's responsibility, the masochist can "get revenge," as Stoller claims: "She has demonstrated the alleged attacker's cruel inhumanity" (*Sexual Excitement* 14, 116).

Paradoxically, the masochist insists that she is a blank page but, in demanding that the author who so inscribed her be known, makes public her own identity and signature. Her masochism maintains that it is not she who is at fault, as Greif observes. "Masochism provides an affective release from shame because the other is endowed with total power, responsibility, and insight, while the self is left depleted but nonculpable" ("Historical Synthesis" 6).[15] Ruth-Jean Eisenbud also emphasizes that shame decreases with the use of pain, while there is "an increase in confidence," a confidence unique to the martyr. The rebel tries to overthrow; the martyr is a witness. As Eisenbud dryly notes, "Martyrdom is satisfactory until fatal" ("Masochism Revisited" 575). The masochist's accusation of the other flirts with her own destruction, but that is a familiar game: only a pawn during her formation, she may now hope to become a more powerful piece or even a player.

The most overt expression of the masochist's need to see her own existence confirmed through her effects on others is when her masochism temporarily becomes its active twin instinct, sadism. Within the analytic situation, interpretation can lead to fear of deprivation until "the sadist emerges and the patient acts out the hated tyranny on another helpless victim" (Eisenbud 577). This sadism may be di-

---

[14]As quoted in Stoller, *Sexual Excitement* 125.

[15]The reference to "depletion" suggests that the other Berliner epigram Stoller cites—"Masochism is a way of hating without great risk" (*Sexual Excitement* 125)—is erroneous. The self is at great risk, whether the source of attack is primarily external or internal in a given case. Psychic integrity and even physical survival are at stake.

rected at the analyst, and hatred of the oppressor becomes contempt for the therapist now revealed as nonthreatening and hence powerless as the patient perceives it. As Alan Parkin points out, "The shift from hate to contempt signifies a shift from an inferior to a superior position" ("On Masochistic Enthralment" 309). In other contexts, such women may, while still accepting their own subordination, do to others what has been done to them and thus confirm their own agency and relative power. Two small girls attest to this handing on of oppression. One, beaten because she is a "big girl," solemnly explains her compensatory treatment of a younger brother to her therapist. "She told me he was still 'too young to be punished' according to Nanny, and confided, 'so I try to make up for it when I can,' hitting the brother on the sly" (Melitta Schmideberg, "On Fantasies" 305). Another "sedate" and "studious" "father's girl" helpfully tutors her small brother. "She would make him sit immobile and repeat things till he wept" (Edward Joseph, *Beating Fantasies* 41). In dealing with others, the masochist replicates the interpersonal relations she knows: she may appropriate the power of the sadist and, in so doing, reproduces masochism.

The masochist seeks affirmation of her existence whether through taking up the cross of martyrdom and assuring that others respond to her passivity and pain, through implicit accusation of her victimizer, or through reenactment of sadism. The masochism that traditional analysis assures us is her innate preference is instead an adaptive behavior and one on which her culture insists if she is to be appropriately feminine. Within the confines of masochism, she still tries to avoid pain and to seek pleasure, to achieve recognition and agency. Even the pain she may inflict upon herself can be a way of maintaining control of her own identity and of warding off more dangerous external threats. Her acceptance of the suffering others impose is necessary to her psychic and physical well-being: she, like all of us, must have whatever form of "love" is available to create and preserve a coherent identity. To secure the recognition and mirroring that lets her know she exists, she will repeat her own experiences time and again—in life, in fantasy, and in the Gothic novel. And perhaps, as she views a woman being beaten, she begins to see other strategies for survival.

The Spectator's Curious Gaze

Within the beating fantasy, the array of Gothic images is refined and stilled to a single, frozen tableau of cruelty: someone watches a beating. Neatly condensed, displaced, and pictorialized, the Gothic dream is thus framed for our consideration. According to Freud's description of the fantasy in "A Child Is Being Beaten" earlier versions ("My father is beating a child," "My father is beating me") are superseded by the formulaic vision "a child is being beaten." What, however, is one to make of such a picture? Is it sadistic? Masochistic? Voyeuristic? Why is it so unvarying? Is its persistent repetition an attempt to recover from trauma? To maintain the image? Is it pleasure? Pain? And why must there be a spectator? These uncomfortable questions demand our attention because, as Benjamin claims, within sadomasochistic fantasies—and, I would add, the Gothic novel—"we can discern the 'pure culture' of domination—a dynamic which organizes both domination and submission" (52).

The beating fantasy's static, invariant, repetitive formula insists that there are no options outside the fantasy's borders. It is within them that we must take our stand as beaters, beaten, or spectators. And, of course, if we opt for the last, we must choose once again: are our sympathies with the beater or the beaten? We thus enter into what Claude Lévi-Strauss points to as "a collaboration between collective tradition and individual invention," the elaboration and modification of a structure quite unlike anything T. S. Eliot ever had in mind. Such consolidation, Lévi-Strauss claims, is achieved through "a system of oppositions and correlations integrating all the elements of a complete situation where sorcerer, patient, and spectators, the representations and the procedures each find their place. And it is necessary for the spectators, like the patient and sorcerer, to participate, at least to a certain extent, in the abreaction, this lived experience of a universe of symbolic effusions."[16] These "symbolic effusions," no matter what their nature, maintain the structure in question. The screams of the beaten or the averted eyes of the spectator do nothing to change what is taking place. Given that fact, one may assume, as the protagonists of the Gothic often do, that there is no other drama,

---

[16]As quoted in Cixous and Clément, *The Newly Born Woman* 10. Criticism of the Gothic often notes the presence of sadism and masochism, and sometimes addresses their dynamic interplay as well. Indeed, in his classic study *The Romantic Agony*, Mario Praz saw fit to add an appendix on "Swinburne and 'Le Vice Anglais,'" a quite lively and uncritical survey of compulsive viewers of executions, beatings, and other sadistic practices. Just as countries indulged in international projection of venereal diseases in earlier periods (variously identified by those from other countries as English, French, Spanish, German, or Italian maladies), the nineteenth-century British see sadism as a continental practice and the French as one only the English would consider. Praz, like Freud switching to another language to defend his explicit discussion of sexuality ("J'appelle un chat un chat"), adds an interesting twist to his own analysis through his French title.

no other reality. Moreover, no matter which role they adopt, all, no matter what their rationalizations, exist under the aegis of the beater so long as the scenario remains intact.

Dominance or submission seem to be the main options of the Gothic, as William Patrick Day argues. "In the Gothic world, the self is defined through conflict, as a giver or receiver of pain in a sadomasochistic dynamic" (*In the Circles of Fear and Desire* 85). To be a spectator rather than the beater or beaten suggests a range of other possible responses: resentment at exclusion, endorsement of the scenario, belief in one's own transcendence or superiority, careful study of the scenario with an eye to either participation or its destruction. The trick, of course, is to see without being seen, like the black man in Walker's *The Temple of My Familiar* who "had perfected the art of doing the most intimate things to and for white people without once appearing to look at them. It was an invaluable skill" (35).[17] The onlooker sees more than the actual participants and enjoys what David Allen, speaking of Freud himself, calls "the cultural binocularity of the inside outsider" (7): servants know what goes on upstairs and downstairs; minorities know both white codes and their own; women recognize masculine and feminine worlds.

I discuss the beating drama as a structure that organizes gender roles. As always, however, emphasis on one axis of differentiation does not exclude others. Class and race roles also are organized through this model. If what the spectator—subordinated through one or several systems—sees is that to have power means you can act freely, and if the only way to be acknowledged as a presence seems to

---

[17]Judith Hall notes the way in which subordination can both limit and enable women's gaze, which can be interpreted "both as a signal of low status and as a means of gathering vital information about others' attitudes toward them and expectations for their behavior" (74). Patricia Webbink adds that women, despite what seem to be "superior decoding abilities," may suppress that ability if the other person seems to want to hide something, perhaps "because they are socialized to be more accommodating to others" (61). There is an extensive empirical literature on gaze and dominance patterns (see, for example, Irene Frieze and S. J. Ramsey's "Nonverbal Maintenance of Traditional Sex Roles" and Clara Mayo and Nancy M. Henley's *Gender and Nonverbal Behavior*). To simplify considerably, the dominant and the subordinated have inverse gaze strategies. Those of inferior status look at the dominant, particularly when she/he speaks; the dominant do not look at subordinates. Another gauge is the adult version of the children's game of "chicken": a competition to see whose eyes drop after mutual gaze begins. Webbink observes that, "although women look more, they usually modify their looking behavior with submissive gestures, such as looking down or frequently breaking eye contact. . . . Staring is considered to be a masculine form of behavior and dropping the eyes when stared at is feminine" (59). All of the studies comment on how, for women in particular, gaze as a means of dominance intersects with gaze as a mode of affiliation.

be through the recognition of the person with power, it is tempting to assume that being beaten is only a necessary apprenticeship to becoming a beater and having one's own power. The beater becomes an angel to wrestle with in the fond belief that one will somehow come away with a blessing. The spectator must thus prove her/his worthiness to be a contender by accumulating knowledge of the system. In this variant, the beating fantasy is yoked to a version of family romance through the onlooker's belief that he/she will be recognized as an exception and welcomed into the inner sanctum of privilege.

Frankenstein's creature, dutifully taking cultural lessons from the de Laceys as he spies upon them only to have them run shrieking in terror instead of adopting him, is one obvious instance of such an endeavor (as is his subsequent decision to become a scourge to humanity). Walker's Grange Copeland also moves from the position of beaten and its disillusionment to that of beater before entering upon his "third life." Quite often, such petitioners for status feel themselves under an exterior compulsion. As both Sedgwick and Modleski note, subordination is closely associated with both paranoia and class issues when the subordinated partner is a male. Eagerly searching out the secrets of authority, such a man feels himself, as Sedgwick states, not only "persecuted by, but . . . transparent to and often under the compulsion of, another male" (*Between Men* 91). The roles of the spectator and of the beater may seem to offer escape.

In both William Godwin's *Caleb Williams* and Charles Brockden Brown's *Wieland*, along with *Wieland*'s accompanying fragment "Carwin the Biloquist," we see stellar instances of how voyeurism can be an attempt to control the Gothic's core fantasy of subordination and domination and of how Gothic hierarchy is maintained through class discrepancy as well as gender. Both Carwin and Caleb, outsiders of lower rank than the objects of their inquiries, are obsessed by learning more about the dominant. Each attempts to escape subordination through surveillance of the dominant, and each believes his deference and interest will eventually be rewarded by his assuming a dominant position. Neither sees his voyeurism as an overt or conscious threat to the dominant, which it of course is, but rather a fond emulation; both, in their inevitable failures, become the beaten again, frozen exemplars to the next spectator.

Caleb idealizes his master, Falkland: his proof of love is to know everything about him.

> The instant I had chosen this employment for myself, I found a strange sort of *pleasure* in it. To do what is forbidden always has its

charms, because we have an indistinct apprehension of something arbitrary and tyrannical in the prohibition. To be a spy upon Mr. Falkland! That there was danger in the employment served to give an *alluring* pungency to the choice. I remembered the stern reprimand I had received, and his terrible looks; and the recollection gave a kind of *tingling* sensation, not altogether unallied to *enjoyment*. The farther I advanced, the more the sensation was *irresistible*. I seemed to myself *perpetually upon the brink* of being countermined, and *perpetually roused* to guard my designs. The more *impenetrable* Mr. Falkland was determined to be, the more *uncontrolable* [sic] was my curiosity. (107–8, emphasis added)[18]

The language of the passage bespeaks the fusion of the erotic and the authoritative in the eye of the voyeur. To penetrate the forbidden is racy stuff, as Freud himself attested in his exploration of that "dark continent," woman. Caleb too wants to claim that it won't hurt a bit and that his intentions are good, but there is nonetheless a dividend of titillation inexplicable in terms of the actual information he seeks, a surplus of excitement brought about by the very act of scopophilic investigation.[19] Nonetheless, he succeeds in being recognized, albeit not quite as he had planned, for Falkland's gaze is now trained on him in turn.

So too in *Wieland*, Carwin's voyeurism seems to release an orgy of inquiring stares. Carwin claims, "'I cannot justify my conduct, yet my only crime was curiosity'" (205–6). At other times, he claims the same edifying goals as Caleb and Pleyel (another character in *Wieland* who practices surveillance): to learn and improve oneself through identification with the other. Pleyel presents himself to Clara as an altruistic middle man, probing so that he can better women by offering them her as exemplar. His language is very like that of Jane Eyre as she portrays a female ideal, Blanche Ingram. Jane's goal, however, is to remind herself of discrepancy, while Pleyel's is wholesale appropriation. "'You know not the accuracy of my observation. I was desirous

---

[18]For literary critical analyses of Caleb's scopophilia, see James Thompson's "Surveillance in William Godwin's *Caleb Williams*" and Robert Kiely's *The Romantic Novel* (81–97).

[19]Herman Nunberg's analysis of scopophilia/epistemophilia run amok applies precisely to both Caleb and Carwin. The child's sexual "researches" become the motif of adult life, with the constant suspicion that other people are doing secret, interesting things. "There are individuals whose urge to know is unlimited and whose ego seems to lose control over this urge and to become its prisoner. Individuals of this type may be utterly ruthless in their avidity for knowledge and totally unconcerned with the possible consequences of their search. They may not even be deterred by the prospect of comprehensive destruction, including their own, when they hope to come closer to their goal" (78).

that others should profit by an example so rare. I therefore noted down, in writing, every particular of your conduct. I was anxious to benefit by an opportunity so seldom afforded us. I laboured not to omit the slightest shade, or the most petty line in your portrait. Here there was no other task incumbent on me but to copy; there was no need to exaggerate or overlook, in order to produce a more unexceptionable pattern' " (122). Like other voyeurs, Pleyel expects the object of his detailed inquiry to be flattered. (Unlike them, however, he claims the surveillance rights of the dominant, in which the object "knows not.") Carwin, like Caleb, fails to achieve his goal. Caleb in particular finds, through his attempt to close the distance between master and servant, that the power of authority is mobilized, not neutralized or shared, by the knowledge of the voyeur.

Carwin and Caleb's narratives are uneasily poised between the traditional masculine plot of upward mobility (voyeurism as a means to become the beater) and the traditional feminine plot of romance (exhibitionism used to attract the "love" of the dominant). They show self-contradictory impulses: they want to know the secrets of the powerful, but they also seek acknowledgment by having the powerful look at them; they are often hostile in their inquiries, yet they profess genuine love and admiration for their subjects; they want to supplant, be one with, and be loved by the dominant.

In a series of essays, Freud puzzles through such paradoxical desires. In his study of paired or component instincts such as sadism/masochism or scopophilia/exhibitionism, he traces the ways in which one pole evokes or suddenly transmutes into its opposite. Interestingly, although Freud often lists epistemophilia as the third instance, there is no term for "the urge *not* to know" (except perhaps denial or repression itself). Although each active instinct—scopophilia, sadism, epistemophilia—is yoked to its passive counterpart, all of the active and passive instincts are also strongly connected to one another. One exemplary and key pairing, scopophilia and exhibitionism, is especially significant for the analysis of the beating fantasy that follows. To look is a way to know; it can also be a form of aggression, as Stoller comments: "In our time and culture, looking is far more intricate and stylized for males (sadism is the mythic theme in masculinity) and being looked at is more so for females (and masochism is the theme here)" (*Perversion* 98).

Not surprisingly, the active and passive uses of looking are neatly sex-segregated in much of Freud's discussion: the man will excel in gazing, while the woman will come to find her pleasure in being the object of the gaze. The reasons for this in Freud's explanation are an uneasy balance of biological or developmental assumptions and clinical observation. There is a "substitutive relation between the eye and the male organ" ("'Uncanny'" 231). It follows that "the libido for looking and touching is present in everyone in two forms, active and passive, male and female" (*Jokes* 98),[20] a "coupling" that meets us as "biological fact" ("Instincts" 134). Indeed, Karl Abraham asserts that women who stare excessively use their eyes as male exhibitionists do their penises, to terrify: "these women unconsciously endeavour to attain the same effect by means of their fixed stare" ("Manifestations" 121). The gaze that Freud and Abraham ascribe to the male is dominant, like the sadistic stare Stoller describes: in all three cases, it is the stare the beater trains upon the beaten. The subordinated cannot use it, a point Abraham makes clear and which Otto Fenichel further develops in his discussion of Lot. In his classic essay, Fenichel relates the biblical injunction against looking back to being forbidden to look at God. "What is the sin in looking? Surely it is that looking implies identification" (27), an identification both presumptuous and unauthorized when used by a subordinate. Interestingly, Fenichel does not mention Lot's wife, the woman who sins against both her husband and her God, the woman turned to salt for her transgression while her husband talks back to the Lord. The stare that seeks to destroy, injure, and incorporate, thus negating the identity of the other, belongs only to the dominant.[21] The gaze of Lot's wife, which seems to be that of the spectator rather than the beater, is nonetheless judged too assertive and appropriative, since her proper place is below the God-angel-man ranking. Freud is more indulgent than God or Fenichel in his interpretation of the dream of a young woman who wrongly thought marriage would give her the right to look. Her triumphant dream-wish, translated by Freud—"'There! now I may go to the theatre and look at everything that's forbidden . . . !'"—is the transformation of her "recent defeat" and "present anger" (*Introductory Lectures* 225, 220) at the closing of her visual and emotional fields with marriage.

The young woman's expectations are naive, according to Freud: her role is to be looked *at*, to find her identity in scopophilia's passive

---

[20]He goes on to state that the predominance of either will depend on the "preponderance of the sexual character," but this gender flexibility seldom appears in a positive light.

[21]For further discussion of the relation between scopophilia and sadism, see: Fenichel (30–31); Harry H. Nierenberg, "A Case of Voyeurism" (163); Stoller, *Perversion* (109), *The Development of Masculinity and Femininity* (218), and *Observing the Erotic Imagination* (31); and C. W. Socarides, "The Demonified Mother" (187–95).

partner, exhibitionism. Belle, the client of Stoller's who has beating fantasies, describes an adolescent's training in being watched: "You wait endlessly and finally angrily. You are being observed in a special way: your breasts, your legs. You have to get used to the separate parts being there, treated as if they are different from you. And you have to come to feel that that is correct, not crazy. . . . Your changing is being watched by males with kind of a proprietary, anticipatory [interest]" (*Sexual Excitement* 139). Snitow, in her study of mass market romance, shows how Belle's belief that "you have to come to feel that this is correct" progresses to a feeling that being watched is wonderful, a sign of one's erotic value. Romances "revitalize daily routines by insisting that . . . a woman doing what women do all day, is in a constant state of potential sexuality. You never can tell when you may be seen and being seen is a precious opportunity" (145).

When pursued predominantly or obsessively, scopophilia and exhibitionism are the strategies of the beater and the beaten, respectively. The first reinforces his identity through the aggressive gaze that assaults and appropriates the other, while the beaten's main hope for recognition is that she will be pleasing in the eye of her beholder.[22] Both the active and the passive versions of looking present less dour possibilities, however. In addition, I want to emphasize that there is nothing "wrong" with either drive—each is necessary to develop and to maintain adult identity—and that, no matter how emphatic one form may be, its counterpart is always present in some fashion.

[22]I will refer to the beater as "he" and the beaten and spectator as "she," given the usual sexual configuration found in the Gothic novel. There are obviously other possibilities. One of the more vexing auxiliary issues of the literature is, in fact, that of gender identification, even when limited to the female spectator and disassociated from the too-quick assignment of active/passive to male/female. In noting that some of his four women patients in "A Child" see the beaten as male, Freud quickly assumes a "masculinity complex" at work, although not Alfred Adler's "masculine protest" which he beats down in the essay's last section along with Fliess's theory of bisexuality. (A possible further complication is his later admission in a letter to Marie Bonaparte that all four women were virgins.) Sedgwick acknowledges a male identification in the drama, but specifies that it is with a gay male (133). Robin Morgan finds the male/male beating scene to be second in effectiveness to male/female, and uncomfortably wonders if this might be because it is impossible even to fantasize a woman with enough power to be the beater ("The Politics of Sado-Masochistic Fantasy" 113). The female fantasy in which a male is beaten may be a gender identification rather than a sexual one—that the woman wants what the man has: not his penis but the social autonomy it permits. In such instances, the sex-typed distinction between erotic and ambitious daydreams that Freud makes in "Creative Writers and Day-Dreaming" (143–45) begins to collapse somewhat. Thus, the woman whose identity is defined by traditional femininity may well construct an obviously erotic, heterosexual fantasy and find her fulfillment in its punitive embrace. The woman who wants what the Oedipal pact promises the younger male—power with time—will create, however, a traditionally masculine fantasy of ambition and eroticism.

One way to question the scopic economy that assigns active gaze to the phallic and the dominant is, of course, the role of the spectator. As Kaja Silverman argues, "Scopophilia may also betray desires that are incompatible with the phallic function" ("Fragments" 141). The spectator gratifies scopophilic and epistemophilic urges—she satisfies curiosity through looking—while overtly eschewing the link of either to sadism, whether through choice or inability. Women cannot be blinded by the theoretical allocation of gaze to a masculinist domain. Naomi Scheman also insists on the reality and importance of women's looking: "The lack of authority in women's looking is not, however, reason to conclude that we do not see, nor even that patriarchy does not allow or require that we see. . . . The looking that we do is a good place to seek out cracks in [masculinist] power, even when we look as dutiful daughters and self-sacrificing mothers" ("Missing Mothers Desiring Daughters" 87). Thus, the gaze of the subordinated is a potential means to identify and reconstruct patterns of domination.

Just as the scopophilic's role must be reassessed, so too the seemingly mute and blind part of the exhibitionist beaten demands further inquiry. By averting our own eyes from her degrading position, we maintain it by pretending it's not there or is at most an appalling but freakish occurrence. We are all necessarily exhibitionists in that we find the affirmation of our existence mirrored in the gaze of an other from infancy on. Not being seen (and this is a part of the spectator's quandary) means not to exist. In Isak Dinesen's "The Deluge at Norderney," the elderly Miss Malin tells a young man who feels overly scrutinized that the "opposite misfortune" is at least as severe. Her duty to her young ward, raised by a misogynist uncle, is "'to teach her to be seen. . . . What if nobody could or would see you, although you were, yourself, firmly convinced of your own existence?'" (40–41). Frances, in Anita Brookner's *Look at Me*, explains her fascination with seemingly "magical," self-sufficient narcissists as necessary for the same reason. "I recognize that they might have no intrinsic merit, and yet I will find myself trying to please them, to attract their attention. 'Look at me,' I want to say. 'Look at me'" (15). Lissie, in Walker's *Temple of My Familiar*, equates love and being seen when she remembers her mother pleading with uncles and slavers. "'I know now that she was someone who was never loved, because she was never really seen, except by her children, who did love her'" (62).

Lissie does not confuse the regard of the dominant with love; in a heterosexual context, culture encourages the conflation. Any woman must have visual confirmation of her identity, and she will seek it in the structures most accessible to her. Moreover, the passivity of exhibitionism can be negotiated actively even within the scopic economy. Freud notes one instance with some chagrin. In discussing forgotten intentions, he grumbles about women patients who forget to pay their bills "and thus arrange things so that one has treated them for nothing—'for the sake of their *beaux yeux*'. They pay one, as it were, by the sight of their countenance" (*Psychopathology* 159n). A woman, then, can insist that her status as display object be accepted as tender and, in so doing, confound the spirit of scopic law while hewing to its letter. She has become an appropriately ornamental object: she must be appreciated and cared for. The apparent passivity of exhibitionism can be used still more actively when there are many viewers to affirm identity. Costuming, in which one creates personae by various styles of dressing, can be such an instance of self-definition. As Silverman notes: "The history of Western fashion poses a serious challenge both to the automatic equation of spectacular display with female subjectivity, and to the assumption that exhibitionism always implies woman's subjugation to a controlling male gaze" ("Fragments" 139). The beating fantasy, through its expansion of the beater/beaten dyad to a triad that includes a spectator, also questions the equations of subordination and femininity, domination and masculinism. The female spectator may be a subject who looks actively without dominating and who is not subordinated by gaze. And, although she can be an accomplice of the beater or a would-be beater, she also can be only one of many spectators who offer a recourse to the beaten, who must find a mirror other than the beater to affirm her identity.

"A Child Is Being Beaten"

In "A Child Is Being Beaten," Freud composes a three act drama of women's masochism and exhibitionism, based on several women patients' beating fantasies. In the first act, the scenario viewed is "My father is beating a child." The second, repressed, tableau shows "My father is beating me." The final episode enacts "A child is being beaten." The last, with its erasure of recognizable actors and its shift from active to passive voice, establishes the spectator as consciously related to neither beaten nor beater. Each stage is an embryonic narrative. Furthermore, when taken sequentially, they outline the viewing strategies used by many Gothic protagonists and readers to bridge the cultural split between what experience shows them and what ideology insists the actual meaning of the event to have been. In addition, the positioning of the spectator raises disturbing moral and political questions not only about her possible identification with the beaten, but also with the beater. The morphology of the Gothic fantasy can be as simple as Freud's three-act drama: (1) My father is hurting a woman; (2) My father (or husband) is hurting me; (3) A woman is being hurt. As in Freud's three acts, the second is repressed, but persistently re-presented. Until the second is worked through, the third—"A woman is being hurt"—remains the manifest arena of the Gothic.

While the reader of the Gothic novel usually begins and ends in this space, protagonists and secondary characters may play musical chairs in the course of the novel, variously testing the roles of beater, beaten, and spectator; as Sedgwick observes about the beating fantasy, the display of trauma can serve as "a free switchpoint for the identities of subject, object, onlooker, desirer, looker-away" ("A Poem" 115). As in the parlor game, to lose is to have to drop out entirely. While such a loss may seem one to be eagerly sought, for the nonce these musical chairs are the only game in town recognized as reality, no matter how painful that reality may be. Thus the ten-year-old Jane Eyre, asked after her traumatic experience in the red room if she would like to live with her Eyre relatives if they can be found, responds negatively from the very depths of her misery.

> Poverty for me was synonymous with degradation.
> "No; I should not like to belong to poor people," was my reply.
> "Not even if they were kind to you?"
> I shook my head: I could not see how poor people had the means of being kind . . . : no, I was not heroic enough to purchase liberty at the price of caste. (20)

Distanced by time, the mature, narrating Jane views her victimized younger self with a keenly accurate eye. Identity itself is cruelly bound within the child's confining situation: to relinquish such ties to authority is nonetheless to lose the only power and knowledge she has.

Similarly, the formation and maintenance of often fragile ego boundaries may come to seem possible only within the constraints of the beating fantasy. The stability of the beating fantasy's drama of triangulation itself fosters credence in the strictures of authority thus created. Within the fantasy, the shifting identification of the spectator with the beaten or the beater marks a further risk: those who are beaten may, in their turn, replicate oppression. Few, because of their own experience, can subordinate their actual oppressors or the systems that validate them: instead, they reenact their own gender reification by insisting upon hierarchies of class, race, and age. There is thus in such cases a basic conservative identification with the very system that assures their oppression: their limited status and power are asserted within such a system by damaging other women, children, and servants, for example.

Such repetition can't be averted by adopting the role of spectator. For one thing, the persistent spectator's rationale of noninvolvement to the contrary, the allure of voyeuristic power is all too evident.[23] In addition, the spectator of this ongoing drama necessarily participates. For example, when Clarissa's mother tells her that she will not intervene (and implicitly blames Clarissa for her plight), her self-exemption from responsibility is specious: she has become an accomplice. "'Your father takes upon himself to be answerable for all consequences. You must not, therefore, apply to me for favour. I shall endeavour to be only an observer; happy, if I could be an unconcerned one! While I had power, you would not let me use it as I *would* have used it'" (Richardson, *Clarissa* 45). The witnessing of the spectator can be a mute protest; it can also devolve into complicity, as it does for Mrs. Harlowe, through her fear that she will be the odd woman out if the world of Gothic barbarity she knows comes to an end. Her observer's role cannot be accepted as neutral; when forced to choose, she sides with the aggressor, her husband, and not the victim, her daughter.

In Walker's *The Color Purple*, Celie too at first perpetuates the order she knows. Beaten and raped by her stepfather and abused by her husband, Celie echoes her husband's recommendation that her stepson Harpo beat his assertive wife Sophia.

> Well how you spect to make her mind? Wives is like children. You have to let 'em know who got the upper hand. Nothing can do that better than a good sound beating. . . .

[23]In "A Poem Is Being Written," Sedgwick offers a densely suggestive and troubling meditation upon beating fantasies. In remembering her own spankings, she muses on how her mental picture is cropped even more severely than those Freud describes, to excise "the entire visible mechanism of the gaze to which the child is exposed, the graphic multicharacter drama of infliction and onlooking, the visibly rendered plural possibilities of sadism, voyeurism, horror, *Schadenfreude*, disgust, or even compassion" (115). For Sedgwick, this further condensation and fragmentation enables increased freedom for the viewer/interpreter/poet—a post-modern beating fantasy, as it were. The issues of viewer identification she touches upon are, however, crucial to all versions of the beating fantasy.

I like Sophia, but she don't act like me at all. If she talking when Harpo and Mr. ___ come in the room, she keep right on. If they ast her where something at, she say she don't know. Keep talking.

I think bout this when Harpo ast me what he ought to do to her to make her mind. . . .

Beat her. I say. (42–43)

The beaten's very identity is threatened by women who "don't act like me at all," who think that they have a right to speech and that their own activities are as important as anyone else's. The bruises Harpo displays after following Celie's advice are vivid and continuing testaments to the startling failure of his ongoing attempts to construct stereotypical gender roles. Celie watches one of Harpo's and Sophia's melées, notes fresh injuries, and, after a month's unrest, has a basic insight: "I sin against Sofia spirit" (45). Celie recognizes and repudiates her complicity, just as Shug Avery later accepts the responsibility of intervention for Celie herself.[24]

Celie's transition is simplified by the omission of a key factor: she has never believed any of her oppressors loved her (although she does believe that to be good means to accept their blows). For many other Gothic protagonists, love and pain are almost inextricably linked. Although the "He" and "Mister" of Celie's early letters sometimes fuse with the omnipotent but never-responding God to whom she writes, her credo is never that "the Lord chastiteth whom he loveth." For characters who embrace that logic and their own roles as the chastised, the only option is to kiss the rod. Such whole-hearted acceptance, while rare, is the stuff of pornography: not a pornography of genital display, but the pornography even D. H. Lawrence recognized "by the insult it offers, invariably, to sex, and to the human spirit" (37) and which Susan Griffin, like Celie, defines as "violent to a woman's soul" (202).

In *Wieland* Pleyel explains to Clara that pleasure in causing and watching pain is not the mystery she thinks it. "The process by which . . . we are made susceptible of no activity but in the infliction, and no joy but in the spectacle of woes, is an obvious process" (131–

[24]In *The Temple of My Familiar*, Celie's daughter tells her own daughter that "'the child will always, as an adult, do to someone else whatever was done to him when he was a child.'" The granddaughter uses Celie's example to rebut her. Her own mother hesitates before responding and then tells her how Celie had a dog she consistently treated with "'detached, brutal disregard,'" while he "'worshiped'" her. Shug takes the dog away for a while. "'The next time Mama Celie tried to beat him, he bit her. And Miss Shug laughed. Mama Celie never dared attempt to beat or humiliate Creighton again'" (311–12).

32). The process he finds so obvious, however, is one to which Freud, dissatisfied, returned repeatedly. In "A Child Is Being Beaten," Freud begins by commenting on the frequency of beating fantasies, their early onset (before the fifth year), their association with a "high degree of pleasure" (180), and, finally, their emphatic lack of connection with actual experience. Real beatings at home or school failed to elicit pleasurable response; indeed, Freud suspected an inverse relationship between actual experience and the fantasy (180).[25] Still more striking, "it was always a condition of the more sophisticated fantasies of later years that the punishment should do the children no serious injury" (180).[26] Thus, the relationship of the fantasy to either masochism or sadism, originally so simple and straightforward, is revealed as more contorted upon even preliminary investigation.

For us, as for Freud, the sharply delineated fixedness of the beating fantasy blurs and reconfigures itself the more one stares at it. Our own curiosity demands an answer to how these characters arrived

[25]The Novicks maintain that there is a lack of correlation between actual abuse and eroticized masochistic fantasy. In considering a subgroup within their study, they "find no constant relationship between actual experiences of being beaten and the presence of beating fantasies in these children" (240). Their subgroup is, however, somewhat unusual in that the fantasy appears at puberty, all nine are fixed fantasizers (as opposed to those for whom it is a transitory fantasy during latency), all nine are male (although selection was through fixed or transitory fantasizing, not sex), and most display sadistic behavior. Loren Johnson, discussing a male client whose identification in the beating fantasy is sadistic, voices concern that the client may carry out his vivid fantasies about mutilating women ("A Woman Is Being Beaten" 259–67).

Chris Gosselin and Glenn Wilson also find a correlation to actual physical violence in sadism, but not in masochism. Their empirical study discovers that for the female group "a very powerful association exists between punishment frequency and the incidence of both intimate and sadistic (but not masochistic) themes." Interestingly, they speculate that a woman's sadism may be activated by the wish for "vengeance on encountering the 'aggressive' sexual approach of the male" (Sexual Variations 151). Roy F. Baumeister (Masochism and the Self 146, 151), Kaplan (7–10, 24–26), Theodor Reik (Masochism in Modern Man 214), Andreas Spengler ("Manifest Sadomasochism of Males" 58), Thomas S. Weinberg ("Sadism and Masochism" 107), and Weinberg and Gerhard Falk ("The Social Organization of Sadism and Masochism" 150), among others, also comment upon the apparently low rate of masochistic perversion (those who seek out alliances in order to have physical pain inflicted) in women.

[26]The distinction between the masochistic beating fantasy and actual sadomasochistic practice is emphasized repeatedly in the literature, and the absence of pain in the fantasy itself is often noted as well. "Pain played no part in the fantasy" (Joseph 50). "In the story, she is humiliated; in reality, she is safe" (Stoller, Sexual Excitement 68). Women do not have masochistic fantasies because they want to be beaten or raped; the fantasies do mark, however, varying degrees of eroticized subordination. See also Marissa Jonel's "Letter from a Former Masochist," Robin Morgan's "The Politics of Sado-Masochistic Fantasy," and Molly Haskell's "Rape Fantasy." Kathleen Barry (Female Sexual Slavery) and Alice Walker ("A Letter of the Times, or Should This Sado-Masochism Be Saved?") also insist powerfully on brutality's reality for women and African-Americans.

here, a narrative causality to set the stilled scene in motion. Freud's inquiries, like those of the voyeur, move in two directions: the use of knowledge to explain and illuminate and an uneasy retreat from the secrets thus uncovered. The picture begins as a familiar Oedipal drama in clear, primary shades but the father's central placement, the disappearance of the mother, and the attempt to establish gender differentiation while at the same time wresting universal typicality from the pattern undermines any finality. Like the voyeur, Freud contemplates the scenario again and again, seemingly unsure of the source of his dis-ease, "an uneasy suspicion that this is not a final solution of the problem" (183).

Over time, the picture is refurbished with rich new colors. The binary play of the component instincts establishes a ceaseless exchange between beater and beaten. The instinctual concatenation of anality, sadism, knowledge, power, and sexuality densely overdetermines the figure of the spectator and its relation to the beater and the beaten. And the picture is constantly rotated, because it is never quite clear which of the three figures is its apex or nadir. Is the beater, overvalued and assigned subject status by the beaten and the spectator, the source of this painful drama? Does the beaten "naturally" embrace her own hurt as proof of existence, insist on its continuation, and thus control the beater and the spectator through her demand? Is the spectator the wishful puppet-master of the scene or is she at the triangle's nadir, passive and alone while the couple rules? The first possibility, in which the father/sadist/subject controls, is the placement that least pleases Freud. His aversion to it in part explains his increasing elaboration of how much and how thoroughly the beaten and the spectator really *want* it thus. Masochism, not sadism, is what he is most interested in understanding, explaining, and justifying.

In "A Child Is Being Beaten," Freud explains the search for a first cause, as it were, of infantile perversion, "a provisional end somewhere or other in tracing back the train of causal connection" (182). He tentatively postulates that "it does not seem impossible" that "the origin of infantile perversions from the Oedipus-complex can be asserted as a general principle" (192). In particular, he stresses that both male and female beating fantasies have the father as their center: "*In both cases the beating-phantasy has its origin in an incestuous attachment to the father*" (198). When he considers the sources of that "incestuous attachment," however, this powerful paternal figure begins to fade, and it is the child that comes to the foreground. Nature, in the form of "congenital constitution" explains an individual child's premature development of the sexual impulse; environment, which supplies unwanted siblings, furthers the process; infantile sexuality "acts as the chief motive force" (204).

Neither father nor mother is an agent in this process: Freud mentions their roles only to rapidly dismiss them. "The affections of the little girl are fixed on her father, who has probably done all he could to win her love, and in this way has sown the seeds of an attitude of hatred and rivalry towards her mother. . . . But it is not with the girl's relation to her mother that the beating-phantasy is connected" (186). The emphatic unyoking of the fantasy from the father who has "done all he could to win her love" and the disappearance of the mother[27] serves a threefold purpose: (1) it negates the inherently hierarchical structure of the fantasy; (2) it advances the date of the father's centrality to the anal period; (3) it emphasizes the fantasy as the child's mental event, unrelated to the actual attitude or behavior of the parents.[28]

The analyst, according to Freud, restores/creates this chronology, raising "his voice on behalf of the claims of childhood," supplanting/supplementing the voice of the adult patient, who already speaks "loudly enough" (184). Maintaining that "theoretical knowledge is still far more important to all of us than therapeutic success" (183), he shapes an "earlier history" (184) to structure the years from two to four or five.

In this history, the girl's fantasy goes through three distinct stages, as previously mentioned. Precocious development of the psychic genital organization and jealousy at the love the parents show a

[27]Schmideberg is unusual in her insistence that the child being beaten is often a substitute for a parent. While she views this as a mark of the child's hostility, she also argues, interestingly, that "the phantasy of being beaten is a substitute for being *actually* beaten" (305, emphasis added). "In most cases, however, the child who gets beaten in the phantasy is a substitute for the parent. To beat the latter is a too guilty desire, so he is substituted by a naughty child. One patient changed her phantasy under the influence of the analysis. Instead of imagining that a child was being beaten, she now developed the phantasy that her mother was being beaten, humiliated, and ill-treated, but such phantasies often produced anxiety" (305). As is the case with other famous daughters, Schmideberg's particular family connections (she was Klein's daughter) might in part explain her unusual ability to note the issue.

[28]Greif's comments on the mother's and the father's roles in masochism add a useful corrective that insists on considering experience: "It is the mother's own life experiences of shame, regret, and disillusionment shaped and sanctioned by cultural norms, as well as heightened by biological givens, that foster the same depressive and masochistic vulnerabilities, usually in her more socially responsive daughter. . . . Why not interpret these fantasies more literally and in concert perhaps with the masochistic identification with the mother . . . ? That is, why not interpret beating fantasies as metaphors for the cruelty of the father, whether it was in the form of deadening indifference to the child's need to individuate from the mother or in the form of direct assaults to the child's self-esteem?" (5, 7–8).

younger child prompt its manufacture: (1) My father is beating a child; (2) My father is beating me; (3) A child is being beaten. The unspoken addition to the first stage is the child's antipathy: "My father is beating the child *whom I hate*" (185). "It means: My father does not love this other child, *he loves only me*" (187). This pleasing vision, according to Freud, is "quite apart from whether he [the father] has actually been seen doing so [beating a child]" (187). The second stage is both a reprimand and a restatement. "The sense of guilt can discover no punishment more severe than the reversal of this triumph: 'No, he does not love you, for he is beating you'" (189). But again the beating also confirms "I am loved" (202). The third stage disguises both beater and beaten (the beaten imagined by the girl is sometimes is a boy), and the girl watches. According to Freud, both the first and third stages are sadistic, the repressed second stage masochistic. "This second phase is the most important and the most momentous of all. But we may say of it in a certain sense that it has never had a real existence. It is never remembered, it has never succeeded in becoming conscious. It is a construction of analysis, but it is no less a necessity on that account" (185). The reasons for that necessity are manifold: the need to locate the father centrally while insisting that desire originates in the daughter, as mentioned above; the analyst's need to construct his own tale of causation; the need to create/recreate that "most momentous" repressed phase of masochistic feminine desire in which being beaten and being loved become one and the same.

Early on, Freud announces that he will confine his discussion to the four female cases among the six he has studied, "in order to make it easier to follow these transformations in beating-phantasies" (184). Later in the essay, he nonetheless returns to his two male patients to establish what he calls a "feminine" attitude which becomes implicitly linked to both passivity and masochism.[29] Thus, as in other essays, the troubling parallel that he himself warns against develops

[29]Although Freud repeatedly inveighs against the equivalency of passivity and femininity, he as repeatedly violates his own injunction. In particular, "inversion" (homosexuality) and femininity work as mutually constitutive constructs. Femininity is proven by material in male case histories, as it is here; male inversion is affirmed through femininity. In "The Economic Problem of Masochism," he sets forth feminine masochism as the "most accessible," "least problematical" form, and announces "we will begin our discussion with it." The paragraph that immediately follows, however, restricts femininity to what is seen "in men (to whom, owing to the material at my command, I shall restrict my remarks)" (161). Freud goes on to draw his examples exclusively from men. This strategy is not unique to Freud, of course. It persists strangely in Cixous and Kristeva, for example, who often find the feminine voice most convincingly present in the male writer.

among the pairings of masculine/feminine, active/passive, sadistic/masochistic, scopophilic/exhibitionist, knowing/not knowing. A further major sexual division develops when the three stages we have accepted as typical are revealed to be exclusively feminine. The boy's stages do not correspond to the girl's.[30]

Intriguing and important as the distinctions between Freud's formulation of male and female fantasies are, they remain generally outside my scope here except to note the obvious: the construction of the female fantasy again normalizes passivity and masochism.[31] "There can be no doubt that the original phantasy in the case of the girl, 'I am being beaten (i.e. I am loved) by my father,' represents a feminine attitude, and corresponds to her dominant and manifest sex" (202). It is only insofar as the girl identifies herself as what Freud calls a "whipping boy" (191), potentially sadistic and masculine instead of a whipped girl, that a problem arises. "When they turn away from their incestuous love for their father, with its genital significance, they easily abandon their feminine role. They spur their 'masculinity complex' into activity, and from that time forward only want to be boys" (191). When active identification happens (it does not in all cases), their evasion of proper femininity by escape to the spectator's role seems fraught with anxiety for Freud, and the motive that spurs their refusal strangely absent. "The girl escapes from the demands of the erotic side of her life altogether. She turns herself in phantasy into a man, without herself becoming active in a masculine way, and is no longer anything but a spectator of the event which takes the place of a sexual act" (199).

The refusal to join in the fun that so disturbs Freud is a commonsense decision for Joan Foster, the costume Gothic author in Atwood's

[30]According to Freud, in the boy's untriangulated, unrepressed, two-part sequence, he moves from "I am being beaten (loved) by my father" to "I am being beaten by my mother" (198). He paradoxically arrives at a heterosexual object choice through a passive homosexual stance instead of developing "masculine instinctual impulses—sadistic tendencies, for instance, or . . . lustful feelings towards his mother" (203). In "Preliminary Phases of the Masculine Beating Fantasy," Edmund Bergler attempts to establish a male scenario that begins with the boy's activity, turned in "sadistic aggression against the breasts of the mother" (518). Interestingly, Bergler posits that the punitive father figure of stage two is a "'transcription' of executive power from mother to father" (518). Nonetheless, for Bergler, as for Freud, the sadistic mother is "phallic" and the boy's final, passive identification is with the "castrated mother" (520).

[31]For excellent and detailed discussions of variations in male/female development and analysis of Freud's discussion of women, see Nancy Chodorow's *The Reproduction of Mothering*, Luce Irigaray's "The Blind Spot of an Old Dream of Symmetry" in her *Speculum of the Other Woman*, Kaplan's *Female Perversions* (78–122), Sarah Kofman's *The Enigma of Woman*, the section on Freud in Juliet Mitchell's *Psychoanalysis and Feminism*, and Stoller's *The Development of Masculinity and Femininity*.

Lady Oracle. Wondering if her mother perhaps named her after Joan of Arc rather than Joan Crawford, as she's always been told, she repudiates both Mommy Dearest and the martyr, the beater and the beaten. "Didn't she know what happened to women like that? They were accused of witchcraft, they were roped to the stake, they gave a lovely light; a star is a blob of burning gas. But I was a coward, I'd rather not win and not burn, I'd rather sit in the grandstand eating my bag of popcorn and watch along with everyone else" (370–71).

For those who want to be stars to an admiring multitude, the "event which takes the place of a sexual act" is being burned or beaten. The genital demand is repressed and also regresses to an earlier stage of development, the anal. According to Freud, "this being beaten is now a convergence of the sense of guilt and sexual love. *It is not only the punishment for the forbidden genital relation, but also the regressive substitute for that relation. . . .* Here for the first time we have the essence of masochism" ("A Child" 189). The repression of the second stage, necessary only for the girl, "is a direct expression of the girl's sense of guilt" (189), which is "perhaps more exacting" (190) in female cases. Freud is adamant about the need for guilt: "So far as I know, this is always so; a sense of guilt is invariably the factor that transforms sadism into masochism" (189). The girl's inexplicable guilt, which brings about the shift from active to passive, seems to stem from an inherent sense of inferiority according to Freud's explanation. It is like the "notorious 'sense of inferiority' " and "seems to correspond to a scar-like formation which is similar to the sense of inferiority" (193, 194).

Several intriguing problems stem from this formulation. First, as Freud reminds us elsewhere, "the formation of the super-ego must suffer" ("Femininity" 129), as must the sense of guilt, in the girl: the castration threat that civilizes a boy is futile for her, given the "fact" that she is already castrated. Girls consequently, according to Freud, show little sense of justice, make ethical decisions through emotion rather than judgment, and lack boys' ability to sublimate.[32] Yet, how strange, then, that in this one instance, their sense of guilt (versus

[32]Although there are frequent references to women's weak superego formation and their poor capacity to achieve the sublimation that propels civilization, the clearest discussions of their supposed limits are in Freud's other two "women" essays, "Some Psychical Consequences of the Anatomical Distinction between the Sexes" and "Female Sexuality." Conversely, *The Ego and the Id* is a fascinating study in how the superego becomes the father's preserve. In the course of explaining how sublimation may in fact be related to secondary narcissism, Freud suggests intriguing possibilities for how women's (pejorative) narcissism can be argued as sublimation, although those possibilities are in no way pursued.

shame) comes to be so well formed. We thus move from the actual father to his internalized representative, the superego. Even that metaphoric identification with the paternal becomes increasingly attenuated as the essay continues, however, so that the girl's shift from activity to passivity, from sadism to masochism, becomes the inevitable result of her own hopeless desire. All this activity is once again only the urge for the penis, and the outcome of her ill-fated quest for mastery turns on the futility of her search for that evanescent Grail, as we are told in another essay. "After a woman has become aware of the wound to her narcissism, she develops, like a scar, a sense of inferiority" ("Some Psychical Consequences" 253). She errs if she thinks this "wound" or "scar" is the mark of any violence other than that self-inflicted.[33] In Freud's early construction, her guilt and inferiority become naturalized internal processes that train her to subordination if she steers between the "masculinity complex" of sadism and the attempted asexual escape of being a spectator—the same three routes later mapped so carefully in "Femininity."

The very issues of agency, order, and causation Freud addresses in "A Child Is Being Beaten" echo strangely in the development of his own argument. In later essays, he seems troubled that his overt epistemophilic aim and search for a first cause were so occluded. Even emphasizing the "normal" heterosexual desire of the girl seems to pose the question of the father's role too pointedly, as we see in Joseph's restatement of Marie Bonaparte's cheery endorsement: "*Every girl* . . . must have unconsciously fantasied being beaten on the clitoris by the father's penis" (56). While again musing on beating fantasies six years after the publication of "A Child Is Being Beaten," Freud moves still further from the paternal representation when he suggests that the girl is simply doing it to herself: "The child which is being beaten (or caressed) may ultimately be nothing more nor less than the clitoris itself" ("Some Psychical Consequences" 254). The problems of a big person doing something to a little person are minimized by the synecdochal shift, while the relative scale remains constant. The beaten is not the mother, and not even the girl; the beater is

[33]I am not arguing here for the preservation of narcissism as a specifically "feminine" mode of nondifferentiation. All children, male or female, suffer a massive "wound" to their grandiose omnipotence. What I object to is the attempt to localize or essentialize that wound through the binary play of genitalia, whether the penis's full presence is created through the vagina's "lack," or the labia's self-enclosure is taken as a pledge of perennial wholeness and plenitude. For excellent discussions on the problems involved with making the maternal into a lost Eden, see Janice L. Doane and Devon Hodge's *Nostalgia and Sexual Difference* and Kaja Silverman's *The Acoustic Mirror*, particularly the chapters on Kristeva and Irigaray.

now not the father (or even his internalized superego representation) but the girl herself. In 1931, Freud's persistent search for and disavowal of causation identifies a new agent through whom actual seduction may occur: the mother.[34] And it is against the mother that the girl's hostility should be rightfully directed; her anger at her father is only a later substitution. "We find the little girl's aggressive oral and sadistic wishes in a form forced on them by early repression, as a fear of being killed by her mother—a fear which, in turn, justifies her death-wish against her mother, if that becomes conscious. It is impossible to say how often this fear of the mother is supported by an unconscious hostility on the mother's part which is sensed by the girl" ("Female Sexuality" 237). Thus, father still knows best and is the ultimate source of authority, but his presence becomes strangely hollow as he is protected from the possibility that the vicissitudes of female development might be laid at his door, that he, like the mother, might display "unconscious hostility" or seduction. If there is any seduction, it is at the daughter's behest.[35]

Because she cannot come to terms with her inferiority, the girl only *thinks* that father might hurt mother, other children, or herself. Yet, ironically, the hierarchical vision of normal sexuality that theory gives for her perusal is the same as that at which she stares in her fantasy; the problem for the analyst seems to be that she will not assume the position of beaten.[36] Freud gives a strange warning at the close of his

[34]In both "Female Sexuality" and "Femininity," the treatment of the mother's role and the intensified interest in the pre-Oedipal period is fascinating. On the one hand, the father must be exculpated from any wrong-doing, and so other children, women, and servants become the agents of seduction, when real. It is the mother who excites precocious sexual development through her fondling of the child and then forbids gratification. On the other hand, the mother must not be given too much power, and so she is "phallic." For a more thorough discussion, see Chodorow's *The Reproduction of Mothering*.

[35]Clearly, much of this material relates to the seduction controversy, in which some argue that Freud abandoned credence in actual abuse in favor of screen memories for personal reasons and for professional advancement. The best known (and most argued about in its own right) statement of this is Jeffrey Masson's *The Assault on Truth*. See also Marie Balmary's *Psychoanalyzing Psychoanalysis* and Jane Gallop's *The Daughter's Seduction*.

[36]Freud's feminization of masochism applies to boys as well as girls. To oversimplify, in many instances aggression is defined pragmatically: it is feminine and masochistic if the patient doesn't "win," sadistic and masculine if he does. In application, then, nomenclature has much to do with the relative power of the parties involved. For example, according to Freud, the Wolf Man uses rage sadistically in dealing with his Nanya; with his father, his aims become masochistic, although the initiative for this is ascribed to the Wolf Man alone. "By bringing his naughtiness forward he was trying to force punishments and beatings out of his father, and in that way to obtain from him the masochistic sexual satisfaction that he desired. His screaming fits were therefore simply attempts at seduction" (*From the History of an Infantile Neurosis* 28).

discussion of girls, one that simultaneously insists on the "delusional" status of "My father is beating me," the stage the analyst has so carefully constructed, and at the same time promises patriarchal retribution. "People who harbour phantasies of this kind develop a special sensitiveness and irritability towards anyone whom they can put among the class of fathers. They allow themselves to be easily offended by a person of this kind, and in that way (to their own sorrow and cost) bring about the realization of the imagined situation of being beaten by their father" (191). Baldly paraphrased, this means "Your father does not beat you, but if you say so one more time, he'll give you a good whack."

Finally, then, Freud's discussion of the beating fantasy in girls recreates the fantasy's own hermetic enclosure while erasing hierarchy. The girl interweaves love and pain for her own complex psychic purposes. Her vicarious identification with power ("My father is beating the child whom I hate") and with subordination ("My father is beating/loving me") exists to satisfy her own needs, and not as a response to the impossibly contradictory relationships she sees around her. And, because there never was a problem, her distanced, rapt observation of "a child is being beaten" remains her futile attempt to escape the heterosexual dynamics of sadomasochism.

3

All You Need Is Love:
Training the Instincts

Caleb Williams describes his motivation with great accuracy: "The spring of action which, perhaps more than any other, characterised the whole train of my life, was curiosity. . . . I was desirous of tracing the variety of effects which might be produced from given causes" (Godwin 4). Caleb typifies what Herman Nunberg, like Freud, sees as an overwhelming drive originating in the anal period: "the *need* for causality, a psychological phenomenon. Everyone feels it as a wish to find, to establish the relationship between cause and effect" (*Curiosity* 76). What the beating fantasy's static portrayal seems to insist is that there is *no* causality: the players just happen to be cast into their fixed, statue-like molds. The formulaic consistency of the players' poses and their demand that the same story be told again and again belies the denial of causality, of course. Furthermore, as Laura Mulvey suggests, the affect and content of such a scene move us to discover, like Caleb, "the spring of action": "sadism demands a story," a narrative to explain how this appalling scene came to be ("Visual Pleasure" 15).[1]

"A Child Is Being Beaten" thus relates an enigmatic fairy tale whose point of origin remains vaguely "once upon a time." Despite its undoubted resonance, the tale's last frozen shot of beater and beaten, seen through the unblinking gaze of the watcher, also lacks proper closure. In traditional marital Gothic, the plot would move to a "happy" ending, asserting (albeit fatuously) that reality principle has ban-

---

[1]Sedgwick adds to this insight: "Isn't anger almost necessarily the most diachronic, the most narrative of emotions, the one most *necessarily* mistranslated in the freeze-frame?" ("A Poem" 124–25). I think that their observations on the connection between anger and narrative are extraordinarily astute, although I wonder whether grief doesn't demand its story as well.

ished horror and that pleasure can now be experienced under its beneficent regime. It would read something like this: "A bad man was hurting a woman. A bad man tried to hurt me. A good man saved me. Now we will live happily ever after." In contrast to this causal and temporal progression, the beating fantasy has no tenses: all time is simultaneously present. And, although in certain versions the figure of patriarchal authority can be split into "good" and "bad" between the characters of beater and beaten, more often both aspects are embodied within the beater. Just as his loving/hating embrace remains deeply ambivalent, so too the affect of the whole scene insists on the simultaneity of pleasure and pain. Furthermore, where traditional marital Gothic closes with ecstatic merger into "we," the beating fantasy insists upon separation, hierarchy, and a viewer.

Within the beating fantasy and the Gothic novel, the beater's fury is manifest. What, though, becomes of the rage and sadism of the beaten? Here, I trace both the early turning inward of the girl's aggression and its later, convoluted path toward the outside world. To follow that path, I want to look also at two of the ways in which the course of the beaten is determined by external as well as internal forces: cultural overvaluation of the male and the emphasis in heterosexual social models on repression rather than sublimation for women. The repeated intertwining of "love" and aggression that the girl experiences in her relations with authority encourage her to redirect her active instincts, to idealize the men who so insouciantly exercise their own aggression, and to control herself through repression instead of entering the social realm via sublimation. To see and understand the beating fantasy at the center of her psychic maze is one way in which she and we can find a path out.

The Turning Inward of Instinct

In order to understand the beating fantasy's drama of triangulation, we need to consider another group of ideas so that we can begin to identify what, besides a victim, is at stake here. The concept of component instincts, most usefully set forth in Freud's "Instincts and Their Vicissitudes," gives us our own specular aid so that we begin to see the prohibition of activity (sadism, scopophilia, epistemophilia), the acceptance of passivity (masochism, exhibitionism, not knowing), and the impasse of the female watcher more clearly. Furthermore, the association of hostility and sexuality, the assigning of subjectivity to an other, the seemingly willing erasure of the self, and the suspension of the viewer start to form their own coherent cultural plot. Briefly stated, the viewer is caught in a moment of decision that can last a lifetime. What the beating fantasy offers her is a Faustian pact of heterosexuality: she can have public identity and existence if she will become the beaten and give up the inquiring gaze that, after all, affirms herself only to herself.

A key passage from "Instincts and Their Vicissitudes" outlines the process of instinctual transformations and their first mutation, and suggests some of the significance of those transformations for the component instincts.

> Observation shows us that an instinct may undergo the following vicissitudes:—
> Reversal into its opposite
> Turning round upon the subject's own self
> Repression
> Sublimation
> . . . . Bearing in mind that there are motive forces which work against an instinct's being carried through in an unmodified form, we may also regard these vicissitudes as modes of *defence* against the instincts.
> Reversal of an instinct into its opposite resolves on closer examination into two different processes: a change from activity to passivity, and a reversal of its content. . . .
> Examples of the first process are met with in the two pairs of opposites: sadism-masochism and scopophilia-exhibitionism. The reversal affects only the *aims* of the instincts. The active aim (to torture, to look at) is replaced by the passive aim (to be tortured, to be looked at). Reversal of *content* is found in the single instance of the transformation of love into hate. (126–27)

The process described is very like that in the beating fantasy: (1) my father is beating a child (reversal from love to hate); (2) my father is beating me (turning round upon the subject's self); (3) a child is being beaten (repression/sublimation). Whereas "Instincts" assumes activity as the starting point for development, though, there is no analogous activity posited for the girl in "A Child": there is no hypothesized early stage in which *she* wants to beat someone. Her desire for her father, anachronistically resituated in the anal period, stands as her sole active expression of yearning. I focus in this section primarily upon the first two possibilities Freud sets forth—reversal of an instinct and its turning upon the subject—to explain how Freud's theory of the instincts' development becomes coterminous with the "natural" female masochism of later life through the prohibition of activity. Each active component instinct (scopophilia/exhibitionism, sadism/masochism, epistemophilia/not knowing) must be relinquished and its passive counterpart adopted.

The Gothic protagonist—and the viewer in the beating fantasy—defends against all expression of active instincts with the limited exception of the gaze. For her, the "motive forces" that work against instinctual discharge demand unusually extensive reinforcement so that she can fit one day into the glass slipper ideology holds forth for her. To defend the ego and to obtain some limited satisfaction, she must trade in the active for the passive. In addition, the original desire must be masked by the reversal of not just aim but content, which shows itself in three forms: love/hate, loving/being loved, love and hate/indifference ("Instincts" 139–40).

Freud points to the second antithesis, love/hate, as being the most clearly related to passivity/activity, but so too are the others. For our analysis, then, it suffices to say that the woman must exhibit love, not hate, will prefer being loved to loving, and may even, like the spectator, try to opt out of the economy entirely by choosing indifference rather than loving or hating.[2]

In reversal of their aims, the component instincts nonetheless remain paired, and each evokes its opposite, as in the instance of the patient who dresses in a distinctive, conspicuously muted style "as if he were saying, 'See how I don't want to be seen' " (Nierenberg, "A Case of Voyeurism" 145). Freud emphasizes this Noah's Ark mating of the component instincts in "Sexual Aberrations." "Every active perversion is thus accompanied by its passive counterpart: anyone who is an exhibitionist in his unconscious is at the same time a *voyeur*; in anyone who suffers from the consequences of repressed sadistic impulses there is sure to be another determinant of his symptoms which has its source in masochistic inclinations" (33). Freud reiterates the presence of activity and passivity in the instincts through a number of essays; indeed, at the end of "Instincts and Their Vicissitudes," he identifies the antithesis as one "*of the three great polarities that dominate mental life*" (140).

Subject (ego)	Object (external world)
Pleasure	Pain
Active	Passive [133]

[2]The second transformation is thoroughly objectified and domesticated in "On Narcissism," published one year earlier, in which some women show "the charm of certain animals" such as cats and "large beasts of prey" as well as that of children, for their supposed need lies not "in the direction of loving but of being loved" (89).

Each polarity is given its own realm: biological (active/passive), real (subject or ego/object or external world), economic (pleasure/pain) (140).

To oversimplify, the desideratum of development is to be a subject (i.e., one who understands the separation between self and other and acknowledges reality principle) who is active and experiences pleasure. This formulation, of course, aligns one side of the three polarities and assumes their predominance. When we think about the routes of female and male development set forth in "A Child" and elsewhere, though, we see that the universalized subject is necessarily male. The "normal" female must find her pleasure in pain, satisfy active strivings through passivity, and know her subjectivity only through an other. She must come to find the malformation comfortable and insist that it is what she herself wanted.

In Emily Prager's "A Visit from the Footbinder," six-year-old Pleasure Mouse is excited at the initiation that will make a woman of her the next day. While admiring her older sister's thousand pairs of tiny shoes, she asks about the ceremony and if she'll be hurt. " 'And it didn't hurt me in the least. It only hurts if you're a liar and a cheat or a sorcerer. Unworthy. Spoiled. Discourteous. . . . But perhaps . . . the pain is so great that one's sentiments are smashed like egg shells. Perhaps for many seasons, one cries out for death and cries unheeded, pines for it and yearns for it. Why should I tell you when no one told me?' " (4). The "normal" Freudian woman must go through much the same process, preferably without the consciousness shown at the end of the passage that something has been done to one or that there was any coercion before acceptance. The result is beauty in the eye of the beholder and one's own: an entire internalization of restriction that insists it didn't hurt at all, that only the "unworthy" feel any pain, and that the suffering of other women is their own problem.

To become such a woman, training must begin early. The active/passive antithesis, based in the anal period, "coalesces" with and is "soldered" to the later masculine/feminine division ("Instincts" 134, *Introductory Lectures* 327). Almost every time Freud draws this analogy, he warns us that we must not confuse masculine/feminine with active/passive. There is no gender identification before the phallic stage, he emphasizes,[3] and every individual has bisexual traits. Yet

[3]I disagree strongly with this premise. The Oedipal period is indeed crucial, but access to language, distinction of self from other, and formation of what Robert Stoller calls "core gender identity" (*Presentations of Gender* 14) take significant shape during the pre-Oedipal period through interaction with the mother or primary caretaker.

his discussion shows a consistent pattern of gender differentiation in the supposedly neutral drives, particularly those in their ascendancy during the anal stage: scopophilia/exhibitionism, sadism/masochism, epistemophilia/not knowing. What we might expect to be the most egalitarian of organs becomes instead a new site for gender colonization. For both sexes, feces are the first substantial commodity, a treasure that can be either hoarded or gifted graciously upon the admiring recipient.[4] Something valuable seems to be at stake in this gift's transformation into gender differentiation, something as precious as the productions of the period are to the child itself.

In "Anxiety and Instinctual Life," for example, Freud comments "that sadism has a more intimate relation with masculinity and masochism with femininity, as though there were a secret kinship present" ("Anxiety" 104). As usual, his tracing of this secret genealogy over time is a brilliant description of what happens; the problem, needless to say, is in the insistence that this is how it must be.

The component instincts are neatly marshalled into alignment with later antitheses. So too their objects and aims reform themselves to more socially acceptable expression. The active poles lead to particularly valued cultural outlets. Young voyeurs, "eager spectators of the processes of micturition and defaecation," will, if possible, continue their investigations with the genitals later, and their voyeurism will modulate itself to "curiosity" and "gaining knowledge" ("Infantile Sexuality" 192, *Five Lectures* 44, *Introductory Lectures* 327). If their activity is stopped, there may be "a permanent injury to the instinct for knowledge," or the later development of obsessional neurosis, in which "procrastination in *action* is soon replaced by lingering over *thoughts*" ("Infantile Sexuality" 197, *Notes* 245).

There must be purposive activity directed to the outside world: sadism. Sadism is the "instinct for mastery which easily passes over into cruelty," "the instinct for mastery, or the will to power"—a Nietzschean formula Sedgwick extends to an "aggressive will-to-narrate and will-to-uncover" (*Introductory Lectures* 327, "Economic Problem" 163, "Poem" 133).[5] The active component drives work with one another, as they do with their passive counterparts, so that the in-

---

[4]See particularly "Character and Anal Erotism" and "On Transformations of Instinct as Exemplified in Anal Erotism," in which the equivalencies feces = money = gift = penis = baby are developed.

[5]In *Sadism and Masochism*, Wilhelm Stekel argues that "psychic processes stand in the service of two forces . . . , *the will to power* and *the will to submission*." Although he views these forces as sex-identified, he suggests that the cause of that identification is social (1: 139, 138).

stinct for knowledge, for instance, although not itself a basic drive, "corresponds on the one hand to a sublimated manner of obtaining mastery, while on the other hand it makes use of the energy of scopophilia" ("Infantile Sexuality" 194). Indeed, "the instinct for knowledge can actually take the place of sadism. . . . It is at bottom a sublimated off-shoot of the instinct of mastery, exalted into something intellectual" ("Disposition" 324).

Such extreme sublimation can almost choke off affect but, while pointing this out, Freud also retains a strange admiration for the Nietzschean feat. "A man who has won his way to a state of knowledge cannot properly be said to love and hate; he remains beyond love and hatred" ("Leonardo" 75). While still within earthly bounds, however, such a man shows, like the patient Nunberg describes, the confluence of sadism, curiosity, and voyeurism in his "sharpened thinking processes" and his ability for "complicated reasoning," "speculation," and "logical thinking" (*Curiosity* 69).

According to Freud's own analysis, then, the active accumulation of principal during the anal period leads to eventual dividends of knowledge, power, and wealth. The beneficiaries may also be somewhat orderly, parsimonious, obstinate, or defiant but, all told, it seems a highly successful transaction. As if this anal cornucopia of bounty weren't enough, ambition too stems from this time, through its more up-front connection with micturition.[6] Unfortunately, those who reap such profits are usually boys. The legacy of the anal stage for little girls is, not surprisingly, quite different. While she may become accultured to giving—a talent for which she will be much lauded later—she will also learn a good deal about giving up and about being properly neat and clean instead of engaging in messy investigations.[7]

Both sexes form the same sensible hypothesis (the cloaca theory) from early investigation. If a large object—a baby—must be expelled from the body, the anus is obviously the most suitable organ. Thus the anus becomes identified with the vagina, and the feces with the baby, another "gift." For both, feces and baby have a third metaphoric

[6]See "Anxiety and Instinctual Life" (102) and "Character and Anal Erotism" (175) for the genesis of "burning ambition."

[7]Anna Freud and Dorothy Burlingham's description of a "typical" child's training seems to suggest the experience of the female authors to some extent, just as Sigmund Freud's assumption that applause greets the accomplishment of the boy appears rooted in the experience of a much-loved son. According to Anna Freud and Burlingham, children must learn to dislike dirt, to feel pity instead of hostility, and to restrain sexual impulses. "The curiosity of the child is left largely unsatisfied, and its natural desire to be admired is criticised as a wish to 'show off'" (*War and Children* 57).

identity, the penis, "all three solid bodies" ("Transformations" 133). The possibility of losing valuable body parts assumes even greater retroactive significance for the boy and enters into the composition of his castration complex. Much of the feces' value as gold or money—if not gift—is also transferred to the penis, while the drives' aims continue to be achieved through later expressions of mastery, curiosity, and looking.

For the girl too, the anal stage is recast in the light of later developments. Its richness of gifts—wealth, knowledge, power, ambition—is available to her only through the vicarious route marked by feces→penis→baby. She can draw on these resources only through a "system of credit, or even usury," as Luce Irigaray argues (*Speculum* 73).[8] She cannot have the penis nor ought she to have the active attributes of the anal period. She can have the baby, and the sensible woman will realize, as Freud claims, "that nature has given babies to women as a substitute for the penis that has been denied them" ("Transformations" 129). "A rational wish then leads from the wish for a baby to the wish for a man" ("Transformations" 132). Even the child may be something the man "gives" her, as Freud points out (although, as he says, the reverse formulation is also common). If she is fortunate enough to have a son, he will embody her own active desires. "A mother can transfer to her son the ambition which she has been obliged to suppress in herself," a conveyance of psychic capital Anna Freud also notes ("Femininity" 133).[9] Thus, her only access to the active attributes of the anal period is to "put up with the man as an appendage to the penis" ("Transformations" 129). Through him she will get the penis, baby, wealth, knowledge, and power. In the course of Freud's discussion, the feces are gradually eliminated, while the baby and penis loom large. The pattern we see in Gothic relationships restores the chain of signification: the protagonist who assumes that through the man she will get knowledge, power, and wealth only too often finds that what she's gotten is shit.

In "Femininity," Freud notes that "to achieve a passive aim may call for a large amount of activity" ("Femininity" 115). In that essay, his

[8]See *Speculum* (73–80) for a strong critique of anal eroticism and the feces/baby/penis equation in Freud.

[9]The ambiguity of Sigmund Freud's "obliged" (by society? by the constraints of "natural" feminine development?) is echoed in Anna Freud's statement, which seems to hint mildly at social reality: "Perhaps even the purely altruistic relation of a mother to her son is largely determined by such a surrender of her own wishes to the object whose sex makes him 'better qualified' to carry them out. A man's success in life does, indeed, go far to compensate the women of his family for the renunciation of their own ambitions" (*The Ego* 131–32).

comment is something of a sop to his own argument of bisexuality and a condescending reassurance to women. In general discussion (i.e., not specifically concerning women), however, he is more willing to cede that such prodigious expenditures of energy do not occur spontaneously but may originate from without.[10] If the demand for repression of sexual investigation is too strong and augmented by later religious and educational "inhibition of thought," development is distorted. "Research shares the fate of sexuality; thenceforward curiosity remains inhibited and the free activity of intelligence may be limited for the whole of a subject's lifetime" ("Leonardo" 79). Such systemic inhibition is normative, however, for the woman: the mysteries of domesticity and of Gothic plots may be her sole outlets for investigation—if she is still able to initiate such investigations.

If she is active, intelligent, and curious, she is demonstrating her "masculinity complex." If she is too passive, too sedulous in her suppression of the drives for mastery and knowledge, she joins the parade of drudges to which so many patients' mothers belong in the case references, or she becomes one of the zombie army Freud castigates at the end of "Femininity." Unlike a man of about thirty, who can "make powerful use of" analysis, who seems still "youthful" and "unformed," a woman of the same age often appears mysteriously brain-dead. "A woman of the same age, however, often frightens us by her psychical rigidity and unchangeability. Her libido has taken up final positions and seems incapable of exchanging them for others. There are no paths open to further development; it is as though the whole process had already run its course and remains thenceforward insusceptible to influence—as though, indeed, the difficult development to femininity had exhausted the possibilities of the person concerned. As therapists we lament this state of things" ("Femininity" 134–35).[11]

The girl whose active sexual curiosity is suppressed is, unlike the

---

[10]As mentioned previously, this position is altered somewhat in *The Ego and the Id* where there is a double maneuver very similar to that found in "A Child." On the one hand, the father is foregrounded (in this instance, through his centrality in superego formation); on the other, his possible causative effect on the ego's development is minimized in favor of internal processes (anxiety, not inhibition).

[11]Anna Freud's comments on the instinctual "onslaught" of adolescence are to the point here. If the ego has been restrained within too-narrow limits, "No use can be made of the increased libido," and there must be a "constant expenditure" of energy to maintain defenses and "hold it in check." The result, "permanently injurious to the individual," is, I suspect, Sigmund Freud's thirty-year-old woman. "Ego institutions which have resisted the onslaught of puberty without yielding generally remain throughout life inflexible, unassailable, and insusceptible of the rectification which a changing reality demands" (*The Ego* 149–50).

boy, usually offered no alternative routes for investigation. She is a living exemplar of Michel Foucault's hypothesis about repression: she is supposed to know, think, and do nothing overtly sexual, and yet everything in her life is shaped around and points to this great "secret," one that finally works to deploy power. Latency begins a long dream of passivity from which not even the transformations of puberty entirely awaken her. She, like the Gothic protagonist, is moved by others and by events while she herself seemingly can move nothing. Her own body is cordoned off as a place to explore, as a child by others and later by herself. The masturbation that so often marks the guilty close of the beating fantasies Freud's virgin patients imagine may, like the role of spectator, remove her from the marriage economy and is to be avoided. Certainly, she cannot prematurely practice activity in the service of passive aims by letting someone else do the exploring or by instigating joint investigations. For the young adult, genital sexuality becomes *the* secret, the only route allowed her for investigation. If girls show great pleasure in looking or curiosity, it can become "a powerful motive for urging them to an early marriage": "Simple-minded girls, after becoming engaged, are reputed often to express their joy that they will soon be able to go the theatre, to all the plays which have hitherto been prohibited, and will be allowed to see everything" (*Introductory Lectures* 220). Even such "simple-minded" girls, however, as Freud implicitly acknowledges, find that anticipation exceeds the event: the marriages that they assume will be the beginning of experience, the authorization of expansion, just usher in a new course in passivity.

Freud's varying uses of the biological, economic, and real realms with which he equates his three "great polarities" (active/passive, pleasure/pain, subject/object) create, defend, and sometimes decry this passivity. In "The Dissolution of the Oedipus Complex," the biology of the girl's "atrophied" penis mandates passivity. "The comparatively lesser strength of the sadistic contribution to her sexual instinct, which we may no doubt connect with the stunted growth of her penis, makes it easier in her case for the direct sexual trends to be transformed into aim-inhibited trends of an affectionate kind" (179). As usual, the form of biology through which he makes a concept into a physiological reality is the least persuasive. In his more utopian economic musings, such as " 'Civilized' Sexual Morality and Modern Nervous Illness," and brief reflections in the course of other essays, he sometimes comments trenchantly on how unsurprising the prevalence of frigidity and neurasthenia is, how unlikely it is that Sleeping Beauty will ever awaken after such an education. In general, however, his analyses operate in the realm of the real, although they do draw on the other two areas for support, particularly the biological. In his most pragmatic mode, his tone seems to indicate that "this is how the world is, and best one adjust to it accordingly."

Thus, the many ambitious, frustrated young women who trudge through Freud's case references must accept the insight that it is their masculinity complex that moves them toward curiosity, knowledge, and power. Many can and do agree to the label, continue their activities, and even find it an enabling alternative to the cultural confines of femininity: the first generation of women analysts that trained with Freud is a stunning instance. As he responds to their hypothetical objections in "Femininity," he is able to dismiss them with a back-handed compliment: " 'This doesn't apply to *you*. You're the exception; on this point you're more masculine than feminine' " (116). And, of course, he is quite right in one regard: these women *are* the exceptions. They have accepted that when they look, speak, act, and explore actively they do so by dint of their masculinity, but their acceptance does let them move within the world. For whatever reason of upbringing, community mores, or constitution, the active drives of the anal period were either not strongly inhibited from without or these women did not internalize those restrictions through repression.

Women who are *not* exceptions—the vast majority, of course— begin the rechanneling of active to passive during the anal period. This is an extraordinarily delicate psychological and social negotiation. Too much passivity, and the nascent ego risks being overwhelmed and destroyed; too little, and the girl will not be properly receptive to the advent of the castration complex and the necessary transition from feces to penis and, later, baby. If all goes well, reversal of her active drives to passivity is already under way, but she must now also turn much of that energy against herself and assign a part of the ego function to another. To do so, she must renounce a good deal of the will to know, to see, and to master. In the rest of this chapter, we will see how subjectivity may be assigned to an overvalued other, how successful the renunciation achieved through repression and sublimation is, and how she may learn to use her passive instincts for active ends.

Assigned Subjectivity and the Overvalued Other

There must be a story—many stories, perhaps—that lead to the scene of the beating fantasy. *Story of O*, as we will see in Chapter 4, tells us one not too different from the one Freud relates in "A Child Is Being Beaten": a woman finds her "natural" satisfaction in masochism's painful pleasures. We have begun to trace another variant through the gloss of "Instincts and Their Vicissitudes," in which the loss of activity and the taking on of masochism seem anything but "natural." The fuller story of "Instincts" gives us a new opening chapter that shows how the active aims—to look, know, and master—are reversed for the girl so that their predominant expression becomes passive. At an early age, she is encouraged to prefer being looked *at*, not knowing, and being mastered. In addition, by the end of the anal period, her bent will be to *be* loved. The transformation of active drives to passive ones is not a clear, neat reversal, however: that is simply the first of their transformations. The active drives must be channeled, expressed, and used in some fashion, for it is almost impossible to erase them entirely. They therefore are turned "round upon the subject's own self" ("Instincts" 126) so that the self becomes its own object. Then another who can act out active urges with impunity is assigned the role of subject. These maneuvers, together with repression and sublimation, efficiently defuse and diffuse a woman's activity. For such defenses to succeed properly, the other to whom one yields one's own subjectivity has to be held worthy of such a gift. Given the gift's value, the other is necessarily overvalued. Furthermore, there must be a pay-off in pleasure, a grafting of sexuality onto the aggression of the overvalued other. Just as the child must believe "My father is beating me *because* he loves me," so the woman, like the protagonist of "The Yellow Wallpaper" and countless other Gothic novels, must assert "He's only's hurting me *because* he cares so much." Finally, then, beating, abuse, and abnegation of the self must be installed as intimacy and object relations, the proof that someone else really cares and that the self "deserves" such caring.

The active drives' use of the self as object is coterminous with the reversal from active to passive. The source and impetus (or force) of the instinct remain unchanged, but it has a new object, and a new, more circuitous route to discharge (aim inhibition). Instinctual needs are still satisfied, but not through the direct line indicated by subject-verb-object order (I am hurting someone, I am looking at something) but instead through a passive formulation (I am being hurt, I am being looked at). In outlining how this comes about, Freud uses sadism as an example of "Instincts and Their Vicissitudes."

In the case of the pair of opposites sadism-masochism, the process may be represented as follows.

(a) Sadism consists in the exercise of violence or power upon some other person as object.

(b) This object is given up and replaced by the subject's self. With the turning round upon the self the change from an active to a passive instinctual aim is also effected.

(c) An extraneous person is once more sought as object; this person, in consequence of the alteration which has taken place in the instinctual aim, has to take over the role of the subject.

Case (c) is what is commonly termed masochism. (127–28)

In giving up the immediately and directly gratifying violence of (a), the power with which it is equated is also transformed. In (b), the girl foregoes both in the exterior world, but reflexively uses them upon herself: she becomes the end of her own anger and aggression. If all stops at (b), what results is obsession—and, perhaps, something of the spectator's role. In that case, the subject will hurt herself through repeated accusations and guilt, but will also control herself.[12] To have a Gothic plot, however—to have a full heterosexual drama—(c) is necessary: someone else has to take over the role of subject. The brusque and grandiose seigneurs of the Gothic, to whom heroines resign their fates with varying degrees of reluctance, are those subjects. This sequence holds true for scopophilia as well, in which (c) becomes the "introduction of a new subject to whom one displays oneself in order to be looked at by him" (129). And the turning inward of curiosity, interdependent on the fate of the other component instincts, achieves the same end: the woman will be known while not knowing, just as she will be displayed and hurt.

The concept that another takes on the role of subject is startling in its implications for women's ego development. In "A Child," Freud professes to find causation a puzzle, and begs the question by emphasizing the internal processes that generate guilt. "Little light is thrown upon the genesis of masochism by our discussion of the beating-phantasy. . . . Instincts with a passive aim must be taken for granted as existing, especially among women. But passivity is not the whole of masochism. . . . The transformation of sadism into masochism appears to be due to the influence of the sense of guilt which takes part in the act of repression" (193–94).

In "Instincts," on the other hand, the possibility that the subject

---

[12]Anna Freud's warning about the lack of activity is seen in the results of routine feminization: "Again, the child's aggressiveness must have an outlet in the outside world, so that it does not become dammed up and turned inward, for, if it does, it will endow the superego with cruel characteristics" (The Ego 56).

might be extraneous and that the instinct's reversal and turning upon the self might be defenses initiated to protect the ego is clearly spelled out in relation to passive scopophilia and masochism. "And in both these cases the narcissistic *subject* is, through identification, replaced by another, extraneous ego. . . . [The passive] instinctual vicissitudes are dependent on the narcissistic organization of the ego and bear the stamp of that phase. They perhaps correspond to the attempts at defence which at higher stages of the development of the ego are effected by other means" (132). In addition to the illumination the explanation sheds on the beating fantasy, an important note is struck about the extent to which the ego is at risk, a risk it attempts to defend against through masochism.[13]

Anna Freud emphasizes this risk and its link to external reality in *The Ego and the Mechanisms of Defense*. Although she does not consider gender roles, her analysis illuminates the dilemma of the girl whose active behavior is met by external suppression. In Anna Freud's reading, the immature ego must not only defend against the instinctual demands generated internally but also endeavor "in all kinds of ways to defend itself against the objective unpleasure and dangers which menace it" (*The Ego* 70). To do so, the child trains herself in reality by learning to connect cause and effect. "Objective anxiety is the anticipation of suffering which may be inflicted on the child as a punishment by outside agents, a kind of 'fore-pain' which governs the ego's behavior, no matter whether the expected punishment always takes place or not" (143). The elegant idea of "fore-pain" aids the child's self-regulation through negative reinforcement. If, however, the child is punished precisely for the ego's development, she must employ ever more stringent defense mechanisms.

Just as, in "A Child," the repudiation of genital desire for the father leads not only to repression but regression to the anal stage, so in "Instincts" the urgency of defense is marked by further regression to narcissistic organization. To preserve the sense of self-worth that is indispensable to survival, the self both turns inward for safety and

[13]Freud develops this point further in his aptly named essay, "Splitting of the Ego in the Process of Defence." The child caught between gratification of an instinct and danger faces "a conflict between the demand by the instinct and the prohibition by reality. . . . On the one hand, with the help of certain mechanisms he rejects reality and refuses to accept any prohibition; on the other hand, in the same breath he recognizes the danger of reality, takes over the fear of that danger as a pathological symptom and tries subsequently to divest himself of the fear" (275). (For further discussion of splitting in the process of defense, see Ulman and Brothers's *The Shattered Self*.) The girl child and the Gothic heroine display precisely such a split between denial and recognition; both of their "plots" can be seen as an attempt to reintegrate the ego.

obscures the boundaries between self and other by letting the other function as the ego.[14]

The other to whom one assigns such a role must be worth a great deal—indeed, is overvalued, one might suspect.[15] In *A Taste for Pain*, Maria Marcus sketches the compensatory strategy that invests the other with full subjectivity while reserving doubt and inadequacy for the self.

> I felt that the man I was going to love had to be the subject, i.e. *someone who was something in himself*, who dealt with things himself and was active of his own free will. I felt that before I could love a man, he had to make me into an object, i.e. *someone who wasn't anything in herself*, who did not deal with things, but who was dealt with, and who was passive because there was no free will for me. . . .
>
> I think there was another reason why I wanted to be the object. I felt that would be the safest. . . . If a man looked at me, I seemed to exist more clearly. (61)

Without that other to reflect the self to the self and to mediate between it and the environment, the self fears its own disappearance. What Marcus describes is indeed narcissistic in its emphasis upon the potential rather than the kinetic. The pattern is specifically feminized, though, in that the potentiality is limited to heterosexual endorsement. Whereas the stereotypically masculine narcissist is a would-be polymath waiting for the applause of the world, the stereotypically feminine is more modest and necessarily finds her world, the testament of her existence, in only one other. The path for her achievement is love alone.[16]

Like the Gothic heroine, so demurely exhibitionist and so dutifully

---

[14]This narcissism is re-presented as the donnée of femininity in "On Narcissism," and its implications are further spelled out in "Female Sexuality" (230–31) and "Femininity" (133), where Freud argues that husbands are often the inheritors of girls' relations to their mothers.

[15]Even when in fantasy (or reality) the other is a grotesque, the implication seems to be that his status is nonetheless higher than the girl's. In addition, degradation can be and often is fused to the fantasy of being an exception, so that the range and depth of humiliation only serve to underscore one's value as martyr.

[16]The vicissitudes of narcissism itself are outside the scope of this study. The particular variations of secondary narcissism I describe here are only two gender-typed redactions among many possibilities. For further discussion of the relationship between masochism and narcissism, see: Baumeister (195–99); Arnold M. Cooper, "The Narcissistic-Masochistic Character"; Maria Carment Gear, Melvin A. Hill, and Ernesto Cesar Liendo, *Working Through Narcissism*; Otto F. Kernberg, "Clinical Dimensions of Masochism"; Herbert A. Rosenfeld, "On Masochism"; Susanne P. Schad-Somers, *Sadomasochism* (53–57, 111–19); and Roy Schafer, "Those Wrecked by Success."

subordinate before her all-powerful other, the masochist uses her passivity to seek recognition and to preserve a coherent identity as best she knows how. She follows the plot of heterosexual romance, the only plot in which culture allows her a leading role. Her very helplessness becomes the means through which she achieves acknowledgment, whether loving or punitive. As Karen Horney argues in "The Overvaluation of Love: A Study of a Common Present-Day Feminine Type," "The function of this masochistic attitude is therefore a neurotically distorted means of attaining a heterosexual goal, which these patients believe they cannot reach in any other way" (*Feminine Psychology* 211). Furthermore, the apparently abject masochist seeks vicarious gratification of the active drives through her idealized other. Her self-sacrificing ethics are potentially her entrée to a larger world. Benjamin's comment on masochistic women's goals is to the point here: "in ideal love, as in other forms of masochism, acts of self-abnegation are in fact meant to secure access to the glory and power of the other" (117).

In Sigmund Freud's discussion of how women and men exalt the other, strangely different mechanisms seem to be at work. According to his reasoning, women introject prized qualities of men—attributes that can be theirs no more than can the penis. When men overvalue women, however, they project their own strengths. In both instances, then, the construct of the male ego assumes plenitude and power, while that of the female marks inadequacy. In his lecture "The Dissection of the Psychical Personality," for example, Freud notes, via common opinion, that women are particularly influenced by their object choices, who represent the capacities they themselves have lost or never had. "It is said that the influencing of the ego by the sexual object occurs particularly often with women and is characteristic of femininity. . . . If one has lost an object or has been obliged to give it up, one often compensates oneself by identifying oneself with it and by setting it up once more in one's ego, so that here object-choice regresses, as it were, to identification" (63). Although libido is diverted from the ego to the object, it is restored to the woman through the narcissistic mirror, Freud argues. In presenting this process as "characteristic of femininity," Freud again naturalizes psychic processes to buttress gender differentiation. The process he describes basically leaves women in a permanently melancholic position, but it is themselves they mourn.[17]

---

[17]See, for example, "Mourning and Melancholia." This is something of a wishful overstatement on my part. If "normal" female development is followed assiduously,

According to Freud, though, overvaluation occurs mostly in men; one can only assume as a corollary that the value women attach to male objects or subjects is true currency. For example, in the early *Studies on Hysteria*, Freud is startled by his own "blindness." "I was afflicted by that blindness of the seeing eye which is so astonishing in the attitude of mothers to their daughters, husbands to their wives and rulers to their favourites" (117*n*). Here, and in fact throughout much of Freud's work, overvaluation is a mistake the dominant make about the subordinated. The reverse possibility—that the subordinated may ascribe strengths to the dominant that the latter don't have, or may even define the dominant through their fealty—is hardly considered as a possibility, particularly within a heterosexual frame.

To a feminist reader, Freud's definition of overvaluation in "Sexual Aberrations" seems to describe culture's inscription of masculine authority if the passage is read using "she" as universal pronoun. "The subject becomes, as it were, intellectually infatuated (that is, his powers of judgement are weakened) by the mental achievements and perfections of the sexual object and he submits to the latter's judgements with credulity. Thus the credulity of love becomes an important, if not the most fundamental, source of *authority*" (150).[18] The pattern of behavior Freud outlines is precisely that found in every naive Gothic protagonist who suspends her own judgment in deference to her beloved's authority. Astonishingly, the overvaluation Freud describes is the man's of the woman—a fatuous adoration most extensively set forth through the famous whore/madonna splitting of "Contributions to the Psychology of Love."[19]

The asymmetrical valuation of the other sex that Freud posits is crucial to how society and Gothic fiction represent and regulate "nor-

---

the little girl doesn't have enough of an ego to be a melancholic, as Irigaray scathingly demonstrates. "In fact the little girl will not choose melancholia as her privileged form of withdrawal. She probably does not have a capacity for narcissism great enough to allow her to fall back on melancholia" (*Speculum* 71; see esp. 66–70). Silverman adds to this point significantly by considering the mother's psychic representation in relation to the girl's insufficient narcissistic reserve: "the only identification with the mother which would be available to her would be one predicated upon lack, insufficiency, and self-contempt" (*Acoustic Mirror* 156).

[18]In a footnote added in 1910, Freud includes what is a rather strange instance of overvaluation in this context: that of the subject for the hypnotist. The woman becomes a *belle dame sans merci* in her fascinating power, and the male hypnotist her hapless prey. Here as elsewhere, the uncomfortable haunting by a female power supposedly exorcised long ago seems to me a clear return of a pre-Oedipal repressed.

[19]See "A Special Type of Choice of Object Made by Men" and "On the Universal Tendency to Debasement in the Sphere of Love."

mal" adult heterosexual relationships. A woman must "look up to" her man: unless she is carefully trained to do so, patriarchy falters. Every girl, and every Gothic heroine, learns that it is only in the mirror of his regard that she exists, only in the plenitude of his subjectivity that she is whole. Her assignment of subjectivity to and overvaluation of the other is, however, an analytic and cultural con game in which she's asked to believe that she's a winner. An economic metaphor best describes the transaction. A worker is told her labor has wage-value, the amount she is paid. The labor also generates the surplus value we call profit, which is reaped by others. The woman in conservative analytic and Gothic fictions is such a laborer emotionally. Love is her wage; the surplus value of her nurturing and self-abnegation funds the autonomy of the idealized other. She, like the wage-laborer, does not recognize the product as her own and remains alienated from the power so "naturally" appropriated by others. In order to maintain this system of subordination, it is imperative that girls learn proper passivity. My argument, then, is that women's devaluation enables and maintains men's overvaluation, a transaction shielded behind Freud's emphasis upon the overvalued woman.

Freud's analysis of object choice for girls and boys highlights the key significance of active and passive choice. Like a docile job applicant, the girl must be ready to accept any offer without pointing to her own qualifications; her getting a job is luck, not merit. All power resides in the employer/lover, and unions, which suggest another locus of power, are an abomination. She must choose to identify with that which is *not* like herself.

The small boy, according to Freud, has two choices: to love his mother (anaclitic object choice) or himself. Although choosing the former primes the boy for adult heterosexuality, it also leads him to overvalue his adult mate, as he once did the woman who cared for him. The small girl also has two choices: to love her mother (or the person who cares for her) or to love herself. Both sexes can have elements of both choices in love (and an individual of either sex can make predominantly anaclitic or narcissistic object choices).

The girl clearly has a problem or, to put it more accurately, Western culture has a major problem whose symptom is the girl. Her narcissism, so often discussed pejoratively, is nonetheless the adolescent girl's consolation prize for passivity. "This is unfavourable to the development of a true object-choice with its accompanying overvaluation. Women, especially if they grow up with good looks, develop a certain self-contentment which compensates them for the social restrictions that are imposed upon them in their choice of object" ("On Narcissism" 88–89).[20] The passage's struggle with logic, seen in the unreconciled conjunction of "unfavourable" *and* compensatory narcissism, points to the impasse in which culture places the girl. If, however, she aspires to "true object-choice" rather than narcissism and makes a fully anaclitic choice, she will choose another woman or a man who has her mother's attributes. Ergo, as a woman seeking a woman's qualities, she will have made a narcissistic object choice. Furthermore, if she thinks she can choose and somehow evade "social restrictions," she strays too far into activity.

Thus, the eighteen year old in "The Psychogenesis of a Case of Homosexuality in a Woman" is masculine in her assumption of the role of courtly lover to older women. Her "acuteness of comprehension and her lucid objectivity" (154) are the first tip-offs, followed by clues indicating "that she must formerly have had strong exhibitionist and scopophilic tendencies" (169). Of "greater importance," however, is her behavior toward the beloved. "She displayed the humility and the sublime overvaluation of the sexual object so characteristic of the male lover, the renunciation of all narcissistic satisfaction, and the preference for being the lover rather than the beloved" (154). She is the exception that proves the rule: "real" heterosexual women love narcissistically and so in "feminine" ways. Freud is careful to distinguish the sex of one's object choice from one's own attitude of masculinity or femininity; finally, though, the least plausible combination is for a woman to love a man in the "sublime" masculine mode ("Psychogenesis" 170).[21]

For Freud, overvaluation is, in the end, an almost exclusively male phenomenon in love, a sentimental overestimation of the mother by the boy that carries over to his eventual mate. "The significance of the

[20]The whole of the discussion on anaclitic and narcissistic object choice is drawn from this essay.

[21]Freud's sensible observation that a man may have a "feminine" attitude and yet be thoroughly heterosexual in his object choice, and that gay males or lesbians can be masculine or feminine in relating to the object is marred by his difficulty in conceding the same flexibility for heterosexual women. This becomes a not-so-subtle appropriation, as we see in "Analysis Terminable and Interminable," where he speaks of the analyst's exasperation in trying to convince male patients that it's okay to be feminine, and female patients that it's seldom acceptable to be masculine. "At no other point in one's analytic work does one suffer more from an oppressive feeling that all one's repeated efforts have been in vain, and from a suspicion that one has been 'preaching to the winds,' than when one is trying to persuade a woman to abandon her wish for a penis on the ground of its being unrealizable or when one is seeking to convince a man that a passive attitude to men does not always signify castration and that it is indispensable in many relationships in life" (251–52).

factor of sexual overvaluation can be best studied in men, for their erotic life alone has become accessible to research. That of women—partly owing to the stunting effect of civilized conditions and partly owing to their conventional secretiveness and insincerity—is still veiled in an impenetrable obscurity" ("Sexual Aberrations" 151). Freud's own wishful suppositions create some of that obscurity. Adult women, secretive and insincere, never quite love men enough—certainly not as much as the idealized, adoring mother of his own narcissistic stage, the mother who, at least in the son's nostalgic reconstruction, finds her own apotheosis in his perfection. "In typical cases women fail to exhibit any sexual overvaluation towards men; but they scarcely ever fail to do so towards their own children" ("Sexual Aberrations" 151n [added 1920]).[22] The value women attach to men is left in the realm of the real: it is what men are actually worth. And women's worth, devalued so ruinously and early, can only be measured as collateral to men's. Women's worth is generated through the men to whom they are attached, just as we are to understand that poor governesses "become somebody" through the love of wealthy men.

The overvaluation of men that Freud implicitly accepts as real value and, finally, a "natural" determinant of the order of things is itself a cultural construct, as Horney so cogently argues in "The Overvaluation of Love." Here, as elsewhere, my interest is not in the analysis of male motives or of the often self-evident benefits that accrue to the male through this structuration. Instead, my concern is what it means to be a woman who must define herself through such a system. The boy's possession of great wealth during the anal stage becomes rarefied into his great value as an adult. The girl, reduced to a beggar during the first major commodities exchange, must find her own adult value through what an other is willing to dower her with.

By signing over subjectivity to another (whether or not the endorsement is coerced), she achieves some vicarious satisfaction of her own active drives, which are directed both to the outside world and herself. Forbidden from exercising the "mastery" of sadism and the will to knowledge that epistemophilia and scopophilia provide, she ekes out what pleasures she can from the reversal of these instincts. She lives out the catch-22 Foucault calls the "cycle of prohibition":

[22]Freud makes the same point in "On the Universal Tendency to Debasement," where "universal" turns out not to include women. "In the case of women, there is little sign of a need to debase their sexual object. This is no doubt connected with the absence in them as a rule of anything similar to the sexual overvaluation found in men" (186).

"Renounce yourself or suffer the penalty of being suppressed; do not appear if you do not want to disappear. Your existence will be maintained only at the cost of your nullification" (*History* 84). She values the knowledge and power she cannot hold and invests them in another.[23] Like the nameless protagonist of du Maurier's *Rebecca* and numerous others, she enviously watches the idealized other, whose unfettered existence is so unlike her own, and forlornly hopes that a magical look or word from him will make her "somebody."

Repression and Sublimation

The masochistic woman's active drives, inhibited and channeled in an exclusive course early on, continue to express the raw, unreformed aggression of the anal stage, augmented by her own rage. Repressed, these drives remain gargantuan, according to "Repression." "This deceptive strength of instinct is the result of an uninhibited development in phantasy and of the damming-up consequent on frustrated satisfaction" (149). She defends against this formidable instinctual energy. Sadly and inevitably, she abets the system that forbade instinctual expression in the first place: the energy she must expend just to maintain repression is not free for use elsewhere, she uses it to monitor herself (thus freeing others for alternate forms of surveillance), and she employs it actively only in preparing another generation of girls for divesture. She survives, although it may be as a much diminished thing.

Anna Freud's neglected analyses of repression and sublimation show her keen awareness that both defenses are necessary maneuvers to preserve coherence of the ego when it is faced by external threats. Although her focus is primarily children, her explication of powerlessness and the genuine need for adaptive strategies sheds light upon the development of women and Gothic heroines as well. Most important, Anna Freud argues that sublimation—the achievement of active drives through a socially valued means—is possible for

[23]One might allocate active drives to several others, in part to lessen the threat to the self. One person could then have the right to know everything about you, while another would be allowed to punish or point out failings, and neither would be the same as the one permitted to look at you. To some extent, of course, this does describe the perquisites of friends and lovers. Within Western heterosexual arrangements, however, such multiplication and diffusion is often discouraged for women and all these functions are condensed and represented through the figure of patriarchal authority, whether father or husband, thus reinforcing that figure's authority.

the subordinated heroine of the beating fantasy. Sealed within her enclosed space, she nonetheless wants to act, speak, and be recognized as a subject.

Anna Freud points to the enormity of the need that generates—and the danger that attends—wide-scale, intense repression. "But repression is not only the most efficacious, it is also the most dangerous mechanism. The dissociation from the ego entailed by the withdrawal of consciousness from whole tracts of instinctual and affective life may destroy the integrity of the personality for good and all" (*The Ego* 50). To the child who must make such a decision, the cessation of pain may outweigh the active seeking of pleasure. "But the ego of the child who has solved her conflicts by means of repression, with all its pathological sequels, is at peace. It suffers secondarily through the consequences of the neurosis which repression has brought upon it. But it has, at least within the limits of the conversion hysteria or obsessional neurosis, bound its anxiety, disposed of its sense of guilt, and gratified its ideas of punishment. The difference is that, if the ego employs repression, the formation of symptoms relieves it of the task of mastering its conflicts" (*The Ego* 48). The girl can hand this impossible task on to an other and, if she is lucky, be assured in so doing that she has become all her world wants of her.

A woman's only path to sublimation, the fourth of the instincts' vicissitudes, may be the roundabout route idealization of the other maps. Loving is not traditionally one of the higher cultural aims; what she *can* do is free the other from mundane demands so that he has the time and energy for the sublimated activities that advance civilization.[24] Or perhaps the beating fantasy itself, "one of which almost rose to the level of a work of art," as Sigmund Freud tells us in "A Child" (191), will be her métier for sublimation.

In "The Relation of Beating-Phantasies to a Day-Dream," Anna Freud traces the artistic transformation from nasty to "nice" daydreams in the same patient—Anna Freud herself.[25] Her elaborate

[24]According to Sigmund Freud, woman, "little capable" of sublimation (*Civilization and Its Discontents* 103), has an ill-formed superego that "cannot attain the strength and independence which give it its cultural significance" ("Femininity" 129). Moral acquisitions belong to the male; "they seem to have then been transmitted to women by cross-inheritance," (*The Ego and the Id* 37). The ability to think is linked to sublimation as well. See Carol Gilligan's *In a Different Voice* for its analysis of gender and moral development.

[25]See Elisabeth Young-Bruehl's *Anna Freud* for an excellent analysis of both essays (103–9). Neither Anna Freud nor Sigmund Freud makes this identification in their respective essays. Interestingly, Helene Deutsch also wrote a lengthy novel/journal in adolescence that seems to have some of the motifs of the beating fantasy, although Paul Roazen's discussion is somewhat confusing (*Helene Deutsch* 18–27).

episodic constructions follow the repeated trials of a boy, held captive in a castle by a knight who punishes him and yet, oddly, loves him as well. The story she constructs is, not surprisingly, a Gothic narrative, and its core concern the tormented protagonist's need to love her torturer. The "beating-theme sometimes formed the actual content of a nice story" if "the humiliation connected with being beaten" was left out (98): blows are inflicted unintentionally and suffering becomes self-inflicted. To Anna Freud, the "nice" stories are definitely sublimations. "While the phantasies of beating thus represent a return of the repressed, i.e., of the incestuous wish-phantasy, the nice stories on the other hand represent a sublimation of it" (99).

The short story Anna Freud eventually writes after years of the fantasy shows a fully successful transformation via sublimation. The frame structure is a conversation between the knight and the boy's father, and the setting vaguely medieval; the events of the plot are now in the past. The story has a clear beginning and middle, while the end anticipates the boy's and the knight's eventual accord. "It began with a description of the torture he underwent and ended with the prisoner's refusal to try to escape from the castle. His readiness to remain in the Knight's power suggested the beginning of their friendship" (100). The renunciation of "single scenes" and "various single climaxes" (101)—like the renunciation of the masturbation that accompanied the beating fantasy—and the choice of sustained interpersonal relations through writing allow the girl to bring together her ambitious and erotic desires. She can be "regarded as a poet" *and* "win in that capacity the love and esteem of others" (102). At the essay's end, she celebrates her turning to "reality" in language reminiscent of that with which Dora's case history closes. "By renouncing her private pleasure in favour of the impression she could create in others she turned from an autistic to a social activity, and thus found her way back from the life of imagination to life in reality" (102).

The protagonist's internment in the castle, self-recrimination, refusal to escape, and willingness to believe that the master's cruelty is love describe, of course, a Gothic plot. Through public articulation in the form of fiction, the girl does not necessarily resolve her dilemma, but she makes it the stuff of a highly satisfactory, sublimated compromise. A story can do this. The implications of this fantasy being a *woman's* fantasy are never addressed by Anna Freud. Both her work with gay men and with children, however, show a sharp awareness of the reality of exterior causation, the difficult achievement of active aims through passive means, and the necessity for sublimation.

In two unpublished lectures on inequitable gay male relationships that Elisabeth Young-Bruehl excerpts, for example, the particular dynamic Anna Freud focuses on is the same we have been investigating in a heterosexual context. One partner sees "the relation to a love object exclusively in passive terms. To love means: to be maltreated, kicked about, impoverished, tormented, possessed." Thus, love and abuse are entwined but, given their interdependence, the ego still works to maintain itself through its very subordination. Furthermore, the patients' own active drives are evident in their choice of partner and in vicarious gratification through the man who "represents to them their lost masculinity, which they enjoy in identification with him. This implies that these apparently passive men are active according to their fantasy, while they are passive only so far as their behavior is concerned" (*Anna Freud* 326, 325).[26] (Masculinity here, as in much of Sigmund Freud's work, clearly signifies activity and the imagined full subjectivity that the subordinated assign to an other.)

In *The Ego and the Mechanisms of Defense*, Anna Freud shows a further subtle expansion of sublimation in two new defense categories, "identification with the aggressor" and "altruistic surrender," both of which are clearly recognizable as strategies used by Gothic heroines. She again demonstrates a strong understanding of how the weaker— in this case, children—must accommodate themselves to the demands of the more powerful. The child's identification with the aggressor shows "a preliminary phase of superego development" (120). The child internalizes the aggressor's behavior and projects its own outward without recognizing any causal connection; it thus does to others what it feels has been done to itself. "By impersonating the aggressor, assuming his attributes or imitating his aggression, the child transforms himself from the person threatened into the person who makes the threat" (113). By striking out against the world, the child transmutes passivity to activity and, potentially, to mastery.[27]

[26]See also the discussion of Freud's comments on active/passive attitudes and object choice in "Psychogenesis of a Case of Homosexuality" (n. 21 above).

[27]Such emulation, if unrecognized, can be an obstacle in analysis, for the aggression the child displays is originally not his own, one might say. According to Anna Freud, his "aggression is due to his identifying himself with what he supposed to be our criticism" (*The Ego* 121); it is not the acting out of his own impulse. The client then treats the therapist or other *as* the self: full transference does not happen. One girl's use of "ridicule and scorn" at certain times in therapy "was explained by her identification of herself with her dead father, who used to try to train the little girl in self-control by making mocking remarks when she gave way to some emotional outburst" (*The Ego* 37). Similarly, the little boy who identified with his "ill-treated" mother in Sigmund Freud's *Moses and Monotheism* is a new man in his dealings with his wife after his father dies. "He developed a completely egoistic, despotic, and brutal personality which clearly felt a need to suppress and insult other people. It was a faithful copy of his father as he had formed a picture of him in his memory" (79).

The symptom disappears only when "the dread of punishment and of the superego has been dissipated" (121)—when both interior and exterior threats have been addressed.

The idea of identification with the aggressor is important simply in its recognition that there is an aggressor. Equally significant, however, is Anna Freud's mapping of projection and introjection as potential pathways to aggression. As we see in texts such as Lois Gould's *A Sea-Change* or Fay Weldon's *The Life and Loves of a She-Devil*, in both of which a woman quite literally *becomes* the character she recognizes as her attacker, this process need not be confined to the boy. In *The Ego and the Mechanisms of Defense*, however, identification with the aggressor and altruistic surrender remain implicitly sex-typed. In the identification with the aggressor chapter, five boys and three girls are discussed. The prototypical example is a little boy who, after running into the fist of a games master (?), appears at a session clad in armour and carrying a toy pistol and sword.[28] During the session, he dashes off a note to his mother urgently requesting a knife as well. Two other little boys express much interest in having or getting knives, one of whom also lays about him with a rod and roars like a lion.

Two of the little girls, in contrast, reproach those around them for secrecy and persist in trying to get information. For both girls, aggression is scopophilic and epistemophilic, and their perceived wrongdoing is their failure to exhibit everything about themselves to analysts or parents. The same mechanism is at work for both boys and girls, but, leaving aside the issue of possible diagnostic and treatment bias, there seems to be a gender discrepancy in what the boys and girls perceive as wrong, what they perceive as aggression, and the form acting out takes. The girls are presented as suspecting themselves to be in the wrong for not being properly exhibitionistic (passive scopophilia), feeling aggression in intense epistemophilic inquiry, and acting out through primarily verbal means. The third girl, afraid of the dark, makes a lovely and poignant statement about her strategy for keeping her fears at bay, a statement that applies to all the children and women who feel they must identify with the aggressor. " 'There's no need to be afraid in the hall,' she said, 'you just have to pretend that you're the ghost who might meet you' " (111).

[28]Novick and Novick cite a little girl with similar behavior, and note its cessation with approval. "One girl repeatedly played that she had a magic sword and used it to smack all the soldiers coming to invade her land. In contrast, the increasing ability to take the passive role in beating games indicated a move towards the positive oedipal position" (239).

Anna Freud's final example of identification with the aggressor seems to show its own haunting, some uneasy recognition that the pattern so clearly set forth might be sex-related. Toward the essay's close, Freud declares that the defense mechanism "can be regarded as normal only so long as the ego employs this mechanism in its conflict with authority, i.e., in its efforts to deal with anxiety objects. It is a defensive process which ceases to be innocuous and becomes pathological when it is carried over into a person's love life" (120). Anxiety and love life are sharply separated in the formulation, and the hypothetical instance she adduces underscores the wish to assert their jointure implausible in relations between adult women and men. She speculates that a husband who wants to be unfaithful and so reproaches his wife with infidelity acts "to protect himself not against aggression from without but against the shattering of his positive libidinal fixation to her by disturbing forces from within" (120). The possibility that there might be "conflict with authority" within one's love life is adroitly evaded by use of an example where there is no exterior threat, where the subject is the aggressor, and where emphasis is placed upon his wish to preserve object love.

In setting forth altruistic surrender, Freud identifies a pattern that fits more comfortably within current mores for women, but one that also illuminates the array of Gothic women who are more distressed by a man's pain than their own. Their altruism dramatically modifies and calls into question their "surrender." In addition, it suggests effective agency and self-esteem for the altruist, although the beneficiary of her interventions is an other. Five girls or women provide the demonstrations of altruism; the one male example, Rostand's Cyrano, apparently has to be sought in literature, not life. Altruistic surrender, like identification with the aggressor, uses projection and introjection in tandem, but in altruistic surrender the girl introjects inadequacy and guilt while she projects gratification of inhibited instincts upon others. Unlike projection that "accuses others" and is "excessively intolerant" (123), hers helps others to achieve their desires and rejoices in gratifications forbidden to herself.

Matchmakers, benefactresses, and involved friends thus help others to make demands and fulfill desires. Projection in this case enables "us to form valuable positive attachments and so to consolidate our relations with one another. This normal and less conspicuous form of projection might be described as 'altruistic surrender' of our own instinctual impulses in favor of other people" (123). As Freud acknowledges in a note, masochism is "another and easy route to the same goal" (134n). I would argue that these roads converge, so that a part of the girl's helping others to instinctual gratification may include letting them beat her, as they do so unremittingly in *Story of O*, if such is their pleasure.

Nonetheless, Freud, like Horney in her brilliant analysis of the secondary gains the self-effacing type discovers (*Neurosis and Human Growth*), rightfully insists that there are compensations for the altruistic. The governess who, as a little girl, wanted "to be admired for her cleverness" finds a socially approved way to gratify the child's cry of " 'Me too!' " (124), despite her own renunciation. Her interest in friends' clothes and social lives, her devotion to others' children, and her ambition for the men she loves let her actively strive for and take pleasure in the goals of others. Their appreciation and love gratify her still further.

Unlike Sigmund Freud's discussions of masochism, Anna Freud's regularly emphasize the need for the defense mechanisms and the activity exerted within them: "As in the process of identification with the aggressor, passivity is transformed into activity, narcissistic mortification is compensated for by the sense of power associated with the role of benefactor, while the passive experience of frustration finds compensation in the active conferring of happiness on others" (*The Ego* 134n). Despite the problems that are attached to the idea of women putting the needs of others above their own, the modification of "surrender" by altruism is important within a psychological frame because of the way it points to the outside world and its connection with sublimation. Like Anna Freud's and Gothic novels' successful recrafting of the beating fantasy, altruism emphasizes that a woman can and will wrest activity, self-esteem, and voice from the most unpromising restrictions.

Finally, then, Anna Freud does not apparently recognize any sex difference in the "choice" of defense mechanisms. Cyrano, for example, is the "finest and most detailed" study of altruistic surrender (132). Not too surprisingly, neither does she question the cultural economy of entitlement and subsistence that leads to that difference. What she does do consistently is to assume discrepancy in power through the parent/child relationship and to complicate binary oppositions of active/passive, inner/outer. In so doing, she potentially, if problematically, provides the subordinated with sublimation as a means to gain the place in culture otherwise denied them.

Love, Pain, and Power

The child desperately needs love, approval, and acknowledgment of her own existence. She will give up anything to get it, will hope for a caress, but will accept a cuff rather than nothing. If she is told repeatedly that a cuff *is* a caress, she can and will believe it.[29] If she is told the cuff is to make her caressable, she will accept that too, and work for that forever distanced time when she will be judged worthy of love. She keeps busy with her girlish little projects until then, a spendthrift in the "persistent expenditure of force" ("Repression" 151) she uses to embroider over her repression and idealization of the other to make them prettier. Somewhere and sometimes, though, a part of the self watches the ongoing enactment of the beating fantasy. It may display the anaesthetized regard Charcot described as "la belle indifférence des hystériques" ("Repression" 156),[30] or perhaps it wonders about what it sees, with whatever residue of curiosity remains.

What the spectator looks at, whether permanently or only in preparation for her own turn as participant, is a woman being beaten. Her feeling may be enormous satisfaction ("He is beating her because he *hates* her" or "He is beating her *for* me"), envy ("He is beating her because he *loves* her"), horror ("He is *beating* her"), or an admixture. No matter what her response, she must hear cruelty and love used synonymously and see beating eroticized. The combination may eventually seem the only worthwhile form of object relations to her, as Freud jovially claims it to be for the peasant woman who understands the man's need for aggression. "The love-object will not al-

---

[29]Something of the child's enormous resiliency and resistance to trauma is evident in Anna Freud and Dorothy Burlingham's monograph, *Young Children in War-Time*. What need *not* cause trauma underscores the seriousness of what *does* in gender differentiation. The chapters matter-of-factly, succinctly, and chillingly sketch the children's responses to bombing, shelter sleeping, evacuation, and the illness and deaths of parents. In general, children replicate the responses of their mothers; if she does not seem unduly agitated, they do not see external events as traumatic. The direct effects of war (barring personal injury) are negligible compared to separation from the mother. "Observers seldom appreciate the depth and seriousness of this grief of a small child" (52), a point reinforced in *War and Children* (21). The children can accept separation from the father and his reappearance in new guises such as a uniform, while they deal poorly with such shifts in the mother if she is primary caretaker (*War and Children* 17). Even this separation, however, is not necessarily trauma. It can be negotiated in a surprisingly short time by intermittent visits and reassurance: "it does not seem to be the fact of separation from the mother to which the child reacts in this abnormal manner, but the traumatic way in which this separation takes place" (*War and Children* 103).

[30]There may be no onlooker. As Freud comments in "Repression," entire success is conceivable and "the instinct is altogether suppressed, so that no trace of it is found" (153). One way to achieve this is by splitting the instinct into two, repressing one part and identifying the second, idealized part with an other (150)—precisely the heterosexual dynamic we are looking at here. In such cases, the result would be the "total woman," a dream of unresisting receptivity like the automaton Olympia in Hoffmann's "The Sandman." More often, though, there is a residue of affect or anxiety from the process that might be seen, for instance, in the flashes of hostility apparently successful repressors show toward other women.

ways view these complications with the degree of understanding and tolerance shown by the peasant woman who complained that her husband did not love her any more, since he had not beaten her for a week" (*Civilization and Its Discontents* 106n).[31]

The wife who is beaten like a piece of meat "to make her tender," as the joke goes, often learns to be more "understanding" quickly. She learns—if she hasn't already—to be a masochist and make her man happy. No particular merit attaches to her achievement; it is part of the basic job description of femininity. What Freud so sympathetically portrays in Dostoevsky is the least she can do. "Thus in little things he was a sadist toward others, and in bigger things a sadist toward himself, in fact a masochist—that is to say the mildest, kindliest, most helpful person possible" ("Dostoevsky" 179). The masochism of the woman, unlike Anna Freud's "altruistic surrender," is worthy of neither praise nor note: it becomes so in the breach rather than in the observance.

The troubling, complex, and sometimes insightful association of passive/active, feminine/masculine too often become neatly polar and cast in concrete for the weary sons of Freud, encouraged by the assent of Deutsch and Bonaparte. Whereas a man may gain limited social credit for passivity, activity—or sadism—is preferred. Thus, a male who switches from the fantasy of being beaten by female pirates to that of whipping his father's secretary is making real progress. (The move to an actual person is apparently insignificant.) "This fantasy represents, in a sense, a progress from passivity and homosexuality to activity and heterosexuality" (Nunberg 29). The activity and sadism of a woman, however, is an abomination. "The symbolic sadism of women constitutes one of the most remarkable aspects of sexual pathology. . . . Feminine sadism is invariably totalitarian. . . . The woman sadist is a sadist through and through and her sadism is the dominant factor in her professional as well as in her social and sexual life."[32] The man is able to leave his sadism at home where it belongs. The label of "symbolic sadism" for the woman becomes a diagnostic prod used for social control: any active woman can be so labelled. Her analytic goal is cheerful acceptance of her own passivity and natural masochism. Thus, the woman's progress is marked by the "desire for a child from the analyst," becoming "more feminine and softer," and fantasizing being underneath during intercourse (Joseph 44, 45). The

---

[31]See also Horney's comments on the passage in "The Problem of Feminine Masochism" (*Feminine Psychology* 224).

[32]M. Hirschfeld, *Sexual Anomalies and Perversions* (1925), as quoted (not approvingly) in Gosselin (45).

astute analyst realizes that "to some degree the need to feel beaten and the pleasure in it persist in the woman's subsequent development" (Lester, "Analysis of an Unconscious Beating Fantasy" 30).[33] Little girls with beating fantasies do encouragingly well if, as adolescents, "the beating wish had been adequately sublimated in the development of appropriate feminine passivity" (Novick and Novick 239). The flat, unipolar insistence on receptivity and passivity for a woman assures her masochism. If she recognizes cruelty or experiences pain (and, depending on the degree of repression, that awareness is by no means automatic), she is only registering reality.

As we have seen in "A Child" and "Instincts," Freud elegantly explains ambivalence through the simultaneity and counterplay of the component instincts. A particular example of the interfusion of love and hate, aggression and passivity is children's sadistic theory of intercourse through which, as Novick and Novick point out, "the beating wish becomes sexualized" ("Beating Fantasies in Children" 238). The frequency of this association throughout the sadism/ masochism literature is striking. As in other instances, though, Freud's interpretation of the child's stricken recognitions works through its own vicissitudes. At issue again here is the way in which social gender arrangements give rise to and shape structures of oppression. The results of these arrangements can then be analyzed with great acumen and clarity, but the very force of the explanation obscures and denies their origin, which becomes displaced as an unavoidable, naturalized intra-psychic process.

As usual, Freud himself gives much of his own counterargument. In "On the Sexual Theories of Children," he observes that children see coitus "as something that the stronger participant is forcibly inflicting on the weaker" (220). He further cedes that there often may be a familial context that encourages the child's supposition. Children can notice the signs of a wife's reluctance to have intercourse, whether its source be disinclination, frigidity, or avoiding further pregnancies, as he notes. If intercourse nonetheless occurs, the child may well believe that her mother is "defending herself against an act of violence. At other times the whole marriage offers an observant child the spectacle of an unceasing quarrel, expressed in loud words and unfriendly gestures; so that he need not be surprised if the quar-

---

[33]He continues to say that there are negative and positive attributes, "all generally considered feminine," in her masochism. "Among the former are the propensity to silent reproach, ready tears and martyred forbearance. Among the latter are willingness to bear hardship, generous devotion, and steadfastness" (30). "Positive" seems to mean suffering cheerfully; it becomes negative if you point out that you *are* suffering.

rel is carried on at night as well" (221–22).[34] There need not be physical violence in a house for a child to conclude that daddy is the boss
and that mommy, like the children, had best obey him.[35] For the boy,
the spectacle is a promise of the perquisites that becoming a man will
bestow; for the girl, it is a training lesson for her own future in
subordination.

The general tendency in Freud's presentation of children's equation
of intercourse and sadism, though, is to move from analogy to metaphoric identification that collapses all distinction in his own discussion. Thus we begin with what is undoubtedly a frequent observation
by the child, recounted *as* the child's equation. Intercourse "appears
to them to be something hostile and violent" and "they inevitably
regard the sexual act as a sort of ill-treatment or act of subjugation:
they view it, that is, in a sadistic sense" ("Leonardo" 79, "Infantile
Sexuality" 196). Insensibly, the analogy becomes the only possible,
"inevitable" response so that coitus in the missionary position "cannot fail to produce the impression of being a sadistic act" (*History*
45*n*). Finally, the child's analogy assumes the force of reality in explication. Thus, for example, little Hans expresses "sadistic impulses
(premonitions, as it were, of copulation) towards his mother" (*Analysis of a Phobia* 138). As in "A Child," cause and effect get confused.
Something carried forward to a later stage is identified with that
stage, and the new compound assumes retroactive causal force. Thus,
in "Beyond the Pleasure Principle," "erotic mastery" becomes a single
concept discernible in each instinctual stage. For the infant, it means
wholesale "destruction" of the object (incorporation) until "the sadistic instinct separates off" (anal stage). Erotic mastery reaches its full
sociobiological and psychological telos when "finally, at the stage of
genital primacy, it takes on, for the purposes of reproduction, the
function of overpowering the sexual object to the extent necessary for
carrying out the sexual act" (*Beyond the Pleasure Principle* 54). Civiliza-

[34]Joseph, who refers repeatedly to the sadistic theory of intercourse, also cites many
instances of this belief, but fails to note any oddity worth pursuing into the real world.
For example, he reports one patient who concludes hostility from verbal (as opposed to
the more simple aural sounds a couple might make during intercourse) as well as
physical indications, "sounds which to him were of intercourse, that is, of a vicious
attack in which father was beating mother verbally or physically" (Joseph 39). Similarly, the allegiance of the child who provokes punishment from his father "to identify
himself with his ill-treated mother" (particularly when it is the mother who threatens
him) is not fully explored by Freud except as the boy's own (feminine) passivity and
masochism (*Moses and Monotheism* 79). For a radical critique of the intercourse = sadism
formula, see Andrea Dworkin's *Intercourse*.

[35]This astonishing change in the child's perspective of the all-powerful mother is
surely as disillusioning as discovering that she herself has no penis.

tion then becomes a rape best carried out behind the nuclear family's closed doors, and only the small-minded would impede its progress through their discontent.[36]

According to Freud, aggression and the will to mastery propagate the species and advance knowledge. Suddenly, the apparently innocuous biological goal of the nervous system in "Instincts"—"*to master stimuli*" (120)—begins to seem a tad troubling. It may be reassuring that "when the genital organization is established . . . love become[s] the opposite of hate" (139), but the full love of the ego for its sexual object becomes as ominous in its implications as what the child believes she knows. "The word [love] can only begin to be applied in this relation after there has been a synthesis of all the component instincts of sexuality under the primacy of the genitals and in the service of the reproductive function" (138). In light of *Civilization*'s "overpowering" drive for purposes of reproduction, I suspect that the primacy is that of the phallus and the servitude a handmaid's tale.

The girl who is disabused of her belief that daddy hurts mommy is being told the truth (one hopes) in relation to intercourse itself. The issue of coitus can serve as a red herring, though, to dismiss all of the child's perceptions that there is indeed something fishy going on and to encourage her to disregard and doubt the evidence of her own senses. Her doubt, offshoot of her curiosity, will then apply only to herself and she will agree that what she sees is love. She will use denial to reverse facts so that she can believe in external harmony and love, a highly useful measure employed, as Anna Freud says, "in situations in which it is impossible to escape some painful external impression" (*The Ego* 93). Like Matilda, the dutiful daughter of *The Castle of Otranto*, she will believe her parents' relationship to be exemplary and will excuse daddy's harshness to mommy and herself as a sign of his solicitude for their well-being.

Through such a reversal, as well as the transformation of activity into passivity, the turning of instinctual energy upon herself, assignation of subjectivity to an other, repression, and sublimation, she will find true love. She will forge a self through pain, and identify each fresh injury as a new token of affection. The case histories (and popu-

---

[36]In *Civilization and Its Discontents*, Freud dismisses such grumpiness as the woman's ire because the "business of men," civilization itself, takes his attention away from her. Women, "little capable" of sublimation, "represent the interests of the family and of sexual life" and pit these against civilization, thus exercising a "retarding and restraining influence" (103–4). Apparently, the family and sexual life have little to do with civilization in advanced cultures.

lar advice columns) are filled with accounts of children who are tick-
led until they scream, verbally denigrated until they weep, and sometimes beaten until they die. They are the symptomatic carriers of
others' behavior, like the girl who has rape fantasies and anorexia.
Her "father bites to show his affection. As a child, when she cried
because he bit too hard, he was surprised and hurt—he only meant
love" (Joseph 86). Her ego and body pay so that she can credit that
love, like a little boy Anna Freud mentions. "He flies into violent
tempers, turns against the people he loves most, attempts to destroy
furniture, toys, etc. At the end of the scene he suddenly becomes
gentle and affectionate, demands to sit on the teacher's lap and sucks
his thumb. His father is known to act in a similar manner towards the
mother" (*War and Children* 72).[37] Although the active/passive split
(and their auguries for the future) are very obvious here, both children are victims who cling to their oppressors and know object relations only through beating.[38]

The beating fantasy and its constellation of affect can be sought
after and valued "as a way of maintaining or establishing some sort of
relationship with the world of objects," the beater adored "because
this is the only kind of intimacy that [the beaten] knows" (Joseph 60,
Sack and Miller 247). As one patient cries out, echoing Freud's antithesis between love/hate and indifference, " 'It's better to be beaten
than ignored' " (Lester 29). To be ignored—not to merit any kind of
attention, no matter what form it takes—is to disappear as a self. To
be beaten is proof of existence and even of lovableness for many
protagonists, as the character Marie Rogers discovers in Agnes
Smedley's *Daughter of Earth*. "Thus I learned that if you are sick or
injured, people love you; if you are well they do not. Another paradox impressed itself upon my being, that the way to love lies through
suffering" (38).

Those who embrace such suffering find their worth in it. They

[37]*War and Children* 72. In *Toward a New Psychology of Women*, Jean Baker Miller points
out that "truly blaming the person(s) who hurt you can seem much harder than
continuing the masochistic circle of self-condemnation" (123). Caplan too comments on
how "masochists stunt their own development in order to protect their image of their
parent as all-good" (88), and Greif adds to the insight by pointing to the parents'
example. "Love is confused by the power inequalities between the parents, and becomes equated with the giving over of autonomy and control" (8).

[38]The children's "ingratiating and appeasing" responses to their victimizer is very
similar to what Alexandra Symonds calls "traumatic psychological infantilism." For
adult victims of violent crime, this is a second stage of response, preceded by disbelief
and followed by self-accusatory depression. Children—or protagonists fully inculcated
in Gothic mores—may never show the first stage: such infantilism will be their fixed
identities (169).

insist, sometimes with great dignity, that they are beaten by choice, not necessity. Prager's Pleasure Mouse has an hallucinatory moment of decision before her feet are bound and, after deliberation, responds, " 'The only way to escape one's destiny is to enjoy it. I will stay here' " (30). Atwood's Joan Foster reaches the same conclusion in *Lady Oracle*, ever mindful that there is an audience. "If you find yourself trapped in a situation you can't get out of gracefully, you might as well pretend you chose it. Otherwise you will look ridiculous" (166).

Joan's sage observation uses humor as one way to insist that the self is very much still present and looking on, even if there indubitably are situations "you can't get out of." In Réage's *Story of O* a less divided and infinitely more disturbing character "chooses" her own annihilation through what seems to be an entire abdication of the active drives and of the self. In considering a character who celebrates the role of beaten, we will satisfy some of our own curiosity about why any woman would assume that position.

4

Kissing the Rod:
The Beaten and *Story of O*

The most extreme instance I know of Gothic pornography is
Pauline Réage's *Story of O*. The novel Angela Carter calls "that mon-
strous book" (*Nothing Sacred* 161) intrigues and appalls through its
excruciating refinement and jointure of the unspoken assumptions of
both genres. *Story of O* has been vehemently defended and reviled in
print and in countless women's groups. It is the ultimate in degradation; it is erotic, and part of the erotic *is* degradation. It is a text of high
aesthetic merit that represents a mystical spirituality achieved
through the body's purification; it is a dangerous instance of pornography as what Judy Grahn calls "the poetry of oppression." Debate
still surrounds the author's identity and sex: only a woman could
have written it (and what is a woman to make of what that says about
herself?), or no woman could ever have written it.[1]

Story of O confounds the neat sex segregation that, as Sally Roesch
Wagner notes, usually divides pornography and romance (at least in
public parlance).[2] The novel collapses the distinction between por-

---

[1]Judy Grahn, as quoted in Griffin 2. Kaja Silverman's "*Histoire d'O*" is a thorough
and astute analysis of how pornography transfers its "structures and significance" to
"real bodies" that internalize them (345). Some sense of the intensity and range of
response to *Story of O* is evinced by Griffin's excellent reading of the novel as a "desperate alienation from the female self and from nature" (226) in her chapter on "Silence,"
Susan Sontag's defense of its aesthetic and metaphysical attributes in "The Pornographic Imagination," and the adoption of "Samois" (the women-run house to which
O is later brought) as a group name by a lesbian sado-masochistic organization. See
also Andrea Dworkin's "Woman as Victim."

[2]Wagner explains the complementary gender tasks of pornography and romance
thus: "Pornography is the propaganda which indoctrinates men into the sexual power
they have over women and teaches men how to manifest that power. Patriarchy gives
women a different medium that reflects our experience and educates us for 'proper'

nography and Gothic romance in its joyful insistence that the two are one and the same. Readers, regardless of gender preference or evaluation, thus are drawn unusually close to the text—or perhaps become unusually aware of the visceral implications of "reader response." Each must decide whether to identify with beater or beaten, and each must be aware, if the act of reading continues, of assenting to the voyeur's role, just as O consents to every stage of her progress. To continue reading, a woman must agree to be the beaten in her own identification with O or must be a spectator to another woman's being beaten, a position the third-person narration encourages. (It is also of course possible, although less likely, for her to identify with the men who are beaters. Later in the novel, the option of identification with women who beat is also offered.) Thus one of the implicit themes of the Gothic becomes conjoined to the celebratory "affirmation" of the pornographic. By glaringly highlighting the masochism that the Gothic casts in chiaroscuro, *Story of O* dramatically presents the psychological progression of the Gothic heroine who embraces the systems that traumatize her.

A woman is taken by her lover to a secluded manor, Roissy. She does not know why, nor does she understand the reasons for her ordeals there. Nonetheless, she continues to love him unquestioningly. This, of course, is the stuff of the Gothic. The specifics of her trials are not, however, typically Gothic, although their rationale is uncannily familiar. A woman's body—her vagina, anus, or mouth—is open to a man. Her sole pleasure is his pleasure; she has no demands of her own and no judgment to pass on his desire. This, needless to say, is the pornographic.

The two genres are linked by their similar ideological messages; in conservative versions, their only difference is in choice of vehicles. The Gothic uses the woman's whole body as pawn: she is moved, threatened, discarded, and lost. And, as the whole person is abducted, attacked, and so forth, the subtext metaphorically conveys anxiety about her specifically genital risk. Pornography reverses the synecdochical relation by instead using the part to refer to the whole: a woman is a twat, a cunt, a hole. The depiction of explicitly genital sexual practice which is pornography's métier can be simply a difference in degree, not in kind, from the Gothic's more genteel abuse. The yoking of the two genres in *Story of O* is strengthened by the

feminine sexuality: the 'cult of romance.' Through romance we learn to be passive, to wait and to submit to the pain and humiliation of loving someone who has power over us. He has his *Hustler*: she has her Barbara Cartland novel" (24).

protagonist's voiced assent to her own disappearance at every stage, her consciously choosing the identity of the beaten as her own, and her continuing credence in the love thus idealized and requited.

The flat, obsessional, and hackneyed Ur-plots of both genres assume new and disturbing form through their alliance. At their center is a woman's body that proclaims a new dispensation. There is no split between body and mind; the polymorphous perverse now rules. The screening and repression Freud sees as inevitable for women patients in the beating fantasy is no longer necessary. O is able to discard such subterfuge and claim direct gratification from the unrepressed second stage of the beating fantasy, "My father is beating (loves) me." The text functions assuredly to present her not as the abject Other but as the utopian subject who speaks the body.

The text, like O, seems calmly confident, matter-of-fact and without defensiveness. No tortured search for motivation exists, and the pleasures of pain need not be apologized for or argued. Unlike standard pornographic texts, the novel shows austere restraint: it overflows with neither adjectives nor bodily fluids.[3] We simply witness a woman straightforwardly experiencing her own pleasure by resigning her will to her lover's and being beaten. And there, of course, is the psychological and generic rub. The text works to assure us, as both pornography and the Gothic always do, that O's changes are both natural and consciously chosen. The body, fettered, speaks its own unmediated desire and thus liberates the mind and spirit. Freed from cultural restraint, O will "choose" the body's exquisitely tutored language of passivity and sufferance. I agree with Benjamin, however, when she argues that even O is only "willing to risk complete annihilation of her person in order to continue to be the object of her lover's desire—to be recognized" (*Bonds of Love* 60).[4]

The turning inward of desire and the assignment of subjectivity to another nonetheless leaves a structural and motivational gap in the novel. O must *learn* how to be a natural masochist. *Story of O* insists on a specific, individualistic rationale, but the rigidly patterned social practices it represents, like the book's own sparse and ordered form, point to a systemic regulation of the woman's body. The text needs to

---

[3]Characters ejaculate, lubricate, urinate, and defecate in *Story of O* and its sequel, *Return to the Château*, but there is no lovingly detailed Sadean excess. The sequel also explains how women's bodies and their fluidity are managed to prevent pregnancy and disease by douching, etc. Strangely, the one fluid never mentioned or explained (given the perennial availability of every woman at Roissy) is menstrual.

[4]As Benjamin makes clear, the exchange is worthwhile because of O's belief in the superior knowledge and power of her idealized other (61).

assert that this regulation, like her beating, is her own desire. As paradoxically, the novel, so very much about sexual practices, seeks to erase gender hierarchy as cultural, create it as natural, and glorify it in so doing.

In attempting to bypass gender, the hierarchical structure must be displaced—or even sublimated—to another register. And so the union of the Gothic and the pornographic is sanctified by a third genre, spiritual autobiography. In *Story of O*, the unequal status of beater and beaten is exalted and normalized by the persistent invocation of the divine—not the Divine Marquis, but a godhead that looks down upon its suffering creation and finds it good. The novel's overvaluation of the male makes of him a god, and blesses O for her worship at his shrine. The destruction of a body and mind is thus rewritten as the journey of a soul. This arrogation of a godly model for gender relations is itself not strange, alas.[5] What is strange is the enthusiastic endorsement of the preface, introductory notes, and some criticism. At the moment when a woman's body is most exposed, most open to all comers—which I suppose to be much of the point of pornography—commentary carefully rearranges the limbs and covers her decently. O's body, so blatantly present, disappears as a transcendent emblem in a new chain of signification. Just as *Story of O* offers a recognizable and significant mutation of the Gothic, so its criticism distortedly reflects that of the Gothic. At stake is a woman's body again, and authorization will be sought from heaven itself if necessary to keep it there.

The Mystical Way and Criticism

Freud knows that "the craving of mankind for mysticism is ineradicable, and that it makes ceaseless efforts to win back for mysticism the territory it has been deprived of by *The Interpretation of Dreams* ("Psychogenesis" 165). We want to preserve the dream and the unconscious as the sites of truth and the divine, undisturbed by sexual constructions. In "God and the *Jouissance* of ~~The~~ Woman," Lacan warns against any equally erroneous corrective move "to reduce the mystical to questions of fucking" (147). The Other, vested with all

---

[5]See, for example, Valerie Martin's *A Recent Martyr*, in which one character seeks illumination through religion and one through masochistic sexuality, and Atwood's *The Handmaid's Tale*, in which a theocracy mandates women's subordination and forced pregnancy. The society of Gilead, like that of Roissy, appropriates conventual codes governing dress, daily behavior, and ritual to reinforce cultural control of women.

knowledge and power, partakes of the divine and marks our own separation from imagined plenitude. Courtly love is one instance of such a construction, "an altogether refined way of making up for the absence of sexual relation by pretending that it is we who put an obstacle to it," "the only way of coming off elegantly from the absence of sexual relation" (141). Lacan's perspective in his description is that of the man; romance is the woman's fairy tale. Romance too wrests divinest sense and pleasure from unpromising material: it is often the only way of getting off graciously from the *presence* of sexual relation by pretending that it is we who chose it.[6]

Story of O displays both wrong-headed strategies: the woman religiously watches the god she has helped to bring into being, while other characters and we watch her, ourselves devoutly wanting to believe that there is no fucking, only a mystical sublation. Like Lacan ogling Bernini's Theresa and urging his auditors to do likewise ("You only have to go and look at Bernini's statue in Rome to understand immediately that she's coming, there is no doubt about it" [147]), we gather around O, the representation made by who knows whom, and peer at her exposure while wondering what it means.

According to Lacan, God is anaclitically supported by feminine *jouissance* (147), by an unmediated relation to the Imaginary. But the women analysts he questions about this *jouissance*, like the exasperatingly obdurate women of Freud's "Femininity," refuse to yield. Just as Dora's father claims to "get nothing" (26), so Lacan bemoans his own plight: "We've been . . . begging them on our knees to try to tell us about it. . . . We have never managed to get anything out of them" (146). The analyst and critic excel in nothing so much as getting something from nothing, however, in filling in those intriguing gaps that inform texts and dreams. O as mystic needs us (or so we believe), for "the essential testimony of the mystics is that they are experiencing it but know nothing about it" (147), just as "the woman knows nothing of this *jouissance*" (146). We, like O's gods, know. Thus, like the analyst or interpreter whom Lacan describes as *"the subject supposed to know"* (139), our position as spectator becomes uncomfortably allied to that of O's beaters. O, at first seemingly exalted in her mystical *jouissance*, is cast down again. The subject "whom I suppose to know, I love" (139); O knows nothing.

Unlike that knowing subject, and like Lacan's portrait of himself divested of his knowledge by critics, O experiences the reversal of an affect into its opposite: "When I say that they hate me, what I mean is

---

[6]I am aware of Lacan's argument on the impossibility of sexual relations.

that they de-suppose me of knowledge" (139). We too, fascinated by O's testimony of the body and its pleasures, de-suppose her of knowledge about their significance. Nonetheless, while knowingly speaking for the woman (or for the man who, as he says, can also be a mystic), Lacan simultaneously and polymorphously places his *Écrits* in "the same order" of "mystical ejaculations" (147). He too seems to be coming as he gazes at Hadewijck of Norwich and at Theresa, a man's construction of a woman.

The equally rapt contemplation of O's transcendence in criticism points to sublimation as the cultural high road of denial. As Silverman rightfully notes about the novel's prefaces, "What Paulhan and Mandiargues call O's 'soul' is nothing other than a psychic registration of the power relations by means of which her body has been mapped and defined" (*"Histoire d'O"* 339). These power relations are enthusiastically normalized by those critics who want to make the welts that score her flesh into stigmata. Thus, the book's fantastic reprise of the beating scenario is made flesh: O submits to men as unto the Lord and we, witnessing, can only be edified, not titillated. Carter's comments on the "clever confidence trick" of universalizing female experience is to the point here. "Pornography, like marriage and the fictions of romantic love, assists the process of false universalizing. Its excesses belong to that timeless, locationless, area outside history, outside geography, where fascist art is born" (*Sadeian Woman* 12). By removing the text from its historical and cultural specificity, by claiming the body's miraculous assumption to a noosphere of eternal verities, such criticism intriguingly and troublingly enacts its own fantasies.

We all recognize the form of curiosity that seeks out the sexual in texts whose primary function is not pornographic. Children search for the "dirty" stories in the Bible or studiously look up forbidden words in the dictionary; Freud's beating fantasists have an inordinate fondness for *Uncle Tom's Cabin* and similar texts ("A Child" 180); Severin, in Leopold von Sacher-Masoch's *Venus in Furs*, delights in the lives of the martyrs (90, 97). The particular form of inquiry that interests me in relation to *Story of O*, however, vehemently denies *any* prurient interest as it examines graphically sexual material.[7] Placed as

---

[7]This strand of scopophilia is part of all our inquiries, of course; it is potentially dangerous and falsifying if repudiated. It is implicated in not only scholarly endeavors, but large areas of social and religious reform, for instance. Thus, those who avidly sought accounts of demonic possession, who were engrossed by the detailed reports Acton and others issued relative to England's Contagious Diseases Acts of the 1860s, or who repeatedly view pornography to demand censorship often have goals and objects

"the subject supposed to know" in relation to the text, partner, or patient, it insists that the other articulate or embody the desire it denies for itself and pays for the show by writing a good review declaring it free of dross and heavenly.

The translator's note by Sabrine d'Estrée, critical note by André Pieyre de Mandiargues, and preface by Jean Paulhan of the French Academy are a hallelujah chorus to O's solo performance. All use the same key of admiration, but there is a slow crescendo as they proceed. D'Estrée, the lowest in status and the only woman among them, replicates the text for us and has the briefest say. She relates what is known of the text's provenance and claims that the novel "demands a woman translator, one who will humble herself before the work" (xii); she duly pays her homage. Mandiargues, in his longer note, begins the "interpretation" and "elaboration" d'Estrée identifies as not her part (xii). He insists that the novel "is not, strictly speaking, an erotic book," but "a mystic work" (xvi). "The subject is the tragic flowering of a woman in the abdication of her freedom, in willful slavery, in humiliation, in the prostitution imposed upon her by her masters, in torture" (vxi-xvii). "Woman, through the decline of her flesh [becomes] pure spirit" (xviii). O's "complete spiritual transformation" might well be titled "*A Woman's Progress*" (xvii), although not the progress of every woman, for her peers are to be found among the Portuguese Nun, Theresa of Avila, the Nun of Dülmen (xvii, xx). O "is about to enter that small circle of blessed and accursed creatures which constitutes the only aristocracy which one can consider today with any degree of respect" (xx). Mandiargues, like Lacan, clearly admires the mystic. His effusions, which insist upon what he perceives as the signified without any reference to the signifier, are bizarre. Mandiargues's enthusiasm, his eager willingness to rise up and call O blessed, is linked to the text's replacement of God by man, for which he is duly thankful.

Whereas the woman translator disappears within the text, Mandiargues stands apart while lauding O's elevation. In the last part of the critical progression, Paulhan, the most prestigious of the three, speaks and situates himself *above* the novel: he is to Mandiargues as

---

quite different from those they claim. This is made more evident when the prerequisite to redemption or reform is mandatory confessions, whether in the confessional proper, British Magdalene houses where the inhabitants had to provide accounts of their "falls," or contemporary commissions on pornography engrossed by first-person narratives. As Susan Stewart argues about the Meese commission, "Here the whore, whose sexuality has been objectified and dispersed from her body, makes the final gesture of disclosure in the outpourings of her writing" (190).

Sir Stephen is to René in the novel. He approvingly sees the specificity of the body disappear: "it is an idea, or a complex of ideas, an opinion rather than a young woman we see being subjected to these tortures" (xxxiii). Both he and Mandiargues imagine O and Réage as possibly, enticingly, the same. Whereas Mandiargues simply wonders if he might one day see a woman with an iron ring (the insignia of Roissy) and know her to be Pauline Réage, Paulhan wants to examine her more fully and inquire into the status of her knowingness. Is she a woman "who knows whereof she speaks?" (xxvi). Has that "busy little bee," by leaving some things unsaid, "kept part of the honey for herself" (xxvi), like the woman hoarding the *jouissance* she cannot know? Whereas Mandiargues's O is a hallowed exception, Paulhan's is honored for her willingness to admit "what women have always refused till now to admit": "At last a woman who admits it! . . . Something that men have always reproached them with: that they never cease obeying their nature, the call of their blood, that everything in them, even their minds, is sex. That they have constantly to be nourished, constantly washed and made up, constantly beaten. . . . In short, that we must, when we go to see them, take a whip along" (xxv). Paulhan believes in that whip as wholeheartedly as does Sade, whom he ranks as "un écrivain qu il faut placer parmi les plus grands [a writer who definitely has to be ranked among the greatest]" (Praz xvii). He is not the passive spectator but a would-be participant, for surely *Story of O*, "the most ardent love letter any man has ever received" (xxxii), is addressed *to* someone (xxiv).

Unable to be that addressee except in fantasy, Paulhan instead appropriates the voice of O and writes a letter from her. "'Keep me rather in this cage, and feed me sparingly, if you dare. Anything that brings me closer to illness and the edge of death makes me more faithful. It is only when you make me suffer that I feel safe and secure. You should never have agreed to be a god for me if you were afraid to assume the duties of a god, and we all know that they are not as tender as all that. You have already seen me cry. Now you must learn to relish my tears'" (xxx). Paulhan's letter from O is exemplary for the way in which it creates a female voice to insist that he or others "assume the duties of a god." The woman is even "virile," "descended from a knight, or a crusader" (xxv), in her courageous willingness to demand her own suffering. Thus, as in Freud's discussion of the beating fantasy, the novel's beaters are exonerated from any responsibility as they stoically perform their duty. "So far as we can tell, they do not enjoy themselves. There is nothing sadistic about them. It all happens as though it were O alone who, from the outset, demanded to be chastised, to be forced in her retreats" (xxviii). Paulhan's protest that the woman "made them do it" is crucial in its construction of masochistic desire as separate from the sadistic long-ings of the beater, as Silverman comments: "A very different strategy of reading is proposed. . . . Instead of reading 'outward,' as we are encouraged to do in the case of the signifying complex 'donor of welt/sadistic subject,' we are told to read 'inward,' to locate the mas-ochistic subject within an interior space" ("Histoire d'O" 337).

Finally, Paulhan's authority in acknowledging and erasing the body of O is most evident in his willingness to extrapolate a global annun-ciation of oppression from the letter he's sent himself. He frames his preface, titled "Happiness in Slavery," with an account of two hun-dred natives of Barbados who, in 1838, "came one morning to beg their former master, a certain Glenelg, to take them back into bond-age" (xxi). Glenelg refuses, and is massacred. Paulhan creates the slaves' missing notebook of grievances, as he does O's letter, quite sure that it would state "that the only freedoms we really appreciate are those which cast others into an equivalent state of servitude" (xxii). Each slave, like O—and unlike Jean Paulhan, member of the French Academy—has the admirable ability "to surrender oneself to the will of others (as often happens with lovers and mystics) and so find oneself at last rid of selfish pleasures, interests, and personal complexes" (xxii). The hierarchies of race, class, and sex intersect neatly: the subordinated, void of vexing identity, know that their place is to create the freedom (or perception thereof) of the dominant. Why, lessen the weight of their chains, and they may even rise up and massacre their oppressors in resentment. It is only our prudery, according to Paulhan, that obscures this truth. "Strange, that the notion of happiness in slavery should today seem so novel" (xxxiii). In closing, Paulhan returns to the Barbados uprising to reconstitute the voices that would not be found even in the notebook of grievances. What they say for Paulhan is "the truth, which is that Glenelg's slaves were in love with their master, that they could not bear to be without him. The same truth, after all, which lends *Story of O* its resolute quality, its incredible decency" (xxvi). Paulhan's "decency" is the sense of propriety or appropriateness that maintains the ordering of social rank: the "decent" subordinate tugs his forelock or lifts her skirt as the master passes by brandishing his whip.

Susan Sontag's song of praise is outside the text's own critical appa-ratus, but is nonetheless a part of the continuum I have outlined here. In her reading, O is etherealized almost past recognition. Neither the means (O's psychic and physical abasement) nor the end (merger of her identity with her master's) is significant: what does matter is her putative transcendence. "But O is an adept; whatever the cost in pain and fear, she is grateful for the opportunity to be initiated into a mystery. That mystery is the loss of the self. O learns, she suffers, she changes. Step by step she becomes more what she is, a process identical with the emptying out of herself. In the vision of the world presented by *Story of O*, the highest good is the transcendence of personality" ("Pornographic Imagination" 220). Sontag is willing to credit O as the acolyte of enlightenment, the oracle of the mystery. The novel unfolds "a spiritual paradox, that of the full void and of the vacuity that is also a plenum" (220). That a woman's tortured body embodies that pregnant emptiness is peripheral, a "metaphor" for the "religious imagination" "working in a total way" (230). In her reading of *Story of O*, Sontag maintains that to hang on to the sorry remnants of mortality and female flesh is to remain enmired in the mundane. "The need of human beings to transcend 'the personal' is no less profound than the need to be a person, an individual" (231).

Ethel Spector Person makes much the same point about love in general from a psychological perspective, arguing that our culture places excessive emphasis on autonomy and too little on surrender. "In surrender, it is a purged "reconstituted" self that is saved: the very act of surrender is a kind of recovery of radical innocence. No self-will stands between the lover and her secular god. This it shares with the religious impulse and it yields the same gratification. . . . As Dante has it, 'In la sua volontade e la nostra pace.' (In His will is our peace.)" (*Dreams* 146). Like Sontag, Person conflates the human and the divine and thus "transcends" gender specificity. She sees no apparent problem in the investment of another with divinity nor with the relinquishing of identity to "His will."

My objective in reviewing what seems to me an extremely perverse and significant strand of critical commentary is not to examine the possibility of transcendence, or even, assuming its possibility, to question love for an other as its means. Nor, for that matter, do I doubt in the least that the text presents a woman's surrender of identity as ecstatic. What impresses me as highly noteworthy is the willingness of some very sophisticated readers to genuflect before O's gods by crediting a transcendent, universal metaphysics that erases difference. As they do so, the text's ideology is recognized, masked, and further replicated through other systems. The most salient common effect of their willingness to credit the transubstantiation of man into God is to equate the discrepancy between woman and man with that between created and creator. Just as the novel insists on O's supernal excess, so the criticism obligingly leaves the God/ordinary human division behind and takes up its most intense articulation, that of the mystic.

O's idolatry, like that of O by some of her critics, doesn't bear psychological or theological scrutiny as an ideal. The text appropriates the stages of the mystical way to insist that the vicissitudes of O's development are explicable in terms of a higher authority. O is a sexual quietist, wanting to believe that she has found illumination in her stasis and surrender of identity. Her utter passivity remains suspect, however. She enters what Evelyn Underhill, in *Mysticism*, calls "the danger-zone of introversion," where the mystic can come to believe herself "exempt from the usual duties and limitations of human existence" (322).[8] Such absorption "leads to the absurdities of 'holy indifference,' and ends in the complete stultification of the mental and moral life" (323). As Underhill repeatedly emphasizes, the true mystic is passive *and* active: "Personality is not lost" (323). Just as healthy psychological development requires activity as well as passivity, so too the life of the soul. If endless gazing at the navel is dubious, so is believing one has found the universe in rapt contemplation of any other organ.

Feminist and psychoanalytic analyses call the text's hierarchy into question as well. Silverman's precise study of O's "secret," of "the territorialization and inscription of a body" ("Histoire d'O" 320, 346), Griffin's identification of the novel's center as "negation of the self" (226), Louise Kaplan's explication of slave and master's mutual regulation (*Female Perversions* 337–38), Benjamin's analysis of O's attempt to gain access to a more powerful self (61), and my own reading of the novel note the same features as other critics. The difference, however, lies in a shared unwillingness to adopt the text's ideology as normative or ideal.

Most psychologists describe the deification of the other as a problematic phenomenon as well. Stoller, for example, situates secrecy as the spur to sexual excitement. When secrecy develops into mystery, though, the lover aggrandizes the mysterious other through her belief that "a Will—God's, Woman's, Nature's, the Universe's, Fate's—has been at work to move the unknown toward divinity" (*Sexual Excitement* 16n). Parkin, like Freud, comments on the power of repressed instinctual characteristics that, unmodified by active, exter-

---

[8]I make general references to stages of the mystic way that rely upon Underhill's delineation and, to a lesser extent, upon some of the concepts in Frits Staal's *Exploring Mysticism*.

nalized usage, "are held as part of the self-ideal, usually in the most primitive and grotesque form, of the submissive one." The submissive partner believes such characteristics "may be magically attained in a *unio mystica* with the dominant partner" (307).

O, like many another Gothic heroine, yields the active drives, her own agency, and identity itself to René and, later, Sir Stephen. We are encouraged to keep our eyes on her, to agree that the beater acts at her behest, but the text inevitably calls our attention to the beater as well as the beaten. Only at our own critical and psychological peril can we say "a woman is being beaten" rather than "a man is beating a woman." O embodies what Day presents as the feminine archetype in the Gothic's "dynamics of sadomasochism, bondage, and domination": "the desire to submit and serve." Her subordination enables the masculine archetype to have his way as well, however, in his "desire to become godlike, or even to become God" (76). In other words, the divine is persistently invoked to justify the ways of the beater to the beaten. Though O's temporal and spatial progress in the course of the novel undeniably parallels the mystic's path, my focus is on how this system masks another kind of progress altogether: the reversal, turning round upon the self, repression, and sublimation of instincts that finally allow a woman to define herself proudly as the beaten.

The Purgative Way and the Reversal of Instincts

O's name follows the nomenclature of many of the Gothic's nameless protagonists: it signifies nothing, a cipher, a figure that marks order for other figures while having no value itself. Her name suggests what Wanda, the dominatrix of Sacher-Masoch's *Venus in Furs* asserts: "'*Woman's character is characterlessness*'" (113). O's chronological beginning place is not self-abnegation, however: she has financial and social authority in her job as a high-fashion photographer. Thus, her first position is that of the subject who acts, knows, and sees— the activity presumed in "Instincts and Their Vicissitudes" but never displayed in the woman's pattern of "A Child Is Being Beaten." Through the camera's eye and her other behavior, she achieves scopophilic and epistemophilic aims. Furthermore, the use of her own power to "hunt" other women constitutes her as a "beater" as well. It is she who initiates discussions, rendezvous, and caresses; she glories in her partner's yielding but "never return[s]" it (99, 100). "Indifferent," "cruel," and "fickle," she hunts female and male partners, but what she thinks "to be desire was actually nothing more than the thirst for conquest" (93–94). She remembers her enjoyment of such pursuits, "probably not for the pursuit itself, however amusing or fascinating it might be, but for the complete sense of freedom she experienced in the act of hunting. She, and she alone, set the rules and directed the proceedings (something she never did with men, or only in a most oblique manner)" (99). During this first stage, O's aggressive sexuality, social authority, and "freedom" mark her emphatically active instincts in a psychological frame and her decidedly natural and sinful self in a religious context. She enacts with satisfaction the first, active stage that "Instincts and Their Vicissitudes" supplies for "A Child": "*I* am beating someone." Her satisfaction is not quite entire, however, as the pecking order suggested above (and contradicted elsewhere) indicates: O is to other women what men are to her.

O relinquishes her problematic authority when, at novel's beginning, her lover René simply orders her to get into a cab, remove her undergarments, and hand over her identification. He brings her to Roissy not as a specific person, but as a chattel identified by her owner; she is, as René tells her, "'merely the girl I'm furnishing'" (5). (During her two weeks there and during subsequent interruptions, her profession seems increasingly unreal: no one from the office ever seems to find her absences somewhat strange, nor are finances an issue.)

Her stay at Roissy begins the conversion both of instincts and of the natural self. René takes her out of the sinful, active world and introduces her to a new order, marked by the removal of her blindfold and freeing of her tied hands after entrance. Instinct is reversed into its opposite: instead of looking, knowing, acting, and beating, she will be looked at, known, acted on, and beaten. She has faith in René: now, flesh and spirit must be mortified so that she is a fit worshiper at his altar. Her purgation begins immediately. Two other women, garbed in strangely eighteenth-century costumes, undress and bathe her. After she is thus purified, they do her hair, make her up (rouge her mouth, nipples, and labia), and perfume her. She is not allowed to touch herself or bring her legs together, and, after their ministrations, she waits in her red room, surrounded by mirrors and perhaps scrutinized through a peephole (7). Like Jane Eyre, confined in her own red room, she is ready to learn about authority. After being measured for and fitted with a leather collar and bracelets, her hands are chained behind her back, and she is introduced to four of the gentlemen of Roissy, who are having after-dinner coffee in the library.

Through these preliminaries, O is divested of the physical reminders of the external world and, along with them, of the conventions that maintain bodily and psychological integrity. She is objectified to herself as she sits spraddle-legged and surrounded by
mirrors, prepared to enter what Silverman terms "pornography's
scopic regime" (333). As Griffin points out, O "gradually unlearns all
the knowledge of her body" through training that reverses that of an
infant learning about its own body, its power, and its relations to
others (219).

The novel presents this transformation as the spiritual awakening
and purification of the self through purgation, contrition, and self-
knowledge. In both the psychological and the mystical patterns, the
self is radically reformed: *Story of O* achieves much of its force through
its insistence that the psychological transformation to passivity and
mystical enlightenment are one and the same in their deferral to a
higher authority. The Gothic's name for feminine transcendence via
abnegation, "true love," further supports the same goal on a secular
level, as the title of the novel's first section, "The Lovers of Roissy,"
sardonically suggests.

During her first night at Roissy, O begins her purgation and training in passivity. She is beaten, gang-banged vaginally, anally and
orally, and chained before sleep. She learns the rules: she is not ever
to speak unless spoken to (and not at all to the other women there),
she cannot lift her eyes to those of any man, she cannot use her own
hands. She cannot close her lips or her legs. She will be whipped at
the end of every day for her infractions, and chained nightly. She is
corsetted, garbed in a flowing green gown that allows full access to
her body (and whose color marks her as a veritable *fille verte* by
Roissy's standards), and shod in high-heeled mules.

The regimen at Roissy clearly parodies that of a convent. The sharp
break with the outer world emphasizes the resemblance, as do
Roissy's costumes and customs, its injunctions against "special
friendships," regulation of the day, custody of the eyes and other
disciplines, and the wedding band worn upon completion of training.
What at first seems the mechanical invocation of a tired convention,
however (no one from Diderot on seems to escape the titillating wonder about what all those women *do* together), acquires resonance as
the novel continues, for, within the world of this novel, women worship overvalued men as nuns adore their God.

The novel explains and justifies O's self-annihilation by constituting the men of Roissy as gods. The inward turn of instinct is accompanied and enabled by their overvaluation and the assignment of ego

function to them. Anything that might indicate that O's disciplining occurs because she is desirable or to satisfy male need is avoided in the speech of the men who set forth the terms of her perpetual receptivity. From the initiation on, the text repeats that, like gods, the men of Roissy do not need their creatures, and that they are in no way dependent for their being or pleasure upon the female bodies with which they surround themselves. Nonetheless, René and Sir Stephen, to whom he later "gives" O, make the creature of their dreams, just as Victor Frankenstein does. The men will "use" O; she will properly "honor" them by her obeisance (17). The illuminati of the boudoir represent a higher authority, as they tell her the first night. The whipping "'is less for our pleasure than for your enlightenment. . . . Actually, both this flogging and the chain . . . are intended less to make you suffer, scream, or shed tears than to make you feel, *through* this suffering, that you are not free but fettered, and to teach you that you are totally dedicated to something outside yourself' " (17). In order to stress that her "enlightenment" is necessitated by her need, not theirs, they tell her that her nightly whipping will be administered by a valet should one of the masters choose not to do it himself. The perquisites of class are again apparently subsumed by those of sex.[9]

Although not the speaker, René is one of the four men present. O does not know which of the penetrations or blows might have been his: her god is now part of a pantheon. Yet when he tells her that he loves her, "O, trembling, was terrified to notice that she answered 'I love you,' and that it was true" (18). Ministered to by two other women, he sits on a table's edge and has O fellate him while the other three men adjust a lamp so that they can better observe and comment on her technique. "O felt that her mouth was beautiful, since her

[9]As in Wharton's "Mr. Jones," sex and class intersect interestingly to form the text's hierarchy. The lower-class valets, like the women, must wear costumes, and their commands are always politely phrased. Like the masters, though, they cannot be looked at in the face or spoken to directly, and their genitals, token of privilege at Roissy, are exposed. They can rape or discipline the women at will when alone, but must also do so when ordered to, and they of course must defer their own gratifications when the masters (white, male, and upper-class) are present. The valets' class status is raised through masculinism, while the women's social rank is lowered through their duties in sweeping, waiting on tables, and so forth (15). The net status, if you will, of sex and class is sometimes similar enough that "it was possible to bribe the valets" (37).

The servants at Roissy in *Story of O* are all male. As O perfects herself in humility and humiliation, her "progress" is emphasized later in the novel by Sir Stephen's assigning his "Negro maid" (178) to whip her. Norah, subordinated through class, race, and sex, nevertheless has more authority (albeit delegated, like that of Mr. Jones) than O—and Norah, like Pierre the valet and unlike O, merits a proper name.

lover condescended to thrust himself into it, since he deigned publicly to offer caresses to it, since, finally, he deigned to discharge in it.
She received it as a god is received, she heard him cry out, heard the
others laugh, and when she had received it she fell, her face against
the floor" (19). O's mouth is "beautiful" only because it magnifies the
Lord, and Rene's ejaculation becomes sacramental.[10] Like one of
Freud's patients, she rejoices in the painful mark of his esteem, inflicted *because* he loves her. Released from the gentlemen, she is
chained in her red room and again whipped in the early morning
hours by the valet Pierre. Before and after her second flogging of the
night, her thoughts center upon René. She is mildly surprised that
the first whipping "left her so untroubled, so calm" (23), and, after
the second, continues to repose her will in his. "She did not wish to
die, but if torture was the price she had to pay to keep her lover's
love, then she only hoped he was pleased that she had endured it. All
soft and silent she waited, waited for them to bring her back to him"
(27). This peace that passes all understanding is made possible by the
assignment of subject status to another.

O's purgation continues through the repeated mortification of her
flesh. Whipped, raped, and wearing a dildo to enlarge her anus, she
works at improving her obedience daily. She is contrite for her active
sins, and sedulously tries to avoid further ones of omission or commission. She easily maintains the rule of silence (38), although finding
it more difficult to control the wish to look men in the face (37). In an
order where "an advance toward one of the masters seemed quite
naturally inconceivable" (36), O examines her conscience for vestiges
of active longing, for signs that it is her will and not another's that she
follows. When another man has sex with her as René watches and
participates, O is aghast—not at the event itself, nor even at the
disloyalty to René she fears, but in the pleasure that points to a
residual self that seeks gratification from others rather than giving it
unquestioningly. The stranger begins with cunnilingus, a "caress to
which she never submitted without a struggle and which always
filled her with shame." Her shamed struggle at this "sacrilege" is no
misplaced modesty, though, but displaced authority: "she deemed it
sacrilege for her lover to be on his knees, feeling that she should be on

[10]As Silverman insightfully comments, René is nonetheless feminized in relation to
Sir Stephen. I agree: René is demoted to demi-god and, eventually, minor sainthood.
His worship of Sir Stephen assures his devaluation, as does his "cry" at ejaculation
during this scene. The other men laugh at his loss of manly control as well as at O's
reverent blow job. The impassive Sir Stephen is Real Presence. René eventually becomes a mere penis; Sir Stephen remains the forever-erect and self-sufficient Phallus.

hers" (30). Excited by the stranger's ministrations, O fails in her self-discipline. She has gained pleasure from her own responses rather than vicarious satisfaction. "In a flash, O saw herself released, reduced to nothing, accursed. . . . She felt debased and guilty" (31). O will submit to anything René asks, because she believes that she is loved in return for her faith and her surrender of will. The sources of her debasement and guilt are, like her instincts, a reversal of what we might expect: her sin, in her own reckoning, is too much, not too little, self.

O's willingness to surrender is countered by the need of René and others to force that surrender, to have it be the effect of their will, not hers, as René carefully explains: "'It's because it's easy for you to consent that I want from you what it will be impossible for you to consent to, even if you agree ahead of time, even if you say yes now and imagine yourself capable of submitting. You won't be able *not* to revolt. Your submission will be obtained in spite of you, not only for the inimitable pleasure that I and others will derive from it, but also so that you will be made aware of what has been done to you'" (32–33). O almost responds that "she was his slave and that she bore her bonds cheerfully" (33), before she is interrupted; she misses the point. Her dutiful eagerness to be what is wanted still maintains, however perversely, that it is she who decides. René and the others need some flicker of awareness to remain, some part of personality that will watch and "will be made aware of" the self's destruction, but it is necessary that that destruction be a sacrifice, not a self-chosen martyrdom. O will know "what has been done to" her; she will be the object, not the subject, of that action.

Throughout O's "purification," what she finds most difficult to yield is monogamous (albeit strictly psychic) exclusivity. She needs to believe that the bond between her and René is special, that, like the speaker of Dowson's "Cynara," "I have been faithful to thee . . . in my fashion." Blessed among women because maltreated more than others, she nonetheless needs training to see herself as exchangeable with any other woman. At the same time, any man can stand in for René. The cultural inscription of masculinity and femininity thus becomes essentialized to male and female, at least within the elite society of Roissy. Anyone with a penis has the right to the uninhibited exercise of authority, while anyone with a vagina is receptive, passive, and unquestioningly obedient.

To emphasize that point, René fondles another woman in front of O, so that she realizes she has no unique properties. "What pleasure was she giving him, yes she, that this girl or any other could not?"

René's lesson is quite intentional, as his knowing question, "'That hadn't occurred to you?'" (35), indicates. As the spectator watching another woman being beaten, O is still further distanced from the activity she has eschewed. She wants nothing more than again to be a participant, than again to be the one specially elected for chastisement.

In this scene, O enacts the first woman's stage Freud postulates for women in "A Child"—"'My father is beating a child whom he loves/hates.'" The antithesis to that ambivalent love/hate is indifference, as Freud suggest in "Instincts": the indifference that erases existence itself. *Story of O* has not gone beyond love and hate but, perhaps, before them. O or the woman being beaten no longer deliberates between the niceties of love and hate, loving and being loved, so much as between having her existence ratified in any fashion and the void of indifference. And she is as helpless in evoking that recognition as her penates are arbitrary in bestowing favor: while she must always be prepared for grace, she cannot demand it or hasten it. The passivity demanded of O has little to do with good works and much to do with blind faith.

The deployment of power at Roissy privileges all the men; their courteous accord grants René no special status. René tells O that the interdiction against visually or vocally addressing a man "'applies to me as well: with me you shall remain silent and obey'" (33). Nonetheless, there is room for O to continue her fantasy that the relation between herself and René is somehow unique, despite his casual loaning of her to any taker. René encourages the fantasy by insisting that she obey all men, insofar as they are aspects of himself.

> She must greet them and submit to them with the same respect with which she greeted him, as though they were so many reflections of him. Thus he would possess her as a god possesses his creatures, whom he lays hold of in the guise of a monster or a bird, of an invisible spirit or a state of ecstasy. . . . The more he surrendered her, the more he would hold her dear. . . . One can only give what belongs to you. He gave her only to reclaim her immediately, to reclaim her enriched in his eyes, like some common object which had been used for some divine purpose and has thus been consecrated. (32)

René is a god and the others his priests, as it were—sanctified, due all honor, but ultimately "reflections of him." O's "consecration" is bait for her swallowing the hook of herself as thing, along with whatever else she swallows at Roissy. Like Freud's Dora or Walker's Roselily, O is "*re*claimed" as an object of exchange in a masculine economy.

O docilely follows René's edicts: "'The only times you will open you mouth here in the presence of a man will be to cry out or to caress'" (33). She does not cry out when, at the end of seven days, René leaves, promising to return again at the end of O's two-week stay. His departure underscores both O's weaning and his installment as the overvalued other to whom she assigns her subjectivity. The fort/da game of surveillance reverses the child's, in which she, repeating "gone/here," comes to understand that she continues as a self when the loved one leaves. Both the child and O must learn to tolerate the other's absence, in part by internalizing the other's values. The child practices her own growing control, however, while O is schooled in the loss of autonomy and the knowledge that she will never really be alone.

During René's absence, other caretakers aid O's socialization. Her very tractability, like that of Sade's Justine, excites new excesses that only serve to perfect her discipline. Like "a young girl in her parents' living room," she tends to her daily tasks with lowered eyes (45). So irresistible is her meek obedience "that all it took for the men whom she was serving was to order her to remain by their sides while they were violating another girl to make them want to violate her as well; which doubtless explains why she was treated worse than before" (45). Her self-denial helps to create their self-assertion, of course. But, within the novel, the men's status is presented as absolute and not subject to change. What instead unrolls as overt plot is the testing of O's vocation and the examination of her devotional aptitude.

O is unsure whether the departure of her overvalued other is a punishment for her or a thoughtful politeness to the other men (45–46). She wonders "Had she sinned?" and she is given ample opportunity for contrition and penance. Two days after René leaves, Pierre the valet again blindfolds her and O, for once, welcomes the loss of vision. "Blessèd darkness like unto her own night, never had O greeted it with such joy, blessèd chains that bore her away from herself" (47). For five days and nights, she is left in darkness, beaten and raped by anonymous bodies. During this time of sensory deprivation and torture, her conversion process is completed, as is the turning inward of instinct. Her contrition, purgation, and self-knowledge make her postulancy successful: she is heartily sorry for ever having acted willfully or believing that she had a self. Her acknowledgment is a distorted Act of Contrition in which she detests her sins because of René's "just" punishments and because they offend him—a startling, grotesque aggrandizement of the male that assumes normal proportions on the book's scale of values.

During her first stay at Roissy, O achieves illumination through the Purgative Way. She is infused with an abiding sense of divine presence and often reminded of it by more substantial effusions. She remembers her stay fondly. "And yet nothing had been such a comfort to her as the silence, unless it was the chains. The chains and the silence, which should have bound her deep within herself, which should have smothered her, strangled her, on the contrary freed her from herself" (38–39). The text claims spiritual awakening, a new birth after near suffocation, but O is more like a placidly smiling instance of Cixous's silenced, decapitated women. Her submission and the men's domination are given connotations of spiritual struggle and she, like the speaker of Donne's "Batter My Heart," is represented as needing force to accept her own salvation: "Take me to you, imprison me, for I / Except you enthrall me, never shall be free, / Nor ever chaste, except you ravish me." The language of her own paradoxical metamorphosis draws heavily upon the same devotional tradition. "That she should have been ennobled and gained in dignity through being prostituted was a source of surprise, and yet dignity was indeed the right term. She was illuminated by it, as though from within, and her bearing bespoke calm, while on her face could be detected the serenity and imperceptible smile that one surmises rather than actually sees in the eyes of hermits" (44).

O's "dignity," "calm," and "serenity" hallow her renunciation of self. No longer conflicted, she rests content in her cloistered existence. Her active aims are reversed into passive; she herself is now their object and René their divine subject.

The Illuminative Way and the Overvalued Other

Transformed, O can return to the world after having successfully negotiated the Purgative Way. In the world—back in her own apartment and again working—she knows herself and others differently: she is illuminated. This stage that she, like some mystics, believes permanent is but a way-station, however, albeit a crucial one. She believes that she apprehends the divine although, as Underhill says of this stage, it "is the 'betrothal' rather than the 'marriage' of the soul" (240). The phenomenal world is seen with a new perception through the "clarity" she has gained at Roissy. Lastly, she experiences "automatic activity" in which her god appears and speaks to her. Needless to say, O is deceived by self and others in her evaluation of her progress.

During this stage, O is perfecting her passivity and her object status. Like a well-broken animal, she is allowed into society because her training assures that she will act under orders and not of her own accord. Nonetheless, her handler must now refine her skills and broaden the range of commands to which she will answer. In addition, the work of repression must be continued and subtilized. The crass physical and psychological oppression of Roissy has done its work but, during her illuminative stage, O must internalize her restrictions entirely so that they continue to function despite the temptations of the outer world whose values are not overtly those of Roissy.

Towards these ends, O reinforces her credence in a love that surpasses that of normal man for woman and intensifies the superhuman attributes of her owners. In so doing, she at the same time scourges consciousness to excise the sin of willfulness or activity. While working to assure her worthiness for the beloved, the loss of self accelerates so that their will may be as one—his. Finally, the fruition of "enlightenment" and her still imperfect sanctity is evident in her dealings with a potential new convert, Jacqueline.

O continues throughout the book to believe that her idol loves her also, and that the rationale for her suffering can and should remain beyond her ken. Within this section, though, she discovers that René has only been a "transitional subject," as it were. Just as D. W. Winnicott sees baby blankets as "transitional objects" on the infant's route to object love, so René proves to be a preliminary avatar of O's externalized subjectivity. His older British half-brother, Sir Stephen, becomes the ultimate godhead to whom O assigns all self-interest. On first returning home, however, O knows only her familiar spirit, René. His presence infuses all, even on her first day back. "She was alone, her own sole spectator. And yet never had she felt herself more totally committed to a will which was not her own, more totally a slave, and more content to be so" (60). René personifies that will for the nonce, and it is his commandments she follows, not yet realizing that he is lawgiver for another.

René carefully explains how she must continue Roissy's regime and how difficult it will be to maintain seemingly simple disciplines (57–58). Her mouth and legs must always remain open, she cannot wear underpants, and all other garments must open up the front, so that she is as readily available to any initiate as she was at Roissy.[11] (The

---

[11]That O's new style attracts admiring attention but no surprise suggests that the mores of Roissy and Paris are not as separate as we might at first think. Indeed, later in the novel, an assistant remarks about O's pronounced pallor and outfit that she looks like a *"femme fatale"* (93), when a *femme fatalisée* might be a more accurate description.

band she wears on her finger will serve to identify her to such cogno-scenti.) Here and throughout the rest of the novel, O is asked to consent—a request as farcical as asking any broken and trained ani-mal if it agrees to perform its tricks. "He began by saying that she should not think that she was now free. With one exception, and that was that she was free not to love him any longer, and to leave him immediately. But if she did love him, then she was in no wise free. She listened to him without saying a word" (56). Well-taught, O no longer needs chains: her mind-forg'd manacles are strong enough to assure that she will use her freedom to remain with her owner.

René's "one exception" is impossible for O, as the "if . . . then" logic of the next sentence indicates. If she loses the externalized sub-jectivity that she calls love, then she indeed loses all. René too seems to know this, for no explicit response is called for or given by her. Instead, reminded to open her legs, she dutifully squats "on her heels in the manner of Carmelites or of Japanese women,"[12] overcome by "a kind of internal prostration, a sacred submission, as though a god, and not he, had spoken to her" (57). O continues to hear and obey her voices, as it were, throughout the novel, never doubting but for a minute that they are genuine visitations and she well-beloved.

When René introduces O to Sir Stephen, she quickly realizes that this new man, unlike all the others, is no mere instrument of René. More troublingly still, she perceives that the strongest bond among the three of them is that between René and Sir Stephen, who so coolly and convincingly embodies what Praz, in *Romantic Agony*, describes as the French view of *le vice Anglais*. They affirm their homosocial bond through her body and, indeed, come to resemble a bizarre little family in which O is the child. At their first dinner, O, child-like, wants dessert and is indulged. "She wanted to order ice cream for dessert, with lots of almonds and whipped cream. For she was feeling light and happy. . . . They let her have the ice cream, but not the coffee" (70). Later on, O simply hands the menu to Sir Stephen so that he can decide for her (118). Her new style, described as "'very little-girl-like'" (63), makes her look like a "well-brought-up little girl," who is often mistaken for Sir Stephen's daughter or niece (168–69), in part because he tutoyers her, though she always addresses him using "vous" or "Sir Stephen" (112, 169). The two men strengthen their bond by deciding together how to dress their toy and rearrange her

[12]The equation of equally stereotyped Carmelites and geisha-like Japanese women assumes a supine passivity that is inaccurate as a generalization and in this instance: Carmelites do not "squat," but kneel upright.

body, as when they agree that she must always have welts, because she is "'infinitely more moving'" (115) thus. In being looked at, spoken about as the object of their knowledge, and acted upon, the O whose instincts have been reversed and turned inward is happy.

When again asked for her consent—this time to their shared ownership of her—O is hesitant. Her relationship with René as the overvalued other assigned subjectivity is necessarily dyadic: a third mandates a radical realignment. Before the celebratory whipping that follows her agreement, she suddenly remembers a print in which a child and dog play in a corner while a woman, skirts raised, kneels before an armchair and is whipped. The picture "bore a title which she had found disgusting: 'Family Punishment'" (79). The picture suggests that the sexual authority of the sadist may in fact not be unique, that it may have another, more recognizable source in family dynamics. The need to avoid that recognition mandates René's eventual demotion to demigod or even sibling, augured by his quasi-maternal role in their own holy family,[13] well before Sir Stephen assumes exclusive ownership of O. Furthermore, René's role as spectator in the beating relationship assures his loss of status. As spectator/panderer/mother he must assuage the possible ire of an angry Father and guarantee his satisfaction. He defers to Sir Stephen that first night in a number of ways, including giving him sole use of O's anus, Sir Stephen's preferred organ.

O seems to sense the twilight of her god that first night. She fears the bond between the two men, and quickly realizes that she must somehow get the aloof Sir Stephen "to love her" (82), love being the sole justification for her existence as the beaten. Moreover, from the stance of the beaten, the only recognizable "love" is having the beater realize that he must have you, and you only, to beat. To be solely the medium for the two men's exchange does not suffice. "And today, this sharing derived its meaning from René's relation to Sir Stephen much more than it did from his relation to her. What each of them would look for in her would be the other's mark, the trace of the other's passage" (83). If used thus, O's body becomes a dead letter to her while constituting a means of communication to them. "O realized that through the medium of her body, shared between them, they attained something more mysterious and perhaps more acute, more intense than an amorous communion, the very conception of

[13]For a perceptive analysis of an equally strange family in which two male vampires raise a girl-vampire who will never change, see Janice Doane and Devon Hodges's "Undoing Feminism."

which was arduous but whose reality and force she could not deny" (105). While acknowledging the "mysterious" arcana of homosocial bonding, supposedly so much more elevated, "arduous," and "intense" than the knowledge wrung from her body, O nonetheless displays her first signs of resentment and competition at being shuttled aside.

O originally fears Sir Stephen—not because of the excruciating refinement of his beating techniques but because he threatens to break up O's and René's fantastic dyad of beater and beaten, lover and beloved. She clings to René that first night and for some time thereafter, insisting that it is he whom she obeys, he who is her god. When Sir Stephen slaps her in the face and says that René's training of her "'leaves a great deal to be desired,'" O's response—"'I always obey René'" (88)—is an attempt to maintain René's status and to establish Sir Stephen as the interloper.

That first night points to the close of O's postulancy in being the beaten with René and the beginning of her novitiate with Sir Stephen. He promises no love, entirely objectifies her, increases her pain, and detects reserves of self-will René never perceived. He recapitulates the process of self-divesture that she has undergone, demanding that she search within herself and yield more. Whereas René's "look was one of constant tenderness, of unflagging gratitude whenever he saw her mouth open to moan or scream" (84), she does not exist for Sir Stephen. "But, in Sir Stephen, she thought she detected a will of ice and iron, which would not be swayed by desire, a will in whose judgment, no matter how moving and submissive she might be, she counted for absolutely nothing, at least till now" (84). His indifference threatens all O has "achieved" with René; she runs the risk of becoming the excluded third even if the two men define and create the primacy of their bond over her beaten body.

By flicking ashes on O (82), slapping her in the face (an unusual blow), and denigrating her training, Sir Stephen shows contempt and indifference even according to the standards of Roissy. O is no longer much beaten because much loved. Instead, she is fully commodified: "a trip, a boat, a horse" that the two men might share (83), a pawn in a "game" (85), a "machine" that must be checked for proper functioning (85), a horse examined for sale (84). Sir Stephen nonetheless insists that she consent, thus forcing the full attachment of her will to his without the luxury of overt coercion or the lure of love as rationale. "But she could not move of her own free will—an order from them would immediately have made her get up, but this time what they wanted from her was not blind obedience, acquiescence to an order, they wanted her to anticipate orders, to judge herself a slave and surrender herself as such. This, then, is what they called her consent" (75). After René leaves her and Sir Stephen for the evening, O is bent over, waiting for what she thinks will be a beating. She remembers with nostalgia those simpler days when she was actually chained, "a happy prisoner" (80).

The good old days when she was the star pupil, acknowledged and loved for the perfection of her self-abnegating discipline, seem to be gone. "And however humiliated she was, or rather because she had been humiliated, was it not somehow pleasant to be esteemed only for her humiliation, for the meekness with which she surrendered, for the obedient way in which she opened?" (80). No longer "esteemed," O is insignificant and inadequate to Sir Stephen. Furthermore, he accuses her of sin, of active pleasure after she fellates him. "'You are easy, O,' he said to her. 'You love René, but you're easy'" (86). It is when she says that she "'can't'" (87) masturbate in front of him that he slaps her and calls her poorly trained. (In fact, O has always felt "disgust" at the autoeroticism of masturbation, in which one's self is both subject and object.) As he coldly tells her, "'You're confusing love and obedience. You'll obey me without loving me, and without my loving you'" (88).

Sir Stephen demands that O bring forth the hidden traces of active will, desire, and subjectivity and that she make them over to him without any return of the love she so values. When he tells her that she will obey without love and proceeds to rape her anally until she bleeds, she screams as she never did at Roissy—a scream of rebellion rather than agony. "With that, she felt a strange inexplicable storm of revolt rising within her. . . . She screamed as much out of revolt as of pain, and he was fully aware of it. She also knew—which meant that in any event she was vanquished—that he was pleased to make her cry out" (89). Rather than being angry (and thus allowing O a measure of masochistic control), Sir Stephen is "pleased" that there is something there for him to appropriate and subdue.

On that first night, O begins to realize that a new order has come into being. When René assigns her anus to Sir Stephen, O is "stunned" at "the sign that her lover cared more about Sir Stephen than he did about her" (84). By caring more for Sir Stephen than Sir Stephen seems to care for him, René is feminized and declassed. He brings O to Sir Stephen, escorts both to Sir Stephen's house after their dinner, relays Sir Stephen's commands to O, holds her hand "in a viselike grip" (79) to better demonstrate her best features while Sir Stephen masturbates her, and politely excuses himself for the rest of the evening. Given René's deference to Sir Stephen, O must get some response from this cool British overlord—not only to preserve her own precarious position, but to avoid devaluation and indifference from René as well. "Here he was not the master any longer. On the contrary. Sir Stephen was René's master, without René's being fully aware of it. . . . René would probably go on loving her insofar as Sir Stephen deemed that she was worth the trouble and would love her himself. . . . She did not expect any pity from [Sir Stephen]; but could she not hope to wrest some slight feeling of love from him?" (90).

O's valuation of Sir Stephen is thus on the one hand a pragmatic assessment of his worth to René. On the other hand, his aloofness, self-sufficiency, and contempt are a challenge and an incitement to her own overvaluation of him. After O's scream of revolt—and vanquishment—Sir Stephen gallantly helps her to her feet and remarks that, by the time she learns what she has consented to in becoming his and René's slave, "it would be too late for her to escape" (89). O's "retaliation," explained as the need to help René, is simple: Sir Stephen too must come to love her. "Listening, O told herself that perhaps it would also be too late for him to escape becoming enamored of her, for she had no intention of being quickly tamed, and by the time she was he might have learned to love her a little. For all her inner resistance, and the timid refusal she had dared to display, had one object and one object alone: she wanted to exist for Sir Stephen, in however modest a way, in the same way she existed for René" (89–90). O's need for anything rather than indifference is evident here, as is her covert knowledge that, in their "precise relationship of master to slave" (90), there is no master without a slave, no subjectivity, as René and Sir Stephen understand it, without an abject object.

O's own desire, brought to the foreground by Sir Stephen's rejection, is highlighted by the end of that first night. She and Sir Stephen both want the same thing—a beating relationship—but they are engaged in a conflict of will in which each insists that the other be responsible for articulating desire. Taken to Sir Stephen's guest room, O, suddenly the most clichéd of Gothic protagonists, "wept, and did not fall asleep until dawn" (91). Torn apart by her desires and a bleeding rectum, O goes to bed that night crying like a lovesick girl after a disappointing first date. Her tears and her sleeplessness, like her screams, are different than at Roissy; it is her complicity and possible failure she must now consider as much as the actions of others. She weeps for her "useless and scorned womb" (86)—Sir Stephen uses only her mouth and anus—and the lack of at least a good-night kiss: he "condescended only to place his lips upon her fingertips" (91). And perhaps, in some fashion, she weeps for the last reaches of selfhood she will surrender in order to be loved.

O weeps but will be comforted. The following day, after she is returned to her apartment, René is elevated to new heights in her mind. The very fervor of her adoration, comparable to her nostalgia for Roissy, implies comparison of René to Sir Stephen and suggests the compensatory excess of emotion that often precedes a leavetaking one won't yet admit. Alone in her room, she apostrophizes René. "'I love you, do whatever you want with me, but don't leave me, for God's sake don't leave me'" (93). She owes René gratitude for her captivity. "She was no longer free? Yes! thank God, she was no longer free" (94). If she is base and sinful in her willfulness, then René is all the more magnanimous. "What if she actually enjoyed her debasement? In that case, the baser she was, the more merciful was René to consent to make O the instrument of his pleasure" (96). He always returns to her in his infinite loving kindness and through no merit of her own. "Oh, let the miracle continue, let me still be touched by grace, René don't leave me!" (97). Referring to O's fear that René will stop loving her and leave, the text sententiously comments: "Who pities those who wait? They are easily recognized: by their gentleness, by their falsely attentive looks" (93).

O's fear of abandonment is that of a child overly reliant upon one other; René *is* her self, and their umbilical bond is, horrifyingly, "the only network through which the current of life any longer flowed into her" (94). Yet, her repeated pleas that René not leave her suggest that she will soon be leaving him. So too, her "falsely attentive looks" at others while she waits for René soon become the gaze attached to René as she waits for Sir Stephen's pleasure. During this day, there are two extended passages in which O remembers her days as an active huntress and praises the contentment she now finds through René. Her recollection is stirred by Sir Stephen's search for vestiges of will and identity the previous night, but it also presages repetition of her renunciation of self.

In imagining abandonment, even O's fear of full annihilation is cast in passive terms: if René "was on the verge of ceasing to love her, then everything was choked and smothered within her" (95). The suffocation one might identify with his too intrusive presence is instead associated with his absence. The instinct she has turned upon herself demands an other as its agent. O now needs that agent in order overtly to maintain her passivity and covertly to gain what vicarious satisfaction she still can. While her "impassioned submission" (95) to prostitution is proof of René's potent ownership, the "pain," "shame," and "outrage inflicted upon her by those who compelled her to pleasure when they took her, and at the same time delighted in their own without paying the slightest heed to hers, seemed to her the very redemption of her sins" (95–96). As long as there is any "pleasure" for herself that is not "compelled"—as long as O is alive—there will also be sin.[14]

Although it is René who has the status of subject, in O's theology it is her sinful self who will be at fault if deserted.

> For she was guilty. Those who love God, and by Him are abandoned in the dark of night, are guilty, *because* they are abandoned. They cast back into their memories, searching for their sins. She looked back, hunting for hers. . . . Her total submission to René rendered her vulnerable, irresponsible, and all her trifling acts—but what acts? For all she had to reproach herself with were thoughts and fleeting temptations. Yet, he was certain that she was guilty and, without really wanting to, René was punishing her for a sin he knew nothing about (since it remained completely internal), although Sir Stephen had immediately detected it: her wantonness. (95)

O no longer has self-initiated deeds with which to reproach herself and few words for which she could be culpable; it is thought and emotion that damn her in her own reckoning. Her own irresponsibility (since another makes decisions for her) doesn't matter a whit in the grand illogic of guilt *because* of abandonment. O has not been passive enough, has withheld a nest egg of pleasure instead of transferring all to René.

Sir Stephen in his omniscience knows what René cannot: O's "wantonness," the trace of pleasure and will. O remembers a motto that hung in a house in which she stayed as a child.

---

[14]The different valuation of masochism for men and women is as pronounced in fiction as in the case histories discussed earlier. Sade's worthies take inordinate pride in their masochistic abilities, for example, and in both *Justine* and *The 120 Days of Sodom* maintain control by forcing others to beat them. Sacher-Masoch's Severin, like O, feels "'there was something sacred in sex'" (97). When he explains his "sensitivity" to Wanda, she immediately feminizes him. "'In other words, reason has little power over you, and you are by nature, soft, sensual, yielding.'" He indignantly refutes her by comparing himself to martyrs in their strength and virility. "'They were *suprasensual men*, who found enjoyment in suffering. They sought out the most frightful tortures, even death itself, as others seek joy, and as they were, so am I—*suprasensual*'" (89–90).

IT IS A FEARFUL THING TO FALL
INTO THE HANDS OF THE LIVING GOD
No, O told herself now, that isn't true. What is fearful is to be cast out of
the hands of the living God. (96)

For her, this is true: to be left alone would be to be cast into outer darkness. When she most fears immolation, however, she is vouch-safed further illumination: René is only the type and promise of the true god. In Sir Stephen, René admires "the stern master he himself was unable to be" (108). O's willingness to be prostituted "sanctified" (108) her and established René's masculine worth; Sir Stephen's willingness to "tame" (108) her elevates both to new heights. "Each time she emerged from his arms, René looked for the mark of a god upon her" (108–9). While busily engaged in tracking god spoor on O's body, René's own aura of divinity necessarily fades.

When, after a month of transition, Sir Stephen goes to O's apartment for the first time, the visitation marks the full ascendancy of Sir Stephen and O's successful completion of her novitiate. Although René remains present for much of the remainder of the novel (and at one crucial point O again needs to be told that he loves her), he slowly becomes laicized. This day is the last on which the two men confer together about how best to manage their property as co-owners: in the future, René simply admires the improvements that Sir Stephen makes. They agree that she must always have welts, "irrespective of the pleasure they might derive from her screams and tears," not only because she is "infinitely more moving" thus mutilated (she still shows the scars of the beating inflicted a month ago), but because "these marks made it impossible for her to cheat" (115).

By physically emblazoning O with the signs of their "secrets" (116), they make her a marked woman. She can "cheat" neither by alliances she chooses herself (assuming her capable of such decisions) nor by pretending to own herself and be her own subject. The welts further circumscribe her movement in the world, for much physical activity, "such as playing tennis or swimming" (116) is now impractical. O is relieved at her new mnemonics. "That these things were forbidden her was a comfort to her, a material comfort, as the bars of the convent materially prevent the cloistered girls from belonging to one another, and from escaping" (116). From now on, O will belong neither to herself nor to anyone other than Sir Stephen: she frets not at her convent's narrow room, but instead finds comfort in its stifling enclosure.

O learns of her new restrictions in a semihypnoid state. Legs dan-gling, she lies back on a table covered with photographs she has taken, in the position into which Sir Stephen "rudely shoved her" (114) when a moan, apparently of pleasure, escaped her as he fondled her. She is languidly detached, "as though it did not concern her"; for "what she had to do, and even what she had to be, was decided without her" (114). O is in full mystical bliss.

O believes her new god to be all-knowing and all-present; at the end of her Illuminative Way, she has reason to think that he may be all-loving as well. When O meets his gaze during the lunch that concludes the section, "what she read in it was so clear this time, and it was so obvious to him that she had seen it, that now it was his turn to blanch" (117). O is at first disappointed by the items sets forth for her consent—masturbation and possession by others in his pres-ence—for none is rigorous enough to gauge justly the depth of her devotion. Subsequent stipulations are exacting enough to match O's need to prove her reverent mettle: she will be further marked, in ways yet unclear to her, and she is to have relations with a co-worker, Jacqueline, with the aim of recruiting her for Roissy. O's ambiguous new marks, in some way related to irons, still leave her obliged to accommodate all, but will "reveal her to be a personal slave" (121), Sir Stephen's own. She will be the beloved's fully.

The day she is transferred to Sir Stephen is a day of joy, fulfillment, and lucidity for O. She has found the one true god, the ultimate vicarious subject, and she is his. "Henceforth there were no more hiatuses, no dead time, no remission. He whom one awaits is, be-cause he is expected, already present, already master" (111). Herself always and already lacking because a subordinated woman, O finds a celestial supplement. Time itself dissolves in Sir Stephen's omnipre-sence: she is at narcissistic peace in the full merger of her identity in his. Like Stoller's client, Bella, whose beater in fantasy is a cruelly indifferent Director, O believes Sir Stephen's very aloofness to be a guarantee of his divinity. "Still, there is this comfort: as she believed was true with God, she might not be able to stir him but he is always present, dependable, potent, watching her" (*Sexual Excitement* 80).

As Sir Stephen speaks to René, O is further soothed into quiescence by the seeming omniscience that lets her declare her version of "Not my will, but thine." "She had the feeling that by some strange sub-stitution Sir Stephen was speaking for her, in her place. As though he was somehow in her body and could feel the anxiety, the anguish, and the shame, but also the secret pride and harrowing pleasure that she was feeling" (115–16). The sense of Divine Presence, faultily embodied in René, illuminates O. Emptied of self, she and her body are the seemingly transparent media for the indwelling presence of Sir Stephen.

The text presents O as an initiate of the Illuminative Way at the end of her second stage of development. Existing in the world, she has a new sense of its significance, infused as she is by the immanent presence of her living god. Further perfected in her discipline, she prepares to embark upon her third and most arduous path, the Unitive Way. O's painstaking progress, cast in mystical terms, vehemently denies the physical, psychological, and religious abomination of her torture. Her faith, which works by love, extols subordination by simultaneous reification of the woman and deification of the man. The veneer of religiosity that overlays the text masks its warped psychosocial base.

O's "progress" is in fact a devolution. Although in both mystical and psychological paradigms, processes occur simultaneously and continuingly rather than in neat sequentiality, nonetheless certain functions assume primacy during different times. O's component instincts reverse from active to passive emphasis and turn upon herself: thus, she is "purged." An overvalued other becomes the repository for activity and subjectivity; in this manner, she achieves "illumination." Beating becomes proof and assurance of intimacy in object relations. Both the inhibition of instinct that has been at work throughout the text and the sublimation that is the novel's ostensible rationale become O's final tasks of self-mastery as she begins what we are supposed to credit as her Unitive Way.

The Unitive Way and Sublimation

For the mystic, the Unitive Way is, according to Underhill, "'the life in which man's will is united with God'" (413). As she emphasizes, this union is no supine erasure of self: "All that we value in personality—love, action, will—remains unimpaired" (423). O's Unitive Way is the disappearance of a woman's will within a man's, the extinction of self-initiated action and volition with love as the rationale. Furthermore, whereas the mystic on her Unitive Way demonstrates "an access of creative vitality" (429) and activity, O exhibits only stagnation and a quietist stasis. O does seem to demonstrate a newfound spontaneity, freedom, and urge to proselytize after a last struggle with her willfulness, but her seeming vitality is, horrifyingly, not her own, but instead the sign that all self has been extinguished.

O's final two trials before entering upon the Unitive Way are to recruit another woman, Jacqueline, and to bear a definitive mark of her fealty to Sir Stephen. The rigors of her tests affirm both his overvaluation and her worthiness as worshiper, much tried because much loved: "to the very degree that his love and desire for her were increasing, he was becoming more completely, more minutely, and more deliberately exacting with her" (139). Eager to please the master of novices, O undertakes both examinations. The first task, recruiting another woman, is a positive temptation, evoking the sinful, active desires of O before conversion. Seeking active and direct pleasure will lure her to failure, while the second task, bearing new marks, presents the avoidance of pain as its risk. To successfully pass both ordeals, O must repudiate direct pleasure and choose pain.

Upon first being urged to seduce Jacqueline for Sir Stephen, O demurs: the residue of her own active desires, the possible loss of her unique status, and the troubling, if vaguely expressed, implications of involving another woman in Roissy combine in her resistance. Told by Sir Stephen that she herself is the "bait" (122), O pictures Jacqueline in the tableaux of Roissy and concludes, "No, it was impossible, not her, not Jacqueline" (123).

René, still occasionally present to watch Sir Stephen and O, or to hold O down, is to be her accomplice and witness. She feels his evaluating stare at Sir Stephen's house to be that of a panderer assessing the prostitute he's handing over, but also "that he was watching her the way a lion trainer watches the animal he has trained, careful to see that it performs with complete obedience and thus does honor to him" (104). The animal performs impeccably, but its training stands in the way of the kill: it can only stalk on command now. Wondering why she hasn't pursued Jacqueline for herself, O decides that it is precisely because of her apparent freedom, which she "loathed." "But O was henceforth like those wild animals which have been taken captive and either serve as decoys for the hunter or, leaping forward only at the hunter's command, head off the game for him" (103).

A trace of ego remains in O: attracted to Jacqueline, she resents her decoy function and, as an ex-huntress, she is reluctant to have her prey see her as simply a retriever. In addition, she acknowledges in the beautiful, uncaring, and opportunistic Jacqueline the subject status she herself has lost. René's arrogant stare doesn't faze Jacqueline, but it troubles O. "By a curious contradiction, O was disturbed by it, judging an attitude which she considered quite natural and normal for herself, insulting for Jacqueline. Was she taking up cudgels in defense of Jacqueline, or was it merely that she wanted her all to herself?" (129). When Jacqueline moves in with O, and shortly before they have sexual relations, old instincts take over. She does not want to "defend" Jacqueline, except insofar as she herself is defended by her "protectors"; she does want to justify her own status by replicating it. "O, contrary to all expectations, was amazed to find herself obsessed with the burning desire to have Jacqueline at any price, even if attaining her goal meant handing her over to Sir Stephen. . . . And what if she were to be reduced to what I have been reduced to, is that really so terrible?" (134–35). Herself vampirized, O begins to feel an interest in battening on others, in reproducing more of her own kind.[15]

At the end of June, O has been pledged to Sir Stephen for one month; the month of July is dedicated to her second test.[16] Toward the end of the month, Sir Stephen brings O to Anne-Marie (the manager of the women's house, Samois) for a preliminary check-up of sorts so that she can "'wear my mark and my irons'" (141). Although exactly what either emblem means remains unclear to O, and the only fresh indignity is tight corsetting to reduce her waist, the visit is unsettling to her.

Though she needs further reassurance from René and Sir Stephen to steel herself for this new ordeal (it is after this visit that she demands René tell her that he still loves her), the existence of others besides those two begins to fade. Increasingly, the only pseudo object relations of which O will be capable is her merger of identity with Sir Stephen. Repression of ego is almost entire; the sublimation of instinct to "higher" aims is nearly complete. Thus, O, who at the beginning of the month found it "impossible" and "insulting" that Jacqueline might become Roissy's next victim, feels quite differently by month's end.

[15]Angela Carter's comments on Sade's perpetual ingénue, Justine, are to the point here. Although Justine is always a shocked and unwilling victim, she "resolutely eschews the purchasing power of self-sacrifice" (Sadeian Woman 52); her principles never let her stop another woman's suffering, even when given the opportunity, or rebel against the impositions of her oppressor. Thus, she, like O and all masochists who internalize the strictures that bind them, replicates her condition.

[16]The novel's temporal and spatial precision provides a sharp counterpoint to O's increasingly atemporal and placeless perceptions. As the external world fades away, her grasp of place, time, and events regresses until she registers little more than local sensation. (See Silverman for discussion of the novel's use of space and setting.) The passage of time in relation to the body specifically is never raised. What happens to an old, scarred O who must believe herself loved? Does she take the place of Norah, Sir Stephen's maid, and tell herself that she has a special place in his heart because of her offices as she whips girls for a raddled roué?

"You'll never get her to agree to go to Roissy," O said.

"I won't? In that case," René retorted, "we'll force her to."

. . . O, who a month before had been horrified at the idea of seeing this delicate wisp of a body scored by the lash, these narrow loins quartered, the pure mouth screaming, and the fair down on her cheeks streaked with tears, O now repeated to herself René's final words, and was happy. (149)

O departs for her month at Samois with August and Jacqueline's initiation to look forward to. This time is her retreat from even the limited world she now recognizes, a time of introversion in which to renew her vows and vocation. During this period, she recollects, contemplates, and finds ecstasy in the full annihilation of self. O begins by pledging her troth to Sir Stephen as she kneels before him. "'Do you consent, O, to bear the rings and the monogram with which Sir Stephen desires you to be marked, without knowing how they will be placed upon you?' 'I do,' O said" (151). There are no reciprocal vows, of course: O is fully responsible to Sir Stephen and he, by terms of their bond, not at all to her.

Samois's regime can be less carefully regulated than Roissy's because only true believers reside there. Its gynocracy, headed by Anne-Marie, is a grotesquely and cynically enabling commune: these women have power, for they can now beat other women. The idle quiet of Samois's days is broken by one unvarying midafternoon ritual, when lots are drawn to see who will be beater and who beaten. O suspects the point to be less Anne-Marie's "making a spectacle of her power" than establishing "a sense of complicity" (156). In addition, these Total Women are purportedly being taught pride in and intensification of their femininity. "She was bent on proving to every girl who came into her house, and who was fated to live in a totally feminine universe, that her condition as a woman should not be minimized or denigrated by the fact that she was in contact only with other women, but that, on the contrary, it should be heightened and intensified" (157). Once done screaming, the women politely thank their beaters. For most, Samois is an interlude or a refresher charm course before returning to their male owners. Others, like Claire, belong to women who are as "anonymous" and "impersonal" (163) in their pleasures as any man.

The structure of Samois both asserts the "normalcy" of gender hierarchy outside its walls (none of its inmates ever mutters imprecations or contemplates mutiny) and deflects any critique of that hierarchy by the spectacle of women beating other women. The continued deployment of power through gender is thus guaranteed; as in

Ellison's "King of the Bingo Game," in which the "winner" is kicked in the head, the possibility of success in this particular lottery of power is chimerical. In *Story of O* the prize for agreeing to be beaten is that you may get to beat others: not, however, the same people who first beat you.

Samois's beating raffle enacts this pattern literally. O, upon first drawing her lot as beater and beginning her task, "hesitated," "recoiled," and "cringed" (162). Entire power over another is too much to resist, though: "as soon as she had started in again and Yvonne's cries had echoed anew, she had been overwhelmed with a terrible feeling of pleasure, a feeling so intense that she had caught herself laughing in spite of herself, and she had found it almost impossible to restrain herself from striking Yvonne as hard as she could" (162). O's pleasure, laughter, and increased force in striking reflect that of the men who find abuse a fit token of power. In becoming a beater, O affirms the propriety of her own beating, and thus assures the perpetuation of the system that has reified her.[17]

The culmination of O's retreat is having her flesh engraved. Anne-Marie pierces her labia, and Sir Stephen appears for a double-ring ceremony. Rings with both their names inscribed are permanently affixed to O, but her body itself is marked as Sir Stephen's when they brand her buttocks with his initials. No anaesthesia is used for either procedure. Her half-inch deep scars and irons give O "inordinate pride" (167) as proof of the new and everlasting covenant between them. She is fully engaged in the Unitive Way, in ecstatic communication with her god. Or, to phrase her transmogrification more accurately, the vestiges of selfhood have been literally burned out. O retains just enough ego to keep her functional, and no more.

The branding is O's epiphany, the prelude to her rebirth and freedom in the lord. The site of the branding is appropriate (as is Sir Stephen's preference for anal intercourse), because the active instincts, originating in the anal period and attached to it as an erotogenic zone, are cauterized. O seldom looks, knows, acts, or speaks any more; as events occur, she exhibits little curiosity, but remains placidly vegetative. Time, place, and others remain generally indifferent to her as she basks in the full flow of her illumination. As Griffin argues, the text constructs an *"impossibility"*: O, fully "natural," is opposed to culture, language, knowledge, and being itself

---

[17]As Silverman observes, repetition of oppression is no hallmark of change. "That history [of the female subject] will never read otherwise until the female subject alters her relation to discourse—until she succeeds not only in exercising discursive power, but in exercising it differently" (346).

(228). Her regression is to a time earlier than the anal, and is emphatically not in the service of the ego but rather of the ego's destruction. Statically preserved in full, blissful narcissistic merger with Sir Stephen—the merger an infant experiences as the beginning, not the end, of development—O is no longer adult and hardly human.

Like all of Paris, Sir Stephen's entourage goes on vacation in August. O, he, René, Jacqueline, and Jacqueline's fifteen-year-old sister, Natalie, decamp for Cannes. O is no longer self-conscious about what others might think of her stigmata: that, and much else, is a matter of indifference to her beatified self. Jacqueline is "terror-stricken" when she first sees her scarified body, but O "burst out laughing and made as though to kiss her" (178). O's laugh, a dreadful variant of the laugh of the Medusa, proclaims her joy in speaking the body, her fearlessness, her acceptance of herself. It dystopically announces that, as O is, so Jacqueline and others will be. She laughs at those not among the elect, as she does at the young man who wants to "save" her (172) and at Natalie's questions about her love-making with Jacqueline (195); she remains distantly bemused at the uncomprehending "horror," "disgust," and "contempt" others feel at the sight of her mutilated body (199, 203).

Even the once-adored René becomes an object of "pity" (186) as she observes his diffident affair with Jacqueline from her lofty stance. The obdurate Jacqueline, on the other hand, manages to strike a spark of anger when *she* laughs at O (190). Jacqueline scorns the system in which O finds her apotheosis, O herself, and Sir Stephen's omnipotence: O relishes the prospect of Sir Stephen's surreptitiously watching the two women have sexual relations. "O was pleased to think that she would deliver Jacqueline by an act of betrayal, because she had felt insulted at seeing Jacqueline's contempt for her condition as a flogged and branded slave, a condition of which O herself was proud" (180). Nonetheless, when Jacqueline simply leaves, O hardly registers the change: whatever is not sensorially and immediately present to her no longer exists.

O panders as René once did, sure, like him, that the sacrifice is pleasing to her god and that she has taken on some of the attributes of the godhead. Whereas René experiences pleasure both vicariously and directly, however, O can only know gratification indirectly. The training of her eyes upon the male groin at Roissy has taken its effect: her own scopophilic and epistemophilic aims are now only tortuously carried out through the circuitous route of male penis, male eye, and herself or another woman as object. Even when she herself has relations with another woman, it is as proxy for the real thing, Sir Stephen. "Moreover, it seemed to her that the girls she caressed belonged by right to the man to whom she belonged, and that she was only present by proxy. . . . She would have spread her charge's thighs and held them apart with both hands, without the slightest remorse, and in fact with the greatest of pleasure, if it had pleased Sir Stephen to possess her. . . . She was apt at hunting, a naturally trained bird of prey who would beat the game and always bring it back to the hunter" (196). Willing to "beat the game" in whatever manner Sir Stephen thinks necessary, O functions now as a physical and psychological extension of him. Her eyes and hands, so carefully trained, now act only as temporary replacements for his, just as O's own sexual activities serve merely as foreplay to the "real thing," his gratification.

All returns to its source, Sir Stephen. O, like René, is a dim but useful type of his full presence. The young Natalie worships O as O once paid homage to René, willing to risk anything but indifference from her idol. "'Even if you don't want to kiss me, O, keep me with you. Keep me with you always. If you had a dog, you'd keep him and take care of him. And even if you don't want to kiss me but would enjoy beating me, you can beat me. But don't send me away. . . . Teach me, O, please teach me,' she started in again, 'I want to be like you. I'll do anything you tell me. Promise me you'll take me with you'" (184). Natalie's plea for love, like O's own, will be requited: she will be brought to Roissy.[18]

The acme of O's perfect subordination is the novel's closing scene, a party.[19] Natalie, dressed in black, leads a naked, fully depilated O (who wears an owl's mask) by a dog's lead attached to her labial ring. Silent, vision occluded by her mask, O is the gathering's visual and conversational piece. All wonder to whom this inverse Cinderella belongs, but none question her, "as though she were a real owl, deaf to human language, and dumb" (202). No narrative informs her ap-

[18]The role of other women as *exempla* is further emphasized in *Return to the Château*, when Natalie accepts Sir Stephen's authority because O does. "O's submission was so absolute and so constantly immediate that Natalie was quite incapable of conceiving, so great was her admiration for O, that anyone might ever contradict or disagree with Sir Stephen, since O knelt down before him" (22).

[19]A stranger from Roissy, the "Commander," appears to examine O. In a fugue state like that in which she lay on photographs in her apartment while René and Sir Stephen consulted about what to make of her, she dimly hears the two men confer on further modifications. She also realizes that she will be prostituted again (a suggestion that the time in Cannes has been indeed only a vacation) and that she is grossly mistaken in her belief that oppressed individuals can ever mean as much to their oppressors as the dominant do to the subordinate or as much as the dominant mean to one another. (Some of these possibilities are further developed in *Return to the Château*.)

pearance for the spectators (except perhaps that the girl may become such a woman), no masculine causality is suggested by the girl leading the woman, no reading aids help to decipher the signification of this icon.

O's own regression, repression, and sublimation have so refined even her passive instincts that she is dead space: no exhibitionist pleasure mars her smooth surface. Even what Clément sees as the hysteric's insistent articulation through display is no longer possible for O: there is no self except for the vestigial core exclusively attached to Sir Stephen.[20] There is no gaze and no knowing that matters besides his. After a boy brings a young girl in a party frock to touch O and "said he planned to do the same thing to her, she did not seem shocked" (203), and neither is O.

O is indifferent to all around her except Sir Stephen, in whom resides the last of her life. Secure in her constant "imprison[ment] by these all-encompassing eyes" (196), lulled by "her certainty that all he cared about was his own desire" (191), O finds the justification for her own emptiness in his omnipotent plenitude. Eros and Thanatos exist only as authorized by him.

The part of the mystical way O cannot even mime is the dark night of the soul, when, seemingly abandoned by the beloved, the grievously isolated self mourns the absence of divine presence. The envoi to *Story of O* suggests that even in death the will of Sir Stephen is not divided from that of O and that her death, like her life, will be his.[21]

> In a final chapter, which has been suppressed, O returned to Roissy, where she was abandoned by Sir Stephen.
> There exists a second ending to the story of O, according to which O, seeing that Sir Stephen was about to leave her, said she would prefer to die. Sir Stephen gave her his consent. (204)

[20]See "The Guilty One" section of *The Newly Born Woman*, in which Clément analyzes the simultaneous articulation of pain, resistance, and insistence on connection that inform the hysteric's display.

[21]In Jean Rhys's *Wide Sargasso Sea*, Antoinette (one day to be Bertha Mason) also believes that her salvation is in a man. The narrator plays with death linguistically, evoking the repetition Freud yoked to the death instinct and extinction. Antoinette tells Rochester that his word can be made flesh: she will die at his command. For the nonce, he prefers the *petit mort* of orgasm. "'If I could die. Now, when I am happy. Would you do that? You wouldn't have to kill me. Say die and I will die. You don't believe me? Then try, try, say die and watch me die.' 'Die then! Die!' I watched her die many times. In my way, not in hers" (92). Eventually, Bertha dies in her own way, in a death that is perhaps the only thing that belongs to her.

That subdued, chillingly matter-of-fact close is the foreordained end of the beaten and her painful belief that she exists only as reflected in the regard of the beater.[22]

Story of O sells masochism by invoking religious systems, just as a good pimp might huckster raw sex as romance and glamour. Its finely detailed tracing of O's development insists that no shame or guilt need attach to what is, after all, fulfillment of the woman's own desire. Repression itself is ostensibly overturned as O triumphantly enounces her fully conscious knowledge that her lover beats her because he loves her. The Purgative, Illuminative, and Unitive Ways into which I organize the novel's mystical claims mask and legitimize the studied, precise progression of O's destruction as a discrete identity.

Within the beating fantasy's drama of triangulation, the only recognizable power is the force always exercised by the sadist and sometimes used in more roundabout fashion by the masochist. That power, fraught with problems, is nonetheless what all participants acknowledge as activity. The right to see, know, *and* act is the perquisite of the beater alone. The spectator looks, and may even know, but she is ambiguously distanced from the central drama. The beaten, locked in the beater's fatal embrace, nonetheless achieves a secondary access by acting out the vicissitudes that shape her active drives: she thinks that she is a part of things. The reversal of scopophilic, epistemophilic, and aggressive instincts and their turning inward objectifies her to herself. Someone else must become the grammatical and psychological subject and, within the gendered culture in which she hopes to find her place, a male is the appropriate choice. "He looks at me," "He knows me," and even "He beats me" become possible and defensible because "He loves me."

In investing an other with such authority, the beaten must repress the activity that could be seen as her own claim to power and find a culturally validated mode of sublimation that will yield self-approval and the esteem of others in return for her self-abnegation. For Gothic protagonists (and most women in Western culture), heterosexual love and romance is the system that initiates and endorses their doting passivity. Any number of other systems can be drawn upon to support and reinforce romance's ideology: *Story of O* uses religion, but

---

[22]In *Return to the Château*, O contemplates death when she suspects that Sir Stephen is acting through "indifference," not love: "She held herself in abhorrence because she was no longer loved" (26, 28).

education, science, or psychoanalysis, among others, can also serve the same purpose.

Story of O, with its retrospective predication of activity as O's starting point, traces O's shocking transformation to passivity and the role of the beaten. In du Maurier's *Rebecca*, there is a more subtle, insidious shift in which a spectator, disenfranchised through class and sex, looks longingly at the active, enticing world from which she seems so decisively excluded. Her own gradual understanding of the dynamics of power and her adoption of both the beaten's and the beater's positions are the subjects of the next chapter.

5

This Hurts Me More
Than It Does You:
The Beater and *Rebecca*

In *Story of O*, the relations among beater, beaten, and spectator disappear as issues of heterosexual power, normalized, sublimated, and masked by invoking the divine imbalance between creator and created. In Daphne du Maurier's *Rebecca*, other hierarchies—most conspicuously, class—intersect with gender distinctions so that the various structures of oppression obscure and reinforce one another.[1] While *Story of O* claims a mystical sublimation as its rationale, abuse works on a horizontal plane of displacement in *Rebecca*, with romance as its justification. The cruelty of Maximillian de Winter to his un-named bride, enabled by heterosexual and class dominance, is replaced as the text's central issue by the mystery of his relation to his first wife, Rebecca.

Different as both novels at first seem because of their variance in the representation of graphic brutality and in the systems used to cloak a woman's beating, both enact the same beating fantasy and trace the psychological paths of characters who proudly declare that they are beaten because they are loved. In *Rebecca*, as in *Story of O* or the beating fantasy, the explicit and implicit "becauses" that smoothly yoke love and pain emphasize the dynamics of domination. Indeed, *Rebecca*, in drawing on the familiar and thus seemingly innocuous codes of romance, is in many regards a more dangerous text than

---

[1]As Alison Light comments, becoming mistress of Manderley is as crucial as becoming Maxim's wife. "Class and gender differences do not simply speak to each other, they cannot speak *without* each other" (19). Manderley, first seen by her on a postcard when a young girl, affects her much as Pemberley does Elizabeth Bennet in her appraisal of Darcy. For a discussion of this dynamic in texts other than *Rebecca*, see Jan Cohn's *Romance and the Erotics of Property*.

Story of O. Most readers will wince at the vision of an O mutilated and whipped for love; fewer will shudder at a woman tongue-lashed because of her husband's supposed passion for another woman. Instead, like the readers who bought the two series of Gothic romances inspired by *Rebecca*'s popularity (Radway 31), many of us are led by the logic of romance to believe all pain soothed and over once its cause is allied to love. Moreover, the Gothic eroticizes that pain: he beats her because he loves her; her masochistic acceptance is the testament of her own devotion.[2]

As the novel's famous retrospective first lines indicate, however— "Last night I dreamt I went to Manderley again"—the purported erasure of all mystery has not put an end to the need for repetition. The conservative narrator who wants to forego knowledge assures her own subordination: she will never have Manderley or be Rebecca. Subordinated by class, age, and sex, the nameless woman is excruciatingly aware of what she herself regards as her own inferiority and her status as outsider.

Despite her first-person narration, her text is named for another: neither we nor she are sure what her own identity is. *Story of O* graphically portrays the turning inward of instinct and the gradual extinction of identity and activity with O, as beaten, always at center stage. *Rebecca* too enacts the Gothic's beating fantasy, but its emphasis is upon the activity necessary to achieve passive masochistic ends, the need to become a participant in the drama at any cost. For both O and the protagonist of *Rebecca*, the role of spectator is lowest in the beating hierarchy; this is the place where the protagonist of *Rebecca* begins. O gives up her active role as the beater who preys on others to become the beaten: the woman in *Rebecca* finds indifference, not validation, in that role, and moves to a mutation of the beating fantasy in which *she* is in control.

The woman in *Rebecca* shows fragile ego boundaries, as repeatedly seen in her conflation of reality and fantasy, her need to rehearse her actions by miming the responses of others, and her easy merger with others. In the course of the novel, she provisionally adopts each role in the drama of cruelty to achieve identity and agency, although her position of retreat is always that of the passive spectator. Her active drives for looking, knowing, and acting are minimal and highly re-

---

[2]Two of du Maurier's non-Gothic romances, *Frenchman's Creek* and *Jamaica Inn*, exemplify this distinction. In both, the Heathcliff-spawned male characters are aggressive brigands, but the female protagonists are not masochists. Indeed, the couples come together because the women's wills, aggression, and lust for adventure is finally as strong as the men's.

pressed: she is far more able to direct aggressive urges inward and against herself than outward. Indeed, her goal is to have another become subject and take over the job of looking approvingly at her: this she understands as being loved. To be the beaten—to be O—is not her goal, but she is tempted to accept even that if it makes her a participant in the beating drama, the only arena she recognizes as worthwhile. In her final, most powerful role—that of the passive-aggressive dominator of the novel's narrating frame—she can enforce recognition of the only identity she wants to claim, "Mrs. de Winter."

In the novel's measured minuet of cruelty, the woman moves from the passive spectator's role, through that of the beaten, inadequate mate whose passive exhibitionism brings only negative evaluation, to that of the active spectator who seeks vicarious knowledge and power. Finally, through identification with the dominant, active powers of both Maxim and Rebecca, she believes that she has won acknowledgment as a subject and as the positive object of Maxim's regard. Her victory is evidenced by her appropriation of the role of beater from a husband now infantilized in his turn. In *Rebecca*, then, the beating fantasy is never worked through but instead is compulsively repeated. Through this repetition, the protagonist gains just enough knowledge to reverse and replicate the very structures of sex and class that have oppressed her.

Wallflower at the Beating Orgy: The Passive Spectator

At the novel's chronological beginning, set in Monte Carlo, the protagonist is a paid companion acutely aware of the link between her lack of social rank and her bystander's role. She feels herself to be a "parlour-maid," "a juggler's assistant," "a little scrubby schoolboy," "a maid" (19, 13, 35, 46). While on the one hand she painfully assumes that no one would want to look at her because of her plainness, dress, and status, on the other, she bitterly resents her exclusion and finely registers the way in which even servants seem to denigrate her, to sense her "position as inferior and subservient" (10), to inflict numerous perceived slights upon her (10, 48).

The term I use to describe the narrator's position, "passive spectator," suggests both exhibitionism and its active counterpart, scopophilia. For the passive spectator, however, the external reality of her social status (no one wants to look at her) and the internal repression of even indirect activity (she will not or cannot risk making others look at her) deny the roundabout recognition that exhibitionism can give. Furthermore, both epistemophilic and aggressive drives remain dissociated from her viewing: she looks at things, but, unlike Jane Eyre, doesn't incorporate the knowledge gained or act upon it. In *Rebecca*, the passive spectator minimally registers the beater/beaten pattern as a function of unjust class authority (as opposed to an assumed just system) unallied to heterosexual practice. Indeed, courtship seems to promise an escape from subordination. While willing and eager to achieve vicarious subject status and so finally be an insider, she does not begin by assuming sado-masochistic relations: she only learns these in the course of the novel. Needless to say, her wholesale repression of the active drives leads to an intense sexualization of any form of forbidden knowledge.

Within the no-woman's-land of the paid companion who passively views all, the narrator has no coevals and is in effect asexual, a commodity not fit for the marriage market. She is not a person but "a thing called a companion" that costs ninety pounds a year. Maxim comments: "'I did not know one could buy companionship . . . , it sounds a primitive idea. Rather like the eastern slave market'" (24). What at first seems to be ironic recognition is, like Rochester's references to Oriental harems and pashas, more problematically recast as simple acceptance of a good bargain when he reminds himself "'to congratulate Mrs. Van Hopper. You're cheap at ninety pounds a year'" (25).

The woman's nebulous status of gentility is allied to her liminal position as passive spectator: in both instances, she is a bystander and others are "real." Her reference to the reality of her poverty (and loneliness) is a "lack of tact" (25) quickly superseded by the importance of *his* plight. Himself secure, Maxim sees her as puzzlingly "choosing" to be a companion (just as other women choose to be governesses), a job in which you "'either have to give in . . . or stay as you are and be broken'" (27). The only future she sees is in the army of "young women in reduced circumstances" (27) who seek out cheap boarding-houses and support in old age, but of course there is another economy, the marital, which promises women don't have to "give in" or "be broken."

The protagonist loathes her current wifely tasks of social facilitator, household manager, and nurturer, not because of their nature, but because of their unnatural context: they are performed for another woman in a paid economy. Trapped, she sees her only possible role as participant in Mrs. Van Hopper's circle as that of surrogate beaten, a contemporary sin-eater for the wealthy. As sensitive register, she responds to the slights Van Hopper is too gross to feel, "left to writhe in her stead, feeling like a child that had been smacked," "dragged with her as I was into humiliation," ordered to do penance for others' sins, and "a whipping boy again, blushing for her" (16, 15, 18, 40). No martyred exaltation meliorates her loathsome surrogate role, nor does she find her existence mirrored in the regard of another.

Despite the woman's keen sense of subordination, however, she does not question the economy in which she exists, nor does she question the hierarchy that confines her. Instead, there is a splitting into just and unjust authority, a strategy that deflects inquiry from systemic issues of class and gender and so preserves the status quo. Van Hopper, as an older, single American woman, embodies power improperly held, behavior that is active, aggressive, and masculine in the protagonist's accounting. "Her curiosity was a disease, almost a mania. At first I had been shocked, wretchedly embarrassed; I would feel like a whipping boy who must bear his master's pains when I watched people laugh behind her back" (12). Van Hopper remains an unnatural grotesque even in retrospect, filled with inappropriate appetite for physical, visual, and epistemophilic pleasures. The protagonist suspects and dislikes her, as she does every other woman in the novel.[3]

From his first appearance, when he moves her from a hard chair to a comfortable sofa, Maxim promises the restoration of rightful authority wielded by a male of rank and wealth, authority that will draw her within the charmed circle of social existence. He epitomizes power hallowed by tradition to the young woman, as her association of him with the all-seeing portrait of a Gentleman Unknown indicates: "He would stare down at us in our new world from a long distant past— . . . a past of whispers in the dark, of shimmering rapier blades, of silent, exquisite courtesy. . . . The eyes followed one from the dusky frame" (15). Maxim proves his right to that rapier (if not his "exquisite courtesy") by using it on Van Hopper. Although she remains generally impermeable to the "swift lash," "sting," and "shaft" (16, 18, 18) of his remarks, the protagonist gets to view what is for her a highly unusual and satisfying spectacle: a man of power acting as *her* surrogate against a woman she loathes.

Maxim's scrutiny cedes her worth while devaluing Van Hopper's. The curiosity that is a "disease" (12) in Van Hopper and repressed in herself seems his by right to the protagonist: "It seemed natural for him to question me" (27). She makes over her "secret property" to

---

[3]The sole, limited exceptions are Beatrice and Clarice, who are nonthreatening and the only ones she sees as willing to know her as "Mrs. de Winter."

him, saying that her "family history was mine no longer, I shared it with a man I did not know. For some reason I felt impelled to speak, because his eyes followed me in sympathy like the Gentleman Unknown" (24). In her eyes, Maxim's proper, sanctified role is to be "standing on the steps of a gaunt cathedral, his cloak flung back, while a beggar at his feet scrambled for gold coins" (38). His gold— the property of the aggressive anal period—is hers only through his charity.

Because of Maxim's interest, the woman is temporarily no longer a bystander. She cherishes the golden days that she thinks will be the capital of future memory. The narrating self suggests no overt erotic interest by her younger self, although she and we respond automatically to the stimuli of the Cinderella story and of the beating fantasy, in which the beating of a hated other hints that perhaps oneself is loved. Curiosity and interpretation are almost entirely repressed through the brief period of their courtship, which she does not recognize as such.

During their time at Monte Carlo, then, the woman is seemingly content with Maxim's largesse, because she believes the coins he scatters to be true currency, the manner of their distribution the proof of gentilesse. She has no sense of any entitlement or of the rules of exchange O knows so well. After Maxim suggests that she use his first name, she is "cocksure, jubilant," and thinks the privilege "like a plume in the hat, though from the very first he had called me by mine" (41). There can be no reciprocity here, only gratitude for favors, an economy not of grudgingly paid salaries but of noblesse oblige.

The woman has no desire to lift the veil behind which power stands (or, to use Lacan's image, to lift the father's robe and view the phallus). She needs to believe that there are no secrets, no strange negotiations in the transmission of natural power through class or sex. Her unusually frequent and vivid fantasies throughout the novel point to the extent and intensity of suppressed knowledge, of course, but also to the depth of her need to believe that all is well with the pecking order.

Not surprisingly, knowledge itself becomes sexualized. For example, the sentimental fantasy of discrepancy that she constructs around a dressmaker, embellished by details of deserving poverty, crumbles when the dressmaker offers her a kickback or a free frock, "her tone intimate and unpleasant" (26). The woman's response is disproportionate to the event, as her sexualized language indicates: "Somehow, I don't know why, I had been aware of that sick, unhealthy feeling I had experienced as a child when turning the pages of a forbidden book" (26). Knowledge, particularly of a "forbidden" kind, is not for her, and she, like the child who sees or imagines the primal scene of parental sexuality, perceives the entanglement of sexuality and power as aggression. The tension between the dressmaker's suggestion that they are alike in their knowledge of how things really work and the protagonist's wish to believe in how she is *told* they work elicits a symptomatic nausea at the nearness of the "sick," "unhealthy," and "unpleasant."

Her need to believe Maxim's power particularly uncorrupted is strengthened by his apparent willingness to use it on her behalf. She willingly accepts his scolding attention to her as well, "like a little scrubby schoolboy with a passion for a sixth-form prefect" (35). Whether Maxim is admonishing her to stop biting her nails, to eat her food, or to not wear black satin, the woman meekly accepts the "degrading" rebukes as proof of her own inadequacy, of his benevolent ascendancy, and of her finally "belonging."[4] When, on their first drive, Maxim broodingly contemplates a precipice, "so lost in the labyrinth of his own unquiet thoughts that I did not exist" (29), she is frightened. Nonetheless, she assumes her terror is "misjudged" (29) as soon as he turns his attention to her again.

In a still more crucial scene, her willingness to accept and internalize Maxim's punitive judgments highlights the woman's justification of his aggression. She asks Maxim why he has chosen her for his "charity," and comments that "'I know nothing more about you than I did the first day we met'" (37). Maxim breaks his long silence with a bitter, accusatory diatribe that invokes the mysterious sorrows driving him from place to place, and he implicitly forbids any further inquiry. Like Bluebeard, Victor Frankenstein on the eve of his wedding, Rochester, Hoffman's Nathaneal in "The Sandman," and a host of other demon lovers, the proof of her love is her unquestioning, silent enshrinement of his great pain. "'You have spared me all those wanderings. Damn your puritanical little tight-lipped speech to me. Damn your idea of my kindness and my charity. I ask you to come with me because I want you and your company, and if you don't believe me you can leave the car now and find your own way home. Go on, open the door, and get out'" (39).

The savage speech seems to demand adult equality and to repudiate the repression and imbalance of "charity" and puritanism. Both

---

[4]Like her visions of herself as scapegoat, the protagonist's repeated use of the word "degrading" points to her fear that her only place as a participant can be as the beaten (e.g., 37, 48, 232, 252). In *Reading the Romantic Heroine*, Leslie W. Rabine stresses the significance of such terms (174–75), as does Stoller (*Observing the Erotic* 31).

tone and final option offer only limitation, however: to accept the relationship on his terms or to leave. Like a child with no recourse to adult logic or power, she can only say "'I want to go home'" (39) and weep, "plumbing the depths of humiliation" (40). As her tears fall "untouched," she is distanced from her own grief, which becomes transposed from her response at his hurting her to that of her failing him.

Later, remembering the "fever of first love," the narrator attempts to use a rueful, wry tone of recollection to separate the narrating self from the experiencing self, the unique, defended woman she is now from the typical, beaten girl, "so easily bruised, so swiftly wounded" (34), she once was. Even in retrospect, however, the source of her emotion is strangely bifurcated, identifiable as her response both to wounds inflicted on her and to her guilt about having secret knowledge that she believes is necessarily an aggression against others. Thus, the passage moves from description of her being hurt (and now invulnerable to such pain) through the fearsome possibility of aggression against others (she lies to Van Hopper shortly afterward) to self-chastisement. The active instincts that might be used against others are firmly redirected against the self. "They are not brave, the days when we are twenty-one. . . . To-day, wrapped in the complacent armour of approaching middle age, the infinitesimal pricks of day by day brush one but lightly and are soon forgotten, but then—how a careless word would linger, becoming a fiery stigma, and how a look, a glance over a shoulder, branded themselves as things eternal. . . . The adult mind can lie with untroubled conscience and a gay composure, but in those days even a small deception scoured the tongue, lashing one against the stake itself" (34). The careful now/then distinctions that the retrospective opening also emphasize are suspect in their insistence that the present is so clearly distinguishable from the past. Furthermore, here and elsewhere in the novel the identification of grammatical and psychological subject, part of the boundary between self and other, collapses.

All of her tentative essays to gain knowledge are heavily defended against by guilt and shame. Her curiosity thus usually limits itself to her vivid fantasies, the donnée of the passive spectator, but even these are extensively censored.[5] When she takes up a book borrowed from Maxim and it falls open at the poem, "The Hound of Heaven,"

[5]Erikson's comments in *Childhood and Society* capture the woman's shame as negative object. "But this, I think, is essentially rage turned against the self. He who is ashamed would like . . . to destroy the eyes of the world. Instead he must wish for his own invisibility" (252–53).

she says, "I felt rather like someone peering through the keyhole of a locked door, and a little furtively I laid the book aside" (32). Like many another Gothic heroine, she clandestinely uses the voyeur's role to seek knowledge forbidden by others and even by herself, but she quickly denies her own scopophilia and the knowledge she might have gained.

In this instance, the poem's first line suggests Maxim to her as the pursued, but the divine "Him" of the line also suggests Maxim as the hunter of the labyrinthine ways of her own mind. The inscription, "Max—from Rebecca" (33), precipitates the vision of a birthday breakfast, notes exchanged, and an extraordinary woman who can casually call Maximillian de Winter "Max" while "I had to call him Maxim" (43). The image of Rebecca, "so certain, so assured" (43), and so unlike herself, rivets her, as does Jane Eyre's mental picture of Blanche Ingram before meeting her. Her comparative reverie is broken off by a second comparison that serves as a reprimand: the unsavory picture of another voyeur, Van Hopper, "her small pig's eyes" (33) comparing their dinner choices and peering at the diners around them.

The idyll of marital bliss between two people who belong to each other is as diametrically opposed to her own marriage proposal as the dream vision of Rebecca is to her own ignoble reality as passive spectator. Maxim's proposal, like that of Sir Stephen to O or Rochester to Jane, sets up the terms of domination at the apex of romance and is worth considering at length: in accepting the man, the woman also accepts his masterful ways and her own subordination. Although it is she who seeks Maxim out, the initiative becomes his when he asks her to go to Manderley as he suavely files his nails over his breakfast.

"Do you mean you want a secretary or something?"

"No, I'm asking you to marry me, you little fool. . . ."

"I don't belong to your sort of world. . . ."

"You are almost as ignorant as Mrs. Van Hopper, and just as unintelligent. What do you know of Manderley? I'm the person to judge that, whether you would belong there or not. . . . "

"I'm sorry. I rather thought you loved me. A fine blow to my conceit."

"I do love you," I said. "I love you dreadfully. . . ."

"It's a pity you have to grow up."

I was ashamed already, and angry with him for laughing. . . .

"So that's settled, isn't it?" he said, going on with his toast and marmalade; "instead of being companion to Mrs. Van Hopper you become mine, and your duties will be almost exactly the same. . . ."

Was he still laughing at me, was it all a joke? He looked up, and saw the anxiety on my face. "I'm being rather a brute to you, aren't I?" he said; "this isn't your idea of a proposal. We ought to be in a conservatory. . . . You would feel then you were getting your money's worth. Poor darling, what a shame. Never mind, I'll take you to Venice for our honeymoon and we'll hold hands in the gondola." (51–53)

An unintelligent, ignorant fool by Maxim's account, she is ashamed, anxious, angry (the most hopeful adjective of the lot), and fears that it is all a joke. Nonetheless, she, like the protagonist of "The Yellow Wallpaper," recognizes his laughter as well within normal range, for "one expects that in marriage" ("Yellow Wallpaper" 9). Like Rochester's teasing of Jane Eyre, Maxim's banter is a thin veneer over aggression. His promise to his "poor darling" that they will "hold hands" in Venice are taunting dismissals of lovers' expectations rather than reassurances. The balance between them is reinscribed, not reweighed. She will get her "money's worth": since she has none, she will get nothing.

Nonetheless, the woman is overjoyed at the move from anonymity to pseudonymity and she trusts to the merger of identity signaled by "Mrs. de Winter."

> My mind ran riot then, figures came before me and picture after picture—and all the while he ate his tangerine, giving me a piece now and then, and watching me. . . . Mrs. de Winter. I would be Mrs. de Winter. I considered my name, and the signature on cheques, to tradesmen, and in letters asking people to dinner. I heard myself talking. . . . People, always a throng of people. "Oh, but she's simply charming, you must meet her—" This about me, a whisper on the fringe of a crowd, and I would turn away, pretending I had not heard.
>
> Going down to the lodge with a basket on my arm, grapes and peaches for the old lady who was sick. Her hands stretched out to me, "The Lord bless you, Madam, for being so good," and my saying "Just send up to the house for anything you want." Mrs. de Winter. I would be Mrs. de Winter. (53–54)

As Mrs. de Winter, she will *be* somebody, although all imagination can show her is a hall of mirrors with her reflection as Lady of the Manor in each. She will exist because she will be reflected back from the eyes of others, the exhibitionist object of positive scopophilic inquiry. Like Freud's newly married patient who dreams that she will finally see the opera, she imagines the new visual vistas in which knowledge, activity, and sexuality will be joined. Before even chanting "Mrs. de Winter," she repeats "He wanted to show me Manderley" (53). Maxim will give her money, as he now gives her bits of orange, and she, subordinated to him, will nonetheless be able to dominate others who, unlike the dressmaker, will love her for her charity. Maxim, of course, will be the subject whose adoring gaze lifts her above others and relieves her from the burden of self-scrutiny. Her continuation of the fantasy is broken by Maxim telling her that the rest of the tangerine is sour, but the "sharp, bitter taste" remains in her mouth (54).

Her fantasies of being a participant, not an onlooker, remain sweet for only a slightly longer time. She accepts the terms of their bargain, never recognizing it as such. She consents to Maxim's need, expressed earlier, to forget everything before Rebecca's death; she is an accomplice in resisting knowledge and the lure of bottled memories when "'the devil in one, like a furtive Peeping Tom, tries to draw the cork. . . . Those days are finished. They are blotted out'" (39). Max's fiat notwithstanding, it is the genie of the past he calls on to banish the possibility of an elaborate wedding by reminding her that she is a duplicate and his experiences the reality: "'You forget,' he said, 'I had that sort of wedding before'" (55).

Looking for a way to categorize her uneasiness at finally becoming a participant, to explain "that pain in the pit of my stomach when I was so happy" (56), she imagines the response of others with renewed vigor. "Romantic, that was the word I had tried to remember coming up in the lift. Yes, of course. Romantic. That was what people would say" (56). She notes that nothing has been said about love: "No time. The tangerine was very bitter. No, he had not said anything about being in love. Just that we would be married. Short and definite, very original. Original proposals were much better. More genuine. Not like other people. Not like younger men. . . . Not like him the first time, asking Rebecca. . . . I must not think of that. . . . I must never think about that, never, never, never" (56). From his silence, she must weave romance; from his brusqueness, originality. Her staccato language points to the strain of believing that it is she, not some ghostly revenant, who is seen. To avoid thinking and to temporarily seal up her own genie, she commits her first overtly aggressive act: she carefully cuts the inscription page from the volume of poetry, burns it in the basket, and reports that she "felt better, much better" (57).

Restored to an equilibrium based on projection and denial, the woman relishes their honeymoon tour. "I thought only of how I loved him, seeing Venice with his eyes, echoing his words, asking no questions of the past and future, content with the little glory of the living present" (68). She hopefully believes that she is at one with Maxim in voice, sight, and the stilling of time itself. This fragile, fault-ridden foundation is all she has to counter the massive weight of Manderley and its past.

She remains the passive spectator of her new world and her own life at Manderley, however; she cannot see it with Maxim's eyes. Her naive expectations that her new title will denote a recognizable identity and automatic power over property and people are promptly deflated, despite her attempts to tutor herself in the perquisites of possession. "I had to teach myself that all this was mine now, mine as much as his . . . , all of this was mine now because I was married to Maxim" (69). What she finds at Manderley, though, is a fixed reality to which she can adjust herself—if she ever figures out the rules—but which will never change for her. Manderley is emphatically not "mine as much as his," nor is it hers so much as it is still Rebecca's. The attempt to define an "I" through the "my" of possession is futile: someone else possesses Manderley. "It came to me that I was not the first one to lounge there in possession of the chair, someone had been before me. . . . Another one had poured the coffee from that same silver coffee pot, had placed the cup to her lips, had bent down to the dog, even as I was doing" (77). As Maxim's wife, she is again a surrogate, as entirely erased as she was while Van Hopper's companion. Indeed, her situation has worsened. She could resent Van Hopper's treatment of her at Monte Carlo; at Manderley all she can do is separate the house and the past from Maxim so that he is not responsible for her poor showing in this well-furnished monument for the dead.

She sits at Rebecca's desk, eats from menus Rebecca chose, wears her coat, smells her scent, and knows herself as an intruder. Maxim has no time for her and, when addressed by that coveted title, "Mrs. de Winter," she can only blurt out "'Mrs. de Winter has been dead for over a year'" (84). She cannot be mistress to Maxim or to Manderley. And, like O fearing that her pain just serves to strengthen the bond between René and Sir Stephen, the protagonist's presence only resurrects the alliance between Maxim and Rebecca.

Her hope that the power of property will give her authority is yoked to her belief that others will now defer to her. She receives no recognition from Maxim as the beloved subordinate; neither does her putative authority yield acknowledgment of her identity by fawning retainers. No one at Manderley seems to want a Lady Bountiful, nor do they gratefully welcome her into their homes, as she imagines (64). Instead, even when she smiles and waves at the woman in the gatekeeper's lodge, "she stared at me blankly. I don't think she knew who I was" (126).

Not knowing herself "who I was," she can only hope that rank will shift the burden of recognition and the responsibility for ignorance to the perceiver, as the tonal ambiguity of the sentence suggests. ("Don't you know who that *was*?") Still an outsider, she believes that others do have identities, do belong in the magical world of Manderley, where "object relations" mean both what one owns and who one knows. She herself knows no one, not even her own husband, and no one wants to know her. Anonymous and excluded, she remains the passive spectator of her own marriage.

Visual Hierarchy and Negative Exhibitionism

During her time at Manderley, the woman, like an outrée Goldilocks, tries several different positions. She finds herself the negative object of scopophilic inquiry, she actively tries to become a positive object by exhibiting herself, and she falls back into her most secure— or at least most familiar—position, that of passive spectator, after each shift in position. The woman has unwittingly entered a Gothic mansion and the beating fantasy, but a beating fantasy whose borders remain cruelly obvious, unblurred by romance's soft focus. She is the object of sadistic inquiry unallied to the ideology of love; even the intensity of Sir Stephen's aloof gaze offers more validation than Maxim's tepid indifference. She suffers the pain of the masochist, then, with no admixture of pleasure. Finally center stage, no audience applauds her loving sacrifice or even murmurs "poor thing." Instead, like the paranoiac, she finds herself under perennial surveillance, and she is always found wanting by her own reckoning and that of others.[6] Her exhibitionism, like her spectating, is controlled by others while she, genuinely suffering, nonetheless resists even indirectly calling attention to—or gaining a mutated self-esteem from—her pain. O, the diva of the Gothic scream, insists upon a grotesque affirmation of her display; the protagonist of *Rebecca*, also subject to what Silverman calls the "scopic regime" ("Histoire d'O" 333), is less than a scullery maid in the same opera, unwilling or unable to admit

---

[6]The protagonist's belief that she is under surveillance functions much like that of the governess in Henry James's *The Turn of the Screw*: better horror than no one wanting to look. Stoller comments on this linkage between paranoia and the beating fantasy in his case history of Belle: "Such harassment certainly proves that you are not unnoticed—abandoned" (*Sexual Excitement* 66).

that she had a part in the casting. The novel represents a gaze as carefully calibrated as that of *O* but the protagonist, unable to exercise scopophilia or epistemophilia herself, can only be its abject object.

Her life at Manderley is no triumphant new beginning but a nightmarish recapitulation of Monte Carlo: whether she is Mrs. de Winter or a paid companion, no one looks up to her; everyone has the right to look at her; she herself has no rights. The faithful retainers she was so ready to patronize are lined up at her entry, "a sea of faces, openmouthed and curious, gazing at me as though they were the watching crowd about the block, and I the victim with my hands behind my back" (66). In part as a displacement of Maxim's response, she also sees disapproving stares from her new peer group, servants, and townspeople. And, of course, she internalizes what she thinks she sees and is filled with guilt and shame. Still, she does not question the economy of beater and beaten, dominator and subordinate, scrutinizer and exhibit, into which she wants so desperately to enter; it is only their negative manifestations that disturb her. Instead, the production of her fantasies accelerates, and increasingly detailed scenarios dramatize her sense of ongoing critical surveillance and her own inability to stare in turn.

Maxim's treatment of her is the most damaging. He seldom looks at her: when Beatrice, his sister, asks her if he likes her hair and wonders why he hasn't bought her new clothes, she can only say "'I don't know'" and "'I don't think he notices what I wear at all'" (99). When he does turn his gaze upon her, it is seldom approving. She doesn't share even his literally visual knowledge of Manderley, and yet she feels herself culpable for her ignorance. When she insists on seeing the beach house that she doesn't know was Rebecca's, Maxim is silent and punitive. His "face was hard, with no expression. He went straight into the hall and on to the library without looking at me" (116). After breaking a china cupid, she tries to tell Maxim how she feels and to draw some response from him, but she only captures his attention when she suggests that he married her because her dullness wouldn't provoke gossip. She, "scared," then pleads "'Don't look at me like that'" (144).

This is her plea to all around her. The utter indifference to her existence that she thought to escape by marriage begins to seems preferable to what she perceives as contemptuous stares at herself as central exhibit in a spectacle of shame. She is sure that their social group, beginning with Maxim's sister and mother, see only a ghastly shadow of what Rebecca was. "I caught her eye upon me now and again, puzzled, reflective, as though she was saying to herself, 'What on earth does Maxim see in her?' " (101). Still, she admires both wom-en, who, "not like" her, exhibit the activity allowable only for women to the manor born, women for whom class modifies sex. "They had guts, the women of her race. They were not like me. . . . I was badly bred" (219). She assumes that others share this insight: "now and again I would find their eyes upon me, doubtful, rather bewildered. I could picture them saying to one another as they drove away, 'My dear, what a dull girl' " (121). They, like Beatrice, eye her to see if she is pregnant and at least managing some form of breeding. Worse, they are audience and jury for the marriage: the reality of life as Mrs. de Winter has banished the wish for crowds gathered around. "They only came to call at Manderley because they were curious and prying. They liked to criticise my looks, my manners, my figure, they liked to watch how Maxim and I behaved to each other" (125). She knows "people are looking me up and down" (131), but Maxim, so unself-consciously used to having others look up at him, cannot fathom her anxiety lest others look down at her.

An outsider, she moves below even the servants in her visual hier-archy. When a maid "looked almost shocked" (135) at her underwear, the woman promptly sends off for new and frets that her knickers are now "a topic of conversation in the servants' hall" (136). She is sure that Frith and Robert watch her and laugh at her (80, 116), positive that workmen know her suggestions are worthless (204), and often determines her behavior according to what the servants will say or do (e.g., 150). Only after imagining townspeople talking about the te-merity of a "chit" like her (220), "'some pick-up in the South of France, a nursery gov. or something'" (221), can she force herself to reappear at a costume ball. Even the fear that her marriage has failed can only be expressed through her dismay at what the servants may see or speculate: she shudders at "the thought of the servants talking about it [Maxim's empty bed] in the kitchen" (231). If her fear about her marriage *is* true, she "believed I could bear it if I were certain that nobody knew of this but our own two selves" (232).

Most fearsome of all the servants is the housekeeper, Mrs. Dan-vers. The protagonist notices on first meeting her "a look surely of derision, of definite contempt. She knew that I would never with-stand her, and that I feared her too" (73). She is right on both counts, and Danvers's "adoration" of Rebecca, whom she knew since a child, her self-appointed role as the guardian of memory, and her function-ing as mistress of Manderley make her a formidable emblem of disci-pline and punishment. Danvers's gaze is steady, unflinching, and disapproving. The protagonist's immediate yielding of Manderley's supervision does not placate Danvers but instead confirms her own unworthiness to wield power. Trying to hide from visitors, "'I felt suddenly that she knew, that she must have watched me" (91). When outside, she repeatedly suspects that Danvers may be watching her from the house's windows. When inside, particularly in the west wing, Rebecca's preserve, Danvers's scrutiny remains trained on the protagonist, who can read nothing in the other woman's gaze. "I could not be certain whether it was anger I read in her eyes or curiosity, for her face became a mask directly she saw me. Although she said nothing I felt guilty and ashamed, as though I had been caught trespassing, and I felt the tell-tale colour come up into my face" (90). Unlike O, contentedly sequestered within confined spaces, or Jane Eyre, always looking outward and longing for wider horizons, the protagonist gives an almost agoraphobic sense of herself overwhelmed in space, the isolated object in others' field of vision. Her own credence in Rebecca's omnipresent ability to occupy space and to belong where she only trespasses is reinforced by Danvers's belief that Rebecca still watches all at Manderley (172, 242, 234) and that Danvers is her agent.

The ignorance the woman clings to makes her the inevitable victim of harsh scopophilic inquiry: she will see or understand nothing, while still distantly recognizing that her blindness will elicit aggression. "It would be easy for Mrs. Danvers to . . . look down upon me from behind the drawn curtains. I should not know. Even if I turned in my chair and looked up to the windows I would not see her. I remembered a game I had played as a child. . . . You knew, with a fatal terrifying certainty, that before long . . . this bold player would pounce upon you from behind, unheralded, unseen, with a scream of triumph. I felt as tense and expectant as I did then. I was playing 'Old Witch' with Mrs. Danvers" (176). The game Americans call "Red Light," British children "Grandmother's Step," and the protagonist the more threatening "Old Witch" is a carefully orchestrated mime of blindness and insight. In the version the protagonist and Danvers play, there are no turns; she cannot move from her role of being the one with always shielded vision, nor can she stop the game's repetition by remembering what happened last time. By refusing to exercise her own scopophilia and epistemophilia—by refusing to see what's going on—the protagonist is always the loser.

Like Norah, Sir Stephen's housekeeper in *Story of O*, or the ghostly majordomo of Wharton's "Mr. Jones," Danvers functions through the delegated authority of her master: her right to look and to know at Manderley is greater than the protagonist's. Because *Rebecca*'s evocation of the past as sole reality is so persistent and powerful, Danvers, the guardian of that past, is usually identified as a surrogate of Rebecca. In addition to that charged erotic link, however, she also functions as Maxim's surrogate. She is the warden of his estate, carefully enforcing his regulations while he remains unseen as agent.

The excruciating scene after a servant is accused of breaking a china cupid, a piece that the woman broke and guiltily hid, foregrounds her part as negative exhibit as well as Danvers's and Maxim's affinity in their aggression.[7] Maxim's counsel before meeting with the servants is "'Don't be a little idiot. Anyone would think you were afraid of them.'" Her response—"'I am afraid'" (141)—is interrupted by the servants' entry. What follows is a bizarre and cruel belittlement of the woman, intensified when she is alone with Maxim and Danvers. "They all looked at me. It was like being a child again. . . . She did not seem to be surprised that I was the culprit. She looked at me with her white skull's face and her dark eyes. I felt she had known it was me all along. . . . It was like being a prisoner, giving evidence. . . . 'It looks as though Mrs. de Winter thought you would put her in prison, doesn't it, Mrs. Danvers?' said Maxim" (141). Maxim's hostile jocularity toward the protagonist shifts to a strange familiarity with Danvers as they together discuss his wife in her presence. She, a criminal child, is silent before the grown-ups. Danvers suggests that, "'if such a thing should happen again,'" she be told directly.

> "Naturally," said Maxim impatiently. . . . "I was just going to tell her when you came into the room."
> "Perhaps Mrs. de Winter was not aware of the value of the ornament?" said Mrs. Danvers, turning her eyes upon me.
> "Yes," I said wretchedly. "Yes, I was afraid it was valuable. That's why I swept it up so carefully."
> "And hid them at the back of the drawer where no one would find them, eh?" said Maxim, with a laugh, and a shrug of the shoulder. "Is not that the sort of thing the between-maid is supposed to do, Mrs. Danvers?"

[7]The accusation of Robert the footman is an instance of class and gender working together to render the object of scopophilic inquiry powerless. Maxim is surprised that the accused Robert, "nearly in tears," should be "so sensitive" (140), and he advises Frith, "'Tell Robert to dry his tears'" (141). The maids, subordinated by sex *and* class, are automatic scapegoats. Nonetheless, Robert's unsought position as victim feminizes him, as do his tears and sensitivity.

"The between-maid at Manderley would never be allowed to touch the valuable things in the morning-room, sir," said Mrs. Danvers.

"No, I can't see you letting her," said Maxim. (141–42)

During this brief and humiliating conference, Danvers and Maxim speak as near equals, while the protagonist is the infantilized third, somewhere below the obedient tweenie who knows her place. Maxim earlier grouses that servants' rows are "'your job, sweetheart'" (140). The protagonist, unlike Danvers, does not fulfill her job description by protecting the master, a perception Danvers later reinforces. Danvers, refusing an order, taunts the protagonist for her lack of even delegated power. "'Go to my room,' she mimicked, 'go to my room. The mistress of the house thinks I had better go to my room'" (245).

The woman accepts the perceived negative scrutiny of Maxim, peers, and servants. Her own aggression is turned against herself: she becomes still more acutely self-conscious, and blames herself for anything and everything. During this stage, then, scopophilic, sadistic, and epistemophilic drives are at their most passive: she refuses to see literally what is happening, is hurt by others and herself, and remains willfully blind to knowledge. She believes that to be a servant is dreadful and degrading and, not surprisingly, this is what she sees as her own role. The similes through which she situates herself are consistently those of inferiority. She likens herself to "a guilty child," "a little untrained maid," "a prisoner," "a schoolboy," "a barmaid," a dog (139, 62, 141, 148, 161, 206). Maxim and she are in accord on her status, each reinforcing the other's appraisal as her stock sinks lower. "'Just like a between-maid, as I said, and not the mistress of a house.' 'I am like a between-maid,' I said slowly, 'I know I am, in lots of ways. That's why I have so much in common with Clarice. We are on the same sort of footing. And that's why she likes me'" (143). During this painful conversation, Maxim, unlike her maid Clarice, shows no signs of liking her. He adds to her burden of self-blame, by claiming that of course others view her as subordinate if she responds "'like someone after a new job, which you did the only time we returned a call together'" (143).

Throughout this period of negative scrutiny, the woman buttresses the drama of triangulation by critiquing herself and not the structure in which she finds herself. Danvers, like the inhabitants of Roissy and Samois, watches coolly while Maxim administers punishment. The protagonist never questions his right: all she desires is to be embraced by him as the beloved rather than the punished, to achieve vicarious power and identity through him. She energetically erases any disturbances to her particular version of family romance. Maxim is her companion, "'my father and my brother and my son. All those things'" (145). He is her world and, like an abused child, she believes she can find validation only within that withering relationship. She attempts to make a meal of the crumbs tossed her way while still praising the generosity of the Gentleman Unknown—unknown to her, certainly. The sting of his epithets—"little fool" and "little idiot" (51, 141)—is supposed to be soothed by a string of dimunitives: "poor darling," "my good child," "my sweet child," "poor lamb" (53, 115, 142, 145).

Both the positive and negative epithets, like positive and negative scrutiny, of course reflect the same imbalance between Maxim and the woman, one she wants to deny at all costs. Just as she corrected for the absent passion of his "original" proposal, so she eagerly transforms details of their twin-bed marriage (231), scanty communication, and rare accord into an idyll of companionate stability, kissing his hands as she begs for the boon of mutual deception.

> "Just like old people, married for years and years. Of course we are happy. . . . You know our marriage is a success, a wonderful success?"
> "If you say so, then it's all right," he said.
> "No, but you think it too, don't you, darling? It's not just me? We are happy, aren't we? Terribly happy?"
> He did not answer. (146)

Her repeated inquiries from him as sole arbiter are met by silence. She dreads his indifference more even than his disapproval, for she then disappears as a personality.

Not surprisingly, she lapses back with something like relief into her now almost-comfortable old position of passive spectator. If social peers and even the servants are active participants at Manderley in a way she cannot be, then it is surely more secure to be safely on the sidelines and recoup rather than run the gauntlet of all those disapproving stares at her failure. Like the little boy Anna Freud treats who avoids repetition by imposing his own restrictions, she adopts "the role of the spectator, who does nothing and so cannot have his performance compared with that of someone else" (*The Ego* 94). If the foiling of erotic expectations is painful, it is still less so than Maxim's gentlemanly regard. His eyes "looked through me and beyond me, cold, expressionless, to some place of pain and torture I could not enter, to some private, inward hell I could not share" (225), to some place where Rebecca stands.

As a spectator again, as passive and unexpectant as when she first met Maxim, the woman simply watches the pageant of life at Manderley. What happens in it remains unconnected to herself, and, while she notes the material abundance and emotional plenty that others seem to possess, she expresses no longing to have or to be what she is not. Desire itself is curtailed as a way of protecting the self, and the woman dreamily insulates herself from the reality of the world around her. She sits before the daily feast at Manderley, described retrospectively in loving detail but, as she comments, "we ate so little" (8).[8] A plaintive waif, she asks for nothing partly because she cannot believe it will be granted her. She also refrains from inquiry, however, because she does not want to draw negative attention to herself and because to gain even trivial knowledge is to press a claim of power. There is very little she can share in the wintry landscape that surrounds Maxim, few ways she can capture his gaze without also calling down his censure.

Looking for Answers: Vision and Knowledge

The protagonist in *Rebecca* doesn't know small things—where rooms are, how lunch is announced, if they will have guests—and she will not ask: "I don't know" (e.g., 94) remains her talisman for much of the book.[9] She consistently thinks "it better not to ask" if "Maxim hasn't said" (107, 104). She has an inkling that there is something strange about her and Maxim's unspoken pact when she wonders what Beatrice would say at knowing "that I questioned him never" (96), but this is a slight shadow of curiosity, easily evaded. By being silently still, she hopes to remain safely invisible to others, free

[8]The description of food, like that of Rebecca's clothes or of objects at Manderley, is startlingly vivid and detailed (8) and exemplifies the protagonist's self-prohibition against expressing desire and her austere regulation of needs. The young Jane Eyre, in contrast, knows very clearly that she wants something else when facing a bowl of burnt porridge (and she savors Miss Temple's seed cake when it is offered). The protagonist of *Rebecca* cannot find pleasure even in a groaning board. The issue, then, is not simply one of deprivation versus gorging in any sensory realm, but atrophy of the ability to take pleasure in reasonable appetite. In the physical realm as well as the psychological, the protagonist's inhibition makes her apathetic before or an accomplice to the spectacle of others' deprivation. "There was enough food there to keep a starving family for a week. . . . The waste used to worry me sometimes" (8).

[9]Milton Lester, in "Analysis of an Unconscious Beating Fantasy," reports on a woman who also finds herself "unable to understand" routine problems at home and work. He links her inability, like that of *Rebecca's* protagonist, to her insistent need "to deny her knowledge of the facts of sex" (28).

from the risks attendant upon active scopophilia, epistemophilia, and the sadism with which they are associated. Like Walker's Celie, who feels nauseous when angry and eventually starts "to feel nothing at all" (*Color Purple* 47), the woman is ill at ease with the excitement that usually accompanies her pursuit of the forbidden and so tries to suppress curiosity. And suppressing any urge to know is a small price to pay for the bliss of knowing little and being responsible for nothing.

The woman's passive strategies have failed abysmally, unrewarded by even perfunctory positive response. Relatively secure as a passive spectator, she remains an outsider in that role, mute, ignorant, and null. Being "Mrs. de Winter" provides no ready-made identity when the other to whom she wants to assign subjectivity, Maxim, can barely muster a glimmer of recognition. Willy-nilly, she must forge her own identity through what means she has available. The often self-administered reproaches of "humiliating" and "degrading" that she uses so repeatedly to characterize her passivity give way to the as insistent and more ambivalent "forbidden," which offers the guilt and titillation of active transgression.

In learning a limited, aim-inhibited activity, the protagonist continues to function hierarchically. Appropriating the behavior of two other women, she practices her new skills upon those of lower class. In both instances, she repudiates or depreciates these others after she has conned her lesson: Danvers serves as her exemplar for scopophilic inquiry, while the dead Rebecca is a stellar role model for positive exhibitionism and, later, the aggression allied to sadism. Through her own scopophilia and exhibitionism, she survives and constructs a feminine, upper-class identity that reinscribes traditional gender and class oppositions.

As we witness *Rebecca*'s permutations of the beater/beaten/spectator triangle, its all-inclusive power and self-maintenance is striking. The complex play of the component instincts in the Gothic's beating drama is claustrophobic. The response to this suffocating enclosure by class and sex is that which the Gothic heroine so often elicits: the urge to yell "Get out!" There is no "out" for the protagonist of *Rebecca* and her sisters, though: glimpses of freedom quickly become terrifying possibilities of alienation and are forgotten, as in the single episode of any duration in *Rebecca*, when Maxim is away. Significantly, the day-dream the woman spins while sitting at lunch is of an accident, his death, and the funeral. Her transparent wish sets the stage for a short interlude of alternate possibilities. "I was aware of a sense of freedom, as though I had no responsibilities at all. It was rather like a Saturday when one was a child" (150). She herself recognizes the cause of her release. "It must be because Maxim had gone to London. I was rather shocked at myself. I could not understand it at all. I had not wanted him to go. And now this lightness of heart, this spring in my step, this childish feeling that I wanted to run across the lawn, and roll down the bank" (150). A hitherto unrecognized threat has been removed and being child-like is no longer the occasion for being smacked. Her spontaneity, physical abandon, and sense of release are poignant indications of the severity of her usual restraints.[10] For a brief while, she is self-determined, alone without being lonely. "If Maxim had been there I should not be lying as I was now. . . . I should have been watching him, watching his eyes, his expression. Wondering if he liked it, if he was bored. Wondering what he was thinking. Now I could relax. . . . How lovely it was to be alone again. No, I did not mean that. It was disloyal, wicked. It was not what I meant. Maxim was my life and my world" (151). Her brief expansion is curtailed by her self-reprimand, the repudiation of her own knowledge, and the restoration of another as "my life and my world."

Her moment of freedom, the bit of clandestine information she gains (Favell's visit during Maxim's absence), and Maxim's refusal to acknowledge her for her passivity, even while insisting upon it, together encourage a limited resistant activity. Thus fortified, she shifts her scopophilic activity and tries to be the object of positive scrutiny, the cynosure of all eyes rather than the ignominious wretch. She practices exhibitionism, as it were, with Rebecca as model and competitor and those of lower class as rehearsal audience.

She begins to foment a quiet, limited revolution that aims not at overturning the state of patriarchy but at gaining what small enfranchisement its ideology promises. "I wished he would not always treat me as a child. . . . Was it always going to be like this? He away ahead of me, with his own moods that I did not share, his secret troubles that I did not know? Would we never be together, he a man and I a woman, standing shoulder to shoulder, hand in hand, with no gulf between us? I did not want to be a child. I wanted to be his wife, his mother. I wanted to be old" (196). Although the woman here focuses on age as the key to inequity and her goal is limited, her discontent indicates a shift. Earlier attempts at initiative, such as going to the beach house, exploring the west wing, or having Maxim listen to her,

---

[10]Her sense of physical abandon (on which she doesn't act) is like Catherine Morland's who, as a girl "loved nothing so well in the world as rolling down the green slope at the back of the house" (Austen 2). Catherine, like Jane Eyre, however, never loses her appetite for pleasure.

are rebuffed.[11] She accepts this. What she cannot accept, and what brings forth what anger she can muster, is that Maxim refuses to tell her that he hurts her because he loves her—or that he loves her at all.[12] Maxim's mute refusal of even those sops of esteem with which she might rest content pushes her toward new claims for attention as it stresses that she must know more.

One of her first investigations uses Frank—one of the few characters to whom she'll reveal a form of appetite, curiosity—as its object. She is fascinated by the recovery of Rebecca's body and its condition. "Suddenly I did not want to ask him any more. I felt sick at myself, sick and disgusted. I was like a curious sight-seer standing on the fringe of a crowd after someone had been knocked down. I felt like a poor person in a tenement building, when someone has died, asking if I might see the body. I hated myself. My questions had been degrading, shameful. Frank Crawley must despise me" (130). The vehemence of her self-accusation and the abhorrence she assumes her own on-looker must experience mark both the intensity of her epistemophilic drive and the extent of her repression. Ashamed and guilty for wanting to know what went on between Maxim and that dead body, she readily agrees with Frank that they must forget the past and chides herself for seeking knowledge rather than patiently waiting to have it bestowed on her as a boon.

In another revelatory scene with Maxim, she mimes Rebecca receiving a call from her cousin Jack. As she tells herself her story, her animated, changing face catches Maxim's attention. He is struck by her "different expression," "'a flash of knowledge in your eyes. Not the right sort of knowledge'" (201). Through copying Rebecca's self-possessed exhibitionism, she musters enough confidence to pursue epistemophilic ends by asking questions.

> I felt very curious, rather excited. "What do you mean, Maxim? What isn't the right sort of knowledge . . . ?"

[11]The way in which Maxim reasserts himself as subject and center by claiming the primacy of *his* emotions and encouraging guilty doubt is exemplified by his anger and silence after the beach scene. He refuses to explain what she has done wrong—except disobey his injunction. When he does speak, it is a petulant barrage hours later: "'And if you had my memories you would not want to go there either, or talk about it, or even think about it. There. You can digest that if you like, and I hope it satisfies you'" (115). What the woman learns from this, of course, is that active initiation gains her no new ground. "I was Jasper again. I was back where I had been before" (117–18).

[12]Maxim even doubts her dogged devotion, implying that his unhappiness or anger is her fault. His cold anger—which he will not acknowledge as such—is what she most fears. "'I've made you unhappy. It's the same as making you angry'" (117).

He considered me a moment, his eyebrows raised, whistling softly. "Listen, my sweet. When you were a little girl, were you ever forbidden to read certain books, and did your father put those books under lock and key?"

"Yes," I said.

"Well, then. A husband is not so very different from a father after all. There is a certain type of knowledge I prefer you not to have. It's better kept under lock and key. So that's that. And now eat up your peaches, and don't ask me any more questions, or I shall put you in the corner."

"I wish you would not treat me as if I was six," I said.

"How do you want to be treated?"

"Like other men treat their wives."

"Knock you about, do you mean?"

. . . . "You're playing with me all the time, just as if I was a silly little girl."

. . . . "Get on with your peach and don't talk with your mouth full."

(202)

She captures Maxim's attention by imitating Rebecca, but his catch-22 response is that this is the "wrong" way to do it. Maxim is the rightful knower and custodian of the intimate arcana best kept from daughters and wives by "lock and key." She, like Freud's Dora or the protagonist of "The Yellow Wallpaper," can only be a secret sharer, at best, of forbidden knowledge.

His jovial infantilization ("'eat up your peaches,'" "'I shall put you in the corner,'" "'don't talk with your mouth full'"), like his mocking injunctions to silence ("'don't ask me,'" "'don't talk'") emphasize that they will get on best if she accepts his indulgent superiority. Her lot, after all, is not so bad comparatively: other husbands literally "knock about" their wives. It is a "good idea," he subsequently suggests (202), that she costume as Alice in Wonderland, and perhaps an equally good one that she know him as the master in the looking-glass world of Manderley. Like Alice, she is free to wander about (within certain limits), but she must remember that she does not belong here. Why things happen as they do and what events mean are beyond her ken: they mean what Maxim wants them to mean. Unlike Alice, however, she is apparently larger than no one around her.

All knowledge she seeks seems to be forbidden. Maxim makes no effort to teach her anything explicit: he remains silent about the routines of life at Manderley, the people she meets, and his own past. The most basic question, about their happiness, is fobbed off (146). She imagines Rebecca and Maxim together, mutually adoring newlyweds whose shared knowledge is a critique and explanation of her own marriage. Testing her fantasy, she asks Maxim, "'What are you thinking about?'" but the answer—"'Nothing very much'" (148) shuts her out from the garden of marital bliss she envisions. Her scenario establishes that the problem is not that Maxim lacks the capacity to love, but that he does not love her—a painful conclusion, but one easier to adopt than one that might overthrow the libidinal economy he represents. He has wronged her, but there is nothing inherently wrong with him or his position as lord of the manor. Still, that limited sense of rightful grievance gives her some distance from which to evaluate. "My voice was steady and cool. . . . Not like my mind, bitter and resentful" (148). From her resentment, she generates the energy to try to be seen.

She begins her exhibitionist training with the only group to which she feels she belongs, a motley collection allied to her in their own passivity, low status, and lower expectations—the estate manager Frank, her maid Clarice, the village idiot Ben, and the dog Jasper. They nonetheless approve of her in a way no one else at Manderley does. She recognizes an accord with Frank immediately: both are "dull" (126), reserved, protect Maxim, and minister to "the common wants of the herd" (192) at teas. She repeatedly calls Frank her "ally" (94, 130, 133), but she is comfortable with him and the others in her small troop only because he acknowledges her superiority. Just as Maxim was once "Mr. de Winter" to her while he used her first name, so she remains "Mrs. de Winter" throughout the novel to the man she calls "Frank." Maxim's diminutives for her are matched by the equally condescending epithets with which she seems to accompany every use of Frank's name: "poor Frank," "dear Frank" (e.g., 132, 133, 204, 209). The terms are often paired, and he seems able to be "dear" Frank only because he is "poor" Frank. She feels whole before someone she understands as partial—a man subordinated to another man. Within this frame, she is able to be mildly flirtatious and dismissive at the same time. Her laughter, like Maxim's, is not that of an equal but that of an adult indulgently marking the unknowing antics of a child. "I burst into laughter. 'Oh, Frank, dear, I do love you,' I said, and he turned rather pink, a little shocked I think at my impulsive words, and a little hurt too that I was laughing at him" (195).

Frank has the invisibility of the subordinated: he exists for the woman only insofar as he relates to and serves her. In this way, she mirrors Maxim's model of domination. At one point, when the protagonist says to Danvers that Maxim has "suffered enough," Danvers's angry and justified retort startles her. "'What do I care for his

suffering?' she said, 'he's never cared about mine'" (242).[13] The exquisitely sensitive protagonist is equally callous. "Poor Frank. Dear
Frank. I never asked, I never knew, how much he hated the last fancy
dress ball ever given at Manderley" (224).

The same problematic dynamic holds true for Clarice, her personal
maid. On the one hand, there is an affinity, as she tells Maxim. "'I
have so much in common with Clarice'" (143). On the other hand,
"she was the only person in the house who stood in awe of me" (135).
Thus, she can be "little" Clarice, "my ally and favoured friend" (196,
210) during preparations for the ball, and it is she who weeps at the
protagonist's humiliation (while she herself remains silent), just as
the protagonist acts out Maxim's pain (215).

Ben the village idiot and Jasper the dog are the allies that most
painfully comment on her self-esteem. Ben shares "idiot" status with
the woman and, like her, he "'never said nothing,'" "'done nothing,'" "'never seen 'un'" (113, 154, 338), hoping that his ignorance
will keep him safe. Like her, he acts as if he wonders "'when you're
going to whip him'" (338). He gives her a rare compliment when he
looks at her and sees "'angel's eyes'" (154), and he has the equally
rare distinction of being one of the few to whom she can speak
"firmly" (153). Jasper the dog is the only one she can freely call a
"fool" (153), and yet he still loves her, in the same way that she still
loves Maxim when he does the same. Indeed, she refers several times
to the relation between herself and Jasper as a relative analogy to that
between her and Maxim. "'That's what I do to Jasper,' I thought. 'I'm
being like Jasper now, leaning against him. He pats me now and
again, when he remembers, and I'm pleased, I get closer to him for a
moment. He likes me in the way I like Jasper'" (101).

From this strangely constituted audience she gains a modicum of
self-regard, some conviction that she does exist in the eyes of others.
She seeks to make this reflection real, to solidify it, and finds the
ghostly figure of Rebecca to be the best mentor in exhibitionism. She
can resent Rebecca's power in a way she cannot Maxim's because she
is more able to feel emotion such as anger consciously and to feel
warranted in wanting what another woman has though she can question no upper-class man's right.

Her first visit to Rebecca's room gives her the necessary setting and
part of the plot she needs to construct a self: it elicits acquisitive desire

---

[13]In a similar scene in Rhys's *Wide Sargasso Sea*, a servant weeps as the plantation
burns. "'You cry for her—when she ever cry for you? Tell me that'" (44). In both
instances, the subordinated refuse to do the emotional work of the dominant; they
also, however, run the troubling risk of replicating the dominant's mode of response.

and resentment in a way nothing else at Manderley has. "It seemed to me that the position of the room would make it the one I wanted"; its lush appointments "were things I would have loved and almost worshipped had they been mine" (164, 166). Not for Rebecca the hastily refitted guest room or the spare wardrobe: the kept-up room remains a mausoleum of the visual, insisting upon Rebecca's continued presence. O in her sumptuous red room is gradually dispossessed of her body, desire, and will; *Rebecca*'s protagonist learns about her own in another woman's room. For the protagonist, even experiencing envy is an advance in activity, because it means that she wants something. So too her exploration of Rebecca's room, bed, dressing table, and wardrobe lets her "play at" being Rebecca. She sits at the table and touches the brushes, feels the dressing gown casually laid over a chair, picks up Rebecca's slippers, traces her monogram on her nightdress case, examines her extravagantly filled wardrobe. Most strikingly, she removes the unlaundered gown from its case and holds it to her face, noting Rebecca's scent, as though some imprint might linger that will help her to understand. The passage presents an entire sensory immersion through which she begins to know what it means to be Rebecca, how Rebecca succeeded at capturing the attention of everyone, why Maxim "'would do as she told him'" (169), as Danvers reports. The protagonist is fascinated and repulsed by—but attentive to—the lesson.

When she mimes Rebecca at the dinner table Maxim tells her that she looks "'like a little criminal'" (201). Indeed, by emulating Rebecca's independence and secrecy, she flouts the laws that govern their marriage. The role of Rebecca enables her to answer back to Maxim and, briefly at least, refuse him the ready access to her mind he expects as his right when he asks her to share what she is thinking. "'Why should I? You never tell me what you are thinking about'" (201). By beginning to have her own secrets, she tentatively separates herself from Maxim and suggests the possibility of a discrete identity. Self-knowledge is not her material of choice for constructing that identity: the lives of the mysterious, powerful Maxim and Rebecca are.

Her urge for knowledge, identified as the knowledge of sexual relations and of the power that regulates those relations, becomes explicit and sustained as her exhibitionism increases. Danvers serves as her model for voyeurism, albeit one whose embrace of vicarious satisfaction is inadequate to the protagonist's own gender and class ambitions. Danvers is a servant, and one who still serves and loves another woman, Rebecca. She is depreciated on both counts, op-

posed to the protagonist's wishful views of herself as femininely heterosexual, upper class, and an insider. It is precisely these factors that
make Danvers safe to deal with, just as death limits even the formidable Rebecca. In both instances, however, it is only after her tentative
forays fail that she turns to these depreciated female mentors.

The links between knowledge, power, and sexuality are emphasized in all the woman's eroticized descriptions of gaining information. Her search for knowledge—and the repression of that urge—is
overdetermined and becomes prurient, as seen in her intense desire
to peek one more time and her revulsion against the same qualities in
Danvers. The mystery of the present at Manderley becomes displaced, localized, and sexually charged by becoming the enigma sur-
rounding what happened in the past between Maxim and Rebecca.
Maxim's god-like decree refusing her this knowledge while offering
no substitute inevitably leads to her violating his command. Breaking
such injunctions against knowledge also involves the risk (and temptation) of getting caught, of being punished, of finding out something
you really didn't want to know, as the woman fears when she opens
the closet in Rebecca's cottage. "I had the odd, uneasy feeling that I
might come upon something unawares, that I had no wish to see.
Something that might harm me, that might be horrible" (113). And
yet, of course, she opens the door, just as she later opens the door of
Rebecca's room. The trade-off between possible consequences and
power gained is finally worthwhile.

She is at first highly ambivalent about and defends against her
surreptitious hoarding of information, and yet her curiosity prompts
further discovery. "Somewhere, at the back of my mind, there was a
frightened furtive seed of curiosity that grew slowly and stealthily, for
all my denial of it, and I knew all the doubt and the anxiety of the
child who has been told, 'these things are not discussed, they are
forbidden'" (120). Like a child, she suspects that these "furtive,"
"forbidden" things that evoke such anxiety and curiosity are the secret of adult power and, like a child, the first hypothesis she generates that seems to cover the evidence is sexual. During social calls,
she remains alert for "little snatches of information to add to my
secret store. . . . And, if Maxim was not with me, the hearing of them
would be a furtive, rather painful pleasure, guilty knowledge learnt
in the dark" (121–22). After dropping Rebecca's name for the first
time, she sits, a "flush on my face," and "listened to her [hostess]
greedily, like an eavesdropper at a shuttered window" (123). Her
"flush" does not seem to be a blush: it bespeaks sexual excitement
more than it does shame. So too, asking Frank about Rebecca, she
feels a compulsion to violate her "proper" silence: "A strange sort of

excitement was upon me. I had to go on with my questions" (128). When she decides to enter Rebecca's room during Maxim's absence, it is not surprising that she reports, "My heart was beating in a queer excited way" (163). Doing anything to satisfy herself, to claim the knowledge others seem to possess, is active assertion for her, the identification of self as subject and not object. To look knowingly is a move toward consciousness and away from the amnesia of the passive spectator and, in addition, it reverses the gaze so often trained on her as negative exhibit.

Danvers, who "simply adored Rebecca" (100), is a treasure house of information and the epitome of a scopophilic inquirer; it is to Danvers that she must look. Danvers's own subordination is rationalized and exalted by her love for Rebecca. Sole confidante, she identifies wholeheartedly with Rebecca, accepts Rebecca's interests as her own, and rests content with vicarious satisfaction. She is, in short, a perfectly stereotypical wife. She holds forth Rebecca as a vision of "rightful" feminine power, and briefly seems to offer a pact of complicity by inviting the other woman to become an acolyte at Rebecca's shrine. Her insistence that the other woman should see Rebecca's rooms, like the dressmaker's bribe, made "me vaguely uncomfortable, I knew not why" (90, 91). "Her insistence struck a chord in my memory, reminding me of a visit to a friend's house, as a child, when the daughter of the house, older than I, took my arm and whispered in my ear. 'I know where there is a book, locked in a cupboard, in my mother's bedroom. Shall we go and look at it?' I remembered her white, excited face, and her small, beady eyes, and the way she kept pinching my arm" (91). At this early stage, the protagonist can refuse the knowledge hidden away in others' bedrooms, sure that she'll find it in her own soon enough. Apprehensive and unsure as she is, she nonetheless still believes that being a good girl will pay off, while entering more fully into the power of servants will not.

A connoisseur of the vicarious, Danvers knows that the protagonist will eventually come around and sneak just a taste of the forbidden. Danvers knows her motive for the second trip to Rebecca's bedroom, despite the protagonist's explanations: "'You wanted to see the room'" (167). "I shall never forget the expression on her face. Triumphant, gloating, excited in a strange unhealthy way. I felt very frightened. . . . She smiled, and her manner . . . became startlingly familiar, fawning even" (167). Danvers's "startlingly familiar" behavior is like recognizing like. She is the doyenne of voyeurism initiating a neophyte. Rebecca watches over all, and they will together watch the specter of Rebecca.

As Danvers runs the protagonist through her seminar in voyeurism, she uncannily has her repeat the same actions she has performed alone. Done under Danvers's tutelage, their meaning shifts: secret sin becomes complicity, private indulgence metamorphoses into shared vice, initiative shifts to supervision. "'You've been touching it [Rebecca's unwashed nightgown], haven't you? . . . Would you like to touch it again? . . . Put it up against you . . . ' She forced the slippers over my hands. . . . 'You've seen her brushes, haven't you? . . . You opened it [the wardrobe], didn't you? . . . Put it against your face. It's soft, isn't it? You can feel it, can't you? The scent is still fresh, isn't it? . . . These are her underclothes, in this drawer' " (168–71). Of course, Danvers's voice too becomes a part of her sensory initiation, but its alternating series of imperatives and interrogatives emphasize that all the protagonist would find here is a new servitude. She wants a partner to take over the role of subject, but it is not Danvers. Access to power mediated by another subordinate is less than the woman desires: she wants to be Rebecca, not Danvers, a participant and not an onlooker. The female/female bond Danvers maintains is, for the protagonist, an inadequate reflection of the "real" thing she accepts entirely—power used by a man heterosexually.

The woman seeks to use all her lessons on self-display by insisting that there be another costume ball at Manderley. She is prepared to do what Rebecca once did, ready and eager to exhibit herself in her secret costume, and prepared finally to be recognized as the mistress of Manderley. The secret itself gives her power and makes others look at her differently. "It was new, this sudden unexpected sensation of being important, of having Giles, and Beatrice, and Frank and Maxim all looking at me and talking about my dress" (209). Suddenly, she is worth the speculation of others. The actual event promises a glorious butterfly unfurling in the costume copied from a family portrait that Danvers suggests. Placed within the frame of familial authority, drawing upon Rebecca's precedent, she is startled by her transformation as she gazes into a mirror. "I did not recognise the face that stared at me in the glass. . . . I watched this self that was not me at all and then smiled; a new, slow smile" (212).

Her knowing, seductive smile heralds a new era of poised and proud display. Announced by a drum roll, she poses at the top of the stairs for the applause of the group assembled below.

"What the hell do you think you are doing?" he said. His eyes blazed in anger. His face was still ashen white. . . .
There was a long silence. We went on staring at each other. Nobody moved in the hall. . . . "What is it?" I said. "What have I done?"

If only they would not stare at me like that. . . .
"Go and change," he said. . . .
"What are you standing there for?" he said, his voice harsh and queer.
"Didn't you hear what I said?" (213–14)

Her would-be apotheosis has become her utter failure, and her triumphant exhibitionism only the means to return her to the position of the beaten. By wearing a costume Rebecca has already worn, she is again the surrogate or whipping girl.

Her struggle, as she sees it, is not with Maxim but with Rebecca and Rebecca, dead and forever fair, has won. "Rebecca would always be the same. And she and I could not fight. She was too strong for me" (234).[14] Vanquished, she retreats again to be the passive, increasingly unwilling, viewer of Maxim and Rebecca. Failing as the object of positive regard, she nonetheless cannot lose the knowledge or the glimmer of power she has gained, and she moves to consolidate and increase both by further investigating the possibilities of the active spectator—the scopophiliac who, although not a direct participant, sees all and knows all. In addition, through the figure of Rebecca, she learns that one must do something with the power gained through looking and knowing: dominate others.

Becoming the Beater

Rebecca's power, with its seemingly full access to sadistic aggression, scopophilia, and epistemophilia, disheartens the protagonist

[14]Edward Joseph, among others, notes that the first stage of the beating fantasy ("My father is beating a child") gratifies "sadistic impulses toward the rival as well as voyeuristic drives" (54). Insofar as the beating is identified as love, usually suppressed rage is directed toward the beaten, not the beater; the viewer wants both to supplant and blame her rival for the original scene. *Rebecca* is a stellar instance of this maneuver, as the protagonist exercises the active instincts to look, know, and aggress against an enemy safe by dint of sex and death. In Weldon's *The Life and Loves of a She-Devil*, Ruth vents the same invigorating spleen against her rival: "I sing in praise of hate, and all its attendant energy" (3). Ruth literally *becomes* her rival as her revenge, a metamorphosis the protagonist of Rebecca undergoes less consciously. In a number of other stories the rivals used to displace rage are also dead: e.g., Wharton's "Pomegranate Seed," Mary E. Wilkins Freeman's "Luella Miller," and May Sinclair's "The Nature of the Evidence."
In another fascinating subgroup, however, the women form alliances or find that their loyalties lie with their ghostly rivals. The protagonist of Sinclair's "The Flaw in the Crystal" heals her rival and yields her lover to one who was mad rather than dead. Mrs. Vanderbridge, in Ellen Glasgow's "The Past," renounces battle, as does the protagonist of *Rebecca*, but for a different reason: "'After all, you are dead and I am living, and I cannot fight you that way. . . .' She had won, not by resisting, but by accepting; not by violence, but by gentleness; not by grasping, but by renouncing" (145–46). Lucy, in Elizabeth von Armin's *Vera*, knows that the dead Vera is her only possible ally and source of knowledge. "The only person who could have told her anything, who could have explained, who *knew*, was Vera" (189).

entirely: she cannot compete. Rebecca is arrayed in the panoply of power, while the protagonist can barely cover herself with her tatters of identity the day after the ball. Maxim has abandoned her, the marriage has seemingly failed, and each of her viewing strategies has led to further loss of status, more humiliation. Rebecca has always been a formidable adversary, but the androgynous figure that Danvers places before her during their third meeting in her room is wholly invincible. She is seductive and sexually aggressive, beautiful and muscular, looking "'like . . . a boy with a face like a Botticelli angel'" (278). Wholly masculine in her use of power, passive in nothing save her death (and she stage-manages that), Rebecca adopts the pose of exhibitionist only to manipulate knowingly the response she gets. She sees all and, most appallingly for a "lady," will not only brook no punishment but will wreak her own will. "'He knows she sees him, he knows she comes by night and watches him. And she doesn't come kindly, not she, not my lady. She was never one to stand mute and still and be wronged. . . . She had all the courage and the spirit of a boy, had my Mrs. de Winter. She ought to have been a boy, I often told her that'" (242–43). Danvers celebrates the miracle of Rebecca, never to be silenced or oppressed. Her only possible frame of reference is masculine: Rebecca "ought to have been a boy."

The protagonist listens, fascinated and repelled by the narrative of a woman who wields power as she herself never has, who consciously knows and sees all. Rebecca uses her beauty and her awareness of the forbidden to speak to the elders at eleven. "'She had all the knowledge then of a grown person, she'd enter into conversation with men and women as clever and full of tricks as someone of eighteen'" (243). In recounting the early presages of glory, Danvers' hagiography persistently points to Rebecca's active and open cruelty, the masculine sadism that the protagonist so carefully represses. Rebecca fights physically, "'crack[ing] her whip over [Favell's] head'" (243), and, with "'the strength of a little lion'" masters a horse she is told is too "hot" for her with all the harsh aplomb of D. H. Lawrence's Gerald Crich. "'I can see her now . . . , slashing at him, drawing blood, digging the spurs into his side, and when she got off his back he was trembling all over, full of froth and blood. "That will teach him, won't it, Danny?" she said, and walked off to wash her hands as cool as you please. And that's how she went at life, when she grew up. I saw her. I was with her. She cared for nothing and for no one'" (244). Rebecca's coolness and indifference are signs of her special election to Danvers and she, like all worshipful subordinates, believes herself the sole exception to Rebecca's uncaring ways. She bows before her icon of Rebecca victrix, herself valorized because Rebecca never turned on her. And she applauds Rebecca's bloody lessons, her savage vanquishing of all would-be enemies, just as she lauds Rebecca's narcissistic self-sufficiency and her irresistible appeal. "'Of course he was jealous. So was I. So was everyone who knew her. She didn't care. She only laughed. "I shall live as I please, Danny," she told me, "and the whole world won't stop me." A man had only to look at her once and be mad about her'" (245).

The protagonist cannot withstand the vision. No one is "mad about her"; they just get mad at her. She can't live "as she pleases," for she has no idea what that might be. She does "care," because it is only through others that she hopes to discover herself. Rebecca remains indisputable mistress of Manderley and of Maxim and, in contemplating her omnipotence, she herself fades away, as Danvers tells her. "'You'll never get the better of her. . . . She's the real Mrs. de Winter, not you. It's you that's the shadow and the ghost'" (245–46). Rebecca, like the Bertha Mason of *Wide Sargasso Sea* who sees Jane Eyre as the house ghost, is no longer the specter but the reality.

The woman is at an impasse, then, for each viewing strategy has failed her: neither the roles of active or passive spectator, positive or negative object of scrutiny, have won her the limited self-definition she wants: to know that she exists because reflected in Maxim's eyes and in the eyes of her own subordinates. The impasse is one of both psychology and plot, for neither have anywhere else to go. As she prepares to throw herself from a window at Danvers' prompting, she is stopped by the sound of rockets announcing a ship run ashore.

The sound breaks her resolve, but it also breaks the frozen tableau she has been watching in which Maxim and Rebecca, god-like and self-sufficient, pose for her. It's not just Rebecca's body that has been dredged up in "Je Reviens," her aptly named boat, but also Maxim's past. What she learns as active spectator is the greatest of all secrets: Maxim murdered Rebecca by shooting her.

Her ambiguous numbness gives way to eager complicity and then elation as Rebecca is resketched before her eyes.[15] Rebecca is now the detested object, beaten and killed because unloved. "'You thought I loved Rebecca?' he said. 'You thought I killed her, loving her? I hated

[15]As Alison Light points out, Rebecca's control of her own sexuality threatens the social and the sexual order. She must somehow be contained, and indicting her as "abnormal" in the book's last section does so. "What is at stake in her murder is the continuance of male authority and of masculinity itself, as it is defined through ownership and the power of hierarchy" (15). The film version further obscures the issues at stake by making her death an accident and so lessening Maxim's culpability.

her, I tell you, our marriage was a farce from the very first. She was vicious, damnable, rotten through and through. We never loved each other, never had one moment of happiness together. Rebecca was incapable of love, of tenderness, of decency. She was not even normal'" (271). The woman watches avidly as hagiography is stripped away to reveal a hag. In addition, the new figure of Rebecca helps her to construct a coherent self by uniting her fragmented, episodic fantasies of degradation in a master plot that controls character and narration. Like Anna Freud's "patient" who progresses from daydreams of degradation to writing a story, the woman improves her lot by "abandoning the single scenes and renouncing the pleasure derived from the various single climaxes" ("Relation" 101).

Picturing Maxim killing another woman, she is safe and sure for the first time. "My heart was light like a feather floating in the air. He had never loved Rebecca" (274). "None of the things that he had told me mattered to me at all. I clung to one thing only, and repeated it to myself, over and over again. Maxim did not love Rebecca. He had never loved her, never, never. They had never known one moment's happiness together. Maxim was talking, and I listened to him, but his words meant nothing to me. I did not really care" (273). Her vehement repetition of "never" and her new mantra, chanted "over and over again," is like the earlier chain of "nevers" that emphasized her futile injunction against thinking about Maxim and Rebecca. In both instances, the move to never-never land suggests that some reality is being left behind.

Through the knowledge that Maxim has murdered Rebecca, she gains power. Most important, the beating scenario changes radically. First, the motivation shifts from "Max beat (murdered) Rebecca because he loved her" to "Max beat (murdered) Rebecca because he hated her"—a highly gratifying, if problematic, outcome, as Freud emphasizes. Second, and equally gratifying, is the role reversal her new information unveils: Rebecca beat Maxim, as it were.

Animated by Danvers's and Maxim's revelations, the drama the protagonist represses is that of this new, ghastly Rebecca set in motion—and beating Maxim. In Maxim's "explanation" of his action, he is, for the first time, a victim. Led into marriage under false pretenses, like Rochester, he hears Rebecca's horrifying (and unrepeatable) declaration five days later at Monte Carlo, when "'she told me about herself, told me things I shall never repeat to a living soul'" (272).[16]

---

[16]Like the precipitating act that causes Quint and Jessel to haunt Bly, the "horrors" Flora and Miles know, and the "perverse," "abominable" propensities of Bertha Mason, the lack of specificity creates a Rorschach test for morality and sexuality. In all

Rebecca becomes "'the devil'" (273), offering Maxim a pact that lets them appear as what she calls "'the luckiest, happiest, handsomest couple in all England,'" ensconced at his "'precious Manderley'" (273), if he will remain silent and let her go her own way.

Maxim feebly suggests that his acquiescence is duty to a nobler cause, property—"'I put Manderley first, before anything else'" (273–74)—but his commentary shows him terrified, as the woman has been, by the negative scrutiny of others, "'The shame and the degradation'" (274). "'She knew I would sacrifice pride, honour, personal feeling, every damned quality on earth, rather than stand before our little world after a week of marriage and have them know the things about her that she had told me then. She knew I would never stand in a divorce court and give her away, have fingers pointing at us, mud flung at us in the newspapers, all the people who belong down here whispering when my name was mentioned, all the trippers from Kerrith trooping to the lodge gates, peering into the grounds'" (273). The peering hordes will see what Rebecca already "knew" and what the woman is gradually learning: Maxim's weakness.

In Maxim's recounting, Rebecca is the same figure Danvers presents and, finally, more of a stereotypical man than he. She administers Manderley masterfully. "'Her blasted taste made Manderley the thing it is to-day. . . . It's all due to her, to Rebecca'" (274–75).[17] All defer to her will, and a part of that will is that inheritance will be through her alone. The child she tells Maxim she carries will be heir to Manderley, and there is no suggestion that the child might be his. Thus, Maxim's horror at "'this life of degradation'" (278), like his indignation at her pursuing "'poor shy faithful Frank'" (275), seems based on a double nightmare of revelation: her promiscuity and his impotence.[18]

---

these instances, a strong possibility exists that *any* sexual knowledge becomes translated into unspeakable acts and moral depravity. The reader/spectator is thus asked to join the narrator in prurient speculation and to condone or applaud her/his subsequent acts and evaluations.

[17]The finances of their marriage are somewhat murky, but a distinct possibility exists that much of the wealth is Rebecca's. Maxim says that Manderley's splendor is very recent. The place "'was crying out for skill and care and the money that [my father] would never give to it, that I would not have thought of giving to it—but for Rebecca'" (274). Whether he and his father "would" or "could" not spend and whether Rebecca's buying is with her own checkbook remain unclear. Certainly, their lives after Manderley's destruction show no signs of affluence, nor does the sale of the land for a resort that du Maurier proposed in her unused epilogue ("*Rebecca*" Notebook 48–49).

[18]Losing property through a bastard child's inheriting obviously agitates Maxim, but so too may all issues of sexuality and reproduction. The marriage with Rebecca may

The woman erases this last picture of Maxim as the beaten. She chides herself for having "built up false pictures in my mind" (276), willfully obscures the newly restored past, and represses her knowledge. "'Rebecca is dead,' I said. 'That's what we've got to remember. Rebecca is dead. She can't speak, she can't bear witness. She can't harm you any more'" (282). Still, as her final comment indicates, the past is necessarily more lightly buried now. Sympathizing with Maxim's pain necessitates holding on to the cadaver. To exonerate Maxim, Rebecca must be dreadful; to maintain the fiction of his power, she assumes freakish proportions at the same time. Most of all, the past must remain alive because it is what she has learned from Rebecca and about Maxim that allows her to claim her own power by entering into the role of the beater through her complicity with Maxim.

As a beater, the woman becomes the participant she has always wanted to be. No longer distanced from activity, she can feel herself to be as substantial as those she has hitherto watched. She and Maxim are for the first time full partners as accomplices in the death of another woman. Having found her rightful place, she can now use her newfound authority to dominate others. The servants are her first tutees, but, less obviously, Maxim too experiences a new order. His weakness revealed and his culpability established (even if both are strongly denied by her), he himself can now be safely infantilized. The woman's use of her power is paradoxical and self-contradictory. She buries it, as she did the specter of Rebecca, but uses it to fertilize the old romantic dream of her courtship and marriage. Maxim is now in her power, and she exerts that power to infuse her vision of their blind symbiosis with life. If he is not quite the figure she first imagined, he remains a reasonable facsimile who can fill the part. And their connubial bliss rests uneasily upon her continued identification with Rebecca.

Her complicity with Maxim ushers in a new period. For the first time, he shares his knowledge with her, declares his love—and needs her help to protect himself. The plot she narrates remains Maxim's story as told in her voice, and the subject is still Maxim—but that is

---

have been unconsummated, for those first few days seem the only possibility. She takes lovers but, when he threatens divorce for too conspicuous license, her rebuttal establishes that they have no sexual relations. "'They think we live together at Manderley as husband and wife, don't they? . . . Well, how are you going to prove that we don't?'" (279). The protagonist and Maxim sleep in separate beds, which obviously doesn't preclude intercourse but does suggest something of a barrier. The protagonist mentions wanting children (boys), and, after the revelation, Maxim promises that she will have them. Nonetheless, they have no children. Whether the cause is lack of fertility or lack of intercourse, both marriages are sterile.

precisely what she has always wanted. The means to that end, murder, matters little to the woman.[19] Her demon lover's demand for proof of her love—"'How much do you love me?'" (265)—is suddenly and astonishingly joined to his own declaration. She becomes "'my darling, my little love'" as foreplay to the climax, murder. "'I killed her. I shot Rebecca. . . . Will you look into my eyes and tell me that you love me now?'" (266). Like many another heroine, she passes the test of how much she loves him by accepting the simultaneous declaration of love and murder and by not inquiring too closely into their relationship.

There is a moment's pause when, numb, she waits for the pieces to fall into place, to "fit themselves into a pattern" (268). "At the moment I am nothing. I have no heart, and no mind, and no senses. I am just a wooden thing in Maxim's arms. Then he began to kiss me. He had not kissed me like this before. I put my hands behind his head and shut my eyes. 'I love you so much,' he whispered. 'So much.' . . . . For the first time he is telling me he loves me" (268). At this crucial moment, he faces destruction. She can repudiate the murderer—and thus the identity she has given over to him—or embrace him and shore up the foundations of fantasy. Even for her, the conjunction of events is difficult to reconcile, the protestations of love too opportunistic. She eagerly foregoes her spectator's distance, though, and chooses to be a participant in another woman's beating and death. Finally, they share and are as one. Her inquiries move from "'What will *they* [the authorities] do?'" through "'What are *you* going to do?'" to "'What are *we* going to do?'" (269–70, emphasis added) in a short space. The "we" with which she closes marks her decision and their new accord through the rest of the novel.

Listening to his narrative consolidates her spectating and participating selves.[20] And, of course, her own retelling of the tale emphasizes that she has made the story her own. "I had sat there on the floor beside Maxim in a sort of dream. . . . I too had killed Rebecca, I too had sunk the boat there in the bay. I had listened beside him to

[19]Ethel Spector Person's reading of the text in *Dreams of Love* as an instance of "happy fantasies of Oedipal victory" is incomplete in that she accepts Maxim as an unproblematic father/husband, minimizing the murder by discussion of Rebecca's "taunting" Maxim and her "vicious lies" (272).

[20]Light rightfully notes the significance of the narration, in which the woman "transfers her identification from Rebecca to Maxim, and invites the reader to do the same. Her own identity solidifies and secures itself around this endorsement of murder" (16). The conflict is lesser and more dour than Light suggests: I would argue that the woman's identification with Rebecca is always partial and faute de mieux, while she has fully incorporated the values of property and class that Maxim represents.

the wind and water. I had waited for Mrs. Danvers' knocking on the door. All this I had suffered with him, all this and more besides. But the rest of me sat there on the carpet, unmoved and detached, thinking and caring for one thing only, repeating a phrase over and over again. 'He did not love Rebecca, he did not love Rebecca. . . .' These two selves merged and became one again" (284). The focus must remain upon his suffering, not his act, his immediate need, not her own or Rebecca's. Her "I" is a anaesthetic echo of his agency that marks both her complicity in murder and her merger with Maxim.

His suffering, Rebecca's murder, and current events become linked in a dreamy sequence of causality. Her conjunctive links, like those of the protagonist in "The Yellow Wallpaper," have an underlying logic: "all these foolish inconsequent threads hanging upon one another, because Maxim had killed Rebecca" (336). Much earlier, she repeatedly reminds herself that "all of this was mine now because I was married to Maxim" (69). The "becauses" can be joined: all of this is hers now because Maxim murdered Rebecca. And the protagonist's marriage, the proof that Maxim loves her, is only possible as the staged scene following Maxim's murder of another woman because he hates her. The frightening implications of the causation must be avoided, so the screen explanation of Maxim's act becomes his pain, not his infliction of it. It is not his fault, but Rebecca's. Of course, this reasoning establishes Rebecca as first cause and most powerful figure, but that knowledge too can be blurred by emphasizing her freakishness and his responses. The wrongful feminine authority once embodied in Van Hopper with her pretentious "'je viens'" (19) now becomes fulfilled by Rebecca and her fearsome promise, "'Je reviens.'" By focusing and displacing unjust authority on other women the protagonist protects Maxim, gender arrangements, and class stratification from scrutiny.

The woman's reward for her complicity in defending "'our side'" (287) is Maxim's "love," his no longer critical regard. "We did not talk much. I sat on the floor at Maxim's feet, my head against his knees. He ran his fingers through my hair. Different from his old abstracted way. It was not like stroking Jasper any more. . . . Sometimes he kissed me. Sometimes he said things to me. There were no shadows between us any more, and when we were silent it was because the silence came to us of our own asking" (287–88). She shows no trepidation about the next lesson in this school for wives, no fear that Rebecca's punishment might become her own. She demonstrates a certain interest in the consequences of chastisement when she vaguely wonders what will happen to the corpse of the woman who was buried as Rebecca but, finally, she doesn't much care what happens: other women lie in coffins, not she.

Now that Maxim has claimed her, what she feels with her new knowledge is the absence of restraints and "shadows." "I was free now to be with Maxim, to touch him, and hold him, and love him. . . . It would not be I, I, I any longer, it would be we, it would be us. . . . I would fight for Maxim. I would lie and perjure and swear, I would blaspheme and pray. Rebecca had not won. Rebecca had lost" (285). Whether the troublesome "I, I, I" was hers or Maxim's is moot. Enthusiastically coupled with Maxim, she has no more scruples about aiding and abetting him than did O in bringing Jacqueline to Sir Stephen. He has been a beater, but she will forestall his ever being beaten by Rebecca or by a world that would humiliate and degrade him.[21] Indeed, when the loutish Favell attempts to blackmail Maxim, her participatory fervor is noteworthy. "In a book or in a play I would have found a revolver, and we should have shot Favell, hidden his body in a cupboard" (328). She clearly still maintains some distinction between fantasy and reality, as her references to books and plays indicate, but the easy transition to cruelty is startling.

Knowing the secret of murder, knowing that Maxim must now be hers and she his because of that knowledge, gives her a new access to class authority. She is for the first time a model of managerial efficiency the morning after the confession. She, as Rebecca once did, skims through her morning mail and takes it to Rebecca's morning room. Briskly throwing open windows, she rings for the maid and reprimands her; the "nervous" and "apologetic" response that would once have caused *her* to apologize now only commands a brusque "'Don't let it happen again'" (289). Robert is summoned and given orders for Danvers; when Danvers herself appears, the command is repeated and amplified by a critique of the house's wastefulness (290). Her assumption of the role of mistress draws a stare and an attempted rebuke that she counters forcefully. "'I'm afraid it does not concern me very much what Mrs. de Winter used to do,' I said. 'I am Mrs. de Winter now, you know'" (290). Later, when Danvers appears to weep, "no one moved towards her, to say anything or to help her"

[21]The purposes of this particular triangulation fit neatly into what Freud describes as the role of the third party in obscene jokes. The third person, originally an obstacle, becomes an ally for both sexual and aggressive goals, while the butt of the joke is punished for sexual noncompliance: "the hearer, who was indifferent to begin with, [turns] into a co-hater or co-despiser" (*Jokes* 133). Thus, Rebecca is posthumously the object of a dirty joke, as it were. Because she will not "come across" and do as Maxim wants, she is reviled as a loathsome instance of (natural) female sexual excess. The protagonist and Maxim seal their accord by their shared abuse of her.

(340). The protagonist just turns away, disturbed by but participating in the humiliation of her old enemy. She has come into her own by finally having others subordinated to her.

Her new understanding of power gives her a new sureness in action. She eagerly anticipates many changes: "I should learn bit by bit to control the house" (376). She need not bother to interpret the behavior of "inferiors" any more; she can insist on what that behavior will be. Privy for the first time to the secrets of domination, she can anticipate its workings, as she does when she realizes no will believe Favell's claims of murder because he's the "wrong sort."[22] Beneficiary of gender and class structure through Maxim and Manderley, she feels no need to placate Favell, as she did when she first met him, and she refuses him a parting handshake.

In her new capacity, she no longer feels compelled to share what she knows or has, even with Maxim. Her knowledge makes her someone to reckon with, but she guards the principal carefully while maintaining the interest. Dominant, she needn't respond to inquiries. Clarice disappears as an "ally" (210), out of her league now: "I was not going to discuss it with her" (304). She brushes away Frith's, Danvers's and Beatrice's requests for information. When Frith discreetly fishes for information and expresses his good servant's willingness "'to do anything that might help the family'" (301), she is politely receptive and entirely uninformative. Danvers, wanting to know about the body in the boat, is soundly rebuffed. "'It's no use asking me, Mrs. Danvers,' I said. 'I don't know any more than you do.' 'Don't you?' she said slowly. She kept on looking at me. I turned away" (291). The "I don't know" that was once the protagonist's defense against the risk of asserting any knowledge was hers alone has mutated to a smooth lie that suggests she knows a great deal.

Her unwillingness to confide in either Maxim or Frank attests that her self-imposed silence is not simply the practical necessity to protect Maxim but satisfying in its own right. She repeats nothing to Maxim, while at the same time remaining highly engaged with him. Whereas Maxim once knew everything about her, and she nothing about him, their roles are now reversed. Although she understands after watching Frank protect Maxim that he knows about the murder,

[22]Favell's position as lower-class outsider is obvious in the abysmal failure of his attempt to achieve camaraderie with Maxim over the body of Rebecca. He utterly fails in the alliance Freud postulates, in large part because he shows no more understanding of exclusive property rights than would a poacher on Manderley's grounds. "'I can't think why fellows can't share their women instead of killing them. . . . A lovely woman isn't like a motor tyre, she doesn't wear out. The more you use her the better she goes'" (326).

she discusses this with neither him nor Maxim. "Frank knew. And Maxim did not know that he knew" (297). Still, "dear Frank" is no longer her ally. "I did not look at him. I was afraid he would understand my eyes. I did not want him to know that I knew" (298). She could once gain something from Frank's knowledge, but her account is now larger than his and further transactions have no profit.

The most conspicuous change in her relationships of course has to do with Maxim. She cannot enter fully into the role of beater because she needs to have his overt authority maintained. She can, however, adopt a modified form by infantilizing him precisely because she so loves him. Bolstered by his acknowledgment of his own humiliation, she can even be mildly judgmental. "There was something degrading in the fact that Maxim had hit Favell" (334). She and Frank together protect Maxim against himself, cautioning him against outbursts of anger, aggression which is no longer appropriate for him.

Maxim now garners his own list of pet names. Immediately after his confession, he asks her if she "understands" what he has told her, and her response includes a contextually bizarre barrage of possessive terms of endearment that continue thereafter: "my darling," "my Maxim," "my love," "my sweet" (274). Where once Maxim's wish was her command, she now insists on going to the inquest and to Doctor Baker's. In all three drives, she keeps her hand on Maxim's knee—an affectionate and connective gesture that, in terms of their relationship, also hints at the possessive and controlling. Where once Maxim could admonish her to eat "like a good girl," she can now gently chide him: "'Eat it, darling'. . . . I was using the words he had used to me. I felt better and stronger. It was I now who was taking care of him" (375). In "taking care" of Maxim, she can dotingly infantilize him as he once did her. She lovingly and condescendingly describes the once-mighty Maxim as being "like a child" needing security (270, 352, 358).

At the novel's end, her and Maxim's last ride, with the diagnosis of Rebecca's malignancy and uterine "malformation" (367) at its beginning and Manderley's destruction at its close, shows plot and psychological resolution at odds. There is no closure for her, just the regressus set into motion by unresolved memory that will be the rest of her life. Tucked into the back seat while Maxim drives through the night, she dreams and has no control as phantasmagoric images from the past flood her.

Her final dream, before they see the reddened night sky that lets them know Manderley is no more, holds all she has come to know and all she will work to forget.

I was writing letters in the morning-room. I was sending out invitations. . . . But when I looked down to see what I had written it was not my small square hand-writing at all, it was long, and slanting, with curious pointed strokes. I pushed the cards away from the blotter and hid them. I got up and went to the looking-glass. A face stared back at me that was not my own. . . . The eyes narrowed and smiled. The lips parted. The face in the glass stared back at me and laughed. And I saw then that she was sitting on a chair before the dressing-table in her bedroom, and Maxim was brushing her hair. . . . He wound it slowly into a thick long rope. It twisted like a snake, and he took hold of it with both hands and smiled at Rebecca and put it round his neck. (379)

Within the condensation, displacement, and plastic representation of the dream, the shifting roles of all three are mirrored. She takes Rebecca's place, assumes her room, activities, pen and writing. She wants these attributes, and yet she doesn't want to know what she is inviting. She hides what she has dared to write in that "bold" script, "the symbol of [Rebecca], so certain, so assured" (43), and so unlike her own "unformed" hand, "without individuality, without style" (87). Upon looking into the mirror, there is another brief fusion between herself and Rebecca, like that when Jane Eyre sees Bertha Mason's reflection. Rebecca's knowing stare seems to mock the protagonist's own blindered gaze. Her laugh, so often commented upon in the novel, is not that of the Medusa but certainly that of the dominant. Put in her place, as it were, the narrator distinguishes between "I" and "she." Again spectator to the drama of Maxim and Rebecca in her dream, she represents the metamorphosis of Maxim's seemingly active control into his victimization by Rebecca's erotic and hostile domination.[23] It is Rebecca's enticing hair that becomes the blatantly phallic "snake" and strangling rope.[24] Most chillingly, Maxim, as the

[23]To explain such role reversals and their pleasure, Stoller emphasizes revenge and the dissolution of mystery. "One moves from victim to victor, from passive object of others' hostility and power to the director, ruler; one's tormentors in turn will be one's victims. With this mechanism, the child imagines himself parent, the impotent potent" (*Perversion* 106). Within stereotyped marital roles, we can add "the wife imagines herself the husband." In all instances, the ex-victims replicate oppression, like Ruth, in Fay Weldon's *Life and Loves*, who controls her husband as entirely as he once controlled her. Similarly, in Alice Walker's *Temple*, the white Heath uses his childhood victimization to rationalize his cruelty. "He spoke of this to explain his ability to understand how 'the nigras felt,' but what it really seemed to explain was why he so often tried to make those he knew feel as bad as he'd once felt himself" (135).

[24]The only hint of Maxim's sensuality is in Danvers' report that he used to brush Rebecca's hair. "'Harder, Max, harder,' she would say, laughing up at him, and he would do as she told him" (169). The sexuality of the language and of the scene itself make the hairbrushing an obvious choice for the dream material. The woman envies Rebecca's brushes (166), although Maxim has given her a set of which she "need not be ashamed" (72) as a wedding gift. While he never paddles her with the brushes, neither, alas, does he ever brush her hair as he did Rebecca's.

subordinated, smilingly embraces his own destruction—and the protagonist, using Rebecca as her surrogate, wills it also.

The balance between them has shifted in her favor. The power and
knowledge she gains through scopophilia, coupled with Maxim's loss
of dominance, make them peers. Her aim has been to have this
power; her goal, however, is to recreate the same dream of gender
stereotyped romance and class prerogative that led to her deper-
sonalization throughout the novel. She has gained enough power so
that she can make Maxim be her powerful but adoring husband. And,
as his ever-solicitous wife, attentive to his needs, she succeeds in
active, aggressive control through passive means in their exile. "And
confidence is a quality I prize, although it has come to me a little late
in the day. I suppose it is his dependence upon me that has made me
bold at last" (9). Thus, there is no breaking from the beating paradigm
in their mutual cannibalism but rather a doubling, an exchange of
roles that lets them maintain the relationship through the years.

The destruction of Manderley and the "true death" of Rebecca, like
that of a vampire, promise an end to the pattern—but only if the past
can be integrated with the present, the externalized with the internalized. Neither character shows any such signs. Instead, they continue, as they always have, to function through wholesale denial
(they are content and all to one another), repression (they have no
unfulfilled needs), and projection (Rebecca, not they, is responsible
for all cruelty).[25] Locked together in exile at the novel's beginning and
the plot's chronological end, they are a strangely vitiated pair, joined
in limitation of desire and insistence that they choose it to be thus,
according to the narrator.[26] "I know we are together, we march in
unison, no clash of thought or of opinion makes a barrier between us.
We have no secrets now from one another. All things are shared.
Granted that our little hotel is dull, and the food indifferent, and that
day after day dawns very much the same, yet we would not have it
otherwise" (6). She represents their merger as idyllic accord, but their
unanimity seems possible only because they have so few thoughts,

[25]Danvers shares the negative projection. In the novel, she decamps the evening of
the fire (and is of course the major suspect). In the Hitchcock film, she burns in
Rebecca's bedroom. The film version neatly suggests suttee (since Rebecca is her erotic
object) as well as her function as surrogate victim, through whose destruction Maxim
and the protagonist can consolidate their bond. In addition, of course, the choice of her
as expendable character is overdetermined by sex and class (like the death of other
subordinated scapegoats such as the housekeeper in Wharton's "Mr. Jones," or the
immolations of the creature in Karloff's "Frankenstein" and Bertha in *Jane Eyre*).

[26]In the unused epilogue, du Maurier presents both as physically scarred. Henry
(Maxim), à la Rochester, is crippled by a "maimed body and scarred hands," but she
too has a "disfigurement" (*"Rebecca" Notebook* 40, 51).

opinions, and secrets. Unlike the rank profusion that characterized Manderley—the vivid, lush environs, the abundance of objects in every room, the kitchen's cornucopia spilling forth, the parade of people—their current life is sparse, gray, and muted.

They are finally as one. She maintains their unity diligently, like any attentive wife. She monitors Maxim's world minutely and lovingly; nothing he does escapes her. She reads to Maxim, as she once did to Van Hopper. She watches carefully for all signs of agitation, as she once did as a new bride. She is a "mine of information on the English countryside" (7), no matter how trivial, which she doles out to him as she sees fit. Where once she was unable to fathom the causes or effects of Maxim's disturbances, though, she now understands them well enough to move him toward neutral, safe topics. In her dutiful mirroring of his needs, however, it is she who decides what they may be, since he expresses no desire, and, of course, it is she who controls the narrative, as she does their environment, she who speaks for both of them.

She tells us that they have given battle to their "devil" and "have conquered ours, or so we believe" (5). Yet, the willful misprision she maintains for both of them is given the lie by her own account. Each is haunted by the past, and both re-view it time and again. Maxim "never complains, not even when he remembers . . . which happens, I think, rather more often than he would have me know" (5). The memory and knowledge she thinks she can guard him against (just as he once sought to keep her from the "forbidden" [202]) remain her surreptitious delight, however. Their sharing is not quite so entire as she claims, for she relishes the pain and delight he is too weak to bear as "my secret indulgence" (7).

Her entrapment in a re-vision of the past is our text, of course, her ultimate "indulgence" and excoriating enactment of the vicissitudes of voyeurism. Dominant now in relation to Maxim, she remains forever subordinate to Rebecca. Unable to escape the self-contained logic of the beating triangle, she can only repudiate her affinity with Rebecca, while remaining blind to her own variant of the beater's role.[27] Just as she once rejoiced at Maxim's beating Rebecca because he *hated* her, so the protagonist can justify her beating of Maxim because she *loves* him and thus can deny any association with aggression.

In the span of her dream of Rebecca, the dream that is the novel's

[27]As Light says about the final, repressed identification: "Rebecca acts out in this dream what the girl also desires. Perhaps, then, the de Winters *do* need to go abroad to save Maxim's skin—not from the scaffold, but from his wife" (20).

close, she is spectator, beaten (through identification with Maxim), and beater (through identification with Rebecca). The dream represents her own split self, longing for the power of the beater while claiming the blamelessness of the beaten. Indeed, in the course of the novel she has been beaten. In seeking to escape the passivity of spectator and beaten, however, the only way she sees to gain their rewards of knowledge and verifiable identity is to exercise scopophilia, exhibitionism, and sadism as the dominant use them. An accomplice to the murder of another woman, her knowledge prevents her from becoming the next victim.[28] But the only model of heterosexuality she knows is the beating fantasy's drama of triangulation, and all she can do to achieve her desire is mirror its oppression and live a gray nightmare happily ever after.

[28]Their (and our) position as spectators to a nonstop movie of the past is complemented by du Maurier's use of second-person in the discarded epilogue, where the narrator presents them as they might appear to "your" eyes as traveler/viewer/reader.

6

Looking Out for Yourself:
The Spectator and *Jane Eyre*

In both *Story of O* and *Rebecca*, the protagonists move from self-accusatory masochism to forms of object relations that reproduce the beating triangle. While both texts overtly celebrate the triumph of the heterosexual couple, their thematic concerns and structures as insistently constitute a ménage à trois. In *Rebecca* the first-person account inextricably links the observing, narrating self to the experiencing self who is beaten and beats in her turn; the coolly distanced third-person narrator of *O* frames the Grand Guignol of a woman's suffering through narrative point of view. And, of course, as readers we too are spectators/accomplices to the Gothic's repetitive display of masochism. The insidious lure of audience participation parallels characters' regression from the spectator's analytic scrutiny of "a child being beaten" to center stage's heady, unself-conscious immersion in aggression and sexuality generated by the other serving as subject, beating because he loves. What, however, if the fusion between both drives doesn't happen? What if the viewer watching the reenactment of trauma lacks the early training that would lead to her interpreting the scene as a religious mystery play, a beguiling romance, or the entirely unremarkable portrait of normal adults? What if she doesn't *want* to be an actor?

I would like to suggest that Charlotte Brontë's Jane Eyre is such a spectator, one for whom the early absence of love enables a clear separation between the affection she desires and authoritarianism. No endearments or murmurs of future rewards for being a good girl soften her punishments; no one suggests that she is much chastised because much loved. Love and subordination remain sharply distinct for her as a child and as an adult. The implications of my argument are deeply disturbing, since they suggest that, in this novel's representation at least, a child with the most austere minimum of what D. W. Winnicott calls "good enough" parenting is better prepared to be an adult than others seemingly more fortunate. Yet I find that this reading helps to explain the construction of this particular character, with her preference for spectating, her persistent debates between emotion (which can lead one to the beating dyad) and reason (which urges staying clear), and her two plots of Gothic courtship and its repudiation.[1] Jane's active instincts—scopophilia, epistemophilia, sadism—are sharply and repeatedly suppressed by external sources; she does not, however, internalize these strictures through repression. Thus, she distinguishes between appropriate behavior in given social contexts and who she is.[2] Because she is beaten without claims of love, her identity remains relatively autonomous. Not at fault in her own assessment, she becomes an instance of trauma without self-accusatory guilt.[3]

[1]The scholarship on *Jane Eyre* is so extensive that I can only offer a selective bibliography of those essays that have most influenced my analysis. Several critics comment on specific instances of masochism and/or sadism in the text, such as the "flagellation ceremonies" of the red room (Elaine Showalter, *A Literature of Their Own* 115), or how Brontë "turns Jane's energies upon her self" (Lee R. Edwards, *Female Heroism* 82). Both Helene Moglen (*Charlotte Brontë* 105–45) and Dianne F. Sadoff (*Monsters of Affection* 119–69) consider masochism as a central issue.

Other critics whose arguments bear upon my own, although the central conflict they assume may be cast varyingly as inner/outer, passive/active, passion/rationalism, surrender/autonomy, romance/reality, transcendence/mundane, individual/social, etc., include: Maurianne Adams ("*Jane Eyre*: Woman's Estate"), Nancy Armstrong (*Desire and Domestic Fiction* 186–202, 205–13), Nina Auerbach (*Romantic Imprisonment* 195–211), Elizabeth R. Baer ("The Sisterhood of Jane Eyre and Antoinette Cosway"), Eugenia C. DeLamotte (*Perils of the Night*, 193–228), Terry Eagleton (*Myths of Power*), Sandra M. Gilbert and Susan Gubar (*The Madwoman in the Attic* 336–71), Margaret Homans ("Dreaming of Children"), the Marxist Feminist Literature Collective ("Women's Writing"), Mary Poovey (*Uneven Development* 126–63), Adrienne Rich (*On Lies, Secrets, and Silence* 89–106), Karen E. Rowe ("'Fairy-born and human-bred'"), and Patricia Meyer Spacks (*Female Imagination* 44–96).

[2]I am in no way suggesting that the deprivations Jane reports (or other forms of abuse) are advantages in forming adult identity. It may be that parents or uncle provided enough nurturing and rapport to sustain the infant (although her maximum age at her uncle's death is twenty-three months); it may be that Jane is simply what the literature of abuse sometimes refers to as a "survivor," one apparently and startlingly unmarked by early trauma. In addition, actual abuse may lessen the propensity to masochistic fantasy—and, I would add, it may lessen the tendency to credit the twinned ideologies of romance and the Gothic novel. In any event, Jane's ability to separate love and domination underscores how early and thoroughly the two are fused in supposedly normal feminine development.

[3]In discussing acute, chronic, and cumulative trauma, Stoller emphasizes that adult conflict happens only when parental values are internalized as self-punishment and guilt. "Not all traumas produce conflict. . . . Thus, if a small child has a powerful sensual impulse that is forbidden by his parent, this does not cause *intra*psychic conflict even though the child may change his outward behavior when the parent punishes him" (*Perversion* 34).

Although Jane attaches no erotic value to the beating drama, it is insistently represented in the novel as reality, not fantasy—a reality where the only safety and limited gratification of active drives are to be found in the spectator's role.[4] "Currer Bell," in "his" preface to the 1848 edition, defends the observing truth-sayer who must "mark broadly and clearly the line of separation" between fantasy and reality, "bigotry" and "piety," ideology and experience. "Conventionality is not morality. Self-righteousness is not religion." No "sycophant," Bell insists on the right to witness injustice and be heard, to refuse to "blend" "external show" and "truth" (1–2). The world "may hate him who dares to scrutinise and expose—to raise the gilding, and show base metal under it—to penetrate the sepulchre, and reveal charnel relics: but hate as it will, it is indebted to him" (2). What Brontë enters through her novel and insists upon representing is not the sepulchre, of course, but the analogous nuptial chamber, not the charnel relic but the bridal veil lifted to reveal a madwoman as wedding souvenir.

My intention is not to present either the novel or the character as a triumphant overthrow of the Gothic economy. I do, however, want to argue that the representation of the spectator's role suggests a significant new strategy in its emphasis upon how the viewer can use her curiosity, knowledge, and activity to avoid becoming part of the beating dyad. Jane's position is liminal, as it literally is in so much of the novel: she looks out to the freedom of open spaces, and back to the groups that confine, punish, and exclude but which also constitute social existence. The character's knowledge is not enough to call a halt to Gothic repetition: as generations of exasperated critics have noted, only plot's divine intervention can do this in *Jane Eyre*. This is not, I think, a failure of imagination or craft, but a deeply grounded skepticism about whether a woman's identity can endure in relationship and whether individual insight can have social efficacy. The novel, like the character, tests its own reality; within its culture, the utopian can only be imaged in the most ambivalent of closings, one that hesitates at the plausibility of even two people escaping the Gothic.

Jane Eyre investigates the outer boundaries of the Gothic and, through its re-valuation of the spectator's role, suggests a crucial way in which the individual viewer can recognize the drama of cruelty for

[4]By not ceding that "poor Charlotte Brontë" might also understand the conflation of sexuality and aggression as other than ideal, D. H. Lawrence finds *Jane Eyre* "verging towards pornography" (37). One of his insights about pornography, however—its merging of anal and genital "flows" so that "sex is dirt and dirt is sex," exciting insofar as we "humiliate [sex] and degrade it" (39)—is in fact precisely the arrangement *Jane Eyre* critiques.

what it is and refuse complicity. Jane's hard-won ability to distinguish between love and dominance is what enables her to withstand the temptations of Gothic courtship. Her stance as spectator does not allow her to change what she sees or knows as reality; it does, however, enable her refusal to participate or to replicate oppression. And that refusal, like her repudiation of the role of beater or beaten for herself, promises an eventual end to repetition and to the Gothic.

The Dissociation of Love and Dominance

The young Jane, "scapegoat of the nursery" (13), is imaginative, inquisitive, and wants to be loved as much as any other child. Like any other girl, she might well direct her active instincts inward if in return she could believe her identity validated in an approving eye. What Jane is told repeatedly, however, is that she has no place in anyone's heart or in the world. Firmly checked at every turn, she is often quite unsure what her infraction is, except simply existing. A child can learn to die under such conditions; what Jane learns is to live by unyoking her sense of self from the evaluation of those around her as much as possible and by differentiating between the power that punishes and love. Her active instincts are turned against the self only insofar as necessary to avoid punishment, and they are used whenever possible to gain knowledge, to gratify scopophilia, and to act. Aggression figures strongly in her makeup and yet, in part because to use anger like those who punish her would assume an identification with her tormentors or incorporation of their values, she eventually refuses the identity of the beater as decisively as she does that of the beaten. Although decidedly bound by numerous cultural imperatives of class and gender, Jane vests the beating scene with few ideological overlays. As spectator she, unlike O or the narrator of *Rebecca*, recognizes cruelty for what it is.

No natural prodigy of dispassionate investigation, Jane learns her skepticism with difficulty, working against the bent of an affectionate child seeking approval. In the intensely condensed, brief (only some thirty pages) representation of the ten-year-old child at Gateshead as well as the account of her adolescent years at Lowood, we see the early training in deprivation, separation, and injustice that begin to make her into the spectator who will control herself rather than allowing anyone else to assume that role and who will keep her own distance. She wants love, but only her cousins seem worth that rare commodity, as the child despairingly notes. "Why could I never please? Why was it useless to try to win any one's favour?" (12).[5] After her first punishment at Lowood, she falls to the floor and weeps at her blasted hopes "to earn respect, and win affection" (59): she has never seen love come unsought.

To win that affection, she is more than willing to suffer, for, as she tells Helen, self-approval is "not enough" (60). "'If others don't love me, I would rather die than live—I cannot bear to be solitary and hated, Helen. Look here; to gain some real affection from you, or Miss Temple, or any other whom I truly love, I would willingly submit to have the bone of my arm broken, or to let a bull toss me, or to stand behind a kicking horse, and let it dash its hoof at my chest'" (60). The child's melodramatic images do not evoke the secondary gains of pain (loved because hurt) or the trade-off of the beating triangle (loved because affirming another's power). Instead she vividly describes the strength of her own love, her need, and the price she is willing to pay for a return. At the very least, then, Jane, in contrast to O or the protagonist of *Rebecca*, knows her own desire and that it originates in herself, not in another. Here, and when she describes her desire to please her teachers, "especially such as I loved" (73), she is the subject. Over time, her question shifts from what she can do to earn love to what she is willing to do because *she* loves. The seemingly minor semantic shift from another hurting you because "he loves me" to accepting pain because "I love" bespeaks a significant psychological difference. Pain and love are still in proximity, but Jane knows herself as the agent of her own desire, the only possible subject for such a conjecture.

In *Jane Eyre*, the only way a girl can gain such self-knowledge is through consistent, long-lasting emotional deprivation.[6] Because Jane's punishments are unassociated with love, they can be recognized as what they are: aggression. As a consequence, she doesn't

[5]The bleakness of Jane's childhood is so extreme that readers often recast Bessie as a nurturant exception (prompted in part by class expectations, I suspect). Yet, despite Bessie's greater sympathy for Jane after the red room scene and her sometimes telling the children stories while she irons, there is little evidence of any special caring before then. "Disposed to entertain" a "bad opinion" of Jane (9), Bessie lodges the mysterious complaint that precipitates the punishment with which the novel opens (5), and it is she who first suggests tying Jane down in the red room (9). Bessie's later solicitude, seen in bringing Jane pastry on the painted china plate, is too little too late.

[6]Eagleton touches on this when he claims that "at the centre of all Charlotte's novels, I am arguing, is a figure who either lacks or deliberately cuts the bonds of kinship. This leaves the self a free, blank, 'pre-social' atom: free to be injured and exploited, but free also to progress, move through the class-structure" (26). His reading is itself somewhat romantic—or perhaps even Imaginary, though, in its exaggerated assessment of such a woman as "pre-social" and highly mobile.

idealize her tormentors or eroticize beating. All have more power than she but, whether her assailant is Mrs. Reed, John Reed, the servants with their "partiality" (11) for the other children, or Brocklehurst, their harsh methods of control fail to be internalized by Jane as her own values.

As the character of Mrs. Reed so chillingly demonstrates, abusive power is no sex-linked trait. She and her husband reverse stereotypical gender arrangements, for it is he who cares for the orphan child, she who repels Jane's overtures and exerts the aggressive right of scrutiny allocated to those of rank and wealth.[7] The relationship between Mrs. Reed and Jane, then, is a negative exemplum of Chodorow's thesis that girls, raised by loving caretakers of the same sex, often find separation or differentiation from those they love difficult in adult life.

There is no risk of loving merger with Mrs. Reed for Jane, as the Kafkaesque tribunal of the novel's opening emphatically demonstrates. Before being ousted from the conviviality of the drawing room, Jane tries to find out what her offense might be.

> Until [Mrs. Reed] heard from Bessie and could discover by her own observation that I was endeavouring in good earnest to acquire a more sociable and child-like disposition, a more attractive and sprightly manner—something lighter, franker, more natural, as it were—she really must exclude me from privileges intended only for contented, happy, little children.
> "What does Bessie say I have done?" I asked.
> "Jane, I don't like cavillers or questioners: besides, there is something truly forbidding in a child taking up her elders in that manner. Be seated somewhere; and until you can speak pleasantly, remain silent." (5)

The amorphous accusation, like the paradoxical stipulation for reformation—to be more "child-like," more "natural"—make it impossible for the child to give any response that will gain approval. Jane's specificity and logic is, as Mrs. Reed notes, already adult in some fashion. Whereas love can train a child so that she simply weeps "I'm sorry" in order to restore relationship, heedless of the nature of her

---

[7]The same interrogation of "natural" feminine nurturing is evident in Mary Wollstonecraft's use of the wicked stepmother trope in *Maria or the Wrongs of Women*. When once casually called "dear" by her stepmother, Jemima "thought I could never do enough to please her" (54). Her childish attempts to seek approval and caresses are repulsed, like Jane's, in favor of other children (54). Labeled, like Jane and Helen, by having "Glutton, Liar, or Thief" written on her forehead (56), she dissociates love and suffering and goes on to show unusual independence in adult life.

infraction, the closure of that option for Jane fosters her ability to pass rational judgment. She may "remain silent" for a time, but she comes to use her silence, her vision, and her physical separation to analyze her oppressors and so maintain ego integrity.

In the crucial red room scene, that still tentative integrity almost disintegrates, but love and dominance are sundered permanently so that it need not. Imagining her dead uncle rising to "punish the perjured and avenge the oppressed," the child is not soothed but terrified: "This idea, consolatory in theory, I felt would be terrible if realised" (13). The use of the already rare, quasi-passive "perjured" points both to aggressor *and* victim as those to be punished, as does her assumption that the ghost would appear to her, not to his wife. No theories of affectionate care have been borne out in Jane's experience: "consolatory" authority, whether supernatural or human, is unthinkable. Promised liberation only after "perfect submission and stillness" (14), Jane is also told (as she is later by St. John [361]) that she is the aggressor: "'Silence! This violence is all most repulsive'" (14). The child is past accepting that projection, however: she knows herself to be the victim.

The red room scene, then, is the culmination of a long process that makes Jane radically suspicious of any claim that punishment is "for your own good," that aggression is warranted by love. Strangers are now more congenial and safer to her than acquaintances. When Mr. Lloyd, the apothecary brought to examine her after her seizure, appears, she feels "sheltered and befriended," reassured by "a soothing conviction of protection and security, when I knew that there was a stranger in the room" (15). Nonetheless, Lloyd tries to minimize her trauma by suggesting that only a "baby" would be afraid of ghosts, but Jane insists on her own assessments: "'It was cruel to shut me up alone without a candle,—so cruel that I think I shall never forget it'" (19). And she doesn't. Indeed, the older Jane, trying to explain at her aunt's death-bed that "'I should have been glad to love you if you would have let me'" (210), is, almost relieved to find no new interpretation, no tender reconciliation. What the girl identified as oppression is validated by the woman's analysis. This shocking understanding, so at odds with the sentimental ideology that rosily covers women and children, even provokes a break in narrative point of view when the adult Jane addresses Mrs. Reed directly to assert again the reality of her experience (16).

Jane's life of "ceaseless reprimand and thankless fagging" (16) sharpens her eye for all forms of domination. Despite her desire to love and be loved, she cannot idealize her aunt or persuade herself that her abuse is a mark of solicitude. Neither can she eroticize or excuse the bully of her own age, John, common as such transformations are.[8] No rationale of boyish high spirits or underlying good intentions softens her response: "Every nerve I had feared him, and every morsel of flesh on my bones shrank when he came near" (7). "Habitually obedient to John" (8), Jane endures his insults and blows in part by reminding herself of the actuality of his tyranny: "I knew he would soon strike, and while dreading the blow, I mused on the disgusting and ugly appearance of him who would presently deal it" (8). Such splitting of her own response, more highly developed later, lets her acknowledge the reality of being the beaten while reserving her functioning identity for the role of the spectator who looks on, assesses reality, and judges.

Jane submits to John's interrogations as well as to those of Lloyd, Mrs. Reed, Bessie, and Brocklehurst. Indeed, authority exercises itself via such interlocutory examinations throughout her narrative. Like the narrator of *Rebecca*, she knows that she exists only on sufferance, "like nobody there" and "'less than a servant'" (12, 9). She is the negative exhibit of the drawing room, the red room, and the parlor, all at least temporarily public spaces in which Jane is pilloried, as she later is at Lowood and by the scornful eyes of the house party at Thornfield (155).

What seems coincidental at Gateshead becomes a science of humiliation at Lowood, where public punishment, often achieved via visual aggression, is the norm. On Jane's first day, she sees Helen, "the central mark of all eyes," standing in the middle of the classroom and thinks the punishment "ignominious." "I expected she would show signs of great distress and shame; but to my surprise she neither wept

[8]Frances Restuccia, like Judith Wilt, notes that the patriarch's son may be seen as a lesser evil or even an ally by the Gothic heroine—until he becomes a patriarch himself (see particularly 247, 254, 264). I agree, and think the *Clarissa*-inspired inset narrative of Emily in William Godwin's *Caleb Williams* an excellent instance. (Emily believes in the affection of her cousin, the county bully Tyrrel, until he hounds her to her death.) In other texts, however, it is precisely the cruelty of the heroines' contemporaries that awaken thoughts of love. In Mary Cowden Clarke's infamous *The Girlhood of Shakespeare's Heroines*, for example, a childhood meeting between Kate and Petruchio in which he ties her up and switches her until she owns herself "mastered" (51) is the preface to *The Taming of the Shrew*. "As her woman's frame involuntary [sic] yields to his masculine strength—as her feeble limbs bend beneath his will, and submit to his power, there is an inexplicable acquiescence, an absence of resentment and resistance, altogether unwonted, and surprising to herself" (169). Similarly, in Vita Sackville-West's *The Dark Island*, the stage for Shirin's marriage to Venn is set when, on their first meeting as adolescents, he twists her wrists, tells her that he would like to chain her naked to the coastal rocks "'and beat you and beat you till you screamed.'" Her response, so unlike that of Jane, is "unexpected fascination" (51).

nor blushed: composed, though grave, she stood, the central mark of all eyes. 'How can she bear it so quietly—so firmly?' I asked of myself" (44). Jane watches with horror as the stoic Helen is switched on the neck before her peers or made to wear the sign "Slattern" (46, 64). Later, she even musters a note of grim humor in describing the "remedy" for sleepy little girls who tumble out of lofts during sermons: being stood in the room's center until the end. "Sometimes their feet failed them, and they sank together in a heap; they were then propped up with the monitors' high stools" (53). The regimen of Lowood, like that of Roissy or Manderley, demands perfect submissiveness; Jane, unlike other protagonists, rightly considers the verbal and visual scrutiny to which she is subjected as an assault. Rochester later assumes that the students, consolidating love and power, "worshipped" Brocklehurst "'as a convent full of religieuses would worship their director'" (108), but such a possibility is by now foreign to Jane.

The concept of positive exhibitionism, controlled by the self, is as unknown to Jane as the exacting claims of love. To be looked at is to be threatened, as are the girls whose topknots and curls are shorn after Brocklehurst's examination, and as is Jane herself, the object of perpetual vigilance: "'Teachers, you must watch her: keep your eyes on her movements, weigh well her words, scrutinise her actions, punish her body to save her soul. . . . This girl is—a liar!'" (58). Publicly labelled, as are Wollstonecraft's Jemima, Dickens's David, Smedley's Marie, and Walker's Celie, Jane is also sentenced to silence for the rest of the day, as though her speech might still harbor some vestige of independence and seditious credibility (which it surprisingly and fortunately does). Perched on a stool, she is the still point in a visual gauntlet as all file past her. "There was I, then, mounted aloft: I, who had said I could not bear the shame of standing on my natural feet in the middle of the room, was now exposed to general view on a pedestal of infamy" (58). At Lowood, then, as at Gateshead, power is vested in no kind smile or warm gaze. (The beneficent power of Miss Temple disappears in the presence of Brocklehurst.) Authority remains inimical, to be trusted under no circumstances.

While the strand of development I have been tracing so far might seem to presage the most perfectly meek submission, Jane's ability to distinguish between love and aggression and the splitting of her ego in the process of defense enable her not only to survive psychically but to thrive. Her active instincts are turned against the self only insofar as necessary to avoid punishment; with her highly conscious spectator's gaze, she monitors both others and herself. From this position, she fulfills highly charged active drives whenever possible: Jane gratifies curiosity through her penchant for spectating and listening, the urge for knowledge through painting, education, and stories, and an increasingly subtle aggression. Furthermore, *pace* Freud, she sublimates these drives into higher, socially valued outlets, as her love for painting and narration attest. As her spectating self gains ascendancy, the abused child with her "habitual mood of humiliation, self-doubt, forlorn depression" (13) becomes more quiet, emerging only to debate her ongoing need for loving relationships or to haunt dreams. She is not entirely repressed; there is simply no room for her in the phenomenal world of the novel.

Jane's scopophilia, first developed of necessity as a means of defense, remains her dominant mode of gaining knowledge from the sidelines.[9] What her aunt describes as "'her continual, unnatural watchings of one's movements!'" (203) becomes highly refined, imperceptible except to other proficient viewers. Her invisible gaze is conjoined to listening, and both pressed into service to satisfy her curiosity in the search for knowledge. She looks outward to wider vistas from her window seat at Gateshead, her room at Lowood, and the leads at Thornfield, but she as regularly uses her isolated position to scrutinize and listen to those around her. Carefully watching Brocklehurst as he speaks (53), studying Rochester's face (115), surveying the members of the house party (153), looking upon the tableau of Blanche Ingram and Rochester (162–65, 171), or gravely regarding the spectacle of Bertha Mason (258), Jane uses visual inquiry as a substitute for the verbal querying and action her status and external circumstance often proscribe.

When appropriate, Jane does ask questions, questions that are most direct and persistent when she is in a new place and dealing with someone "safe": Helen at Lowood, Mrs. Fairfax at Thornfield, Hannah at Moor House. An adept and active listener, she draws information from others. Rochester magisterially declares "'It is not your forte to tell of yourself, but to listen while others talk of themselves'" (119). Jane duly listens to his amorous tales, but her true forte is confounding the active/passive split he predicates. She unobtrusively gathers information for herself, whether about Thornfield's mystery from Leah, Mrs. Fairfax, and Rochester himself, about courtship from the gypsy's tantalizing hints (174), or about the romance of Rosamund and St. John (326–31).

[9]See Sadoff for an excellent discussion of the importance of gaze and voice in Brontë's juvenilia and novels (122–29, 147–49), and Armstrong (e.g., 196).

Jane's accumulation of auditory and visual knowledge helps her to defend herself, but it is also a highly pleasurable and sublimated activity. Her love of information becomes a love of narrative in its own right, whether that narrative is found in Bessie's folk tales or the stories of the "racy" Mary Ann Wilson who "could tell me many things I liked to hear. . . . She had a turn for narrative, I for analysis; she liked to inform, I to question" (67–68). Jane evinces a certain exasperation with those who, not "of a descriptive or narrative turn" (96), like Mrs. Fairfax or Sophie, "seem to have no notion of sketching a character, or observing and describing salient points, either in persons or things" (92). They frustrate her interlocutor's skill: "My queries puzzled, but did not draw her out" (92). Jane longs for stories and sights, whether through oral narrative or voyeurism, the *Arabian Nights* or Bewick's colored plates.

In addition, she can fantasize her own production rather than reception of visual and oral stimuli. When she has her first sketching class, she forgets to imagine decent food: "I feasted instead on the spectacle of ideal drawings, which I saw in the dark; all the work of my own hands" (65). At Thornfield, she shapes a mental narrative, opening her "inward ear to a tale that was never ended—a tale my imagination created, and narrated continuously; quickened with all of incident, life, fire, feeling, that I desired and had not in my actual existence" (95–96). Jane's vivid pictures and stories move beyond vicarious experience, through her fantasies, and to actual production: her own paintings and the narrative told to us as *Jane Eyre*.

Both visual and verbal products reflect Jane's knowledge of destruction, the uncanny analysis of the aggression she recognizes in others and in herself. She knows that gaze can be aggression, for she connects her own knowing stare to the violent reactions of John and Mrs. Reed (8, 30). She understands the power of language finely and exhilaratingly when she first says to John Reed "'You are like a murderer—you are like a slave-driver—you are like the Roman emperors!'" (8). The heady knowledge that she too can use aggression tempts her, but finally does not become her dominant mode of response for two reasons: the consequences (her outburst against John brings her to the red room), and the possibility that she might become like her aggressors. In the course of her development, Jane does test various forms of overt aggression, however.

After her verbal assault on John, the young Jane considers turning her anger against herself, "never eating or drinking more, and letting myself die" (12), an option again rejected after leaving Thornfield. Instead, "like any other rebel slave, I felt resolved, in my desperation, to go all lengths" (9) and to relish the power her "deep ire and desperate revolt" (22) bring. Her verbal and physical outbursts satisfy her aggression; at the same time, their effects on others testify to Jane as agent, not hapless victim. After punching John in the nose, Jane interrupts the maternal denunciation of her unworthiness to proclaim "'They are not fit to associate with me'" (22). Her anger insists upon her naming the truth and refusing to be the designated scapegoat for the crimes of others; at the same time, knowing that she too can inflict pain brings its own gratification.

Jane knows triumph for the first time when she moves to active assault against her oppressors. What she has seen and heard becomes her ammunition, fueled by the righteous indignation of the truthsayer. Preparing to leave Gateshead, she turns Mrs. Reed's accusations back against her, secure in the conviction that there is nothing more to lose and much to gain for herself.

> I gathered my energies and launched them in this blunt sentence:—"I am not deceitful: if I were, I should say I loved *you*; but I declare I do not love you. . . ."
>
> "People think you a good woman, but you are bad; hard-hearted. *You* are deceitful!"
>
> Ere I had finished this reply my soul began to expand, to exult, with the strangest sense of freedom, of triumph, I ever felt. It seemed as if an invisible bond had burst, and that I had struggled out into unhoped-for liberty. (30–31)

In asserting control of her own identity through language, Jane declares herself an equal, one not to be manipulated through the empty promises of the beating fantasy.

The subordinated's truthful reflection of inequity is perceived as aggression by the dominant, as is clear when Jane simply and accurately reverses the accusations made against her. Jane moves past that lucid, immediate mirroring, however, when she demands that her assailant internalize Jane's accusation by asking "'What would uncle Reed say to you, if he were alive?'" (23). Just as she later invokes divine higher authorities to escape from the claims pressed upon her as an appropriately loving woman, so here she summons the spectre to whose power her aunt is most responsive. It is no wonder that Mrs. Reed at various points becomes "troubled with a look like fear" (23), looks "frightened" (31), and speaks "rather in the tone in which a person might address an opponent of adult age than such as is ordinarily used to a child" (31). On her deathbed, Mrs. Reed avers: "'I felt fear, as if an animal that I had struck or pushed had looked up at me with human eyes and cursed me in a man's voice'" (210). By refusing her subordination, by exercising her own anger in vocal self-defense, Jane is precociously and precariously a "man," an adult to reckon with.

The allure of aggression remains powerful for Jane at Lowood and extends to anger for injustices perpetrated against others. Watching Helen being switched on the neck, Jane's "fingers quivered at this spectacle with a sentiment of unavailing and impotent anger" (46). She later insists to Helen: "'And if I were in your place I should dislike her; I should resist her; if she struck me with that rod, I should get it from her hand; I should break it under her nose'" (48). Jane tries to teach Helen anger as a means of survival as repeatedly as Helen tries to inculcate forbearance in Jane. They are at odds about the victim's right to rebel against her oppressor, but alike in their refusal to espouse the cycle that another once-suffering child, Heathcliff, claims: "'The tyrant grinds down his slaves and they don't turn against him, they crush those beneath them'" (Wuthering Heights 97).

Jane acts out the anger Helen herself can no longer feel; her grief at Helen's "Slattern" label comes more from Helen's acceptance of what she perceives as "deserved punishment" than from the indignity itself. "I ran to Helen, tore it off, and thrust it into the fire: the fury of which she was incapable had been burning in my soul all day, and tears, hot and large, had continually been scalding my cheek; for the spectacle of her sad resignation gave me an intolerable pain at the heart" (64). Capable of what Helen is not, Jane's ability to feel fury motivates her and helps her to identify the reality of domination. Jane reworks Helen's would-be gift of resignation as the "doctrine of equality of disembodied souls" (208, emphasis added), the doctrine that later lets her address Rochester as a "spirit" and an "equal" (222). Jane's own legacy to Helen is the tombstone inscribed with the enigmatic "Resurgam" (72, "I shall rise"), a word that marks Helen's faith as well as Jane's own hopeful last wish and vicarious resistance for her.

As spectator, Jane witnesses and remembers cruelty. Helen marvels at "'how minutely you remember all she [Mrs. Reed] has done and said to you!'" (50), and insists that her own injustices "brand" no trace upon feeling or memory. For Jane, the recollection of suffering is the only way to work through to survival as an adult: Helen's amnesiac creed of "endure" (48), the perfection of feminine passivity, is a mystery to her until modified to "strive and endure" (279, emphasis added). Jane forgives, but she does not forget. When, returning to

Gateshead as an adult, Jane assures us that "the gaping wound of my wrongs, too, was now quite healed; and the flame of resentment extinguished" (200), she conveys as little credibility as the narrator of *Rebecca* avowing that the past is "conquered" (*Rebecca* 5). Faced with her oldest antagonist's "icily" "stony eye" after identifying herself, Jane traces the steps of domination. "I felt pain, and then I felt ire; and then I felt a determination to subdue her—to be her mistress in spite both of her nature and her will" (203). Her temptation, to which she does not yield, tempts the reader also, but the stages she outlines explain her refusal to progress any further along this route in the use of anger: she would become a dominator in turn.

Woolf argued that "anger was tampering with the integrity of Charlotte Brontë the novelist" in *Jane Eyre* (*Room* 76). Contemporary readers are more apt to celebrate Jane's anger, and to rue its rechanneling as a regrettable capitulation to Victorian mores and gender conventions (both assumed to be utterly unlike our own). Our desire for the woman warrior who vanquishes all challengers, who vicariously enacts for us what Horney calls "vindictive triumph" (*Neurosis* 103), and so restores pride while humiliating the opponent, is our own fairy-tale expectation. Jane's use of anger does indeed change significantly during her time at Lowood, as critics so often note. That shift is not a surrender or an identification with Helen Burn's other-worldly meekness but rather a gradual maturation that assures Jane will define herself outside the beater-beaten dyad, that object relations and abusive power will not be synonymous for her.

The taste of revenge is bittersweet from the first time Jane savors its "bitter vigour" (11). Enjoying her "conqueror's solitude" after routing Mrs. Reed, Jane's martial metaphors give way to those of inebriation and poison. "I was left there alone—winner of the field. It was the hardest battle I had fought, and the first victory I had gained. . . . Half an hour's silence and reflection had shown me the madness of my conduct, and the dreariness of my hatred and hating position. Something of vengeance I had tasted for the first time; as aromatic wine it seemed, on swallowing, warm and racy: its after- flavour, metallic and corroding, gave me a sensation as if I had been poisoned" (32). In her "hating position" she is as locked into the dynamics of the beating fantasy as the victim, as defined by her adversary as the most abject. The sequence she establishes—pain, ire, and the determination to subdue—must find another third stage, an anodyne for corrosive raw aggression.

Helen's saintly distance from "'degradation'" and "'injustice,'" her clear Christian separation of "'the criminal and his crime'" (51), offers

one possibility, albeit one achieved by putting her ego on the altar—
and that Jane cannot do. Responding to Helen's extremism, the
young Jane offers an ethics of aggression as one socialized option for
that third stage. "'If people were always kind and obedient to those
who are cruel and unjust, the wicked people would have it all their
own way; they would never feel afraid, and so they would never
alter, but would grow worse and worse. When we are struck at without a reason, we should strike back again very hard; I am sure we
should—so hard as to teach the person who struck us never to do it
again'" (50). Able to understand the separation between sin and sin-
ner that Helen espouses (and at which she later proves herself no
slouch), Jane is nonetheless adamant about the connection between
the two as well as the need for responsibility and reform.

Without a doubt, Jane loves Helen for her affection and admires her
for her intelligence and the staunchness of her convictions. That admiration is not accompanied by any belief of her own, though, or any
desire to emulate her renunciation of self. Mounted on her stool of
shame, Jane is indeed braced by Helen's lifted eyes as she passes. "It
was as if a martyr, a hero, had passed a slave or victim, and imparted
strength in the transit. I mastered the rising hysteria, lifted up my
head, and took a firm stand on the stool" (58). Terry Eagleton rightly
notices the significant conjunction of "martyr" and "hero": "Martyrdom is seen as both saintly self-abnegation and heroic self-affirmation, a realisation of the self through its surrender" (*Myths of Power*
16). Although I think him right in the general suggestion that virtue
and identity can be wrung from the most dour of necessities, Jane
embarks on no such mystic way. For her, a martyr means one killed
by others, one who knows herself right and her torturers wrong—a
revelation Helen never has. To choose self-sacrifice is as anathema to
her as a child as it is when she contemplates St. John's call to suffering
as an adult. To Jane, the martyr and hero are instead those who aid
resistance, who are willing to comfort or to die for another "slave or
victim." Yet, even in her gratitude and admiration, Jane eschews the
model of what Anna Freud called "altruistic surrender": she will yield
herself as victim to no person or ideal.

By refusing to ground her identity in anger as a young adult, Jane
disclaims the model that might lead her to become a beater in turn.
She neither becomes one of the "great girls" who "coax or menace the
little ones out of their portion" (52) and so survive physically and
psychically, nor does she as a teacher augment her pittance of power
by brutalizing others. Helen's deadly role, one that idealizes and
erases what it means to be a victim, attracts her as little. Insofar as

Helen agrees that she herself has done wrong, she is no more a hero or martyr than O and as much a part of authority's construction. As Helene Moglen argues, "Masochistically oppressed, she participates in the power of the oppressor by accepting his punishment and assuming his blame" (*Charlotte Brontë* 116).[10] Jane's aggression avoids the beater's and beaten's mutations and instead manifests itself in her insistence on clear vision, as much knowledge as she can gain, and her ambitious, unfeminine, and unerotic "desire to excel" (73).

She is a survivor, one who remembers everything that has happened to her and others, whatever name they may choose to give their own suffering. Deeply pragmatic, Jane at eighteen recognizes the limits of her life. Yet she also knows her own desires and longs for what activity she can manage in the world she sees. Love might still hold her to those who love her in turn, but Helen is dead and Maria Temple is married. Free, she begins "to feel the stirring of old emotions" (73): action and new vistas beckon. "I desired liberty; for liberty I gasped; for liberty I uttered a prayer; it seemed scattered on the wind then faintly blowing. I abandoned it and framed a humbler supplication; for change, stimulus: that petition, too, seemed swept off into vague space. 'Then,' I cried, half desperate, 'grant me at least a new servitude!'" (74). Jane's cry before leaving Lowood is a courageous, unflinching victory of the individual: this is what has become of her aggression. If naming a "new servitude" seems poor recompense for the unacknowledged servitude of the beating dyad, Jane's ability to assess reality, "*to think*" and to have "a brain active enough to ferret out the means of attaining" (75) what she deems plausible argue otherwise: insofar as possible, it is she who will control her own course, she who will act for herself.

My reading here clearly puts a high premium on Jane's ability to see and to know the conditions of her own oppression. I do not want to suggest that individual consciousness, independent of social conditions, is all in the novel: it is, however, a crucial, indispensable beginning to the freedom for which Jane longs. So too is her recognition that she is not alone in her plight, a reality emphasized by the spring of death at Lowood and her own thought. In not founding her sense of self upon the uniqueness or severity of her sufferings, or, conversely, the pleasing but grandiose fantasy of herself as liberator of the oppressed, Jane remains firmly grounded in the reality of her world, with all the limitations of perception that implies. Her often-quoted

[10]In reference to the male pronoun, I would point out that women are both agents and initiators of punishment in the novel.

indictment of passivity bears repeating as the extraordinary fruit of that hard-won wisdom:

> It is in vain to say human beings ought to be satisfied with tranquility: they must have action; and they will make it if they cannot find it. Millions are condemned to a stiller doom than mine, and millions are in silent revolt against their lot. Nobody knows how many rebellions besides political rebellions ferment in the masses of life which people earth. Women are supposed to be very calm generally: but women feel just as men feel; they need exercise for their faculties and a field for their efforts as much as their brothers do; they suffer from too rigid a restraint, too absolute a stagnation, precisely as men would suffer. (96)

Jane's passionate outburst argues for a new promulgation of power, for activity as the right of every woman. Her own need to look, to know, and to act have survived through adolescence; others, she assumes, are also in "silent revolt." By painfully coming to know that love and domination are not the same, Jane achieves a psychic autonomy unknown to those who learn that their recognition by the dominant can only come through doing to themselves what loving authority figures first do to them: denying their separate identities. By splitting herself into one self that still/always craves love and a second, reality-testing self that watches and acts in the world, Jane reaches a plateau in development from which she can assay that world and her future. With her aggression channeled to assure survival, she knows that she can work: whether she can succeed at the love that is the second part of Freud's definition of (masculine) normalcy will depend upon how well her autonomy and her dissociation of love and dominance can withstand the temptation of Gothic courtship that draws her from the spectator's role.

The Temptation of Gothic Courtship

At Thornfield, "'poor, obscure, plain, and little'" (222) Jane enters into the most influential Gothic relationship in literature. In the hundreds of texts that draw upon *Jane Eyre* as *the* Gothic novel, the ideology of romance emphasizes that any woman can be swept in good Cinderella fashion from obscurity into the loving embrace of the man in whom she'll find her world. *Jane Eyre* itself is a far more skeptical text, however. Just as contemporary feminist thought insists that violence against women is not sexual or provoked by its victims, so the representation of courtship in *Jane Eyre* warns that becoming the victim of aggression in the name of love is a possible scenario for any woman. As Karen Rowe argues, "Fairy-tale expectations prove unreliable, indeed dangerous," for what is on trial "is not merely the heroine's self-will versus her acquiescence, but also the validity of an entire concept of romance derived from fairy tale" ("'Fairy-born and human-bred'" 71, 82).

Reserved, pragmatic, and ambitious, Jane finds her safety and greatest freedom in the spectator's role; Rochester's regard seems based upon his acknowledgment of that independence, his love to offer expansion. Jane's resistance to merger is lulled because authoritarianism is not the dominant tenor of his approach. Yet, what we see in the periods leading to and following his proposal of marriage is a fractured fairy tale, one in which Rochester increasingly attempts to control Jane's mobility, voice, field of vision, and what is presented to her as spectacle. Different as his mode of approach may be from those in authority at Gateshead and Lowood, his aim is finally the same: total regulation. As Margaret Homans observes about Jane's frustrated drive for transcendence: "The special horror of the Gothic is that Jane's allegiance to the plain and practical truth cannot rescue her from the danger of subjectivity, because it is in the practical world that her fears and subversive wishes take their most terrifying form. . . . Confinement to the object world is itself now recognized as the source of horror" ("Dreaming of Children" 260–61).[11] To modify Homans's argument slightly, I would suggest that it is not just the object world, but the world of object relations that precipitates horror.

Jane is willing to love but not to relinquish her powers of judgment, conflate class and emotional authority, or assign her subjectivity to another. Rochester presents no such threat when she first meets him; indeed, his wry awareness of social hierarchy seems to mirror her own consciousness. Furthermore, in their early interaction her independence is valued and, in the reversal of fairy-tale motifs, *her* activity

---

[11]Eugenia DeLamotte too identifies the frustration of transcendence and limitation to the object world in *Jane Eyre* as "the deadliest but most ordinary peril of a woman's life" (195). Nancy Armstrong and Terry Castle see different uses made of this confinement to the material world. Armstrong analyzes the unused furniture and rooms of Thornfield as the "debris of culture," "a space within culture [that] allows change" (208, 211) by women. She goes on to argue that these defamiliarized cultural fragments gradually become endowed "with another kind of meaning that partially realizes the inchoate motions of mind" (212). Castle expands this perception in a specifically psychoanalytic frame when, as part of the "supernaturalization of everyday life," the metonymic objects evoke absent others ("The Spectralization of the Other" 234, 238).

is endorsed. That it is she who saves the gentleman in distress seems a promising augury: "it was yet an active thing, and I was weary of an existence all passive" (101).[12]

Rochester sardonically identifies the structure of master/servant that informs their relationship and seems to dismiss its significance (as does Max when he muses upon what it means to be a "paid companion"). His ironic identification of what it means to be a master or a servant hints that his self-awareness makes the same old behavior somehow different. He interrogates Jane much as Mrs. Reed and Brocklehurst once did, both verbally and in having her display her accomplishments. Unlike them, however, he is promisingly aware of his imperatives. "'Excuse my tone of command; I am used to say "Do this," and it is done: I cannot alter my customary habits for one new inmate'" (109). His brusqueness actually augments the effects of his empathy, for Jane suspects mellifluous charm and "gallantry" (99). Interested, not irritated, by Jane's scrutinizing gaze (which he warns he is "'quick at interpreting'" [119]), and intrigued by her response of "no" when he asks if she finds him handsome (115), Rochester passes Jane's tests as well as she does his.

Each assays the strength and flexibility of the other in an ongoing negotiation to determine who will speak, who will listen, and on what terms. Rochester, like Jane, wants to hear others' narratives and complacently demands that she be the object of his investigation. "'It would please me now to draw you out—to learn more of you— therefore speak'" (117). He immediately understands the silence that follows his peremptory command. Jane, in turn, recognizes Rochester's maneuver when he tries to reclaim dominance not as her employer but as an older man (117) and demurely rejoins that his ascendancy "'depends on the use you have made of your time and experience'" (118). Jane demands clarification of his mutually contradictory claims: "'I don't wish to treat you like an inferior. . . . Do you agree with me that I have a right to be a little masterful, abrupt; perhaps exacting, sometimes . . . ?'" (117). The skirmish between two well-matched, self-conscious interpreters, then, is exciting stuff as each tests the other's mettle.

[12]Voyeurism is, as I argue, its own pleasure but, although Jane often rests content with the knowledge gained thereby, she also is interested in other pleasures, however unavailable they might seem. In *Villette*, Lucy's voyeurism is more finely honed and internalized, joined to a censoring of other desires that insists, like the protagonist of *Rebecca*, on the meagerness of her needs. Lucy wants to see a ball or opera, but "it was not the wish of one who hopes to partake of a pleasure if she could only reach it . . . ; it was no yearning to attain, no hunger to taste; only the calm desire to look on a new thing" (175).

In calling attention to her status as employee, Jane affirms reality, but also obliquely asks whether he wants consent through coercion. While pooh-poohing the significance of his social status, Rochester nonetheless tries to transfer his advantage to other grounds. Each is generous, finally, although Jane gives as much as he from a smaller store—and perhaps a greater need.

> "Leaving superiority out of the question, then, you must still agree to receive my orders now and then, without being piqued or hurt by the tone of command—will you?"
>
> "I was thinking, sir, that very few masters would trouble themselves to inquire whether or not their paid subordinates were piqued and hurt by their orders."
>
> "Paid subordinates! What, you are my paid subordinate, are you? Oh, yes, I had forgotten the salary! Well, then, on that mercenary ground, will you agree to let me hector a little?"
>
> "No, sir, not on that ground: but, on the ground that you did forget it, and that you care whether or not a dependent is comfortable in his dependency, I agree heartily." (118)

Their badinage, playful and acute, results in a tentative accord that suggests a radical restructuring of authority.

Jane literally thrives under the new regime. The only other prolonged relationships we have seen, those with Mrs. Reed and Helen, differ mightily from this one, in which her skepticism, acuteness, and wit are challenges met in kind rather than with abhorrence or gentle chastisement. She gains weight, relishing her new-found recognition and excusing Rochester's occasional harshness as signifying nothing else. "'I felt at times as if he were my relation, rather than my master: yet he was imperious sometimes still; but I did not mind that; I saw it as his way" (129). Jane feels kinship, a commonplace that is the rarest of treasures for her; at the same time, as an adult, she cannot help but note her status as an exception, a status that seems normal to any child. "In my secret soul I knew that his great kindness to me was balanced by unjust severity to many others" (129). Nonetheless, Jane luxuriates in the unwonted affirmation that she is special, is worthy of regard for those qualities she holds most dear in her definition of self. Jane's value thus appreciates by recognition of her autonomy; Rochester's gloomy hints of his suffering and Mrs. Fairfax's brief references to his victimization by father and brother equalizes them still further.

Both Jane and Rochester acknowledge the arbitrary power of class and employer/employee relations which necessarily mean something different to Jane than they do to Rochester.[13] Still and all, Jane is beguiled, if not entirely persuaded, by the prospect of a relationship in which mutual regard is substantial, social and gender authority only accidental. Because this utopian alterity can never be spoken, because Jane's "place" remains a determinant of her reality, Rochester can nonetheless move her in a way she cannot move him. In departing without notice to call his house party together, for example, he covertly emphasizes the limits of her right to see and to know. By making her an unwilling spectator to his social world and his courtship of another woman, he cruelly exploits her greatest strengths and turns them against her. The "viewless fetters of an uniform and too still existence" (102) she thought removed by Rochester's presence at Thornfield are tightened during their unnamed courtship; the relative sense of release is their engagement to be married.

During their own peculiar courtship—the several months of Jane's isolation that follow their several weeks of growing intimacy—Rochester uses Jane's greatest freedom, that of the spectator, to force her to witness his world and his wooing of Blanche. Jane's testing of reality tells her that she cannot invoke the alternate exchange that finally is nothing more than a few strange talks in a drawing room late at night. From the time Jane first learns of Blanche's existence, through the house party, and until Rochester's marriage proposal Midsummer's Eve, Jane is forced into the position of passive spectator that she and the protagonist of *Rebecca* so loathe.

Unlike that character, though, Jane begins courtship with her own active capital. She stands to lose this and, dwelling only in possibility vis à vis Rochester, to lose as well what she hasn't yet even gained, love. The stakes are high, for Jane's relation with Rochester has more depth than we ever see in *Rebecca*: he is her first adult friend as well as love-object. She is for the first time caught up in the mutual reinforcement of authority and love. She must watch what happens because her employer tells her to do so, but she suffers in believing the regard of the man withdrawn. The sorry consolations of the beating fantasy are absent for her; she doesn't even try to make herself believe that he is doing this because he loves her (the rationale Rochester himself will later offer). Instead she must believe that his behavior means that he

---

[13]Poovey's discussion of the governess's liminal, contradictory status in Victorian England as paid worker/lady, "governor" of unruly emotion/sexual innocent, mother/whore is excellent. As she points out, the reality of Jane's job fades "by subordinating her poverty to her personality and to the place it has earned her in Rochester's affections" (*Uneven Development* 137).

doesn't care for her, and that her own reality testing is no longer reliable.

The activity Jane values as much as she does her clarity must therefore be stopped in its course lest "I love" become only a scourge used to flagellate herself: "It does good to no woman to be flattered by her superior, who cannot possibly intend to marry her; and it is madness in all women to let a secret love kindle within them, which, if unreturned and unknown, must devour the life that feeds it" (141). Like Jane's emphasis on "common sense" (140), her insistence on certain universal moral precepts, or her certainty that "'it would be easy to find you thousands'" (173) of dependents like herself, her stress on "no woman" and "all women" underlines her adamant refusal to see herself as an exception. That way lies the special pleading that dissociates the self from social reality and encourages Gothic heroinism: it is a course that she will not take.

Jane calls back those unruly thoughts and feeling that have been straying in "imagination's boundless and trackless waste, into the safe fold of common sense" (140).[14] Memory and emotion are "arraigned" when Reason comes forward to tell "in her own quiet way, a plain, unvarnished tale, showing how I had rejected the real and rabidly devoured the ideal" (140). The task Reason sternly sets her insists that she continue unflinchingly and accurately to register reality, not dreams, with her vision: her chalk "Portrait of a Governess, disconnected, poor, and plain" and her finely painted ivory of "Blanche, an accomplished lady of rank" (141) are the results. She firmly reminds herself that Rochester is her employer, and nothing more. "'Be sure that is the only tie he seriously acknowledges between you and him: so don't make him the object of your fine feelings, your raptures, agonies, and so forth. He is not of your order: keep to your caste, and be too self-respecting to lavish the love of the whole heart, soul, and strength, where such a gift is not wanted and would be despised'" (142).

At first glance, Jane's actions seem highly masochistic. I would draw a sharp distinction here, however, between masochism in which victimization becomes one's identity, and masochism used as a survival strategy precisely so that one need *not* become a victim. O, agonizing over how she might have offended her arbitrary god, is an instance of the former; Jane, knowing that it is her own respect she

[14]Jane's bicameral debates, which often make students (and sometimes critics) uncomfortable, are a superb instance of what Terry Castle identifies as the modern tendency to believe "in the spectral nature of our own thoughts—to figure imaginative activity itself, paradoxically, as a kind of ghost-seeing" ("Phantasmagoria" 29).

must restore in order to continue functioning, is an example of the latter. There is in truth a certain grim pleasure in her determination to force "my feelings to submit" (141), an austere pride in her own strength as she undergoes her self-imposed punishment. Jane indeed turns her aggression against herself, but she does so to prevent further and greater pain from without and as a temporary measure. She cannot realistically exercise her anger against Rochester, and she does not displace emotion on others who are safely weaker, such as Adèle. As significantly, she, unlike the narrator of *Rebecca*, eschews imaginative scenarios that would let her vent her spleen and shift responsibility to her rival, Blanche. She remains firmly ensconced within the realm of the real as that is constituted in the novel.

Jane's valiantly pragmatic exercises to realign her perceptions do not excuse Rochester. They refuse to take his motives into account, rather, because to do so would be to foster delusion and diminish Jane's own responsibility. Her options for decisive action, though, are few: a new job (which she considers [142, 197]) or standing her ground. Her choice of the second is overdetermined by her need to prove to herself that she can "take it" and her inability to break with her image of Rochester, despite her stringent self-discipline. Having decided to stay, however, she remains subject to her employer's control of her behavior. Her attendance at gatherings is as mandatory as it ever was at Gateshead or Lowood. Her restrained comments on the "wholesome discipline" that barely lets her withstand the prolonged spectacle that is the house party hint at how painful her now-enforced role as passive spectator is (141–42).

Rochester's unannounced leave before the house party, which she can question no more than she can the possibility of his return, emphasizes Jane's powerlessness in his world. Her independence, so nourished by new-found intimacy, suddenly contracts sharply, and both are reintroduced in carefully calibrated stages with Rochester as would-be provider. Like O being weaned from her own senses, Jane undergoes a form of sensory deprivation and attempted retraining. After the physical absence that underscores the absence of love as well, Rochester returns and Jane is ordered to look obediently on him, his world, and his courtship of Blanche as one who has no stake in it and can only be an object to those gathered at Thornfield. Intimacy is gradually resupplied insofar as Jane will see through his eyes and be one with him as his confidante and sole ally.

Jane's and Rochester's gazes are no longer reciprocal; he withholds the look she "feared—or, should I say hoped" (155) for when the rest of the company coolly eyes and discusses her. Instead, he joins in their scrutiny of her as negative exhibit, eager to hear Lady Ingram explain how she sees "'all the faults of her class'" (155) in Jane's face. After quietly listening to the anecdotes of dreadful governesses past, hearing Rochester's and Blanche's amorous duet, and watching them flirt, Jane unobtrusively leaves the room. She relishes being negative exhibit now no more than she did at Lowood on her stool. Intercepted by Rochester in the hall, she is quizzed by him—but he leaves her no space for response. Where he once called for her portfolio to display to company (113), now it is her person he demands. "'I expect you to appear in the drawing-room every evening; it is my wish; don't neglect it'" (159).

The evening gatherings, like the house party itself, become a form of torture to Jane. Reason might keep her away, but the decision to attend is no longer hers, and the ongoing drama abets her unruly emotion. She cannot help but see, cannot help but know the bitter implications of what she sees. Withdrawn behind a curtain, Jane persists in the knowledgeable gaze at painful scenes, "pure gold, with a steelly point of agony" (153) that is the "secret indulgence" in *Rebecca* too (7). Yet, as she confesses to herself, "'while I breathe and think I must love him'" (154). She watches Rochester and Blanche act out the charade of courtship and marriage that leads to the prison of "Bridewell," and, as narrating self, vividly recalls her agony. "I still see the consultation which followed each scene: I see Mr. Rochester turn to Miss Ingram, and Miss Ingram to him; I see her incline her head towards him till the jetty curls almost touch his shoulder and wave against his cheek; I hear their mutual whisperings; I recall their interchanged glances; and something even of the feeling roused by the spectacle returns in memory at this moment" (162–63). The very understatement of the narrator's present-tense series—"I see," "I hear," "I recall"—and the nonspecific "feeling roused" emphasize the strength of the experiencing self's emotion and, perhaps, a mental reservation that persists into the future in which she "still sees."

For even while Rochester adroitly controls Jane's field of vision during this period and uses the employer/employee structure to reinforce her role as passive spectator and auditor, Jane watches and judges. Reality says that Blanche and Rochester will marry. But what Jane sees is no meeting of heart or mind, only cold calculation for "family, perhaps political reasons" (163). The qualities she prizes—independence, intellect, passion, integrity—are absent. Watching Rochester watch Blanche "closely, keenly, shrewdly," with "ceaseless surveillance" (163), Jane evaluates him as well as her. She knows he sees what she does: Blanche's materialism and vanity, the "coldness and acrimony" (163) with which she treats Adèle and Jane, her shal-lowness—and it apparently makes no difference. "It was from this sagacity—this guardedness of his—this perfect, clear consciousness of his fair one's defects—this obvious absence of passion in his senti-ments towards her, that my ever-torturing pain arose" (163).

Jane, subjected to a Gothic regimen of "ceaseless excitation and ruthless restraint" (164), excluded from the increased activity and intimacy she has briefly tasted, should become more dependent upon Rochester, more willing to assign him subject status, and more ready to assume that the one who curtails her activity is the only one who can restore it. This doesn't happen. In certain ways, Rochester's strat-egy succeeds, particularly since he skillfully reinforces her dependen-cy in stages, first reintroducing intimacy by asking her to admire Blanche with him and then going on to suggest that Jane is his sole ally. Yet, Rochester has also misstepped significantly. Jane's love of him continues, but his authoritarian actions continue to be noted in a separate register rather than fully merging with the love. She feels anxiety and envy watching him and Blanche model "courtship" for her, but she also disapproves—not the standard response to "my father is beating (loving) a child." Jane believes that Rochester can love, but all she sees with Blanche is a calculating sangfroid that she in no way confuses with love. The "parental" couple viewed in courtship, then, is no more reassuring a sight than her later one of Rochester and Bertha in their marital embrace.[15]

When Rochester genially offers camaraderie again, he feeds her need for intimacy and activity after enforced deprivation: like the bread and cheese at Lowood after burned porridge, it's not ambrosia, but it's enough to get by on. By making the terms of the renewed friendship their mutual admiration of Blanche, though, he also makes her privy to new scenes that do him no credit. At this point, Jane, like the protagonist of *Rebecca* extolling Maxim's largesse or O praising Sir Stephen's generosity, is grateful for the scraps of emotion: "To taste but of the crumbs he scattered to stray and stranger birds like me was to feast genially" (215). Rochester scatters as much gravel as sustain-ing fare, however. He talks to Jane about his approaching nuptials, requests that she stay up with him the night before the wedding, wants her to admire the coach he orders for Blanche, and asks

[15]As Rowe argues, Rochester and Bertha reenact "a child's distorted vision of paren-tal coupling" that substitutes "a loathsome vision of copulation for the romantic expec-tation of 'happy ever after'" (83). Loathsome both visions decidedly are; neither, horrifyingly, is distorted. Within the novel's context, what Jane sees is no fantasy but the reality of the best families.

whether his intended isn't a rare and "'real strapper, Jane: big, brown, and buxom'" (192, 193, 215). To all of this, Jane can only respond "'Yes, sir,'" while Rochester rejoices that "'to you I can talk of my lovely one: for now you have seen her and know her'" (193). Rochester's taunts insult Jane's emotion *and* reason: he knows that Jane loves him, and he knows what her evaluation of Blanche must be. The greater her pain, the greater his joviality: "If . . . I lacked spirits and sank into inevitable dejection, he became quite gay" (217). Their alliance is limited to her seeing what he wants, hearing what he has to say. Her own power in eliciting narrative is no longer under her control as she becomes what Rochester told her she was early on, an "'involuntary confidant'" (119).

As gypsy, Rochester further confounds Jane's vision by his visual foolery, which tries to make her into an involuntary confider as well. He tests the results of his ongoing experiment and tries to ferret out her impressions of "'the fine people flitting before you like shapes in a magic lantern'" and to know "'which tale you like best to hear'" (174). Dreamily reflective during the cross-dressed interview, Jane tells the old women no more than she might the man until he/she expostulates "'What the devil have you seen, then?'" (176). The "masquerade" over, Jane, veteran of so many interrogations, declares that his attempt "'to draw me out'" is scarcely "'fair'" or "'right'" (178).

Rochester wants Jane's secrets, but will reveal none of those in his "Bluebeard's castle" (93) to his "little friend" (179, 190, 192, 221), as he now calls her. Given his own sense of entitlement, he cannot tell Jane the truth; he can only falsify what is best in their relationship by using his not inconsiderable powers in every area to mislead, blind, and mute her. It is to Jane he turns in the burning bed scene, when Mason arrives, and when Bertha attacks her brother. But Jane, like Mason, must remain ignorant and Rochester all-knowing; they must be powerless so that he is the more secure. "'Well, you too have power over me, and may injure me: yet I dare not show you where I am vulnerable, lest, faithful and friendly as you are, you should transfix me at once'" (191).

In demanding Jane's silence, in searching out her weaknesses, and in trying to coerce unconditional loyalty, Rochester plays the role of demon lover as surely as did Clotilda's, Erilda's, or Immalee's fiendish suitors. He draws on her ready sympathy to soothe his "'hideous recollections'" (179) and repeatedly asks for commitment under duress, without ever specifying what the proof of her vows might be. She tells him, "'I'd give my life to serve you'" (179), but, as he exasperatedly notes, conditions always remain: "'I like . . . to obey you in *all that is right*'" (190, emphasis added). Goaded by Mason's appearance at his carefully orchestrated house party, he quizzes her on the degree and depth of her support.

> "If all these people came in a body and spat at me, what would you do, Jane?"
> "Turn them out of the room, sir, if I could."
> . . . . "Would you go with them?"
> "I rather think not, sir. . . ."
> "And if they laid you under a ban for adhering to me?"
> ". . . I should care nothing about it."
> "Then, you could dare censure for my sake?"
> "I could dare it for the sake of any friend who deserved my adherence; as you, I am sure, do." (180)

The pattern of question and response is striking as the catechism of the demon lover who hopes that she will cleave to him above all others no matter what the circumstances.

Equally striking, however, is the reservation that appears whenever Jane is asked to unquestioningly assign her will to her demon lover. She will give to those who "deserved my adherence," but it is she who will decide. When she is finally asked for the "proof" of her love—when she knows about Rochester's marriage—she, like other Gothic protagonists, is "tortured by a sense of remorse at thus hurting *his* feeling" (267, emphasis added). She nonetheless decides, at whatever cost to herself. She cannot resign her will to his, however strong the temptation, for no invocation of pure love and utopian alterity can carry conviction for that stern judge, reason. Jane fails the demonic pact by refusing to be damned for another, even when that other uses the most basic prop of Gothic identity: "'You don't love me, then?'" (266).

During the whole period of their "courtship," Rochester controls Jane's vision and mobility with the hope that he will ultimately control her will. He follows a pattern of intermittent reinforcement that encourages her to rely solely upon him. Just as, when she asks for her wages before her trip to Gateshead, he gives her too much and then too little, his treatment of her throughout this period works to suggest that what he gives is a gift, not earned or hers by right. Her salary is, for him, on a par with the present he thinks she might expect when Adèle opens her *boîte* (106) and finally with his love. By sporadically depriving Jane of all regard and relationship, he tries to establish himself as their source, their return as generosity and not justice. Through making Jane a passive spectator, reintroducing relationship via joint voyeurism of his marriage-to-be, and then reclaiming intimacy as a "friend," Rochester assures that she imbibes "poison" with her "nectar" (140, 153), that his love is adulterated by domination.

It is only through threatening to withdraw entirely Jane's recently restored object relations, by offering to find her "an asylum" (with the oxymoronically named Mrs. Dionysius O'Gall of Ireland and her five daughters [220]), that Jane is stung into revolt against someone who, like John Reed, claims it all "'belongs to me'" (8) and that her lot is nothing. Now, as when she was a child, she has nothing to lose, and she exerts her full powers in rebellion against anyone who would use authority to control her life, tell her that all she receives is charity, and question her very right to exist autonomously.

> "Do you think I can stay to become nothing to you? Do you think I am an automaton?—a machine without feelings? and can bear to have my morsel of bread snatched from my lips, and my drop of living water dashed from my cup? Do you think because I am poor, obscure, plain, and little, I am soulless and heartless? You think wrong!—I have as much soul as you,—and full as much heart! And if God had gifted me with some beauty and much wealth, I should have made it as hard for you to leave me, as it is now for me to leave you. . . . It is my spirit that addresses your spirit; just as if both had passed through the grave, and we stood at God's feet, equal,—as we are!" (222)

Jane's declaration rings through the centuries as one of the most famous proposals in literature. Its ominous undertone, however, resounds as strongly.

Jane's insistence that Rochester "'thinks wrong'" to deny her soul and heart is as much a salvo hurled against authority as is her denunciation of John Reed as "a tyrant, a murderer" (9) or her accusation of Mrs. Reed: "'You think I have no feelings, and that I can do without one bit of love or kindness; but I cannot live so'" (31). A "thing" (10, 203) and a "dependent" (8, 220), Jane is refused the love and identity reserved for the "sanguine, brilliant, careless, exacting, handsome, romping child" (12–13) that Jane could never be, or the woman of "'some beauty and much wealth'" she is not. Jane rebels with furious activity against all who would deny her very existence: in "passion," "fierce pleasure," and "'independent will'" (9, 32, 223) she seeks "liberty" (31, 223). Our wishful expectations to the contrary, Jane's defiant proclamation to Rochester does not create equality and loving accord but instead announces their absence.

The Danger of Gothic Engagements

The traditional plot sequence of *Jane Eyre*'s first half encourages us to believe that the decision to marry is the capstone of romance. Lowly female and upper-class male meet, he tests her love by playing the part of an authoritarian frog, and she, having passed all tests splendidly, is rewarded by his transformation into the prince of love. Jane comments on the likelihood of this scenario: "'I was not born for a different destiny to the rest of my species: to imagine such a lot befalling me is a fairy-tale—a day-dream'" (227). And so it is. What the first half of *Jane Eyre* shows us is the appalling power of that dream. Jane is an unlikely protagonist, not because of her "lacks"— that she is "poor, obscure, plain, and little" (222)—but because of her strengths—her obdurate opposition to authority, her clear vision, and keen judgment. That these powers fall into abeyance when Jane confronts romance's myth speaks to the ability of dominance to clothe itself in the more seemly garb of ideology, the urgency of her need for love, and, accordingly, her determined attempt to split aggression and love within one figure, Rochester, to maintain that they are as entirely unconnected as they have been in her previous experience.

Throughout the one month of their engagement, we see Jane vacillating between the poles of attraction and resistance. So powerful is her need for love that no other mediating system—such as mysticism in *O* or social class in *Rebecca*—is needed to bridge the distance between the stark alternatives of love and dominance: her need alone is sufficient. Yet, supposedly elevated from knowing spectator to full participant, Jane finds herself more alienated than ever before. Rochester's declaration of love does not remove the scopophilic restraints of the house party. They increase, as do the curbs on her epistemophilia. Then, she was still an other; now, won, she runs the risk of losing her autonomy and becoming an adjunct of Rochester, a silent, acquiescent trophy. The flickerings of moral certainty, the slow dimming of vision, and the blurring of authority's outlines mark a frightening sea-change in Jane. What she fights against now with increasing reluctance are shadows that have no name. Promised to and loving Rochester, she has no way to address what his authority is doing to their love except in her retrospective narrative, which brilliantly represents her increasing anxiety. "The feeling, the [wedding] announcement sent through me, was something stronger than was consistent with joy—something that smote and stunned: it was, I think, almost fear" (227). In the novel, plot must do what character can not to exorcise this fear: it is only the revelation of Bertha's existence that frees Jane once more to think and act. As has so often been noted, the terms of that intervention, a madwoman and a previous marriage, are a displaced commentary on Jane's own plight in relation to "the dread, but adored, type of my unknown future day" (252).

In proposing, Rochester says, "'Your will shall decide your destiny'" (223); upon acceptance, that will no longer exists in his reckoning. He recasts Jane as an extension of himself, minimizes her knowledge and curiosity, and aggrandizes himself. The language of his love is all too often that of possession and she a new bibelot acquired by a discerning connoisseur: "'I must have you for my own—entirely my own'" (224). His defiant proclamation at her acceptance—"'I have her and will hold her'" (224)—echoes the language of the wedding ceremony as forebodingly as does that of Walker's "Roselily." Jane is "'my prize'" (244)—but then again, so was Bertha (259). He can indulge her whims now, for "'I mean shortly to claim you—your thoughts, conversation, and company—for life'" (234). If engagement has moved Jane from autonomy to adjunct status, marriage promises a still further reduction, as he "playfully" assures her. "'But listen—whisper—it is your time now, little tyrant, but it will be mine presently: and when once I have fairly seized you, to have and to hold, I'll just—figuratively speaking—attach you to a chain like this' (touching his watch-guard)" (238). The language of capture and imprisonment—"seize," "have," "hold," "attach"—so precisely corrected and dismissed by "figuratively speaking," suggests that attachment indeed presents problems.

Though Jane expects to gain more knowledge of her beloved as his fiancée, she instead finds her curiosity shunted aside, her active quest for knowledge recast as her passive reception of what Rochester chooses to tell her. As employee, Jane tried to discover what the strange secret of the house might be: "There was a mystery at Thornfield; and . . . from participation in that mystery I was purposely excluded" (144). After each "test," she looks forward to knowledge as her due payment. Following Rochester's near-immolation, she expects the master of house to satisfy "my curiosity" (138) about its mystery. During her silent night-watch with Mason, she wonders what "crime . . . lived incarnate in this sequestered mansion, and could neither be expelled nor subdued by the owner?" (185). As fiancée (which has been its own test), she looks forward to the right she once envied Blanche: "I thought Miss Ingram happy, because one day she might look into the abyss at her leisure, explore its secrets, and analyse their nature" (165).

Her anticipation seems reasonable, for Rochester once told her that he talks to her "'almost as freely as if I were writing my thoughts in a diary'" (119). He still expects to inscribe his version of reality upon Jane, but now he edits far more carefully for the "forbidden" knowledge that Maxim too thinks husbands should keep from wives (*Rebecca* 202) and he is far more impatient when he suspects that she is working from a script of her own instead of "entreating" (231) him for his. When Jane asks that he gratify her curiosity on one unspecified point (his courtship of Blanche), his "stern" and thunderous face is the response to her temerity. "'Curiosity is a dangerous petition. . . . You are welcome to all my confidence that is worth having, Jane: but for God's sake don't desire a useless burden! Don't long for poison— don't turn out to be a downright Eve on my hands! . . . Encroach, presume, and the game is up'" (230). Curiosity is now presumption, knowledge a poaching on Rochester's territory that will lead to "the game" (their love, I assume) being "up." He defers the boon of knowledge to "'when we have been married a year and a day'" and offers that promise as the "'solution of the mystery'" (251).

His "solution," phrased in the language of fairy tale, is none at all, of course, and it infantilizes her with its suggestion that she'll be able to understand when she's all grown up. What knowledge she does gain, unconsciously or consciously, he dismisses. Her dreams of the child make of her a "'little nervous subject!'" (248). Her vision of Bertha, confirmed by the torn veil, is chimerical: "'The creature of an over-stimulated brain; that is certain. I must be careful of you, my treasure: nerves like yours were not made for rough handling'" (250). In denying Jane's perception of reality and judgment, in trying to make her into "'my good little girl'" (231), Rochester, like John in "The Yellow Wallpaper," insists that there is only one authoritative source of knowledge and power, and that is unequivocally he.

Just as Jane experiences enormous pressure to reroute her active instincts into appropriately passive channels and to install Rochester as subject, so too she risks being physically remade into an extension of his status, the proof that nothing can thwart his headstrong will. In response to Mrs. Fairfax's fear that Jane has "forgotten" her station, he angrily retorts: "'Station! station!—your station is in my heart, and on the necks of those who would insult you, now or hereafter'" (231). Whereas the narrator of *Rebecca* gratefully accepts such vicarious re-taliation, Jane does not: what she sees in his lordly ways and "gifts" is "'nothing save Fairfax Rochester's pride'" (247). Nonetheless, despite Jane's attempts to keep what defines her—her job, her schedule, her own clothes—she is fighting a holding action at best. Rochester again gives too much (with the inevitable implication that soon he will once more give too little): in so doing, he underscores his perception that she has and is nothing without him.

If Rochester claims to doubt her grasp on reality when she tells of her nighttime visitor, she, with better cause, suspects his when he insists on decking her out with jewels. "'I will myself put the diamond chain round your neck, and the circlet on your forehead . . . , and I will clasp the bracelets on these fine wrists, and load these fairy-like fingers with rings. . . . I will make the world acknowledge you a beauty too,' he went on, while I really became uneasy at the strain he had adopted; because I felt he was either deluding himself, or trying to delude me" (227). The repetition of "I wills" that declares Rochester sole agent is troubling. So are the problems attached to the family jewels: they are a weight far more onerous than the knowledge of which he wants to unburden Jane. Jane's sense of self restricts as Rochester's expands with his spending. She reminds him how quickly his other cherished toys depreciated: "'Do you remember what you said of Céline Varens—of the diamonds, the cashmeres you gave her? I will not be your English Céline Varens'" (237). Rochester insists that she is the exception, unlike all others, but she still doubts. Jane is humiliated, not ecstatic, at his lavish expenditures: "The more he bought me, the more my cheek burned with a sense of annoyance and degradation" (236). But her objections, like her dreams, are trivialized and labeled foibles, the warnings of the anger inherent in her "annoyance" ignored.

Jane is at great risk in that she loves Rochester. If he were simply a John Reed, a Sarah Reed, or a Brocklehurst, his authority could be recognized and countered insofar as possible. He is not, though: the text indicates that he does love Jane, entangled as his motives nonetheless are with the felt entitlements of sex and rank. Jane recognizes and needs his love: at the same time she, more than any other character discussed so far, also recognizes dominance, which she does not equate with love. That Jane, a poorly trained masochist insulated and enabled by her spectator's role, is still susceptible to self-abnegation isolates and highlights the powerful cultural and psychological dynamics of the masochist's dilemma. Rochester's cynical axiom— "'Most things free-born will submit to anything for a salary'" (118)— is correlated with as dour a sex-based assumption: most women will submit to anything for love.

The narrating self, and possibly the experiencing self, notes the slow drift toward possible merger, but her resistance to the pull of Gothic courtship becomes increasingly weak and sporadic, separation more difficult. Jane extends her stay at Gateshead, but then rushes back to the director of the very scenario she fled. Watching Rochester court Blanche, she is still able to report: "I was growing very lenient to my master: I was forgetting all his faults, for which I had once kept a sharp look-out. . . . Now I saw no bad" (165). Seeing no bad, hearing no evil that cannot be explained away, Jane is lulled into quiescence. The protagonist of *Rebecca* becomes one with Maxim "in a sort of dream" (284) as he tells her of Rebecca's murder. O, in her fugue state, listens to herself discussed, and responds "as though it did not concern her and, simultaneously, as though she had already experienced it before" (*O* 114). Jane, seeing the gypsy revealed as Rochester, experiences the same hypnoid suspension of reality. "Where was I? Did I wake or sleep? Had I been dreaming? Did I dream still?" (177). The barrier between self and other enticingly and terrifyingly dissolves for all three characters. O feels that "by some strange substitution Sir Stephen was speaking for her, in her place" (115); the protagonist of *Rebecca* feels Maxim's actions to be her own. Jane discovers the gypsy's "accent, her gesture . . . were familiar to me as my own face in a glass—as the speech of my own tongue" (177).

The comparison of the characters is only initially startling: what is truly shocking is the dreamy indifference that allows each to lay aside identity and will for those of an other. Walking to the church, Jane wants to see through Rochester's eyes, to feel his thoughts, and is blind to all else: "My heart was with my eyes; and both seemed migrated into Mr. Rochester's frame" (253). O and the protagonist of *Rebecca* also seek to lodge their identities in an other's gaze, an other's frame. Like both, Jane is temporarily willing to be a worshiper at her master's shrine. "My future husband was becoming to me my whole world; and more than the world: almost my hope of heaven. He stood between me and every thought of religion, as an eclipse intervenes between man and the broad sun. I could not, in those days, see God for his creature: of whom I had made an idol" (241). Given Jane's reliance upon religion to authorize her independence, her deification is far more scandalous than O's. O can be minimized or dismissed as an extreme, abnormal characterization. Jane, far more firmly placed within the normal scheme of things and much more sympathetic and easy to identify with for most readers, is for those very reasons a more frightening instance of masochism's draw. Their difference is one of degree, not kind, and the distinction between "normal" and "abnormal" not so sharp as we might want to believe.

Though the level-headedness and intellectual insight that characterize Jane are no more able to effect change in themselves than they are in analysis, she still has most common matter of analytic interpretation with which to articulate her plight: dreams and wit. Jane's dreams of a child who depends upon her, precipitated by the veiled aggression directed against her during the house party and before her wedding (193–94, 247–49), awaken and symbolize the still-needy child within her.[16] They both remind her of what she stands to lose should she lose Rochester and question what security she has gained through his love. Telling him about her prenuptial day, Jane emphasizes how "happy" she was: "'I thought of the life that lay before me—*your* life, sir—an existence more expansive and stirring than my own'" (246). Yet, on that night before her wedding, Jane has two nightmares before awakening to the living nightmare of Bertha. Sleeping, she "'experienced a strange, regretful consciousness of some barrier dividing us.'" Burdened with a small child "'which shivered in my cold arms and wailed piteously in my ear,'" she tries to overtake Rochester on her road but, her movements "fettered" and her voice "inarticulate," he withdraws "'farther and farther every moment'" (247–48).

In the second dream, Jane and the child she "'might not lay . . . down anywhere'" find Thornfield a ruin and Rochester "'departing for many years, and for a distant country.'" She climbs the "thin," "fragile-looking" wall to glimpse him, only to have the wall collapse, the child fall, herself fall and then to awaken (248–49). If the "barrier" that separates Jane and Rochester—Jane's very identity, I assume—crumbles, both the woman and the child are lost. The child that was sometimes "laughing" and "playing" (193) in the first series of dreams can apparently no longer be cared for by Jane alone. Though the dream-logic of the sleeping Jane may argue for Rochester's departure, the need of that child still asserts itself. Later, an awake Jane looks at the "child" again, the love that "shivered in my heart, like a suffering child in a cold cradle; sickness and anguish

---

[16]Although she does not discuss *Jane Eyre*, Margaret Doody argues that nightmare in the Gothic "admits dread as a natural experience" and as a part of reality for female and male characters ("Deserts, Ruins and Troubled Waters" 571). Homans's extended analysis of Jane's dreams is the most thorough of recent feminist analyses, but Adams (149–52), Baer (144–46), Edwards (83–84), Gilbert and Gubar (357–59), and Poovey (*Uneven Development* 138–42) also provide some excellent insights.

had seized it; . . . it could not derive warmth from [Rochester's] breast" (260). Jane still fears for the child's survival, but now she knows that it is she who must leave to save both dream-child and woman.

Jane, like her dream-child, still longs for love, but neither its needs nor those of the responsible, active dream-woman will be met by Rochester. Dream-work, then, gives Jane one way with which to represent what can no longer be acknowledged even to herself. Wit, with its close relation to the unconscious, provides still another. The delightful, sharp, and enormously serious play between Jane and Rochester consolidates amorous and aggressive concerns. Jane consciously adopts this strategy during the engagement period to preserve decorum and to give Rochester what she thinks he needs instead of the loving docility he wants: the "needle of repartee" assures no "lamblike" submission to his "despotism" (240), and she uses it to maintain "'that distance between you and myself most conducive to our real mutual advantage'" (240–41).[17]

What Jane *can* voice through the acerbic, if indirect, content of her badinage is a critique of authoritarianism, skepticism about love's endurance in marriage, and serious reservations about her role as an exception. Her commentary is sometimes nonverbal, as when, irked at Rochester's fatuous smile after their shopping, a smile "such as a sultan might, in a blissful and fond moment, bestow on a slave his gold and gems had enriched," she "crushed" Rochester's hand and "thrust it back to him" (236). At other times, she physically moves away from him and his assumptions of ready compliance to his will. More often, however, her response is in the form of clever, acute teasing. Rochester is Hercules, Sampson, Ahasurerus, or an Oriental potentate.[18] She fends off his advances by invoking the first two: "'However, had they been married, they would no doubt by their severity as husbands have made up for their softness as suitors; and so will you, I fear'" (229). She laughingly doubts whether Rochester's fervor will last any longer than theirs for their "charmers" (229). "'For

[17]In addressing Rochester's internalized representation, as she increasingly does, Jane simultaneously attests to his significance and her continuing powers of observation and judgment as well as to the implausibility of his responding to her concerns in actuality and her growing inability/unwillingness to voice them directly. Rochester, in contrast, increasingly refers to Jane in the third person when she is present: it is himself he really addresses, and her existence is simply the occasion for his soliloquies (e.g., 236, 280).

[18]Elsie Michie rightfully suggests that the representation of Orientalism is allied to that of the Irish and to the most often discussed "otherness" of the novel, Bertha's Creole identity ("The Historical Specificity of the Gothic").

a little while you will perhaps be as you are now,—a very little while; and then you will turn cool; and then you will be capricious; and then you will be stern, and I shall have much ado to please you: but when you get well used to me, you will perhaps like me again—*like* me, I say, not love me'" (228). In provokingly doubting the depth and duration of mythical strong men's love, in casting a future where women's apparent "conquests" (229) are chimerical, Jane presents her own fears, her own wish that "liking," more linked to recognition of identity than "loving," at least may be preserved.

Jane is not alone in her bandying of metaphor, of course. Rochester, delighted at her resistance to shopping, extends his conspicuous consumption to the vision of himself as the purchaser of female flesh. "'Is she original? Is she piquant? I would not exchange this one little English girl for the grand Turk's whole seraglio'" (236). Jane repudiates the equivalency, noting that the "Eastern allusion bit me again" (236), and proceeds to spin out her own fantasy. After Rochester has purchased his "'tons of flesh and such an assortment of black eyes,'" Jane will "'go out as a missionary to preach liberty to them that are enslaved,'" foment rebellion against the tyrant, and not "'consent to cut your bonds till you have signed a charter, the most liberal that despot ever yet conferred.'" Pleased by her own plot, starring herself as the spectator become liberator of the oppressed, she nonetheless is "'certain that . . . your first act, when released, would be to violate its conditions'" (237). Through what passes as banter between them, Jane questions the integrity and reliability of her loving "despot" just as she condenses, displaces, and represents her concerns in her dreams.

Jane's empathy for her mythical and actual female predecessors shows her still able to note and judge aggression. After the revelation of Rochester's marriage, she is able again to see clearly that she will be no reforming exception should she agree to be his mistress, but merely one in a series. The transition in Jane's case from "my father is beating a child" to "my father is beating me" is the source of dread, not eager anticipation: she wants to believe that there will be no repetition. In order to rejoice in the "'great good'" of marrying Rochester, she needs to know that Blanche is not "'suffering the bitter pain I myself felt a while ago'" (231). She terms his treatment of Blanche "'a burning shame, and a scandalous disgrace'" (231), just as she later condemns his response to Bertha as "inexorable," "vindictive," and "cruel" (265).

Jane's affinity with Bertha—underscored through their wifely doubling, passion, appearance (robed on her wedding morning, Jane is singularly like the apparition of the night before)—is explicit when Rochester insists that he would treat Jane differently in similar circumstances. To his demand that she acknowledge that difference—"'If you were mad, do you think I should hate you?'"—Jane can only steadfastly reply, "'I do indeed, sir'" (265).[19] Similarly, when Rochester self-pityingly describes his affairs with Céline, Giacinta, and Clara, she knows that she might well be the next object of loathing, even if no money changes hands. Rochester fastidiously disclaims his experience: "'Hiring a mistress is the next worst thing to buying a slave. . . . To live familiarly with inferiors is degrading'" (274). Jane has no intention of being leased or bought outright by a sham marriage: as she instantly realizes, the very love she sought would be irrevocably lost. "I felt the truth of these words; and I drew from them the certain inference, that if I were so far to forget myself and all the teaching that had ever been instilled into me as—under any pretext—with any justification—through any temptation—to become the successor of these poor girls, he would one day regard me with the same feeling which now in his mind desecrated their memory. I did not give utterance to this conviction: it was enough to feel it" (274). Jane has seen enough pain inflicted to know that "'these poor girls,'" like "'that unfortunate lady'" Bertha (265), suffered. And, whatever their own complicity in the past, she knows that Rochester "desecrates" them in the present through his righteous abuse. Where the protagonist of *Rebecca* merges with Maxim as he narrates the murder of a vilified other woman, Jane cannot do so. The man she loves is in effect beating another woman: she neither calls it love nor justifies it through righteous hate; she can and does silently note it.

Jane's previous knowledge of authority, Rochester's behavior to her during their courtship, and his treatment of other women buttress Jane's resistance to him after the revelation. In addition, however, the crescendo of his aggression from arrogant dismissal during courtship, through jovial management while engaged, to barely controlled violence when faced with the loss of Jane makes it impossible for her to ignore a truth she would rather not see. On what was to have been her wedding day, her hand is "held by a grasp of iron" (253) en route to the church and by a "hot and strong grasp" (255) during the ceremony. She stands at the altar with a man of rock: "Without speaking, without smiling, without seeming to recognise in me a human being,

---

[19]Jane's use of "I do" here, like her triple repetition of the phrase when Rochester later asks if she means to leave (278), obviously echoes the marriage ceremony. In both instances, what she is stubbornly avowing is not only her resistance, but her determination to love, honor, and obey herself.

he only twined my waist with his arm, and riveted me to his side"
(255). The element of physical coercion, no matter what its motivation, is unmistakable and ominous. It is Bertha with whom he
wrestles, and Bertha he binds to a chair after their return (259) but
Jane, who well knows what it feels like to be threatened with such
restriction after rebellion, is wary of what is also her own peril.

During their excruciating final interview, Jane knows herself at moral risk, but the risk is also mortal as Rochester's violence escalates and
he turns from suasion to rage. Even shaking her head increases her
danger: "it required a degree of courage, excited as he was becoming,
even to risk that mute sign of dissent" (265–66). When his specious
logic fails, as it must, to convince a newly alert Jane, he plays his
trump, force. "'Jane! will you hear reason?' (he stooped and ap-
proached his lips to my ear) 'because, if you won't, I'll try violence'"
(266). Rochester demands pity *and* fear when the former only is unavailing: "'Jane, I am not a gentle-tempered man—you forget
that. . . . Out of pity to me and yourself, put your finger on my pulse,
feel how it throbs, and—beware!'" (267). Jane does beware: she, unlike he, is determined that she *can* help herself but even her mute
resistance further inflames Rochester. "His fury was wrought to the
highest: he must yield to it for a moment, whatever followed; he
crossed the floor and seized my arm, and grasped my waist. He
seemed to devour me with his flaming glance: physically, I felt, at the
moment, powerless as stubble exposed to the draught and glow of a
furnace" (279). Jane's "involuntary sigh" in response to his "painful"
grip and the near-exhaustion of her "overtaxed strength" save her: he
and she realize that nothing will be won, no victory achieved, if, as he
says, "'I bent, if I uptore, if I crushed her'" (280).

Paradoxically, Rochester's final turning to violence strengthens and
frees Jane. Her grief is acute but Rochester's physical coercion, like the
existence of Bertha, concretizes the haunting recognition throughout
courtship and engagement that something is wrong. Jane knows that
her love continues, but she knows too that she is seeing authority at
its most loathsome, in however dear a face. She is now within a
reality, painful as it may be, in which she can again see and act.

Alone in her room after seeing Bertha and before meeting with
Rochester, Jane harrows her own psyche. Vision, reason, and activity
resume their ascendancy in her. Feeling yields to thought, which in
turn demands action. "And now I thought: till now I had only heard,
seen, moved, followed up and down where I was led or dragged—
watched event rush on event, disclosure open beyond disclosure: but
now, I thought" (259–60). Feeling speaks, but so too does reason,

which tells her she must now *act*. Jane asks "'What am I to *do*?' " (261, emphasis added). The answer, "'Leave Thornfield at once,'" seems unbearable.

Jane pleads with conscience, begs to be spared the responsibility for making a decision.

> I wanted to be weak that I might avoid the awful passage of further suffering I saw laid out for me. . . .
> "Let me be torn away, then!" I cried. "Let another help me!"
> "No; you shall tear yourself away, none shall help you: you shall, yourself, pluck out your right eye: yourself cut off your right hand: your heart shall be the victim; and you, the priest, to transfix it." (261)

Her self-sacrifice is for herself but is still grievous, as she ferociously turns her anger and aggression against herself. It would avail her little to direct them at Rochester, for that would only maintain their bond. Moving from frozen disbelief to feeling, thought, and action, Jane cauterizes her own wound and prescribes her own cure.

Having come to terms with herself, Jane can come to terms with Rochester. He warns her in their interview that he is "'on my guard'": "'You are thinking how to *act*,—*talking*, you consider, is of no use'" (263). He knows Jane well but, in his overestimation of his powers, he underestimates hers. During the worst of her ordeal, Jane feels a controlling calm in the eye of the storm. "But I was not afraid: not in the least. I felt an inward power; a sense of influence, which supported me" (266). That sense supports her reassertion of personal responsibility and her refusal to accept the "full responsibility" for him that Horney identifies as the imperative of the morbidly dependent (*Neurosis* 119). Responding to Rochester's claim that she will fling him into a life of profligacy, Jane is sternly just. "'Mr. Rochester, I no more assign this fate to you than I grasp at it for myself. We were born to strive and endure—you as well as I: do so. You will forget me before I forget you'" (279). Her terse injunction and her matter-of-fact final statement shows that the shadowy fears of dream and badinage now have substance and can be acknowledged as reality. Separation, however wrenching, has happened.

Jane might yield for love—her own, actively exerted, as well as his received; she will not yield to fallacious reasoning or physical threat. Her real risk comes when conscience and reason join with feeling to reproach her, to seductively whisper that his salvation (and her happiness) rests upon her. "'Soothe him; save him; love him; tell him you love him and will be his. Who in the world cares for *you*? or who will be injured by what you do?' Still indomitable was the reply—'I care for myself. The more solitary, the more friendless, the more unsustained I am, the more I will respect myself'" (279). In denying the murmured incantation's suggestion that she means nothing and he all, in refusing to live her life for him as mistress or wife, Jane is restored to herself, able to withstand and flee the most powerful of Rochester's pleas: his love and pain. "I had dared and baffled his fury; I must elude his sorrow: I retired to the door" (280).

Jane's retreat from the room and from Thornfield is a valiant one in defense of the ego. She follows the moon's edict, "'My daughter, flee temptation!'" (281), and, in so doing, flees the danger of Gothic engagements as well. The temptation Jane puts behind her was present to her as wife or mistress: that of assigning her identity to another, of gradually conflating the self-chosen limits of love and the other-imposed restraints of authority. Gothic love has no answer except yes to Rochester's annexation of her during their engagement; dreams, wit, the lives of other women, and Rochester's increasing aggression identify her problem and insist on another response. The answer that adult identity and the second half of the novel demand is an end to the Gothic beating fantasy and the beginning of a new world in which love and women's identities need not be contradictions, where men and women can meet, as Jane once proclaimed, as "equals."

Autonomy and the Refusal to Replicate Oppression

This study necessarily emphasizes the first half of *Jane Eyre*, in which the Gothic's beating drama figures prominently. As I understand the text, it is Jane's incomplete training in masochism—the early infliction of pain never associated with love—that enables her clear-sightedness, activity, and rationalism. That such a character, carrying the spectator's limited immunity, can nonetheless almost choose to enter the Gothic's arena of loving cruelty points to the ubiquitous strength of the social and psychological linkage of love and dominance.

So strong and so accepted is that linkage in gender arrangements, however, that its very representation, as well as the problem of how to set forth Jane's need to break free, present a narrative quandary resolved only by the intervention of other plots. It is only because Bertha lives that Jane can too, that she can be restored to the relative autonomy of her spectator's role. So too in the second half of the novel Jane's inheritance, the discovery of family, Rochester's fortunate fall, their psychic communication, and the restoration of Rochester's vision work together as a form of nineteenth-century "magic realism" to envision a new social order, one in which love and independence coexist and no woman is beaten.

In my discussion of the novel's second half, I selectively emphasize those issues that best comment on the character's achievements as spectator as well as the inevitable limits of that role. Her recognition of cruelty to others or herself is acute. She uses traditional morality and religion to sanction her own will and freedom. When faced with repetition, whether by St. John's courtship or the return to Rochester, she shows that her knowledge of Gothic courtship has been incorporated, not denied. Most important, she has no inclination to move to the beater's role and replicate oppression. As "the apple" (397) of Rochester's eye, she is beloved and her own sight, activity, and love relatively uninhibited. Yet, a residue of anxiety remains, at least for this reader, and certainly in the novel's strained close, a suggestion that the Gothic continues to haunt even the safest retreat and that compromise formations are, by their very nature, never entirely satisfactory. If Jane, to her credit, harms no one as spectator and consistently refuses to be an accomplice to cruelty, neither, in extricating herself from "the web of horror" (185), does she initiate activity to save others. In saying this, I don't want to measure some supposed failure against a heroic feminist ideal (although that is inevitably a part of the response) but rather to suggest, within the pattern of the beating fantasy, a next step, another stage, that might end the Gothic, if not *Jane Eyre*. To recognize pain, to understand its repetitions, and to save one's self is an extraordinary feat; to stop future repetitions for one's self and other women is a still greater one, as I argue in the final chapter.

Jane's experiences on the moor, as a beggar, and in once again needing "a new servitude" emphasize that reality does not reside solely in psychic events or interpersonal relations. Neither Nature, her Maker, nor society will succor "the poor orphan child" (18) or a woman suspiciously adrift, but Jane herself agrees with their nonintervention, understanding that it is not their "business" (289) to stop the suffering of an unknown other. Within the social sphere, Jane often embraces limits and rules even when she herself is damaged by them. On the one hand, by restricting herself, she can remain relatively free from others' regulations. On the other hand, her pragmatic acceptance of "things as they are" (barring active injustice) predisposes her conservative reluctance to question the social order. She is, for example, ashamed of her loss of status and feels it to be "degrading" (e.g., 286, 289, 298, 299, 316); despite her experiences, she readily accepts the assumptions of her own world about class and origin. Knowing full well how inadequate others' assumptions about governesses are, Jane nonetheless has no doubts about the place of Bessie, Robert, Leah, Grace, Hannah, John, Mary, or her students;[20] the inherent superiority of the "British peasantry" (343) is no more open to question than are the innate "defects" of the French (369).

Jane uses her very conservatism, though, as one of her most effective weapons in protecting herself against domination. Her personal sureness comes in part from her insistence that "'the human and fallible should not arrogate'" the power to endorse "'any strange, unsanctioned line of action'" (121). In rejecting Rochester, she invokes divine and social consensus to say for her what she cannot say for herself. "'Preconceived opinions, foregone determinations, are all I have at this hour to stand by: there I plant my foot'" (279). Paradoxically, then, the common supports Jane in the uncommon, and her doctrinal conservatism furnishes the wherewithal for radical dissent, as we see in her refusal of St. John. "'Keep to common sense, St. John: you are verging on nonsense. . . . God did not give me my life to throw away; and to do as you wish me would, I begin to think, be almost equivalent to committing suicide'" (364). Secular and sacred authority unite in Jane's impatient reply to new wooing.

Jane's second courtship, quite as problematic as the first, offers the textual occasion to examine the central issues of her character: her need for love, ability to stand alone, relation to authority, and willingness to sacrifice herself for a supposedly higher cause. As "inexorable" as Rochester (265, 321), St. John is also as unself-conscious in his demands and in the "curious intensity of observation" (349) with which he scrutinizes Jane. Rochester is "'used to say "Do this," and it is done'" (109); St. John too compels obedience and sensitivity to his moods. "When he said 'go,' I went; 'come,' I came; 'do this,' I did it" (350). Jane imagines that as his wife she would "accommodate quietly to his masterhood" (358), and she can see that he would appropriate her will as surely as would Rochester. "I was tempted to cease struggling with him—to rush down the torrent of his will into the gulf of his existence, and there lose my own" (368).

[20]I would nonetheless note that the very listing of names suggests that, regardless of class presuppositions, each character is assumed to have an identity, as do the most often seen of "my Morton girls," Alice Wood and Mary Garrett (343, 320, 333). The act of naming seems a necessary acknowledgment by the narrating self: even the un-Christian Mrs. Reed is given her Christian name, Sarah, in death, and Mrs. Fairfax remembers when she was "'called by my name, Alice'" (211, 232).

Unlike Rochester, however, St. John offers no love as the veneer for authority. Neither is his power the self-aggrandizement of the Reeds, Brocklehurst, and even Rochester. The absence of love, Jane's affinity for St. John's cold reason, and her newly increased experience in the recognition of and resistance to unjust authority let her rebut St. John as she never could Rochester. St. John and Helen Burns are alike in their ethic of sacrifice for salvation, but Jane's free and direct arguments with both demonstrates the same separation from their values. In rejecting this new call for self-immolation, she also rejects St. John's claim that "'it is not me you deny, but God'" (360). She has confused God and "his creature" (241), Rochester, once; she is not likely to do so again. Neither does she hesitate to name aggression as straightforwardly as she did when a child in this courtship. "'If I were to marry you, you would kill me. You are killing me now.'" St. John characterizes her response as words that "'ought not to be used: violent, unfeminine, and untrue'" (363). His "ought" is outweighed by his one false term: what Jane has to say is true, and she will not let a mistaken propriety make her a silent assenter to violence against herself again.

If aspects of St. John that correspond to Rochester and Helen explain part of Jane's response to him, a still more powerful and less noted doubling influences her strongly and suggests why the novel closes in St. John's voice: his similarity to *her*.[21] St. John's refusal of emotion, his cool self-mastery, and his decision to live for others model an aspect of Jane, a possible future, from which she turns. Rosamond Oliver comments that Jane is "like" St. John (324). Jane, listening to St. John preach, discerns "insatiate yearnings and disquieting aspirations. . . . He had no more found [peace], I thought, than had I" (310). St. John too comments that "'in your nature is an alloy as detrimental to repose as that in mine'" (312). These two measured, self-controlled characters recognize the "ambitious," "impassioned" (313) nature of one another.

Most important, in watching St. John and Rosamond, Jane sees her own courtship again in the "spectacle of another's suffering and sacrifice" (321). She knows what it means to be a subordinate longing for

[21]As I comment above, St. John is most often seen as a double of Helen or Rochester and an antagonist to Jane, thus perhaps bespeaking our own sympathy for authority exercised in the name of passion rather than reason. As several critics suggest, however, the relations between Jane and St. John are more complex in that he is the "male embodiment of Jane's ambitions" (Adams 148), his longings "have a strong affinity to Jane's own" (DeLamotte 216), his "ice is in Jane as well" (Auerbach 203), he "pushes her to further recognition of possibility" (Moglen 135), and he offers her a "larger world" and "action" (Edwards 87).

one of higher rank, and that one available only if independence and ambition are sacrificed. She recognizes his struggle between reason and emotion, for it has been her own. When his chest heaves, she finely perceives that it is his heart making "a vigorous bound for the attainment of liberty. But he curbed it" (321). Jane, who ordered herself to put by her fantasies with "'No snivel!—no sentiment!—no regret!'" (141), comprehends the harsh self-discipline that requires St. John to end his rapt contemplation of "'human love'" (328) after a precise fifteen minutes. She too has been an "automaton" (222, 321) and knows the price of such stern self-command. She draws St. John out, for she realizes his need in her own: "Reserved people often really need the frank discussion of their sentiments and griefs more than the expansive" (328). She understands his perception, so like her own playful speculation that six months will see the end of Rochester's fervor (228), that "'to twelve months' rapture would succeed a lifetime of regret'" (329). Most of all, she empathizes with his disengaged stance that helps him to remain free of emotional entanglements and to channel his activity.

Jane is a potential St. John. He denies his own need for love and forcefully sublimates both it and his aggressive ambition to higher social aims. St. John's Gothic romance is finally religious: he believes that embracing restriction and self-sacrifice will lead to identity through a divine and loving Other. It is, nonetheless, romance. Precisely because of their affinity, however, Jane is able to recognize through another's romance the limits of reflexive masochism and of independence gained by severing all object relations. St. John's self-elected martyrdom has fused with his ambition and become his very identity; to embrace that unity, "'dearer than the blood in my veins'" (329), means to relinquish human love. So too his Christian mission, suggestive of Jane's one-time fantasy of liberating the oppressed, hints uncomfortably at the link possible between altruism and dominance. St. John's authority as an English gentleman, so decidedly renounced, only reemerges in his role as colonizing missionary. Feminized in his other-worldly and human loves, he opts for the former's grander scale.

For Jane, then, St. John's road is a temptation and a warning. More Pauline than Johnian, he is indeed "inexorable" in his impatience with those weaker than he and in his punitive, joyous acceptance of suffering. There is a stern integrity in his decision that Jane esteems, and yet it falls short of what she desires for herself. It is, of course, no coincidence at all that, when self-sacrifice speaks most strongly during St. John's proposal, the voice of love comes wafting telepathically across the moors. Where Rochester would coerce for love, St. John would for God and reason. Jane wants all three and no coercion.

Jane's own distance from the socially or emotionally "deserving poor," whether the village schoolgirls (who might well become her cause) or Adèle, is a problem insofar as we search for an end to Gothic inequity. Yet, to lessen or close that distance would be to violate the hard-won freedom and integrity Jane achieves as spectator.[22] In addition, the text displays a deep skepticism about whether any character with ascendancy ever can or should determine the good of another. The avoidance of repetition thus is often neutrality in *Jane Eyre*, not active partisanship. I mean "neutrality" in this context—the neutrality that lets Jane avoid abetting the devaluation of Adèle, Bertha, Céline, Giacinta, Clara, her students—as a tribute, not faint praise. Jane refuses to be a part of subordinating others: clearly recollected experience hones her vision so that even the "preconceived opinions" (279) to which she is predisposed cannot cloud it.

Nowhere is this refusal more evident than in the return to

---

[22]Several critics argue strongly that Jane's most important relations during development are with other women. Rich's early and influential essay, "Jane Eyre: The Temptations of a Motherless Woman," finds the "image of a nurturing or principled or spirited woman on whom she can model herself" (91) in each setting/stage. Adams stresses the "fostering sisterhood" of Diana and Mary (155), while Moglen points to the "strength and confidence which she derives from their friendship" (134). While I agree that women crucially affect Jane's development throughout the novel, I cannot find Jane's relationships with them to be as central in her representation or her psyche as are those with men. When women organize individual stages, like Helen and Maria Temple, for example, they disappear from later stages: Jane announces that, after Miss Temple's marriage, "my mind had put off all it had borrowed" of her (73); Helen is remembered once, at Mrs. Reed's deathbed (208). Their memories, when compared to the ghostly persistence of Rochester and St. John in other places and times, seem sadly attenuated.

The only explanation I can find for this relates directly to my thesis about Jane's incorporation of the spectator's stance to maintain what anthropologists call "right distance." If there is a problem in maintaining right distance with men, necessarily "different," then the risk is greater still with other women, who are like one's self, as Chodorow argues. (Particularly if one's internal maternal representation is Mrs. Reed, a figure that does endure over time and place.) Thus, Jane values women who are themselves rational and distanced, however kind they may also be—Miss Temple, Diana, and Mary Rivers. Her conversations with Diana and Mary are the only ones in which we see intimate talk with other women as an adult: that with Diana, in which Jane affectionately calls her "Die" and both agree on the impossibility of her marrying St. John [365–66], is a conspicuous instance. She, like they, however, reserves wit and activity for a masculine audience. Diana and Mary tease their brother, Jane teases Rochester, but they do not engage in badinage with one another. What is indeed a promising vision of alterity fades as St. John takes up Jane's time and narrative. Safely distanced from other women by her marriage, as Diana and Mary are by theirs, Jane can see them in another time and place only through their congenial, sedate pattern of annual visits.

Rochester, where there is repetition aplenty. Jane recapitulates and reverses the stages of their first courtship: she watches him, herself unseen; she controls what he can know and view; she presents him with the drama of her and St. John's courtship, as he once did to her with Blanche; she offers a tauntingly companionate relation. And yet, what *Jane Eyre* demonstrates is not the repetition that, in *Rebecca*, reinforces inequity but instead repetition that marks progress and working through. Her spectating and her activity assume literal and figurative importance. "His countenance reminded one of a lamp quenched, waiting to be relit—and alas! it was not himself that could now kindle the lustre of animated expression: he was dependent on another for that office!" (386). The language of the passage points not so much to vision as to emotion itself. Rochester not only sees but also hears and feels through/with Jane. His lordly, narcissistic self-sufficiency gives way to his willing "avowal of his dependence" (387), his own need for object relations. Troubling as the figuration of their new equality is, it nonetheless does not replicate the inequity of merger but instead achieves what Benjamin terms rapprochement: mutual, intersubjective recognition of agency and desire (*Bonds of Love* 102). Jane does not use her newfound power (any more than her newfound wealth) to become an exultant beater, nor is Rochester's dependency that of the subjugated beaten. Instead, for the first time, there is full reciprocity: "in his presence I thoroughly lived; and he lived in mine" (384).

In their "perfect concord," Jane is, she says, "my husband's life as fully as he is mine" (396, 398). The text's close offers not merger, but synergy, not the absorption of a lesser into the will and power of one stronger, but a mutually chosen coming together that creates something more than either individual. Jane sees, acts, and knows with/for Rochester; she loves and works within the compromise formation that is relationship.

The novel's very emphasis on perfect equilibrium, though, also suggests an instability barely controlled, a discomfort at the loss of the spectator's distance that even the most loving closeness does not quite mitigate.[23] The "unhealthiness of the situation" of isolated Ferndean (264) seems not entirely remedied by Jane's being "supremely blest" (396) in her relationship. The act of narration itself and the reintroduction of St. John, that split-off representation of Jane's

---

[23]Brontë's *The Professor* and *Villette* show the same indeterminacy and discomfort at the spectator's distance being lost. Love and independence coexist in *Villette*'s ending, but only through the absence of the beloved, M. Paul. His suspended presence allows for a balance that is unimaginable within the bounds of realism.

autonomy, reason, and ambition are also necessary ballast, reminders that she cannot live entirely for love any more than she could live entirely without it.[24] The divine imbalance with which the novel closes functions simultaneously as reminder, displacement, and denial of the heterosexual imbalance of Gothic love. After her marriage, Jane, unlike St. John, no longer refers to "my master" (398). But if St. John's sacrifice and death will not be Jane's, neither perhaps will his "ambition," the ability to follow "the path he had marked for himself," or his "steadfast" certainty about his future (398). Through her skills as spectator, Jane has recognized and refused the Gothic's beating drama with unflinching courage and integrity. That drama's end, however, can still only be predicated by the most utopian and provisional of resolutions, one removed in setting and tone from the pragmatic realism that elsewhere constitutes Jane's world.

Nonetheless, in *Jane Eyre*, the spectator's role is not apprenticeship for inclusion in the beating drama as beater or beaten. Instead, both plot and character suggest that the spectator's abilities are prerequisites for moving away from, not toward, the spectacle of a woman being beaten. Because love and authority are never joined for Jane she, unlike O or the protagonist of *Rebecca*, feels no envy for the sadomasochistic couple, has no longing to be a participant by taking the place of either. The distance of the spectator is instead her assurance of safety in clearly witnessing the spectacle that models heterosexual relations and social reality in the novel and in the genre. What Jane sees for herself she also sees for other women: she will not be an accomplice in the reproduction of unjust authority. Jane's testimony as spectator identifies what might overturn the Gothic economy: not eroticizing aggression against one's self and becoming the beaten, not repeating the cycle of violence by oppressing others as beater or accomplice, but rather persisting in the search for love *and* independence. As we will see in the final chapter, the path away from masochism Jane so clearly describes in her first steps as spectator is further traveled by those who follow her.

[24]For an analysis of Jane's and St. John's tug of war over literary and Biblical texts to determine who will have voice, see Carolyn Williams's "Closing the Book" and Carla L. Peterson's *The Determined Reader* (105–6).

7

Resisting the Gothic

In this book, I analyze the ways in which representations of masochism in psychoanalysis and in the Gothic reflect and shape cultural patterns of domination and subordination. While these patterns inform the ways we structure and interpret relationships within and among sexes, classes, and races, my focus has been its most deeply entrenched and common form: heterosexual gender roles. My aim has been, as Benjamin says, "to understand how domination is anchored in the hearts of the dominated" (*Bonds of Love* 5) and to begin to understand how that domination might come to an end. The Gothic, a genre of the dominated, obsessively remembers and repeats the masochism in which its protagonists are so well trained. Some novels, however, also suggest how characters can work through their traumatic denial of identity and find recognition without replicating oppression.

As I argue in my discussion of *Jane Eyre*, the spectator's role is an indispensable prerequisite for ending the beating drama. Nothing seems more simple than recognizing pain and looking for its source, but the roots of masochism lie deep within identity, entangled with the need for love and recognition. Masochism may come to be integral to a woman's ego, a part of self-worth, or the learned strategy through which she deals most successfully with her world. In addition, the inhibition of active instincts that goes along with masochism limits a woman's ability to recognize her own suffering, to ask questions about it, and to act even when she gains such hard-won knowledge.

The spectator's active knowledge, then, is a major achievement. It may be limited to what she sees and not extend to herself but, even if she wonders how and why other women "let" themselves be hurt, she witnesses their pain. Even (or especially) if she understands that she herself could be at risk, she may believe that her bystander's role confers a certain immunity and refuse to name domination or to act when she and others are victimized by it. Nonetheless, the active spectator knows that hurting herself is not in her own best interests, unless it wards off a worse punishment inflicted by another. Her position is the first any protagonist must assume before being able to postulate a love whose economy is not that of the haves and have-nots.

Wary as the active spectator is, she knows that victimization happens but that her real identity is not as a victim. Her self-definition points to the next steps in escaping the Gothic: personal responsibility, the knowledge that her own plight is common to other women, and identification of the systemic forces that help to make masochistic Gothic women. Ideally, as in *Jane Eyre*, these steps preclude seeking to become a master in turn and so perpetuating the cycles of oppression. Aggression is used *for* the self, and not to measure and create a self in light of the powerlessness of others.

There are three main possibilities for working through the Gothic which often operate simultaneously: aggression against the dominator that stops domination; self-conscious subversion that mimes cultural expectations of femininity to achieve the protagonist's freedom; and a utopian alterity, always briefly hinted at, that refuses to accept the binary options of subordinated/oppressed and laughs heartily at the very idea. The last is the future, only hinted at because still unrealized; the first two are our Gothic present.

Aggression and *Linden Hills*

In Walker's *The Third Life of Grange Copeland*, Grange believes he has "stumbled on the necessary act that black men must commit to regain, or to manufacture their manhood, their self-respect. They must kill their oppressors." During his "second life," he haunts the streets of Harlem, screaming at parents "'Teach them to *hate*, if you wants them to survive!'" (153). For women schooled to believe that subordination is love, the knowledge that they have been hurt, that there is an exterior source for their pain, and that they can hate is crucial. To *become* the enemy, however, is finally self-defeating (as Grange discovers in his "third life").

Yet, there are gradations of aggression in protagonists as well as differences between them in both motive and aim. Verbal, visual, or even imaginary behavior can articulate aggression, but the most overt form of the "rage at nonrecognition" (Benjamin 119) is physical violence. Violence, which insists that there *is* an active self to be reckoned with, can be manifested as self-defense, altruism, or just reflective sadism. Self-defense and altruism are, I believe, the only ones that work as resistance to and in the Gothic. Reflective sadism simply means that the once-beaten become beaters in turn, as does Ruth in Weldon's *The Life and Loves of a She-Devil* after she succeeds in making her ex-husband entirely dependent upon her: "I have all [power], and he has none. As I was, so he is now" (247). And, of course, as he once was, so she is now. Reflective sadism, then, only reconstitutes the beating drama as sempiternal domination regardless of who plays which role.

Nonetheless, directing aggression against a now-identified exterior source rather than the self marks an important change in the masochist, as Atwood emphasizes in the four "basic victim positions" she outlines in *Survival*. No longer frozen in denial (position 1) or in the limited recognition of victimization by abstract forces that present only "fellow-victims and oneself" (37) as targets for aggression (position 2), the woman in position 3 can repudiate the victim role while acknowledging the reality of victimization. Her anger and action "can be directed against the real source of oppression" (38). Such anger can be a prelude to the individual and social transformations of position 4, in which the binary "Victor/Victim games are obsolete" (39), and to the "real structural transformations" (10) Cixous and Clément also call for to end the embrace of torturer and victim in all its forms. "To emerge from this coupling of remembrance and reciprocal persecutions, to arrive in the present and no longer return to pantomimes of the past, it will be necessary to get out of the look, to leave the exchange of words, and to break up the circus of transference" (13).

The rebellious masochist who acts in self-defense and asserts her own autonomy, though, can draw destruction upon herself even while leaving a record of the dominator's oppression: identifying a local source for her pain does not in itself erase its power. As readers, we are enormously satisfied, for example, when Jane Eyre punches John Reed in the nose, when Antoinette Coswav/Bertha Mason first tries to knife and then bites her brother at the word "legally" in *Wide Sargasso Sea* (184), or when Mem Copeland pulls a gun on Grange's son, Brownfield, to establish new rules for coexistence. "'Long as you live—and that won't be long the rate you going—don't never call me 'out my name!' Mem sat calmly, watching the blood drip. 'To think I let you drag me round from one corncrib to another just cause I didn't want to hurt your feelings,' she said softly, almost in amazement. 'And just think of how many times I done got my head beat by you just so you could feel a little bit like a man, Brownfield Copeland'" (94). The insistence upon recognition of one's own identity through aggression, true in all three cases, finally proves self-defeating, however, because the power of oppressive forces in each instance is such that the victim may pay more than the victimizer. Satisfying as their actions are, for us and for them, Jane, Antoinette, and Mem suffer for their resistance and risk losing more than they have gained.

In Dinesen's "The Monkey," Athena, a veritable Valkyrie, has no idea that she could lose or that there is any possibility other than defending herself. Athena crosses aggression with the utopian possibility of utter nonrecognition of the beating drama. Athena, trapped by her "bad mother," the Prioress of a local convent,[1] refuses the marriage proposal of the Prioress's nephew: "It had not flattered [Athena]; it had probably at the moment made her very angry. And the fact that any live person could in this way break in upon the proud isolation of her life had given her a shock" (141–42). Athena's "inappropriate" anger leads to her being placed in the classic Gothic rape scene with the connivance of another woman who "in a benevolent way . . . had wanted to put her in a cage" (142) where she must wed. "For a moment the light-eyed girl stared at him, bewildered. Then she drew herself up as a snake does when it is ready to strike. That she did not attempt to cry for help showed him that she had a clearer understanding of the situation, and of the fact that she had no friend in the house, than he had given her credit for; or perhaps her young broad breast harbored sheer love of combat. The next moment she struck out. Her powerful, swift and direct fist hit him in the mouth and knocked out two of his teeth" (152). Unsure of exactly what the issue is, Athena (still a virgin) nonetheless promises the Prioress the next morning that she will marry the now-toothless Boris, but calmly vows retaliation. "'I will never tell Papa of anything. And as to Boris, I promise you that I shall marry him. But, Madame my Aunt, when we are married, and whenever I can do so, I shall kill him. . . . These three things I promise you. Then I will go'" (160). As Boris notes, she, with her "sheer love of combat," is an equal: "This

---

[1]The Prioress is split quite dramatically into a "good" and "bad" mother figure through her periodic possession by the spirit of "The Monkey" to which the title refers. As bad mother, she relishes violence and tries to make another woman a Gothic victim.

deadly pale and still maiden was not beaten" (158).[2] Athena succeeds in her violent self-defense, in large part because she cannot conceive of anyone else thinking they have the right to use force against her and because her own aggression has been unchecked.

Anna Freud suggests that the most extreme instance of altruistic surrender and acting for others is "the assassin who, in the name of the oppressed, murders the oppressor" (*The Ego* 130). We, like Jane, who explains to Helen that, when "'we are struck at without a reason, we should strike back again very hard . . . so hard as to teach the person who struck us never to do it again'" (*Jane Eyre* 50), are also captivated by the reasoning. Mattie Michael's mother, in Gloria Naylor's *The Women of Brewster Place*, threatens her husband's death to save her daughter: "'So help me Jesus, Sam!' she screamed. 'Hit my child again, and I'll meet your soul in hell!'" (24).[3] Similarly, in Angela Carter's revision of the Bluebeard tale, "The Bloody Chamber," the young fourth wife, near decapitation, is saved when her mother comes galloping to the castle and shoots the husband. In the Gothic, as Elizabeth Baer comments in reference to *Wide Sargasso Sea*, "the real meaning of sisterhood is the courage of one generation to empower the next" ("The Sisterhood of *Jane Eyre*" 133). Aggression used on behalf of another is one way to break from the spectator's role and to sublimate masochism to supposedly higher social ends.[4] At the same time that the actor asserts her agency, she also adapts the masochist's empathy for others so that it is no longer the needs of the dominant that interest her, but those of the oppressed. The altruistic aggressor necessarily recognizes and responds to the plight of at least one other woman. To become a successful resister, she develops that knowl-

[2]Sibyl James argues in her analysis of Gothic elements in "The Monkey" that Athena and Boris gain "mutual understanding," one available to both sexes ("Gothic Transformations" 152).

[3]In this instance, Sam is decidedly a victimizer. Throughout the novel, however, Naylor questions "victimizer" as a fixed identity as much as she does "victim" by beautifully tracing their complex mutual regulations. See also Toni Morrison's *Tar Baby*, in which oppositions by sex, class, and race are similarly confounded so that everyone is finally stuck with some degree of complicity.

[4]Judith Martin phrases the issue more politely in *Miss Manners' Guide to Excruciatingly Correct Behavior*, but her point is the same. When asked how one can work for women's rights and still be "ladylike," she frames an impeccable response. "A lady is, above all, someone who is passionately concerned that others be treated with dignity, fairness, and justice. It has always been considered ladylike, for instance, to fight for these things on behalf of children, animals, and one's husband. The difficulty you are encountering on the subject is that many people do not consider it ladylike to fight that battle on one's own behalf. Therefore, if a woman truly wishes to be ladylike, she will fight for dignity, fairness, and justice, not for herself, but for all other women" (100).

edge still further into recognition of her own responsibility for herself and others, of the number of women who suffer, and of the systemic cultural systems that endorse that suffering.

Naylor's *Linden Hills* outlines the stages a character goes through before she is able to exercise aggression for herself or for others. Willa Prescott Nedeed, the fourth generation of "Mrs. Luther Nedeeds," is enclosed within the basement of her house, just as her Gothic story is encased within the rest of the narrative. The novel's complex intersections of gender, race, and class oppression qualify Linden Hills as something "'straight out of a gothic novel'" (86), as one character comments.[5]

My focus, however, is upon gender arrangements and my interest is in how Willa gradually relinquishes the lure of being an "exception" by recognizing her plight as one shared by other women, how she comes to claim responsibility for herself, and how aggression is represented as one answer to systemic oppression. Willa Prescott Nedeed's slow recognition that her grievous plight is itself a repetition leads her to recollect and to give voice to other women from the past. Only then can she begin to work through her own trauma. In *Linden Hills*, aggression is imaged as much through plot and structural features of the novel as by the representation of a character's own insight, much in the same way *Jane Eyre* transmits skepticism about loving merger.

Willa is the fourth Mrs. Luther Nedeed. Linden Hills, an affluent development built by the first Luther as an "ebony jewel" and a "beautiful, black wad of spit right in the white eye of America" (9), suffers from its own compulsive repetition without working through in the course of its hundred and fifty year history. Each Luther finds a light-skinned wife and then, through arcane rituals, produces a dark-skinned son, also named Luther, who looks exactly like every other Luther. The Luthers precisely control and replicate their own and the other families that populate Linden Hills through each generation: the power of birth, marriage, mortgages (they own all of the houses), and death itself (they are all undertakers) is theirs. The appearance of Willa's light-skinned son, Sinclair, breaks with tradition, and for this she is locked in the basement with her dying child while food, water, and light are supplied sporadically by Luther (68): she is trained, like O or Jane Eyre, through sensory deprivation. Her whereabouts are a mystery to the community, as is her very name to herself and to

---

[5]My thanks to Keith Sandiford for our conversations about the novel and for the insights of his article "Gothic and Intertextual Constructions in *Linden Hills*."

Willie, a young man who begins a poem, "There is a man in a house at the bottom of a hill. And his wife has no name" (277).[6]

Willa is unsure of her own identity, the identity she thought would be triumphantly created by the name "Mrs. Luther Nedeed," just as the protagonist of *Rebecca* believes that "Mrs. de Winter" will create the only self she needs. "He knew she would never have looked at him if it weren't for the feel of the name *Mrs. Luther Nedeed* as she slipped on that white satin and brocade, the cold smooth rings. The touch of the name in her silver, mahogany, and velvet. The smell of it in her imported colognes. The sight of it on thick, embossed invitations to the best homes in town" (69). Ten years after her college graduation, Willa has long since lost what Luther calls black women undergraduates' "overinflated sense of their uniqueness" (67); romance's promises of special status have also proven chimerical. Having yielded her dreams of being an exception through education, work, or love, Willa nonetheless believes herself unique in the painful isolation of her marriage and her immurement.

No hopeful Madonna, Willa waits for her own death a week before Christmas, with her child dead beside her. She knows that she will never leave the basement alive, "because Luther knows that he's a dead man" (66). She thinks that she can fend off grief by denial: "to mourn she would have to remember. That alone would be enough to kill her" (91). Her sole rebellion is to "die in her own way" (71) and to let Luther think that she had "the courage to mourn" (92) by burying their son. To do so, she looks for a shroud. What she finds are the threads through which the past is rewoven and other women become present to her in her plight. She is no longer alone, and that is the beginning of her working through.

The basement's trunks yield a lace wedding veil in which she wraps her child and seemingly meaningless scraps from the last century: Bibles, recipe books, photographs. These thoroughly domestic collections are the coded histories of three previous Mrs. Luther Nedeeds, articulated with the greatest of difficulties and through the most unlikely of means. Each of the three women painfully inscribes the history of her own erasure, insisting on some record of her passing,

---

[6]As the names indicate, Willie and Willa are doubles to some extent. Subordinated by class (he does not live in Linden Hills) and race, Willie has his own secret record of identity: the 665 poems he has composed and committed to memory. In addition, he is responsive to others whose identities remain unacknowledged. Just as he wonders about Willa because he "had never heard her name" (273), so he insists that a woman Luther maneuvers into suicide be known as something other than "his [her husband's] wife": "'Her name was Laurel'" (252).

before, like Willa, each at least dies "in her own way." Through de-
ciphering their stories and realizing their communalities, Willa gradually determines that *she* will live.

Her first response to their narratives is disavowal, however; she is
nothing like them. Each women records her own destruction through
"trifles," traditionally feminine areas of household management. The
first history she finds, that of Luwana Packerville, begun in 1837, is
the most traditional in its format and its method of transmission: it is
inscribed on blank pages before appropriate books of the Bible. That
of Evelyn Creton, begun in 1892, is far harder to recognize and decipher, because it is only through careful scrutiny of her recipe book-
let that the shift from love potions through skin-darkening creams to
self-administered purgatives becomes clear. Priscilla McGuire's slow
disappearance is traced through a technology common in the 1930s,
the family photograph album. All three women tell a dishearteningly
familiar story of romantic expectations, minutely regulated oppression, and gradual erasure that they incorporate as part of their own
identities. It is a story Willa originally does not want to believe can be
her own, but she slowly moves from denial of the past to recognition
and a form of mastery over trauma.

Each woman is rapidly disabused of her romantic expectations and
faced with the reality of her husband's legal and social authority.
Luwana records her shock at discovering that her husband never
destroyed her sale papers: "O Blessed Saviour, can it be that I have
only exchanged one master for another?" (117). Willa reluctantly remembers her own wedding and how she "thought her marriage
would set her free, and it should have. It should have" (117). All the
women are reminded by their Luthers that "nothing welds our bond
but his will" (118).

The four women try to achieve recognition of their identity through
the traditional sexual strategies romance suggests. Evelyn begins to
mix aphrodisiacs; Priscilla's lively eyes seek the Luther who moves
away from her in photographs. In poring over Evelyn's recipes for
face lotions and love potions, Willa uneasily thinks of her own trips to
New York for cosmetics, trips that deny the knowledge—"pushed
safely into a place that firmly locked in the unthinkable along with all
the other insane nightmares that threatened to break through on
reality" (174)—that her undertaker husband is a bizarrely ritualistic
necrophile. Instead she, like the jury in Wharton's "Kerfol," continues to insist that her husband's coldness and non-recognition of
her "was natural" (149).

All of the "Mrs. Luther Nedeeds" remain unacknowledged physically, verbally, and visually. They have no purpose for their husbands once they produce a new heir; their sons become their fathers at an early age, so maternity is no solace. Luwana envies the apostles, for she writes "to no one and am missed by no one on this earth. . . . But sometimes I do indeed wonder what it is like to have someone to care about what you will say" (120). Evelyn's love potions are replaced by recipes for massive quantities of food, and then by equally vast shopping lists for bulemic purges. The shadow Priscilla's son casts upon her in annual photographs gradually creeps up her body and her smile disappears; "her absence" (209) grows even when her son no longer does. Luwana begins to write to herself for comfort, but the community of isolated sufferers she predicates for herself provides little solace. "There is nothing—do you hear me—nothing that is going on in your home that is not repeated in countless other homes around you" (123).

In finding no way to turn to the outside world and receive affirmation of her identity, each woman turns within. She achieves masochistic mastery by doing to herself what others have previously done to her. She records her own destruction, which is itself a matter of indifference to all around her. Yet, in insisting upon a record of her pain, each dimly suggests that perhaps someone *will* care. Luwana's last letter to herself records that she has spoken 665 times in the past year: one "good morning" and one "good evening" each time the two Luthers were at home. Her explanation for her sureness is chillingly chatty. "I suppose you wonder how I can be so exact. Well, you know the silver hat pin that I keep next to my mirror? I use it to carve a line on my chest and my stomach, which I then rub with black ink until the bleeding stops, for each time I am called upon to speak throughout the year. Once the wound has healed, the mark is permanently affixed and there is no danger of it washing off during my toilet" (124). Luwana writes the feminine body with and as a vengeance; what she inscribes in her own flesh is the mark of the beast. Evelyn's vast quantities of purgatives give way, as did her love potions and cosmetics, to a new recipe: the prussic acid she orders the day before Christmas. The shadows cast upon Priscilla's photograph by both Luthers pale next to her repeatedly cut-out face in the last pictures. "She came to the last photograph. And scrawled across the empty hole in lilac-colored ink was the word *me*" (249).

Willa at first wants to believe that she "wasn't like these other women; she had coped and they were crazy. They never changed" (204). She is angry at them in a way she never is with Luther as their past threatens to erupt into her present. "This had happened a long time ago. She could taste the anger at the back of her throat as her eyes came full circle to her son" (204). Like the character in "The Yellow Wallpaper," she begins to rip at the paper that contains women like her, but her purpose is to destroy those other women: "she gathered huge handfuls and dozens of women disappeared with one pull" (205). Her displaced rage accuses them and excuses herself. She is furious when the beautiful, laughing Priscilla defaces her own photographs. "She had been tricked into . . . another twisted life. What other kind of woman would have kept something like this? A healthy mind would have never . . ." (249).

Finally, in accepting their histories and her kinship, Willa stops unwitting repetition. Looking in a pan of water, she sees that she still exists as a discrete personality, although her pain, like theirs, is real. She weeps and believes "that she had actually seen and accepted reality, and reality brought such a healing calm. For whatever it was worth, she could rebuild" (268). Where once, like the narrator of "The Yellow Wallpaper," with her perennial "Johns says," she could only echo "what Luther said" (121), she now begins to know what *she* wants to say and be.

To rebuild her identity, she starts with her name, Willa Prescott Nedeed. What she remembers about the first element, "Willa," is giving up independence for love from "her first steps to the sound of those two syllables. Pink ruffled dress, matching hair ribbons, and soft-bottom shoes with bells on the laces. 'Come, Willa, Willa.' Yes, when she first got off her knees with the exhilarating discovery that her feet could take her anywhere in the world, she directed them toward outstretched arms calling that name and telling her that her final choice of that destination made her a 'good girl, good girl' " (277). Just as she has always been a "good girl," directing all energy and initiative toward others for their approval, so too she has been a "good mother" and "good wife" (279). And, she decides, she is Willa Prescott Nedeed "by choice. She knew then and now that there were no laws anywhere in this country that forced her to assume that name; she took it because she wanted to. That was important" (278). Like Pleasure Mouse in Prager's "A Visit from the Footbinder," Willa decides that she will choose her binding. In claiming full responsibility for her identity and exculpating parents and husband, Willa believes herself free. "She gained strength and a sense of power from its possession" (280). She sleeps, "her body a mere shelter for the mating of unfathomable will to unfathomable possibility" (288–89), and the "nucleus of self-determination" (289) grows.

Freed from the basement because Willie accidentally unbolts the door, Willa, past and present now integrated, ascends the stairs to an ambiguous future. She seeks to claim the reality of her own life when she emerges from the cellar, but her first action is quietly to clean the kitchen, with her dead son held in one arm. She moves toward life and survival, but her movement is like that of a "wingless [ant] queen" (300) and, when she goes to the den in which Luther stands before the Christmas tree, it is unclear whether she can interpret the language or action of others any longer. When she announces "'Luther . . . your son is dead'" (299), she affirms the child's legitimacy and a new reality principle, but there is no mutual comprehension. As Luther tries to keep her from leaving the room, she thinks only that she is being brought back to the self she was in the cellar: holding him as tightly as he does her, both burn to death when the child's shroud catches fire.

In destroying Luther along with herself, Willa aggressively brings a local structure of oppression to an end: there will be no new Luther Nedeed to rule this house or Linden Hills. Because she dies, others will live free. This particular history will not repeat itself because of what Willa has learned from the lives of other women. Similarly, in claiming full responsibility for herself, Willa moves decisively beyond the masochist's acceptance of another determining her identity and her fate. She repudiates the either/or logic of masochist/sadist, oppressor/oppressed.

In plots that resist Gothic conventions, such as that of *Linden Hills*, the emphasis shifts radically by novel's end to the protagonist finding that she and her motives are the mystery: what she will do about her constraints, and to what extent she may have enabled them. Willa can only begin to understand what has happened to her when she accepts the narratives of the women who have preceded her. As she traces Bibles, recipe books, and photo albums, she is forced through repetition to relinquish the ideology of marriage and the shame of thinking her plight unique. What she finds is a community of suffering and shared experience; her recollection affirms the reality of all of their pain. Finally, Willa's own partial working through suggests a systemic critique of the Gothic structures that confine women.

That critique, like the representation of aggression itself, can only be imaged through plot and closure, not the consciousness of individual characters. Willa, the upper-class black woman trapped by gender domination, never knows Willie, subordinated by class and race. He unknowingly frees her by accidentally unlatching the kitchen door; she unwittingly liberates him and all of Linden Hills by killing Luther. Similarly, the rest of Linden Hills lets its will be known only through passive aggression: they do not call immediately for help when the fire begins, and they quietly watch the conflagration. As Willie, numbed and trying to come to his own understanding of aggression, keeps repeating, "'They let it burn'" (304). What Christmas day's revelation has been is ambiguous, and whether apocalypse or millennium will follow is uncertain. The New Year may bring a new order or mere anarchy to Linden Hills. Yet, the novel's somber close suggests that the fall of one Gothic house is not the end of Gothic barbarity but that it is perhaps the aggressive first step to a freedom where no woman has to give her life to have her story told and heard.

Subversion and *Lady Oracle*

Subversion, unlike aggression, seeks to undermine domination from within. Its mutinies are quiet: no warning salvos mark the opening of its well-behaved rebellion. While open aggression alerts the dominator that there is something new to overcome, some fresh opposition to absorb into himself, subversion, with its gentle, seemingly non-resistant blankness, gradually erodes domination. The dominator cannot "discover the other" (Benjamin 73) or himself in the flawless opacity before him. The dominated, invisible to him, knows herself to exist and, with luck, also knows the signs by which to recognize those self-effacing others who are her community.

Subversion, then, with its letter-perfect miming of what ideology demands, has a secret knowingness. It takes the tools of oppression and renders them impotent. As Day observes about the Gothic, "The passivity and acceptance we see in the heroines is not a surrender to their situation, but a style of resistance and self-assertion" (20). That same stylized resistance is the weapon of the masochist who finds "that the most effective way to exercise manipulative power is by simulating a position of weakness and vulnerability" (Caplan 48). The risk for the Gothic subversive, of course, is that her miming may become reality, its point forgotten over too many years of too thorough acquiescence. At the same time, her exquisite self-discipline may reinforce and not overturn domination: the dominator, originally baffled, may find that he too can get by on fewer psychic resources than one might think and that life is comfortable with the simulacrum of a woman.

Ideally, however, the Gothic subversive knows and remembers that her quiet stillness and meekly lowered eyes are the route to escape for herself and others. Her freedom asserted through her impeccable obedience to patriarchal law, she can anticipate and guide the responses of the unself-conscious dominator who cannot identify the rules by which he lives. Clearly, there is aggression in the means she chooses, but it is an aggression that masks itself, that pretends that, whatever is asked of her, it is her desire also. That aggression can be only lightly covered, as it is when Toni Morrison's Sula, frightened by four teenage white boys harassing her, pulls a knife and cuts off the tip of her finger. By doing to/for herself more than they might have done, she escapes, as her friend Nel later says: "Sula was so scared she had mutilated herself, to protect herself" (101).

Through her self-inflicted punishment, Sula controls her would-be captors. Such graphic, recognizable violence is atypical for the subversive, however: she more often exaggerates ever so slightly the behavior the dominator claims to want, verging on parody in her fidelity to stereotype.[7] The narrator of "The Yellow Wallpaper," placidly eating, sleeping, and taking her medicine before she finally manages to "astonish" a "silenced" John (34, 36), is potentially such a subversive. So too, the nameless, unpublished, and plagiarized narrator of Walker's "Really, Doesn't Crime Pay?" opts for subversion after aggression doesn't work. (She tries to cut off her husband's head with a chain saw, but "this failed because of the noise" [In Love and Trouble 21].) Her body anointed with perfumes and cosmetics, clad in the purchases she makes in her twice-daily trips to the mall, she looks forward to her escape. "I wait, beautiful and perfect in every limb, cooking supper as if my life depended on it. Lying unresisting on his bed like a drowned body washed to shore. But he is not happy. For he knows now that I intend to do nothing but say yes until he is completely exhausted" (22–23). The subversive's doing "nothing but say

---

[7]Jean Muir, the sweet, obliging governess in Louisa May Alcott's aptly named *Behind a Mask: or, A Woman's Power* is a stellar instance of self-conscious acting, although I have excluded her as an instance of resistance because her "escape," finally, is only to the best match she can manage. While she has a keen sense of systemic rules, her aim is to find a place within that system, and she shows no awareness of others who are oppressed. Nonetheless, the "unobtrusive and retiring" Miss Muir sweeps all before her by her thoughtfulness, deference, genteel suffering, and altogether perfect manipulation of the codes that regulate others' expectations about young ladies and governesses. "The very servants liked her; and instead of being, what most governesses are, a forlorn creature hovering between superiors and inferiors, Jean Muir was the life of the house" (28). The delicate, unprotected young thing retires to her room at night to take out her teeth, doff her hair, have a drink, and muse on what it means to turn thirty. Surveying her employer's property and that of a neighboring lord, she coolly assesses the worth of each man: "'Not bad . . . , but the other may be better, and I will have the best'" (14). She triumphs magnificently by wedding the local lord (after both sons of the house also propose) just before public discovery of her subterfuge.

yes," precisely when that is the behavior supposedly demanded of her, can prove unexpectedly enervating to the dominant, many of whom fail to identify the source of their uneasiness.

Cecil, the ward-become-wife protagonist of Alcott's *A Marble Woman*, for example, is raised by a sculptor to be entirely dispassionate. Through her conscious tactic of painstaking obedience, Cecil causes her guardian-husband to regret his Pygmalion role. "'You bade me be a marble woman, with no heart to love you, only grace and beauty, to please your eye and do you honor. Have I not obeyed you to the letter?'" (232).[8] Because of her subversion, Cecil's husband, like Rochester, comes to acknowledge his needs and limitations as well as her rights: the shift in balance between the couple in itself models a certain utopian alterity.

While the Gothic subversive's smooth imitation of stereotyped behavior circumvents the declared will of the dominator, as it does for Cecil, her goal is not to mime eventually his abusive power as well. Instead, she transmits her knowledge of the emptiness at the core of domination to others and so establishes a community of resistance. Multiple, unobtrusive languages encode this knowledge in a sociolect indiscernible to the dominant. Absence and silence themselves may become the means of communication among the knowing, as in Dinesen's "Blank Page," where generations of female storytellers, nuns, and noble women know that "silence will speak" (100).

The secret knowledge of subversion is preserved, guarded, and passed on among communities of women in the Gothic. The community may be small: Nel and Sula, for example, form one. Knowing that "they were neither white nor male, and that all freedom and triumph was forbidden to them, they had set about creating something else to be" (52). Their mutual, intersubjective recognition, so opposed to the subject/object relations of beater and beaten, is the strength of the subversive and the type of the world that will follow if she succeeds in her resistance.

Initiates in subversive communities may not originally register domination as reality, may not know that opposition in an other language is possible, may be startled to discover their clandestine

---

[8]Interestingly, the noteworthy emphasis on social action in Alcott's mainstream novels is usually missing in her potboilers, which display a kind of corrective self-gratification. Where Jo March goes on to found Plumfield for "Jo's boys," the sculptor in *Rose in Bloom* models the woman of the future, or the protagonists in *Jack and Jill* learn to care for those in need, the women in the novels of A. M. Barnard (Alcott's pseudonym) consider their own needs, act on their own initiative, and demonstrate delightful energy and spleen.

kinship. In Ralph Ellison's *Invisible Man*, for instance, the earnest college-bound protagonist is stunned by his docile grandfather's death-bed revelation that he has been a "traitor" and a "spy" who has kept up "the good fight" (19). Entirely unaware that a battle had been going on, the boy suddenly sees familiar, despised behavior revealed as a self-aware strategy hitherto unrecognized by him. "'I want you to overcome 'em with yeses, undermine 'em with grins, agree 'em to death and destruction, let 'em swoller you till they vomit or bust wide open. . . . Learn it to the younguns,' he whispered fiercely; then he died" (19–20).

The community of subversion can be formed through families and across generations, as it is in *Invisible Man* and in Gothic novels where mothers and aunts whisper secrets to young girls who are preparing to enter the world of the beating drama. More often, however, that community constitutes itself otherwise: friends and lovers of whatever age (or sex) become families who will never demand self-abnegation for love. The Gothic novel itself forms such a community through the various communications between and among authors, characters, and readers. In Gothic silences, enclosures, and repeated representation of the beating drama, domination's traumatic haunting can be heard, felt, and seen. For women, the Gothic provides the conditions Wharton deems mandatory for ghosts: "silence and continuity" (*The Ghost Stories* 3). Like Dinesen claiming that no woman can see a witch burned without a special complicity, Wharton claims that the author of "ghost stories"—and the Gothic, I would add—finds a secret accord with her readers: "I was conscious of a common medium between myself and my readers, of their meeting me halfway among the primeval shadows, and filling in the gaps in my narrative with sensations and divinations akin to my own" (*The Ghost Stories* 2).

The Costume Gothics Joan Foster writes under a pseudonym in Atwood's *Lady Oracle* are such a genre. Joan, as much as the genre, is also the medium, however; she literally composes the one text she publishes under her own name (also titled *Lady Oracle*) by automatic writing and figuratively constructs herself while in a trance state that denies her agency and voice. Joan hides from her readers as author, although she acknowledges their embarrassing, hidden affiliation (102, 278). Joan splits herself (and those close to her) into two selves: the proper daughter, friend, and wife who tries to be what all want her to be, and the secret author of Gothic novels. Highly self-aware, with a fantasy life as rich as that of the protagonist in *Rebecca* and with a penchant for secret investigations as finely honed as that of any Gothic heroine, Joan first deals with her Gothic plight through aggression and then through subversion. In order to avoid having to incorporate her insights and change her behavior, however, she uses splitting, the writing of Gothics, and humor to articulate and maintain her dilemma for much of the novel.

Joan's knowingly subversive behavior is at first reactive, not purposive: in her repetition, self-punishment, and splitting, she uses insight "to avoid having to change" (Stoller, *Sexual Excitement* 123). Parody—of the conventions that govern her public feminine identity as well as those of the Gothic itself—is her way of showing systemic knowledge but avoiding its consequences through playful repetition. Joan's comic relief is, of course, a form of aggression directed against herself and others and, when her change begins, much of it is figured through the "inappropriate" humor that begins to seep through the careful separations between her life and her work. Where Willa Prescott Nedeed begins to hear other women's stories for the first time, Joan begins to hear her own and, through them, to discover her community with other women. Her change is not the dramatic, explosive catharsis that often disappears as fast as it came, but the more minute shifts of incorporated insight that endure. Hiding in Italy after staging her own death, the narrating self reconstructs the past for us and herself while also working on a new Gothic novel that we too read: the past, the present, and the metafictional, like the aspects of Joan herself, eventually coalesce.

Joan controls herself and those around her through her friendly malleability and attentiveness. At the same time, her secret identity gratifies her—she knows something they don't—and protects her from too-harsh scopophilic inquiry. She holds to her spectator's role as the fat teenager who is everyone's friend. "Everyone trusted me, no one was afraid of me, though they should have been. I knew everything about my friends. . . . But they guessed nothing about me; I was a sponge" (102). She also affirms, however, that "knowledge isn't necessarily power" (42). Her own wry, self-conscious, and very funny lived restatement of the "The Yellow Wallpaper" 's "But what is one to do?" (10) comes from a deep-seated knowledge of what power is: her mother. In *Lady Oracle*, as in *The Castle of Otranto* or *Jane Eyre*, the Gothic legacy of domination is forcibly handed on by maternal figures who demand that young girls learn to be "natural" women.

Joan's mother looms over all subsequent relationships: her marriage is, as Freud claims many are, a repetition of her relation with her mother ("Female Sexuality" 230–31). *Lady Oracle* is one of those Gothics in which the "central conflict is with the mother" (Fleenor 15) and the deepest fear is the "sensation of actually being possessed" by the maternal (Modleski 70).[9]

As a little girl, Joan clandestinely examines her mother's drawers, carefully watches her apply makeup, and tries to ferret out the secret formulas of femininity. A plump child, she takes dance lessons; a klutz, she industriously tries to carry out the "Good Turns" her Brownie troop recommends by serving others. In both cases, "the results had not pleased her [mother]" (56). The seven-year-old would-be butterfly is made into an impromptu mothball for her recital after her mother and teacher see her overweight body in tights and spangled wings. Her improvised "dance of rage and destruction" (51) draws applause as, for the first time, farce provides the recognition tragedy cannot.

In remembering her own grief, still present to her, the adult Joan nonetheless knows that the woes of fat little girls are the stuff of humor, not sympathy, to an audience. "Instead of denouncing my mother's injustice, they would probably laugh at me" (53). Jane Eyre too knows that she would be treated differently if she were a "handsome, romping child" (*Jane Eyre* 12–13), but she also knows and proclaims the reality of injustice. Joan, unlike Jane, can imagine no way to indict authority that would not add to her humiliation. In her mind, only "good-looking" (53) victims, like Desdemona or the cover models for Nazi atrocities in "the sleazier men's magazines" (53), are worthy of approving attention.

Warned about "bad" men and the mysterious things they "do" to little girls (62), Joan finds, on the contrary, that her greatest danger is from women and language. Other little girls and her mother are her tormentors, and "words were not a prelude to war but the war itself, a devious subterranean war that was unending because there were no decisive acts" (59). Her ready weeping and display of pain just precipitate new rounds of ever-refined torture. She dreams that perhaps her mother will recognize her pain (and her) but, even in a dream, her

[9]"Aggressive and ambitious," raising her daughter alone until Joan is five, Frances Foster never decides "what she really wanted to do" (71). Her daughter becomes "the embodiment of her own failure and depression, a huge edgeless cloud of inchoate matter which refused to be shaped into anything for which she could get a prize" (71). (Joan, of course, is aware of her own failure at being a satisfactory little girl from an early age.) Her self-contained husband also fails to embody her own ambitions. Where Priscilla McGuire directs her frustrated aggression against herself by cutting out her own face in photographs, however, Frances directs her aggression outward: Joan is startled after her death to find the faces of Frances's first suitor and husband cut from all albums (201).

mother will not close the distance between them by saving Joan from a collapsing bridge. "I called out to my mother, who could still have saved me. . . . She didn't even hear me" (68). Unacknowledged and inadequate in her own eyes and those of others, Joan longs for a "decisive act" that would bring her recognition, even if as victim. Left alone in the dark by the other Brownies, she wishes the "bad man" would come. "That way, after I'd been stolen or killed, they would be punished, and they would be forced to repent at last for what they'd done. . . . Even my mother would be sorry" (62).

What Joan *can* do is suffer aggressively in a way that punishes herself while accusing her mother: she gains more weight. "Even" her mother, who wants neither her house nor her daughter to be "different" (74), is sorry, if not repentant, at the sight of her fifteen-year-old, two hundred and forty-five pound daughter. At home, Joan defiantly asserts her weight as "refutation" and "victory": "It was only in relation to my mother that I derived a morose pleasure from my weight" (78).

Joan's weight protects her from her mother while taunting Frances with her powerlessness. Joan is an exhibitionist, "triumphant" in the repeated proof of the pain she can inflict through making her mother look at her. Her procession through the house "was a sort of fashion show in reverse, it was a display" (75). She carefully searches out the most conspicuous, ugly clothes she can find. "Once, when I arrived home in a new lime-green car coat with toggles down the front, flashing like a neon melon, my mother started to cry. . . . My mother had never cried where I could see her and I was dismayed, but elated too at this evidence of my power, my only power. I had defeated her: I wouldn't ever let her make me over in her image, thin and beautiful" (94). Joan's defeat of her mother defeats herself as well: she is not what her mother wants, and cannot be for her own self-preservation. Yet, she still wants that hand extended to save her from the collapsing bridge, the assurance that she is lovable as she is. She survives through aggression, but each "victory" (78) is also a mark of her loss. Furthermore, she remains acutely self-conscious at school and at her "degrading" (104) jobs, where she is the epitome of self-abnegating consideration. Every girl's confidante, Joan forwards no claims of her own.

When Joan inherits two thousand dollars from her much-loved, eccentric, heavy Aunt Lou (who writes menstrual product questions and answers), her companion in countless weepy afternoons at movie theaters, she at first feels betrayed when told that it is contingent upon her losing one hundred pounds. Aunt Lou's legacy, however, is not a demand for Joan's subordination but an incentive for her emancipation from self-definition by hate. Joan sometimes regrets the lost comfort of her second body as people begin to look at her and longs to be "merely an onlooker again, with nothing too much expected of me" (157). More important, though, Joan sees her mother lose her sureness as she gains definition. "While I grew thinner, she herself became distraught and uncertain" (135). Watching her increasingly thin daughter eat a RyKrisp, Frances cannot see what is actually before her: "'Eat, eat, that's all you ever do. You're disgusting, you really are'" (136). Frances's aggression is still more explicit when she tries to stick Joan with a paring knife during the argument that follows. Joan, now eighteen, runs away from home that night.

In her relationship with her mother and in later heterosexual relationships, Joan is faced with explicit and covert intentions—what people say they want for and from her and their actual desires. The self that others love after she loses weight is to her, artificial, a "disguise" (157). She becomes a participant rather than the object of negative scrutiny, but she doubts whether those who applaud her would give their approval to the Fat Lady she imagines as circus exhibit, trapeze artist, figure-skater, ballerina, and opera singer.

As a thin woman, Joan foregoes aggression and opts for subversion: she seems to be what others want. Joan's weight, dancing, and writing serve as assertions of her presence; all seemingly modulate themselves to passive or anonymous formulae. Her aggressive self reappears only as the villainess of her Gothics. Yet, because she wants to be what others demand (if only they wouldn't hurt her), her subversion is at first limited, despite her insight. Her mothball dance of "rage and destruction" (51) continues as a metaphor for what Sandra Gilbert and Susan Gubar consider as the concerns of the artist (*Madwoman in the Attic* 57), but the steps and rhythm of that dance change. When she waltzes with a lover in shoes from another period which don't fit, she remembers Cinderella's stepsisters, who would mutilate themselves for a mate (284).

Thinking of Hans Christian Andersen's little mermaid and of *The Red Shoes* at another point, Joan concludes that splitting, despite its drawbacks, is a better strategy for survival that openly avowing one's love. "Neither of them had been able to please the handsome prince; both of them had died. I was doing fairly well by comparison. Their mistake had been to go public, whereas I did my dancing behind closed doors. It was safer, but. . . . It was true I had two lives, but on off days I felt that neither of them was completely real" (241–42). In Italy later, Joan decides that it is finally time for her own fling—but she dances through broken glass. Daubing at her bleeding feet, she thinks about culture's contradictory demands for assertion and abnegation: "You could dance, or you could have the love of a good man. But you were afraid to dance, because you had this unnatural fear that if you danced they'd cut your feet off so you wouldn't be able to dance. Finally you overcame your fear and danced, and they cut your feet off" (368). Throughout her life, Joan's "unnatural" fear is carried out in reality, yet she continues to assume that the problem is her own, and not that of the gender expectations that make mothers or husbands want adorable models of femininity willing to spend a life following someone else's lead.

Married to Arthur, Joan continues her subversive route and dances in secret[10] while Arthur concerns himself (quite unsuccessfully) with social causes and obscure literary journals.[11] Arthur does not know about Joan's other selves as Fat Lady, Gothic author, or Gothic villainess. Those aggressive, self-punished, and anonymous selves remain sequestered in photograph albums and the novels of Louisa K. Delacourt while his wife is pleasantly vague, ineffectual, and conciliatory. But, like Joan's mother, Arthur anticipates and relishes Joan's failures; unlike her, he applauds the débacles that satisfy his sense of her and of himself. Joan produces dreadful meals of "lumps burning at the edges" and "untransformed blood" as she once did new pounds: "My failure was a performance, and Arthur was the audience. His applause kept me going" (235).

Joan declares that "for years I wanted to turn into what Arthur thought I was, or what he thought I should be" (235), but the self she is willing to adapt still further is, at best, only half a personality. Her pleasure and much of her identity remain with those secret other selves whose existence she must protect. "But I didn't want Arthur to understand me: I went to great lengths to prevent this" (240).

Joan splits her identity in her marriage and, to maintain stability and safety, also splits her image of the other. As a child, she imagined that her demonstrative Aunt Lou was her "real mother," while Frances, who "seldom touched me," took her in for inexplicable reasons (95). So too men are as doubled as they were in Anna Freud's

[10]Sybil Vincent, in her otherwise insightful article, argues that Joan's Gothic writing gratifies her superego and Arthur her id (161). I would argue the reverse: Arthur, with his demand for "proper" moral and social causes fulfills superego functions, while Joan's novel writing, with its emphasis on sensuality (of which Arthur seems singularly unaware) and aggression, gratifies id drives.

[11]The title of one of those journals, "Resurgance," may well be related to the "Resurgam" with which Jane Eyre marks Helen Burn's grave.

"bad" and "nice" stories, puzzlingly presenting the possibility of love and danger simultaneously. Her father is a killer during the war; he also brings the dead back from life as an anaesthesiologist reviving attempted suicides. The man who exposes himself and then gives her daffodils after a Brownie meeting may well be the same who frees her from the tree her friends have tied her to the next week. "Was the man who untied me a rescuer or a villain? Or, an even more baffling thought: was it possible for a man to be both at once?" (67).

The often cruel and always seductive men of her Gothic novels present the same dilemma, of course, as does the sometimes "evil," sometimes "good," hero of her nonpseudonymous *Lady Oracle* (248). The Royal Porcupine, her lover, seems to embody this dichotomy in tandem with Arthur, but he too has another self, as she discovers to her chagrin. "Was every Heathcliff a Linton in disguise?" (300). Even the once-predictable Arthur reveals doubleness in his idealization of another woman.[12]

Others then, are as frustratingly complicated as Joan herself, as she begins to realize. When Joan tells Arthur that she has a book being published that is about "male-female roles in our society" (253), he offers to edit it for her. But the subject matter and the enormous success of *Lady Oracle*, "'reminiscent of a mixture of Kahlil Gibran and Rod McKuen,'" as her editor happily notes (251), nonpluses Arthur. "I'd been expecting him to tell me the book was bourgeois or tasteless or obscure or a piece of mystification, but instead he was acting as though I'd committed some unpardonable but unmentionable sin" (262).

Joan eventually suspects that love itself "was the pursuit of shadows" (315). Like the Lady of Shalott, who figures so prominently in her novel and in her adolescent imagination (159), she slowly finds that she is half-sick of shadows. The outside world hardly seems better, however: the glare of publicity, her love affair, the reappearance of her first lover, persistent contacts from readers, and blackmail all threaten a public exposure of her many selves, a forced exhibition of her neatly segregated worlds of fantasy and actuality.

Joan's ductile receptiveness to Arthur and others begins to erode. Whereas once she "would listen to anyone about anything, murmuring at appropriate moments, reassuring, noncommittal, sympathetic

---

[12]Tania Modleski, following Joanna Russ, notes the division of male characters in the Gothic into "the Super-Male and the Shadow-Male, the former almost always the apparent villain but the real hero, the latter usually a kind, considerate, gentle male who turns out to be vicious" (79): in becoming Chuck Brewer, commercial artist and would-be husband, the Royal Porcupine loses all claims to Super-Male status.

as a pillow" (42), she reluctantly begins to note that her subversive tactics, which never did change others, no longer even protect herself. The indiscriminate, condescending response she earns for what Arthur calls her "naive humanism" (99) is not enough: she must have her own recognition. "What he didn't know was that behind my compassionate smile was a set of tightly clenched teeth, and behind that a legion of voices, crying, *What about me? What about my own pain? When is it my turn?* But I'd learned to stifle these voices, to be calm and receptive" (100). On a vacation with Arthur, during which she hopes "at least for a return to the way things had been before *Lady Oracle*" (281), Joan contemplates a fountain statue of Diana of Ephesus, "draped in breasts from neck to ankle, as though afflicted with a case of yaws," many of which are out of order. "I stood licking my ice-cream cone, watching the goddess coldly. Once I would have seen her as an image of myself, but not any more. My ability to give was limited, I was not inexhaustible. I was not serene, not really. I wanted things, for myself" (282).

Watching how close her various worlds are to colliding and the dangerous emergence of her "I want," Joan begins to display aggression again when she accuses Arthur's group of being like the "Plymouth Brethren" because they won't "'go out there and really change things, instead you sit around and argue and attack each other'" (290). She breaks with her lover, who has accused her of being "emotionally clumsy" (299), just as her mother once bewailed the clumsiness that made "Good Turns" into aggressively mismanaged messes (95). Her own movement toward the outside world, however, is typically elliptical: she engineers her own faked drowning death as part of a complicated plot involving harassment by the CIA. In death she can be a politically correct heroine and perhaps someone will say, as she hoped when a girl, "that I had a lovely face, even if I had to turn into a corpse in a barge-bottom first" (159).

Alone in Italy, Joan begins to adapt her early lesson from her ballerina teacher: "if you're going to be made to look ridiculous and there's no way out of it, you may as well pretend you meant to" (49). Now, however, there is no need to "pretend" that initiative, agency, and responsibility are not her own, and she finds her sudden autonomy frightening. Earlier, her Gothic writing was a necessary balance to life with Arthur. "As long as I could spend a certain amount of time each week as Louisa, I was all right, I was patient and forbearing, warm, a sympathetic listener. But if I was cut off, if I couldn't work at my current Costume Gothic, I would become mean and irritable, drink too much and start to cry" (238). Nothing now stops Joan from writing, but she finds being just Louisa for long periods seems as difficult as being just Joan: she's irritable, drinks, and cries. Her problem, then, is how to end self-sabotage by integrating both selves.

Joan's shifts in consciousness parallel the vicissitudes of her genre problems: work on her new Gothic, the first since *Lady Oracle*, does not go well. Rereading *Lady Oracle*, she decides the book is "quite peculiar," "a Gothic gone wrong": "It was upside-down somehow. There were the sufferings, the hero in the mask of a villain, the villain in the mask of a hero, the flights, the looming death, the sense of being imprisoned, but there was no happy ending, no true love" (259). In coming to doubt the "happy ending" that justifies the masochist's self-restriction and eroticizes her domination, Joan finds that the whole story now seems oddly awry.

The erotic overlay of the beating drama, so persistently maintained by Joan as the route to recognition and autonomy, slowly leaches away. As it does so, her control of the Gothic's language and conventions slips away also, and her split representations of herself as the meek, beloved protagonist and the delightfully spiteful villainess (always finally punished) become oddly confounded. Charlotte, the jeweler repairing Gilbert Redmond's family jewels, is strangely drawn to that abrupt man and to the mansion's Gothic maze, in which other women have disappeared; not so strangely, his peremptory, unfaithful third wife, Felicia, repels her.

Demure, proper Charlotte has one maternal legacy, the cameo her mother leaves her. This inheritor of a "small square two inches of ivory"—Austen's bequest to other novelists—begins to seem unduly and boringly mannered to Joan while Felicia, her red-haired, green-eyed aggressive double, gains in sympathy. Portraying Charlotte peering from a library window, Joan inscribes: "She was trying to see who they were; not that she was nosy, just inquisitive. It went along with her pluck" (349). Just as she makes fun of Charlotte's self-deceptive curiosity, urge to see, and aggression in language inappropriate to Costume Gothics, so the Gongorism of Gothic metaphor undergoes a sea-change. Redmond's eye "slid like a roving oyster over her blushing countenance" (349), while Felicia's extravagance is part of "her figure that spread like crabgrass, her hair that spread like fire, her mind that spread like cancer or pubic lice" (351).

Joan begins to get impatient with the "too pure" Charlotte: "Wearing her was like wearing a hair shirt, she made me itchy, I wanted her to fall into a mud puddle, have menstrual cramps, sweat, burp, fart" (352). Felicia's flawless facade also cracks when she "snuffled," wiping her tears on the back of her hand, "too distraught to bother with the niceties of a handkerchief" (351). As Felicia loses her marble perfection, Joan wonders, "How could I sacrifice her for the sake of Charlotte?" (352)—the same sacrifice she has, of course, always made in sequestering Louisa and the Fat Lady so Mrs. Arthur Foster could live.

Felicia, so like du Maurier's Rebecca, begins to seem ally rather than nemesis. Brushing her hair, rubbing up against Redmond, Felicia wonders if there is any way she can capture his attention, since flaunting her affairs has not succeeded. "'Do you love me?' she asked; she usually had to ask twice, because Redmond didn't hear her the first time, or would pretend he didn't" (350). Redmond, practicing his noteworthy raised eyebrow in a mirror (351), and thinking of the pleasures that await him as Charlotte's husband, is horrified by the reappearance of Felicia, "enormously fat" and dripping seawater, after her drowning. Weeping at the "disgust" in his face, she tells him: "'It was such an effort, *Arthur*, to get out of that water and come all this way, just to be with you again'" (355, emphasis added). As the identities of Felicia, the Fat Lady, and Joan coalesce, Joan's Gothic takes a radical turn in which Redmond/Arthur is no longer the focus of inquiry: Joan and her motives are the puzzle.

Wondering who she will become now, or who she has ever been, Joan finds that it is the ghost of her mother she must come to terms with before any other. In so doing, Joan traces the same stages Irigaray sets forth in "And the One Doesn't Stir without the Other": the early taking in of "ice" along with her mother's milk (60), eager separation from her suffocating embrace in the love of a father and then a husband who seem to promise independence, the longing for closeness, and the final return to the maternal with the wishful plea that both might live.

Her mother's ghost has appeared before, but Joan, like Lockwood, refused to speak to her or to let her in. This time, she asks what she wants and goes to her: "Could she see I loved her? . . . I would do what she wanted" (362). Her mother disappears, but Joan is terrified by her brush with merger. Finally able to let go of the repetition that just recreates her original trauma, she is able to stop being what others want and to recognize her own complicity in the construction of subordination.

> She'd come very close that time, she'd almost done it. She'd never really let go of me because I had never let her go. It had been she standing behind me in the mirror, she was the one who was waiting around each turn, her voice whispered the words. . . . How could I renounce her?

She needed her freedom also; she had been my reflection too long. What was the charm, what would set her free? . . .

My mother was a vortex, a dark vacuum, I would never be able to make her happy. Or anyone else. Maybe it was time for me to stop trying. (363)

In exorcising her mother's ubiquitous ghost, Joan begins to determine what will make *her* happy and to reassess her subversion.

Joan decides that Charlotte too has to come to terms with her world: "Charlotte would have to go into the maze, there was no way out of it" (364). It is, however, the aggressive Felicia who enters the Gothic maze as Joan's doppelgänger and meets Joan's community, the personifications of her fractured self.

A stone bench ran along one side, and on it were seated four women. Two of them looked a lot like her, with red hair and green eyes and small white teeth. The third was middle-aged, dressed in a strange garment that ended halfway up her calves, with a ratty piece of fur around her neck. The last was enormously fat. She was wearing a pair of pink tights and a short pink skirt covered with spangles. From her head sprouted two antennae, like a butterfly's, and a pair of obviously false wings was pinned to her back. Felicia was surprised at the appearance of the woman in pink, but was too well bred to show it.

The women murmured among themselves. "We were expecting you," they said; the first one shifted over, making room for her. "We could tell it was your turn."

"Who are you?" she asked.

"We are Lady Redmond," said the middle-aged woman sadly. "All of us," the fat woman with the wings added.

"There must be some mistake," Felicia protested. "I myself am Lady Redmond." (375–76)

No more an exception than Jane Eyre as Rochester's fifth lover or Willa as the fourth Mrs. Nedeed, Felicia tries to escape from Joan, Louisa K. Delacourt, Aunt Lou, and the Fat Lady. The only door out leads to Redmond, though, and she suddenly knows that "he was a killer in disguise, he wanted to murder her as he had murdered his other wives. . . . He wanted to replace her with the other one, the next one, thin and flawless" (376–77). Terror-stricken, she sees him transform into all the men in her life and fiction. Finally, she murmurs "Arthur" and steps forward, only to see the skull beneath the skin as he tries to strangle her.

Joan recognizes the limitations of the pseudoinsight and subversive strategy which allowed domination—whether practiced by mother, father, lover, or Gothic villain—to continue unchecked while she placed her real self elsewhere. In so doing, she is able to integrate the hitherto fragmented aspects of herself and to incorporate a revised reality principle. Called back to her identity in actuality by the appearance of a reporter whom she smashes on the head with a bottle, thinking him someone else, she knows that she will leave Arthur and that she will write no more Gothics.

The stages of Joan's writing—from the camp but unreflective Costume Gothics that reinscribe the beating drama, through the revised Gothic of *Lady Oracle* without its happy ending, to the breakdown of Gothic scenarios in Felicia's story—trace Joan's own progress. Still funny, still finely aware of the codes of domination, Joan now repeats with a difference, no longer seeking to restore the past but to create a future. The reporter whom she hits knows the aggressive "part of me" (380) and presents intriguing possibilities, but so too do other genres that may create communities of more effective subversion for her. Longing for "happy endings" (352), Joan discards the possibility of writing "a real novel" (352) and considers a genre that maintains the future is one way to change the present. "I won't write any more Costume Gothics, though; I think they were bad for me. But maybe I'll try some science fiction. The future doesn't appeal to me as much as the past, but I'm sure it's better for you" (379). No longer undermining herself, Joan is now ready to put her subversive knowledge to work.

Leaving the Gothic Arena

The masochist's transition from blindness to insight can lead to purposive action through aggression or subversion. As Nunberg points out, "Without active participation there is no effective adaptation to reality" (72 *n*). Insofar as the Gothic masochist recognizes her own pain, identifies its exterior and interior sources, and no longer eroticizes domination, she has made the transition to insight. As she moves to action, she accepts responsibility for herself, knows her dilemma is shared by other women, and begins to understand the multifarious cultural systems that perpetuate oppression. Still, as an active participant, she finds that the reality which would return her to the embrace of the beater also needs adaptation.

As Jacqueline Rose warns, however, we must beware of polarizing the dynamic between the individual psyche and social actuality into "a crude opposition between inside and outside—a radical Freudianism always having to argue that the social produces the misery of the psychic in a one-way process, which utterly divests the psychic of its own mechanisms and drives" (*Sexuality in the Field of Vision* 9). This one-sided emphasis on the social production of identity can thus reduce the psychic to a tabula rasa in which individual variations of adaptation, defense, and resistance disappear.[13] The Gothic masochist, for example, becomes an undifferentiated victim, defined solely in terms of the forces that oppress and shape her. The social emphasis may further imply that the psychic, once (impossibly) freed from culture's malforming influence, would exist in a Rousseauistic state of innocence, integrity, and joy. If, in contrast, we argue that the psychic is primary, we run the risk of seeing the phenomenal world fade as the beating drama becomes only the puzzling fantasy and desire of the Gothic masochist.

My suggestion that there might be a world without Gothic domination, in which neither beater nor beaten eroticize domination, is decidedly utopian. I am not, however, arguing for a unilateral influence but for the psychosocial equivalent of the mutuality Benjamin calls intersubjectivity, which lets us "distinguish two subjects recognizing each other from one subject regulating another" (45). In the interpersonal realm of the Gothic, the beaten *and* the beater must change; in the social realm, individual consciousnesses *and* the educational, legal, medical, and religious systems through which gender ideology is transmitted must come to recognize domination as abomination.

In their different ways, Brontë's *Jane Eyre*, Dinesen's "The Monkey," Alcott's *The Marble Woman*, and Walker's *The Color Purple* hint at a new social order of shared power, whether through couples or through larger groups. The generic problems of representing such utopian alterity,[14] however, suggest that escape from the Gothic is not simply an issue of individual consciousness, which is so often counterbalanced by the crushing weight of social reality.

---

[13]See Erikson's "Reality and Actuality" in Bernheimer and Kahane for an excellent discussion about the significance of a patient's need to name the "historical truth" and how this need may be at odds with the adjustment to "'outer reality,' meaning to what cannot be helped" (49).

[14]Every novel of this type (and there are many) attempts to show the world as it is through verisimilitude; each also in some way tries to show how it *could* be. As I have commented before, that briefly glimpsed utopian alterity necessarily creates a structural tension in texts whose mode is realistic, a tension too easily dismissed as a flaw in genre or craft. The utopian is the positive side of the same structural dilemma in the representation of Gothic horror, which cannot be articulated or imaged by following the conventions that society or fiction acknowledge as realistic.

The noteworthy curiosity, activity, and consciousness of Radcliffe's heroines suggest some ways in which the social contract might begin to be renegotiated. Emily, in *The Mysteries of Udolpho*, knows that she must "suffer *and* reason": she shuns apathy, condemns "turning from the distressed," and espouses "active virtue" (92, 80). Ellena, in *The Italian*, names and resists injustice as firmly and repeatedly as Jane Eyre: "'Shall the guilty oppressor triumph, and the innocent sufferer sink under the shame that belongs only to guilt! Never will I yield to a weakness so contemptible'" (68).[15]

Nonetheless, despite the intriguing possibilities of gender differences in their mostly off-stage suitors, Valancourt and Vivaldi, there is no social realm, including that of the couple, that promises to support the activity of Emily and Ellena at novels' end, nor do they, repositories of their culture's beliefs, expect it. In Gilman's *Herland*, however, we see the representation of a utopian society that unequivocally supports such activity and recoils from domination. The Herlanders see the relationship between the individual and society as one of mutuality, not opposition; they accordingly "put psychology with history" (105) and, one might add, with education, medicine, law, and religion.

Nowhere is the Herlanders' repudiation of erotic domination more obvious than in their response when Terry, one of the three men who discovers their parthenogenetic country, tries to rape his mate, Alima. As Vandyck, the narrator, notes, in Herland "we had no sense of—perhaps it may be called possession" (125). He and the third man slowly begin to understand that perhaps there are relationships without unilateral possession. Terry, however, cannot help but rue the absence of the "'submissiveness'" and "'natural yielding which is woman's greatest charm'" (98); he continues to believe "'there never was a woman yet that did not enjoy being *mastered*'" (131). When "in all the pride and passion of his intense masculinity" (132), he tries to master Alima, the results astound him: she and a friend quickly subdue him.[16]

---

[15]The representation of gender identity in Radcliffe, Alcott, and others, which show women characters using seemingly passive virtues such as duty and renunciation for active aims, is a rich subject for further investigation.

[16]An equally startling turn-around is found in Dinesen's *Ehrengard*, in which the title character must stay in an idyllic retreat for several months so that the announcement of a royal baby's birth comes the proper time after the wedding. The court painter contemplates this "Amazon," the "daughter of warriors" (36, 34), and thinks, like the guardian-husband of *The Marble Woman*, that his "'greatest triumph hides within that block of marble'" (34–35). The "full surrender" Cazotte seeks is as subtle and destructive as anything a Valmont or a Lovelace might desire: she "will know herself to be

As Terry later tells Vandyck indignantly, Alima kicked him in the groin, something "'no woman with a shade of decency'" would do (143). Like St. John angrily telling Jane that her response to his verbal bullying is "'violent, unfeminine, and untrue'" (*Jane Eyre* 363), Terry can neither recognize his own aggression nor understand the universal Herland response of "sick revulsion and horror" (138) at violence against another that demands their harshest punishment, exile. He expects submission after he "force[s] her to love him as her master" (142), and Vandyck too is bemused at the outcome. "Come to think of it, I do not recall a similar case in all history or fiction. Women have killed themselves rather than submit to outrage; they have killed the outrager; they have escaped; or they have submitted—sometimes seeming to get on very well with the victor afterward" (142–43). Like Athena in "The Monkey," the women in Herland recognize rape only as violence: no one eroticizes it, and each is capable of her own self-defense. Even in utopia, violence still exists, but it is considered the most grievous of social diseases rather than a testament to the will, power, and love of the aggressor or to the helpless charms of the victim.[17]

In the world of what we might call "intrapsychic" Gothic, then, the "real" world has no language to acknowledge the abiding psychological and physical dangers of the protagonist: her idiosyncratic trials once over, we are assured that horror is exorcized and social order restored at novel's end. In texts such as *Herland* that privilege the social, however, individual identity recedes in importance as the genotype subsumes the phenotype. Two texts, Gilman's "The Girl in the Pink Hat" and Dinesen's "Angelic Avengers," outline some ways in which the relationship between self and other, individual and society, might become instead a mutuality that puts an end to Gothic domination.

In Gilman's brief story "The Girl in the Pink Hat," individual and

---

ultimately and hopelessly compromised" (54, 56), but it will not be through intercourse. As Cazotte explains, "There are women who give out the fullness of their womanhood in a smile, a side glance or a waltz, and others who will be giving it in their tears" (13): the mark of Ehrengard's fall, he decides, will be a blush. Increasingly ill at ease, Ehrengard rides furiously in "unconscious attempts at escape" and "yearned to be angry" (45, 95). When the royal infant is kidnapped, she claims maternity to protect the parents and, drawing the rarefied seducer firmly within the real, declares his paternity as well. "At these words Herr Cazotte's blood was drawn upwards, as from the profoundest wells of his being, till it colored him all over like a transparent crimson veil" (109). He flees.

[17]To Vandyck's astonishment, he finds that within their matrilineal society neither the foremothers, nor the Mother Spirit demand "'honor, reverence, obedience'" (112): hierarchical subordination is entirely absent.

social consciousness join together to prevent a Gothic plot. An un-
named woman and her sister Polly save a young woman from an
elopement that's become an abduction. The sisters are "romantic"
(39), as the narrator tells us, but their concept of romance does not
encompass violence. The narrator's visual, auditory, and comprehensive abilities are high, as befits a Gothic rescuer. Overhearing a young
couple on a train, "for my ears are unusually keen" (40), the narrator
finds that the wedding the eloping Jess thought would take place in
Ohio has been put off by the elusive (and somewhat drunk) Julius
until their arrival in New York.

As the narrator notices, Jess is "trying to keep control of herself,
not to be frightened, and not to lose faith in him" (40)—is trying, in
short, to juggle the impossible demands of the Gothic heroine. When
Jess suggests that she stop to visit with an old Sunday school teacher
in Albany, Julius is angered by and she apologetic for her temerity.
"She was fairly trembling at her own daring, and quite ready to break
down and cry on his shoulder and own she was a goose—if he said
the right thing" (42).

He does not say the "right thing," and Jess comes to recognize her
susceptibility to Gothic maneuvers. The next few pages show, however, that individual consciousness of danger, when unaided by the
acknowledgment of others, may be unavailing against domination.
More skeptical than Theodore Dreiser's Sister Carrie, in part because
of the lessons mass culture teaches through "romances or at 'the
movies'" (41), Jess insists that she cannot go on to New York without
being married. Appalled at his positive answer when she asks
"'You're not going to try to *make* me go to New York—against my
will?'" (43), she prepares to call the conductor and disembark at the
next station. Julius silences her objections and immobilizes her, however, by showing her a badge and handcuffs and assuring her he will
falsely claim that he is a police officer and she a criminal in custody.

Jess, then, is captive, and the narrator's active role begins. The narrator does not accost Julius or assume that the altruist should force
her will on others: instead, she slips a note to Jess asking for *her* consent to any intervention. After consultation and a trip to the women's
room, sister Polly gets off the train at Poughkeepsie and the narrator
continues on with Jess, who is dressed in Polly's distinctive outfit
(including goggles, veil, and red wig) and reading a detective story.

The two women attempt to save Jess because of their own sense of
affiliation and personal responsibility. Their rescue of her is only complete, however, when individual resistance is joined to social power.
In addition, what Carol Gilligan would consider the feminine, inter-

personal consciousness of injustice is allied to masculine law and order in the person of brother Hugh, who meets them in New York and arrests Julius, wanted on other charges. This rescue from the bad man Joan Foster and every Gothic heroine fears by a brisk and humorous woman rather than by a nice man, is a decisive, utopian shift.[18]

In Dinesen's *The Angelic Avengers*, as in "The Girl in the Pink Hat," two "sisters" save themselves and other women; in addition, the novel also traces the stages of recognition, action, and resistance that allow women finally to leave the Gothic arena. Zosine and Lucan, schoolmates alone in the world and claiming one another as "sister" (e.g., 179), find that there is no joint employment for two impoverished gentlewomen in London, but they are fortunate enough to have a clergyman and his wife take them to France and "adopt" them for a year in memory of a dead daughter. The Pennhallows, actually brother and sister, are in fact slavers and Satanists, both women the last in a long line of young British women in distress.

The novel is unusual because of its use of double protagonists, a use that emphasizes the necessary union between women and the fact that only at her peril can the Gothic heroine believe herself exceptional and her plight unique. The women who precede them, like those who came before Willa Prescott Nedeed or Jane Eyre, further underscore the need to recognize a community of suffering that extends across place and time. Upon first arriving in France, however, Lucan and Zosine think themselves in safe haven, all danger behind them thanks to benevolent authority.

Carefully tutored by Mr. and Mrs. Pennhallow in "'the great heroes who lived long ago'" (163), Zosine and Lucan consider themselves fortunate. Both old people seem stern but loving, so happy in their new daughter/pupils that they indulge in separate, strange lectures. The sister Pennhallow explains that "'man . . . is made in the image of God, so it is written in the Scriptures. But woman is the most hideous of all creatures'" (114). The brother, for his part, inveighs against the fallen woman, a "'terrible contagion of perdition [that] would leap from woman to woman'" (142). As clergyman, he declares that "'It is a sin even to think of her with anything but aversion,

---

[18]Other novels show women trying to save other women, but their efforts always seem unavailing, whether because of external circumstance or the resistance of the victim herself. Anna Howe tries to help Clarissa, for example, but Clarissa thinks such an escape improper, while Miss Mancel and Miss Melvyn, in Sarah Scott's *Millenium Hall*, think of possible recourses for one another but succumb to domination for "duty"; they only escape through their oppressors' deaths. (They do, however, eventually live in the Hall of the title, a utopian community for independent women.)

or to wish her anything but ruin'" (141), and he is appalled at Lucan's suggestion that there is forgiveness and "'infinite grace in the world'" (143). Nonetheless, both young women accept these jeremiads for their souls' well-being, and they are righteously indignant when a local judge (later revealed as an accomplice, as is the housekeeper) appear to ask the reverend Mr. Pennhallow about the disappearance of previous objects of his charity.

When Zosine and Lucan realize the truth of these accusations, they must decide whether their resistance will be as aggressors, subversives—or some other, as yet unnamed and unknown, option. They reject the possibility of becoming helpless victims or silent accomplices out of hand, although, as Zosine points out, the latter would assure their safety. "'We are their two little canary birds in a neat little cage. . . . Who shall dare, when they see the little birds hopping from perch to perch and singing out their happiness and gratitude, to call their master cruel and inhuman?'" (176). They instead plan for their immediate flight. The discovery of a letter detailing the fate of Rosa, one of their predecessors who was strangled for resisting her forced prostitution by burning her face in obdurate "spite" and defiance (183), strengthens their determination.

Each, then, assumes responsibility for herself and for the other in their sisterhood. Zosine, however, who has "'something hard and dangerous'" within her (204), decides that she cannot leave: she must avenge Rosa. Zosine's aggression—fostered by her upbringing as an heiress, sympathetic and even admirable in context—is nonetheless uncomfortably close to the Gothic premises she wants to explode. Proudly asocial and self-determined, she asserts her own will, adhering to the dictum of an aunt who declares, in her own haughty embrace of self-inflicted pain, "'In this way we will, each of us, fulfill the destiny of our nature, and preserve that dignity which consists in accepting our destiny'" (71).

Zosine's need for aggression and her sense of betrayal are the greater because she was willing to worship, "in her great admiration and devotion," the old man she decides to call "Master" (99). Able to solemnly declare that "'he knows more about us than we do ourselves'" (97), her fury at the revelation is augmented by the knowledge that Pennhallow "'represented to me so much of the greatness and wisdom of the world. I have even loved him'" (176). In converting her rage at him and at herself into altruistic aggression for Rosa, she also begins to understand something of what her black servant, Olympia, must always have felt: "'I have thought much of Olympia tonight. Her own people, her brother and sisters, were sold by us,

and we have wronged them greatly. I will beg Olympia's forgiveness'" (178).[19]

The angered Zosine looks forward with pleasure to the Pennhallows' knowing that "'the tables have been turned, and that now
we are chasing them. The canary birds are out of their cage, and on
their track. And they will never leave the blood-trail till they have
hunted them down, till they are dead!'" (202). Lucan is dubious, but
she will abandon Zosine no more readily than Zosine will abandon
the ghost of Rosa. It is subversion they must pursue, then, in seeming
to be the sweet, stupid canaries the Pennhallows think them until
they can effect their own escape and the Pennhallows' arrest.

The women, alone for a night, are joined by Olympia: all wait,
assuming that their fate will be like the image "all their life they
remembered— . . . the unfaithful servant-maidens [of Odysseus
who] had been hanged on a rope like thrushes" (96). Instead, Pennhallow is in their power, as Terry was in Alima's. Suddenly and almost irresistibly, Olympia and Zosine can kill him, and both want to
do so. Pennhallow's jubilation at his own death is genuine: like the
devil of "Young Goodman Brown," he exults "'You yourself, on your
own, have found the path to lies and deceit, and to murder'" (264).
For, as he announces and Lucan affirms, they will become as he.
Lucan screams: "'Do you not see that he is right? We cannot live if we
kill him. None of us can live!'" (265). Lucan repeats: "'There is forgiveness for all human beings! There is an infinite grace in the world.
There is grace for him too. Have pity on him! Have mercy!'" (265–66).
Her mercy destroys him as replicated aggression cannot when, "as if
he fled from an advancing, devouring fire" (266), he kicks over the
stool on which he stands and dies.[20]

Zosine too prepares to die, a murderer in her own mind, until her
future mother-in-law and a priest intervene. "'Zosine, Madame de
Valfonds asked, 'do you not think that a woman may sin in a more
dreadful way than by hating?'" (281). And Mme. de Valfonds is quite
right (as her own narrative shows), as is the priest who decrees that

---

[19]The representation of Olympia, with her mad force, voodoo powers, and adulation
of the white man and his daughter, both of whom she suckled, is undeniably racist.
Nonetheless, the fact that, within the novel's context, she has her own past and, in
confronting Pennhallow, her own rage (for he is the Satanic double of the orgun who
offered up her own child) indicates, like Zosine's sudden recognition of Olympia's
reality, a limited, provisional recognition.

[20]His sister, returning to find her brother dead, hangs herself at his side. The image
of Odysseus' maid-servants, then, is triumphantly reversed but, as Lucan sadly notes:
"'Poor unhappy woman! She could not bear to live when he had died. But in his last
hour, when he spoke to us, he did not once mention her name'" (288).

Zosine, still worthy of sisterhood, must kiss Lucan and accept her penance: "'You are to live among [innocent and honest people] as before. And, among them, you are to learn to accept, and to show, mercy' " (290).

Pennhallow's death, like that of Luther Nedeed, is more than the destruction of a single oppressor: Lucan and Zosine destroy a country-wide prostitution ring. The complicity of legal and religious figures in that plot is now balanced by the intervention of law and religion in order to address what Zosine and Lucas have uncovered through their individual formulations of salvation and justice. Both have refused to replicate oppression, have found aggression and subversion inadequate for their situation, and have situated themselves outside the confines of the beating drama.

Both wed at novel's end and, like the two couples in *Herland*, one goes forth into the world while the other remains in a utopian space. Zosine discovers her own past and her foremothers' history at idyllic, aristocratic Joliet. She feels "'that here live good people, who are kind and helpful to one another, that here nobody hates or lies, but that all work together to the same purpose' " (280). She stays to become more like the gentle, retired Lucan; Lucan, traveling through Europe, develops some of Zosine's initiative and aggression: "soon she would learn to gaze freely and dauntlessly to all sides, to listen to the voices of the world, and to answer them without diffidence" (303).

The language of both marriages is disturbingly that of merger (e.g., 296–97, 302–3). Nonetheless, the bond between the two women remains powerful. They have previously pledged their own troth with two rings; now, Zosine extends their circle by giving the ring to her husband: "'It pleads the cause of the defenseless, the oppressed, and the wronged' " (301). Lucan thinks of Zosine on her wedding journey, and their new alliances are additions to, not erasures of, the old: "no old Nordic heroes, who, according to the Viking custom, had mingled blood, could ever have felt a more eternal and mysterious oneness than the two friends *after* their wedding day" (300, emphasis added). Unlike Jane Eyre recording the sedate annual visits of Diana and Mary Rivers, these two are not separated.

Both "The Girl in the Pink Hat" and *The Angelic Avengers* suggest that, while their social environments have decidedly influenced their protagonists, they in turn have influenced their worlds. All refuse the eroticization of pain that perpetuates the beating fantasy, recognize their accord with other women, and identify the systemic nature of the forces that seek to confine them. In moving from the spectator's insight to action, they step outside the sometimes replicating responses of aggression and subversion to a utopian space from which they declare that neither their identities nor their actions will be determined by the logic of the dominant.

Still, as the structural tensions in the closure of *Jane Eyre*, "The Girl in the Pink Hat," and *The Angelic Avengers* suggest, such utopian alterity is plagued by radical misgivings within the Gothic. We struggle to believe in the new world the landscapes of Ferndean, New York, and Joliet image; we wonder about the surcease of oppression the figures of Rochester, brother Hugh, and the two husbands in *The Angelic Avengers* embody. Perhaps, then, the final step in escaping Gothic masochism is the move to other genres that begin by assuming a distinction between domination and love, genres that figure oppression as inevitably as much a social problem as an individual dilemma: genres such as the detective novel and science fiction.

Not surprisingly, in "The Girl in the Pink Hat" Jess reads a detective novel as she, the narrator, and Polly effect her escape from the Gothic. Increasingly in the last decade, women detectives are Gothic rescuers, as novels by Linda Barnes, Elisabeth Bowers, Katherine Forrest, Valerie Miner, and Sara Paretsky, among others, suggest.[21] The skills of the Gothic spectator join the initiative and activity of the Gothic resister as women detectives insist on bringing once invisible, "domestic," oppression to justice as the social crime it is. Their investigations often solve such crimes, but the mysteries they pursue are not only those for which rational induction provides an answer but also the always unresolved mysteries of relationship.

In bringing her career as Gothic novelist and Gothic masochist to an end, Joan Foster thinks that maybe she'll "try some science fiction" (379), and she is not alone. Extrapolating from the contemporary reality of Gothic gender arrangements, feminist science fiction authors examine the future implications of domination for not only couples but for the worlds and civilizations in which they might exist.[22] They analyze the organization of resistance in a world where

[21]William Patrick Day (27) and Pierre Macheray (27), among others, see the Gothic as a progenitor of the detective novel, although the lineage they trace is male—primarily, I assume, because of the detective novel's emphasis upon "masculine" qualities of independence and rationality in uncovering mysteries.

[22]In "Is Gender Necessary?" Ursula K. LeGuin sets forth some of feminist science fiction's basic assumptions in language much like that of Jacqueline Rose's warning against dichotomies. "If men and women were completely and genuinely equal in their social roles, equal legally and economically, equal in freedom, in responsibility, and in self-esteem, then society would be a very different thing. What our problems might be, God knows; I only know we would have them. But it seems likely that our central problem would not be the one it is now: the problem of exploitation—exploitation of the woman, of the weak, of the earth. . . . Instead of a search for balance and integration, there is a struggle for dominance. Divisions are insisted upon, interdependence is denied. The dualism of value that destroys us, the dualism of superior/inferior,

women are seen as less than animals (Suzy McKee Charnas, Motherlines series), warn against separatism's risk of replication (Sherri Tepper, *City of Women*), suggest that consciousness itself will change when a literal "women's language" structures that change (Suzette Haden Elgin, Native Tongue series), critique hierarchy as a human genetic failing (Octavia Butler, Exogenesis series), or study the implications of masculine and feminine parenting over millennia (Butler, Patternist series). In the instances I cite and many others, contemporary and earlier authors create communities of women (and sometimes of men) who understand, or come to understand, that it is only through their alliances with one another that domination can be brought to an end.

The Gothic too points forward to a time when there will be a cure for the symptoms it has so repeatedly suffered for the last three centuries, to a time when no woman will be lured by culture into the Gothic arena and remain there by her own "choice." When no beaten woman embraces her pain as proof of existing through her dominator's "loving" gaze, when no woman creates her identity by oppressing other women, other classes, other races, when the spectator need not endlessly watch a woman being beaten—then the Gothic will come to an end. And on that day, what will be heard most loudly will no longer be the Gothic scream but the laugh of the Medusa.

---

ruler/ruled, owner/owned, user/used, might give way to what seems to me, from here, a much healthier, sounder, more promising modality of integration and integrity" (159).

Works Cited

Abel, Elizabeth, Marianne Hirsch, and Elizabeth Langland, eds. *The Voyage In: Fictions of Female Development*. Hanover, N.H: University Press of New England, 1983.

Abraham, Karl. "Manifestations of the Female Castration Complex." 1920. In Strouse, ed. 109–35.

Adams, Maurianne. "*Jane Eyre*: Woman's Estate." In Diamond and Edwards, eds. 137–59.

Ainsworth, William Harrison. "The Spectre Bride." 1822. In Haining, ed. 1: 360–70.

Alcott, Louisa. *Behind a Mask: or, a Woman's Power*. 1866. In *Behind a Mask: The Unknown Thrillers of Louisa May Alcott*. Ed. Madeleine Stern. New York: Bantam Books, 1975. 3–117.

——. *A Marble Woman: or, The Mysterious Model*. 1865. In *Plots and Counterplots: More Unknown Thrillers of Louisa May Alcott*. Ed. Madeleine Stern. New York: Popular Library, 1976. 131–237.

Allen, David W. *The Fear of Looking or Scopophilic-Exhibitionistic Conflicts*. Charlottesville, Va.: University Press of Virginia, 1974.

Anne of Swansea (Julia Anne Curtis). "The Unknown! or the Knight of the Blood-Red Plume." c. 1826. In Haining, ed. 1: 230–60.

Armstrong, Nancy. *Desire and Domestic Fiction: A Political History of the Novel*. New York: Oxford University Press, 1987.

Atwood, Margaret. *The Handmaid's Tale*. New York: Ballantine/Fawcett, 1985.

——. *Lady Oracle*. New York: Bard/Avon, 1976.

——. *Survival: A Thematic Guide to Canadian Literature*. Toronto: House of Anansi Press, 1972.

Auerbach, Nina. *Romantic Imprisonment: Women and Other Glorified Outcasts*. New York: Columbia University Press, 1986.

Austen, Jane. *Northanger Abbey*. 1818. New York: Oxford University Press, 1971.

Baer, Elizabeth R. "The Sisterhood of Jane Eyre and Antoinette Cosway." In Abel, Hirsch, and Langland, eds. 131–48.

Baker, Ernest A. *The Novel of Sentiment and the Gothic Romance*. Vol. 5 of *The History of the English Novel*. New York: Barnes & Noble, 1934.

Balint, Michael. *The Basic Fault: Therapeutic Aspects of Regression*. London: Tavistock, 1968.

Balmary, Marie. *Psychoanalyzing Psychoanalysis: Freud and the Hidden Fault of the Father*. Trans. Ned Lukacher. Baltimore: Johns Hopkins University Press, 1982.

Barry, Kathleen. *Female Sexual Slavery*. Englewood Cliffs, N.J.: Prentice- Hall, 1979.

Baumeister, Roy F. *Masochism and the Self*. Hillsdale, N.J.: Lawrence Erlbaum Associates, 1989.

Beckford, William. "The Nymph of the Fountain." 1791. In Haining, ed. 1: 138–75.

Benjamin, Jessica. *The Bonds of Love: Psychoanalysis, Feminism, and the Problem of Domination*. New York: Pantheon Books, 1988.

Bergler, Edmund. "Preliminary Phases of the Masculine Beating Fantasy." *Psychoanalytic Quarterly* 7 (1938): 514–36.

Bernheimer, Charles, and Claire Kahane, eds. *In Dora's Case: Freud—Hysteria—Feminism*. New York: Columbia University Press, 1985.

Bettelheim, Bruno. *The Uses of Enchantment: The Meaning and Importance of Fairy Tales*. New York: Random House/Vintage, 1975.

Birkhead, Edith. *The Tale of Terror: A Study of the Gothic Romance*. New York: Russell & Russell, 1921.

Blake, William. "The Mental Traveller." 1803. In *Blake: Complete Writings*. Ed. Geoffrey Keynes. New York: Oxford University Press, 1972.

Brontë, Charlotte. *Jane Eyre*. 1848. New York: Norton, 1971.

——. *Villette*. 1853. New York: Penguin Books, 1979

Brontë, Emily. *Wuthering Heights*. 1850. New York: W. W. Norton, 1972.

Brookner, Anita. *Look at Me*. New York: Random House/Pantheon, 1983.

Brooks, Peter. *Reading for the Plot: Design and Intention in Narrative*. New York: Knopf, 1984.

Brown, Charles Brockden. *Wieland and Memoirs of Carwin*. 1798 and 1805. Kent, Ohio: Kent State University Press, 1977.

Burke, Edmund. "A Philosophical Inquiry into the Origins of Our Ideas of the Sublime and Beautiful." 1756. In *The Works of the Right Honourable Edmund Burke*. Vol. 1. Ed. James Prior. London: Henry G. Bohn, 1864. 49–181.

Caplan, Paula J. *The Myth of Women's Masochism*. New York: Dutton, 1985.

Carter, Angela. "The Bloody Chamber." *The Bloody Chamber and Other Stories*. New York: Penguin, 1979. 7–41.

——. *Nothing Sacred: Selected Writings*. London: Virago Press, 1982.

——. *The Sadeian Woman and the Ideology of Pornography*. New York: Pantheon, 1978.

Carter, Margaret L. *Specter or Delusion? The Supernatural in Gothic Fiction*.

Studies in Speculative Fiction, 15. Ann Arbor, Mich.: UMI Research Press, 1987.

Castle, Terry. "Phantasmagoria: Spectral Technology and the Metaphorics of Modern Reverie." *Critical Inquiry* 15 (Autumn 1988): 26–61.

——. "The Spectralization of the Other in *The Mysteries of Udolpho*." Nussbaum and Brown, eds. 231–53.

Chodorow, Nancy. *The Reproduction of Mothering: Psychoanalysis and the Sociology of Gender*. Berkeley: University of California Press, 1978.

Cixous, Hélène, and Catherine Clément. *The Newly Born Woman*. Trans. Betsy Wing. 1975. Minneapolis: University of Minnesota Press, 1986.

Clarke, Mary Cowden. *The Girlhood of Shakespeare's Heroines*. New York, 1851.

Clément, Catherine. See Cixous.

Cohn, Jan. *Romance and the Erotics of Property: Mass-Market Fiction for Women*. Durham, N.C.: Duke University Press, 1988.

Cooper, Arnold. "The Narcissistic-Masochistic Character." In Glick and Meyers, eds. 117–38.

Cullwick, Hannah. *The Diaries of Hannah Cullwick, Victorian Maidservant*. Ed. Liz Stanley. New Brunswick, N.J.: Rutgers University Press, 1984.

Day, William Patrick. *In the Circles of Fear and Desire: A Study of Gothic Fantasy*. Chicago: University of Chicago Press, 1985.

DeLamotte, Eugenia C. *Perils of the Night: A Feminist Study of Nineteenth-Century Gothic*. New York: Oxford University Press, 1989.

De Lauretis, Teresa. *Technologies of Gender: Essays on Theory, Film, and Fiction*. Bloomington: Indiana University Press, 1987.

Diamond, Arlyn, and Lee R. Edwards, eds. *The Authority of Experience: Essays in Feminist Criticism*. Amherst: University of Massachusetts Press, 1977.

Dinesen, Isak. *The Angelic Avengers*. New York: Random House, 1946.

——. "The Blank Page." *Last Tales*. New York: Random House/Vintage, 1957. 99–105.

——. "The Deluge at Norderney." In *Seven Gothic Tales*. 1–79.

——. *Ehrengard*. 1963. New York: Random House/Vintage, 1975.

——. "The Monkey." In *Seven Gothic Tales*. 109–63.

——. *Seven Gothic Tales*. 1934. New York: Random House/Vintage, 1961.

Doane, Janice L., and Devon Hodges. *Nostalgia and Sexual Difference: The Resistance to Contemporary Feminism*. New York: Methuen, 1987.

——. "Undoing Feminism: From the Preoedipal to Postfeminism in Anne Rice's Vampire Chronicles." Forthcoming, *American Literary History*.

Doody, Margaret Ann. "Deserts, Ruins and Troubled Waters: Female Dreams in Fiction and the Development of the Gothic Novel." *Genre* 10 (1977): 529–72.

du Maurier, Daphne. *Rebecca*. New York: Avon Books, 1938.

——. *The "Rebecca" Notebook and Other Memories*. London: Victor Gollancz, 1981.

Dworkin, Andrea. *Intercourse*. New York: Free Press/Macmillan, 1988.

——. "Woman as Victim: Story of O." *Feminist Studies* 2.1 (1974): 107–11.

Eagleton, Terry. *Myths of Power: A Marxist Study of the Brontës*. New York: Barnes & Noble, 1975.

Edwards, Lee R. *Psyche as Hero: Female Heroism and Fictional Form*. Middletown, Conn.: Wesleyan University Press, 1984.

Eisenbud, Ruth-Jean. "Masochism Revisited." *Psychoanalytic Review* 54 (1967): 561–82.

Ellis, Kate Ferguson. *The Contested Castle: Gothic Novels and the Subversion of Domestic Ideology*. Champaign: University of Illinois Press, 1989.

Ellison, Ralph. *Invisible Man*. New York: Signet/New American Library, 1952.

Erikson, Erik. *Childhood and Society*. 1950. New York: W. W. Norton, 1963.

——. "Reality and Actuality." In Bernehimer and Kahane, eds. 44–55.

Feldstein, Richard. "Reader, Text, and Ambiguous Referentiality in 'The Yellow Wall-Paper.'" In Feldstein and Roof, eds. 269–79.

Feldstein, Richard, and Judith Roof, eds. *Feminism and Psychoanalysis*. Ithaca, N.Y.: Cornell University Press, 1989.

Fenichel, Otto. "The Scopophilic Instinct and Identification." *International Journal of Psycho-analysis* 18 (1938): 6–34.

Fetterley, Judith. "Reading about Reading: 'A Jury of Her Peers,' 'The Murders in the Rue Morgue,' and 'The Yellow Wallpaper.'" In Flynn and Schweickart, eds. 147–64.

Fiedler, Leslie A. *Love and Death in the American Novel*. 1960. New York: Dell, 1975.

Fleenor, Juliann E., ed. *The Female Gothic*. Montreal: Eden Press, 1983.

Flynn, Elizabeth A., and Patrocinio P. Schweickart, eds. *Gender and Reading: Essays on Readers, Texts, and Contexts*. Baltimore: Johns Hopkins University Press, 1986.

Ford, Karen. "'The Yellow Wallpaper' and Women's Discourse." *Tulsa Studies in Women's Literature* 4.2 (1985): 309–14.

Foster, James R. *History of the Pre-Romantic Novel in England*. New York: MLA, 1949.

Foucault, Michel. *Discipline and Punish: The Birth of the Prison*. Trans. Alan Sheridan. New York: Random House/Pantheon, 1977.

——. *The History of Sexuality*. Vol. 1: *An Introduction*. Trans. Robert Hurley. 1976. New York: Random House/Vintage, 1978.

Freeman, Mary E. Wilkins. "Luella Miller." *Collected Ghost Stories*. 1903. Sauk City, Wis.: Arkham House, 1974. 39–53.

Frenier, Mariam Darce. *Good-Bye Heathcliff: Changing Heroes, Heroines, Roles, and Values in Women's Category Romances*. Westport, Conn.: Greenwood Press, 1988.

Freud, Anna. *The Ego and the Mechanisms of Defense*. 1936. Vol. 2 of *The Writings of Anna Freud*. Trans. Cecil Baines. New York: International Universities Press, 1966.

——. "The Relation of Beating-Phantasies to a Day-Dream." *International Journal of Psycho-analysis* 4 (1923): 89–102.

Freud, Anna, and Dorothy Burlingham. *War and Children*. New York: Medical War Books, 1943.

——. *Young Children in War-Time: A Year's Work in a Residential War Nursery.* London: Allen & Unwin, 1942.

Freud, Sigmund. *The Standard Edition of the Complete Psychological Works of Sigmund Freud.* Trans. and ed. James Strachey et al. 24 vols. London: Hogarth Press, 1953–74.

——. *Analysis of a Phobia in a Five-Year-Old Boy.* 1909. 10: 7–150.

——. "Analysis Terminable and Interminable." 1937. 23: 209–54.

——. "Anxiety and Instinctual Life." In *New Introductory Lectures.* 1933. 22: 81–111.

——. *Beyond the Pleasure Principle.* 1920. 18: 1–64.

——. "Character and Anal Erotism." 1908. 9: 169–75.

——. "'A Child Is Being Beaten': A Contribution to the Study of the Origin of Sexual Perversions." 1919. 17: 175–204.

——. *Civilization and Its Discontents.* 1930. 21: 57–146.

——. "'Civilized' Sexual Morality and Modern Nervous Illness." 1908. 9: 181–204.

——. "Creative Writers and Day-Dreaming." 1908. 9: 143–53.

——. "The Disposition to Obsessional Neurosis." 1913. 12: 311–26.

——. "The Dissection of the Psychical Personality." In *New Introductory Lectures.* 1933. 22: 51–71.

——. "The Dissolution of the Oedipus Complex." 1924. 19: 173–79.

——. "Dostoevsky and Parricide." 1928. 21: 173–96.

——. "Draft L." 1897. 1: 248–50.

——. "The Economic Problem of Masochism." 1924. 19: 155–70.

——. *The Ego and the Id.* 1927. 19: 13–66.

——. "Female Sexuality." 1931. 21: 221–46.

——. "Femininity." In *New Introductory Lectures.* 1933. 22: 112–35.

——. *Five Lectures on Psycho-Analysis.* 1910. 11: 1–55.

——. "Fixation to Traumas—The Unconscious." In *Introductory Lectures.* 1917. 16: 273–85.

——. *Fragment of an Analysis of a Case of Hysteria.* 1905. 7: 3–122.

——. *From the History of an Infantile Neurosis.* 1918. 17: 7–122.

——. "Infantile Sexuality." In *Three Essays on the Theory of Sexuality.* 1905. 7: 173–206.

——. "Inhibitions, Symptoms, and Anxiety." 1926. 20: 75–176.

——. "Instincts and Their Vicissitudes." 1915. 14: 117–40.

——. *Introductory Lectures on Psycho-Analysis.* 1916–17. 15, 16.

——. *Jokes and Their Relation to the Unconscious.* 1905. 8.

——. "Leonardo da Vinci and a Memory of His Childhood." 1910. 11: 59–138.

——. "Lou Andreas-Salomé." 1937. 23: 297–98.

——. *Moses and Monotheism: Three Essays.* 1939. 23: 1–138.

——. "Mourning and Melancholia." 1917. 14: 243–58.

——. *New Introductory Lectures on Psycho-Analysis.* 1933. 22: 1–182.

——. *Notes upon a Case of Obsessional Neurosis.* 1909. 10: 151–318.

——. "On Narcissism: An Introduction." 1914. 14: 67–104.

——. "On the Sexual Theories of Children." 1908. 9: 209–26.

——. "On the Universal Tendency to Debasement in the Sphere of Love: Contributions to the Psychology of Love II." 1912. 11: 179–90.

——. "On Transformations of Instinct as Exemplified in Anal Eroticism." 1917. 17: 127–33.

——. *The Origins of Psycho-Analysis: Letters of Wilhelm Fliess, Drafts and Notes, 1887–1902.* Ed. Maria Bonaparte, Anna Freud, and Ernst Kris. Trans. Eric Mosbacher and James Strachey. New York: Basic Books, 1954.

——. "The Psychogenesis of a Case of Homosexuality in a Woman." 1920. 18: 147–72.

——. *The Psychopathology of Everyday Life.* 1901. 6.

——. "Remarks on the Theory and Practice of Dream-Interpretation." 1923. 19: 109–22.

——. "Remembering, Repeating, and Working-Through: Further Recommendations on the Technique of Psycho-Analysis." 1914. 12: 145–56.

——. "Repression." 1915. 14: 146–58.

——. "Resistance and Repression." In *Introductory Lectures.* 1917. 16: 286–302.

——. "The Sexual Aberrations." In *Three Essays on the Theory of Sexuality.* 1905. 7: 135–72.

——. "Some Psychical Consequences of the Anatomical Distinction between the Sexes." 1925. 19: 241–60.

——. "A Special Type of Choice of Object Made by Men: Contributions to the Psychology of Love I." 1910. 11: 165–75.

——. "Splitting of the Ego in the Process of Defence." 1940. 23: 271–78.

——. *Three Essays on the Theory of Sexuality.* 1905. 7: 125–246.

——. "The 'Uncanny.'" 1919. 17: 217–52.

Freud, Sigmund, and Josef Breuer. *Studies on Hysteria.* 1893–1895. 2.

Frieze, Irene H., and S. J. Ramsey. "Nonverbal Maintenance of Traditional Sex Roles." *Journal of Social Issues* 32 (1976): 133–41.

Gallop, Jane. *The Daughter's Seduction: Feminism and Psychoanalysis.* Ithaca, N.Y.: Cornell University Press, 1982.

Garner, Shirley Nelson, Claire Kahane, and Madelon Sprengnether, eds. *The (M)other Tongue: Essays in Feminist Psychoanalytic Interpretation.* Ithaca, N.Y.: Cornell University Press, 1985.

Gear, Maria Carmen, Melvyn A. Hill, and Ernesto Cesar Liendo. *Working Through Narcissism: Treating Its Sadomasochistic Structure.* New York: Aronson, 1981.

Gilbert, Lucy, and Paula Webster. *Bound by Love: The Sweet Trap of Daughterhood.* Boston: Beacon Press, 1982.

Gilbert, Sandra M., and Susan Gubar. *The Madwoman in the Attic: The Woman Writer and the Nineteenth-Century Literary Imagination.* New Haven, Conn.: Yale University Press, 1979.

Gilligan, Carol. *In a Different Voice: Psychological Theory and Women's Development.* Cambridge: Harvard University Press, 1982.

Gilman, Charlotte Perkins. "The Girl in the Pink Hat." 1916. In *The Charlotte Perkins Gilman Reader.* Ed. Ann J. Lane. New York: Random House/Pantheon, 1980. 39–46.

——. *Herland*. 1915. New York: Random House/Pantheon, 1979.

——. "The Yellow Wallpaper." 1899. Old Westbury, Conn.: Feminist Press, 1973.

Glasgow, Ellen. "The Past." *The Shadowy Third and Other Stories*. Garden City, N.Y.: Doubleday, Page & Co., 1923. 107–47.

Glick, Robert A., and Donald I. Meyers, eds. *Masochism: Current Psychoanalytic Perspectives*. Hillsdale, N.J.: Analytic Press, 1988.

Godwin, William. *Caleb Williams*. 1794. New York: W. W. Norton, 1977.

Gosselin, Chris, and Glenn Wilson. *Sexual Variations: Fetishism, Sadomasochism, and Transvestism*. New York: Simon and Schuster, 1980.

Gould, Lois. *A Sea-Change*. New York: Random House, 1966.

Greif, Ann C. "Historical Synthesis." In Montgomery and Greif, eds. 1–15.

Griffin, Susan. *Pornography and Silence: Culture's Revenge against Nature*. New York: Harper & Row/Perennial, 1981.

Gross, Louis. *Redefining the American Gothic: From "Wieland" to "Day of the Dead."* Ann Arbor, Mich.: UMI Press, 1989.

Haggerty, George E. *Gothic Fiction/Gothic Form*. University Park: Pennsylvania University Press, 1989.

Haining, Peter, ed. *Gothic Tales of Terror*. 2 vols. New York: Penguin Books, 1972.

Hall, Judith A. *Nonverbal Sex Differences: Communication Accuracy and Expressive Style*. Baltimore: Johns Hopkins University Press, 1984.

Haskell, Molly. "Rape Fantasy: The 2,000-Year-Old Misunderstanding." *Ms.*, November 1976, 84–96.

Hennessey, Brendan. *The Gothic Novel*. London: Longman, 1978.

Hirsch, Marianne. *The Mother/Daughter Plot: Narrative, Psychoanalysis, Feminism*. Bloomington: Indiana University Press, 1989.

Hoffmann, E. T. A. "The Sandman." 1816. In *Selected Writings of E. T. A. Hoffmann*. Ed. and trans. Leonard J. Kent and Elizabeth C. Knight. Vol 1. Chicago: University of Chicago Press, 1969. 137–67.

Holland, Norman, and Leona Sherman. "Gothic Possibilities." *New Literary History* 8 (Winter 1977): 279–94.

Homans, Margaret. "Dreaming of Children: Literalization in *Jane Eyre* and *Wuthering Heights*." In Fleenor, ed. 257–79.

Horney, Karen. *Feminine Psychology*. New York: W. W. Norton, 1973.

——. *Neurosis and Human Growth*. New York: W. W. Norton, 1950.

Howells, Coral Ann. *Love, Mystery, and Misery: Feeling in Gothic Fiction*. London: Athlone Press, 1978.

Hull, Helen R. "The Clay-Shuttered Door." 1926. In *What Did Miss Darrington See?: An Anthology of Feminist Supernatural Fiction*. Ed. Jessica Amanda Salmonson. New York: Feminist Press, 1989. 38–57.

Hunt, Leigh. "A Tale for a Chimney Corner." 1819. In Haining, ed. 1: 350–59.

Irigaray, Luce. "And the One Doesn't Stir without the Other." Trans. Hélène Vivienne Wenzel. *Signs* 7 (Autumn 1981): 60–67.

——. *Speculum of the Other Woman*. Trans. Gillian C. Gill. Ithaca, N.Y.: Cornell University Press, 1985.

James, Sibyl. "Gothic Transformations: Isak Dinesen and the Gothic." In Fleenor, ed. 138–52.

Johnson, Loren B. T. "A Woman Is Being Beaten: An Analytic Fragment." *Psychoanalytic Review* 17 (1930): 259–67.

Jonel, Marissa. "Letter from a Former Masochist." In Linden et al., eds. 16–22.

Joseph, Edward D. *Beating Fantasies.* In Joseph, ed. 30–67.

——, ed. *Beating Fantasies* and *Regressive Ego Phenomena in Psychoanalysis.* The Kris Study Group of the New York Psychoanalytic Institute. New York: International Universities Press, 1965.

Kahane, Claire. "The Gothic Mirror." In Garner, Kahane, and Sprengnether, eds. 334–51.

Kaplan, Louise K. *Female Perversions: The Temptations of Emma Bovary.* New York: Doubleday, 1991.

Kernberg, Otto F. "Clinical Dimensions of Masochism." In Glick and Meyers, eds. 61–79.

Kiely, Robert. *The Romantic Novel in England.* Cambridge, Mass.: Harvard University Press, 1972.

Killen, Alice M. *Le roman terrifiant.* Paris: Librarie Ancienne Édouard Champion, 1923.

Kofman, Sarah. *The Enigma of Woman: Woman in Freud's Writing.* Trans. Catherine Porter. Ithaca, N.Y.: Cornell University Press, 1985.

Kolodny, Annette. "A Map for Rereading: Gender and the Interpretation of Literary Texts." In Showalter, ed. 50–54.

Kristeva, Julia. *Powers of Horror: An Essay on Abjection.* Trans. Leon S. Roudiez. New York: Columbia University Press, 1982.

Lacan, Jacques, and l' *école freudienne,* "God and the *Jouissance* of The Woman." 1972–73. In Mitchell and Rose, eds. 137–48.

Lanser, Susan S. "Feminist Criticism, 'The Yellow Wallpaper,' and the Politics of Color in America." *Feminist Studies* 15.3 (1989): 415–41.

Lawrence, D. H. "Pornography and Obscenity." *D. H. Lawrence: Selected Literary Criticism.* Ed. Anthony Beal. 1929. New York: Viking Press, 1966. 32–51.

LeBrun, Annie. *Les châteaux de la subversion.* Paris: Garnier Frères, 1982.

LeGuin, Ursula K. *The Language of the Night: Essays on Fantasy and Science Fiction.* New York: Berkley Books, 1979.

Lenzer, Gertrud. "On Masochism: A Contribution to the History of a Phantasy and Its Theory." *Signs* 1 (1975): 277–324.

Lester, Milton. "The Analysis of an Unconscious Beating Fantasy in a Woman." *International Journal of Psycho-analysis* 38 (1957): 22–31.

Lewis, Matthew. *The Monk.* 1796. New York: Oxford University Press, 1973.

Light, Alison. "'Returning to Manderley'—Romance Fiction, Female Sexuality, and Class." *Feminist Review* 16 (April 1984): 7–25.

Linden, Robin Ruth, et al., eds. *Against Sadomasochism: A Radical Feminist Analysis.* San Francisco: Frog in the Well, 1982.

MacAndrew, Elizabeth. *The Gothic Tradition in Fiction.* New York: Columbia University Press, 1979.

Macherey, Pierre. *A Theory of Literary Production*. Trans. Geoffrey Wall. Boston: Routledge & Kegan Paul, 1978.

Marcus, Maria. *A Taste for Pain: On Masochism and Female Sexuality*. Trans. Joan Tate. New York: St. Martin's Press, 1981.

Martin, Judith. *Miss Manners' Guide to Excruciatingly Correct Behavior*. New York: Atheneum, 1982.

Martin, Valerie. *A Recent Martyr*. New York: Houghton Mifflin, 1987.

Marxist Feminist Literature Collective. "Women's Writing: *Jane Eyre, Shirley, Villette, Aurora Leigh*." In *1848: The Sociology of Literature*. Ed. Francis Barker et al. Essex: University of Essex Press, 1977. 185–206.

Maso, Carole. *Ghost Dance*. New York: Harper & Row, 1986.

Masson, Jeffrey. *The Assault on Truth: Freud's Suppression of the Seduction Theory*. New York: Farrar Straus Giroux, 1984.

Maturin, Charles Robert. *Melmoth the Wanderer*. 1820. London: Oxford University Press, 1958.

Mayo, Clara, and Nancy M. Henley, eds. *Gender and Nonverbal Behavior*. New York: Springer-Verlag, 1981.

Menaker, Esther. *Masochism and the Emergent Ego: Selected Papers of Esther Menaker*. Ed. Leila Lerner. New York: Human Sciences, 1979.

Michie, Elsie. "The Historical Specificity of the Gothic: Heathcliff, Rochester, and the Simianization of the Irish." Forthcoming, *Novel: A Forum on Fiction*.

Miller, Jean Baker. *Toward a New Psychology of Women*. 2d ed. Boston: Beacon Press, 1986.

Mitchell, Juliet. *Psychoanalysis and Feminism: Freud, Reich, Laing and Women*. New York: Random House/Vintage, 1974.

Mitchell, Juliet, and Jacqueline Rose, eds. *Feminine Sexuality*. Trans. Jacqueline Rose. New York: W. W. Norton, 1982.

Modleski, Tania. *Loving with a Vengeance: Mass-Produced Fantasies for Women*. New York: Methuen, 1984.

——, ed. *Studies in Entertainment: Critical Approaches to Mass Culture*. Bloomington: Indiana University Press, 1986.

Moers, Ellen. *Literary Women*. Garden City, N.Y.: Doubleday, 1977.

Moglen, Helene. *Charlotte Brontë: The Self Conceived*. New York: W. W. Norton, 1976.

Montgomery, Jill D. "The Return of Masochistic Behavior in the Absence of the Analyst." In Montgomery and Greif, eds. 29–36.

Montgomery, Jill D., and Ann C. Greif, eds. *Masochism: The Treatment of Self-Inflicted Suffering*. Madison, Conn.: International Universities Press, 1989.

Morgan, Robin. "The Politics of Sado-Masochistic Fantasy." In Linden et al., eds. 109–23.

Morrison, Toni. *Sula*. New York: Plume/New American, 1973.

——. *Tar Baby*. New York: Knopf, 1981.

Mulvey, Laura. "Visual Pleasure and Narrative Cinema." *Screen* 16.3 (1975): 6–18.

Mussell, Kay. "'But Why Do They Read Those Things?': The Female Audience and the Gothic Novel." In Fleenor, ed. 57–68.

Napier, Elizabeth. *The Failure of Gothic: Problems of Disjunction in an Eighteenth-Century Literary Form*. New York: Oxford University Press, 1987.

Naylor, Gloria. *Linden Hills*. New York: Penguin Books, 1985.

——. *The Women of Brewster Place*. New York: Penguin Books, 1983.

Neely, Carol Thomas. "Alternative Women's Discourse." *Tulsa Studies in Women's Literature* 4.2 (1985): 315–22.

Nierenberg, Harry H. "A Case of Voyeurism." *Samiksa* 4 (1950): 140–66.

Novick, Jack, and Kerry Kelly Novick. "Beating Fantasies in Children." *International Journal of Psycho-analysis* 53 (1972): 237–42.

Nunberg, Herman. *Curiosity*. New York: International Universities Press, 1961.

Nussbaum, Felicity, and Laura Brown, eds. *The New Eighteenth Century*. New York: Methuen, 1987.

Olsen, Tillie. *Silences*. New York: Delta, 1978.

Parkin, Alan. "On Masochistic Enthralment: A Contribution to the Study of Moral Masochism." *International Journal of Psycho-analysis* 61 (1980): 307–14.

Person, Ethel Spector. *Dreams of Love and Fateful Encounters: The Power of Romantic Passion*. New York: W. W. Norton, 1988.

——. "Some New Observations on the Origins of Femininity." In Strouse, ed. 250–61.

Peterson, Carla L. *The Determined Reader: Gender and Culture in the Novel from Napoleon to Victoria*. New Brunswick, N.J.: Rutgers University Press, 1987.

Poovey, Mary. *The Proper Lady and the Woman Writer: Ideology as Style in the Works of Mary Wollstonecraft, Mary Shelley, and Jane Austen*. Chicago: University of Chicago Press, 1984.

——. *Uneven Development: The Ideological Work of Gender in Mid-Victorian England*. Chicago: University of Chicago Press, 1988.

Prager, Emily. "A Visit from the Footbinder." *A Visit from the Footbinder and Other Stories*. New York: Berkeley/Simon & Schuster, 1982. 1–33.

Praz, Mario. *The Romantic Agony*. 2d ed. 1951. New York: Oxford University Press, 1970.

Punter, David. *The Literature of Terror: A History of Gothic Fictions from 1765 to the Present Day*. London: Longman, 1980.

Rabine, Leslie W. *Reading the Romantic Heroine: Text, History, Ideology*. Ann Arbor: University of Michigan Press, 1985.

——. "Romance in the Age of Electronics: Harlequin Enterprises." *Feminist Studies* 11 (Spring 1985): 39–60.

Radcliffe, Ann. *The Italian or the Confessional of the Black Penitents: A Romance*. 1797. New York: Oxford University Press, 1968.

——. *The Mysteries of Udolpho*. 1794. New York: Oxford University Press, 1970.

Radford, Jean, ed. *The Progress of Romance: The Politics of Popular Fiction*. New York: Methuen, 1987.

Radway, Janice A. *Reading the Romance: Women, Patriarchy, and Popular Culture*. Chapel Hill: University of North Carolina Press, 1984.

Railo, Eino. *The Haunted Castle: A Study of the Elements of English Romanticism*. New York: E. P. Dutton, 1927.

Réage, Pauline. *Return to the Château*. New York: Grove Press, 1971.

——. *Story of O*. Trans. Sabine d'Estrée. 1954. New York: Ballantine, 1965.

Reik, Theodor. *Masochism and Modern Man*. Trans. Margaret H. Beigel and Gertrud M. Kurth. New York: Farrar & Rinehart, 1941.

Restuccia, Frances L. "Female Gothic Writing: 'Under Cover to Alice.'" *Genre* 18 (1986): 245–66.

Rhys, Jean. *Wide Sargasso Sea*. 1966. New York: W. W. Norton, 1982.

Rich, Adrienne. *On Lies, Secrets, and Silence: Selected Prose 1966–1978*. New York: W. W. Norton, 1979.

Richardson, Samuel. *Clarissa*. 1748. New York: Houghton Mifflin, 1962.

Roazen, Paul. *Helene Deutsch: A Psychoanalyst's Life*. Garden City, N.Y.: Anchor/Doubleday, 1985.

Robertiello, Robert. "Masochism and the Female Sexual Role." *Journal of Sex Research* 6 (1970): 56–58.

Roberts, Bette. *The Gothic Romance: Its Appeal to Women Writers and Readers in the Eighteenth Century*. New York: Arno Press, 1980.

Robinson, Lillian. *Sex, Class, and Culture*. Bloomington: Indiana University Press, 1978.

Ronald, Ann. "Terror-Gothic: Nightmare and Dream in Ann Radcliffe and Charlotte Brontë". In Fleenor, ed. 176–86.

Rose, Gilbert J. *Trauma and Mastery in Life and Art*. New Haven, Conn.: Yale University Press, 1987.

Rose, Jacqueline. *Sexuality in the Field of Vision*. New York: Verso, 1986.

Rosenfeld, Herbert A. "On Masochism: A Theoretical and Clinical Approach." In Glick and Meyers, eds. 151–74.

Rowe, Karen E. "'Fairy-born and human-bred': Jane Eyre's Education in Romance." In Abel, Hirsch, and Langland, eds. 69–89.

Russ, Joanna. "Somebody's Trying to Kill Me and I Think It's My Husband: The Modern Gothic." In Fleenor, ed. 31–56.

——. "Souls." 1981. In *Extra(ordinary) People*. New York: St. Martin's Press, 1984. 1–59.

Sacher-Masoch, Leopold von. *Venus in Furs*. c. 1870. Trans. Uwe Mueller and Laura Lindgren. New York: Blast Books, 1989.

Sack, Robert L., and Warren Miller. "Masochism: A Clinical and Theoretical Overview." *Psychiatry* 38 (1975): 244–57.

Sacksteder, James L. "Thoughts on the Positive Value of a Negative Identity." In Montgomery and Greif, eds. 37–49.

Sackville-West, Vita. *The Dark Island*. 1934. Garden City, N.Y.: Doubleday, Doran, 1936.

Sadoff, Dianne F. *Monsters of Affection: Dickens, Eliot, and Brontë on Fatherhood*. Baltimore: Johns Hopkins University Press, 1982.

Sandiford, Keith. "Gothic and Intertextual Constructions in *Linden Hills*." Forthcoming, *Arizona Quarterly*.

Scarborough, Dorothy. *The Supernatural in Modern English Fiction*. New York: G. P. Putnam's, 1917.

Schad-Somers, Susanne P. *Sadomasochism: Etiology and Treatment*. New York: Human Sciences Press, 1982.

Schafer, Roy. "Those Wrecked by Success." In Glick and Meyers, eds. 81–91.

Scheman, Naomi. "Missing Mothers/Desiring Daughters: Framing the Sight of Women." *Critical Inquiry* 15 (Autumn 1988): 62–89.

Schmideberg, Melitta. "On Fantasies of Being Beaten." *Psychoanalytic Review* 35 (1948): 303–8.

Scott, Sarah. *Millenium* [*sic*] *Hall*. 1762. New York: Penguin/Virago, 1986.

Sedgwick, Eve Kosofsky. *Between Men: English Literature and Male Homosocial Desire*. New York: Columbia University Press, 1985.

———. *The Coherence of Gothic Conventions*. 2d ed. New York: Methuen, 1986.

———. "A Poem Is Being Written." *Representations* 17 (Winter 1987): 110–43.

Shainess, Natalie. *Sweet Suffering: Woman as Victim*. New York: Bobbs-Merrill, 1984.

Showalter, Elaine. *A Literature of Their Own: British Women Novelists from Brontë to Lessing*. Princeton, N.J.: Princeton University Press, 1977.

———, ed. *The New Feminist Criticism: Essays on Women, Literature, and Theory*. New York: Random House/Pantheon, 1985.

Silverman, Kaja. *The Acoustic Mirror: The Female Voice in Psychoanalysis and Cinema*. Bloomington: Indiana University Press, 1988.

———. "Fragments of a Fashionable Discourse." In Modleski, ed. 139–52.

———. "*Histoire d'O*: The Construction of a Female Subject." In Vance, ed. 320–49.

Sinclair, May. "The Flaw in the Crystal." In *Uncanny Stories*. 81–205.

———. "The Nature of the Evidence." In *Uncanny Stories*. 209–36.

———. *Uncanny Stories*. New York: Macmillan, 1923.

Singer, Marie B. "Fantasies of a Borderline Patient." Vol. 15. *The Psychoanalytic Study of the Child*. New York: International Universities Press, 1960. 310–56.

Smedley, Agnes. *Daughter of Earth*. 1923. New York: Feminist Press, 1987.

Snitow, Ann Barr. "Mass Market Romance: Pornography for Women Is Different." *Radical History Review* 20 (Spring/Summer 1979): 140–61.

Socarides, C. W. "The Demonified Mother: A Study of Voyeurism and Sexual Sadism." *International Review of Psycho-analysis* 1 (1974): 187–95.

Sontag, Susan. "The Pornographic Imagination." *A Susan Sontag Reader*. New York: Farrar Straus Giroux, 1982. 205–33.

Spacks, Patricia Meyer. *The Female Imagination*. New York: Avon/Discus, 1975.

Spector, Robert Donald. *Seven Masterpieces of Gothic Horror*. New York: Bantam, 1963.

Spengler, Andreas. "Manifest Sadomasochism of Males: Results of an Empirical Study." In Weinberg and Kamel, eds. 57–72.

Staal, Frits. *Exploring Mysticism: A Methodological Study*. Berkeley: University of California Press, 1975.

Stekel, Wilhelm. *Sadism and Masochism: The Psychology of Hatred and Cruelty*. Trans. Louise Brink. 2 vols. 1929. New York: Washington Square Press, 1968.

Stewart, Susan. "The Marquis de Meese." *Critical Inquiry* 15 (Autumn 1988): 162–92.

Stoller, Robert J. *Observing the Erotic Imagination*. New Haven, Conn.: Yale University Press, 1985.

——. *Perversion: The Erotic Forum of Hatred*. New York: Random House/Pantheon, 1975.

——. *Presentations of Gender*. New Haven, Conn.: Yale University Press, 1985.

——. *Sex and Gender*. 2 vols. Vol. 1: *The Development of Masculinity and Femininity*; Vol. 2: *The Transsexual Experiment*. New York: Jason Aronson, 1975.

——. *Sexual Excitement: Dynamics of Erotic Life*. New York: Random House/Pantheon, 1979.

Strouse, Jean, ed. *Women and Analysis: Dialogue on Psychoanalytic Views of Femininity*. Boston: G. K. Hall, 1985.

Summers, Montague. *The Gothic Quest: A History of the Gothic Novel*. 1938. New York: Russell & Russell, 1964.

Symonds, Alexandra. "Violence against Women—The Myth of Masochism." *American Journal of Psychotherapy* 33.2 (1979): 161–73.

Thompson, Clara. "Cultural Pressures in the Psychology of Women." 1942. In *On Women*. Ed. Maurice R. Green. New York: Meridian/New American Library, 1971. 125–41.

Thompson, James. "Surveillance in William Godwin's *Caleb Williams*." In *Gothic Fictions: Prohibition/Transgression*. Ed. Kenneth Graham. New York: AMS Press, 1989.

Treichler, Paula A. "Escaping the Sentence: Diagnosis and Discourse in 'The Yellow Wallpaper.'" *Tulsa Studies in Women's Literature* 3.1–2 (1984): 61–77.

——. "The Wall behind the Yellow Wallpaper: Response on Carol Neely and Karen Ford." *Tulsa Studies in Women's Literature* 4.2 (1985): 323–30.

Ulman, Richard B., and Doris Brothers. *The Shattered Self: A Psychoanalytic Study of Trauma*. Hillsdale, N.J.: Analytic Press, 1988.

Underhill, Evelyn. *Mysticism: A Study in the Nature and Development of Man's Spiritual Consciousness*. 1911. New York: E. P. Dutton, 1961.

Vance, Carol, ed. *Pleasure and Danger: Exploring Female Sexuality*. Boston: Routledge & Kegan Paul, 1984.

Varma, Devendra P. *The Gothic Flame*. London: Arthur Barker, 1957.

Varnado, S. L. *Haunted Presence: The Numinous in Gothic Fiction*. Tuscaloosa: University of Alabama Press, 1987.

Vincent, Sybil Korff. "The Mirror and the Cameo: Margaret Atwood's Comic/Gothic Novel, *Lady Oracle*." In Fleenor, ed. 153–63.

Von Armin, Elizabeth. *Vera*. 1921. London: Virago Press, 1983.

Wagner, Sally Roesche. "Pornography and the Sexual Revolution: The Backlash of Sadomasochism." In Linden et al., eds. 23–44.

Waites, Elizabeth A. "Female Masochism and the Enforced Restriction of Choice." *Victimology* 2 (1977–78): 535–44.

Walker, Alice. *The Color Purple*. New York: Pocket Books/Washington Square Press, 1982.

——. *In Love and Trouble: Stories of Black Women*. New York: Harvest/Harcourt Brace Jovanovich, 1973.

——. *In Search of Our Mothers' Gardens*. New York: Harcourt Brace Jovanovich, 1983.

——. "A Letter of the Times, or Should This Sado-Masochism Be Saved?" In Linden et al., eds. 205–9.

——. "Really, *Doesn't* Crime Pay?" In *In Love and Trouble*. 10–23.

——. "Roselily." In *In Love and Trouble*. 3–9.

——. *The Temple of My Familiar*. New York: Harcourt Brace Jovanovich, 1989.

——. *The Third Life of Grange Copeland*. New York: Harvest/Harcourt Brace Jovanovich, 1970.

Walker, Lenore. "Battered Women and Learned Helplessness." *Victimology* 2 (1977–78): 525–34.

Walpole, Horace. *The Castle of Otranto*. 1765. In *Seven Masterpieces of Gothic Horror*. Ed. Robert Donald Spector. New York: Bantam Books, 1963. 13–102.

Walpole, Hugh. "Mrs. Lunt." 1926. In *The Ghost Book: Sixteen Stories of the Uncanny*. Ed. Cynthia Asquith. New York: Beagle Books, 1971. 127–42.

Webbink, Patricia. *The Power of the Eyes*. New York: Springer, 1986.

Weinberg, Thomas. "Sadism and Masochism: Sociological Perspectives." In Weinberg and Kamel, eds. 99–112.

Weinberg, Thomas, and Gerhard Falk. "The Social Organization of Sadism and Masochism." In Weinberg and Kamel, eds. 149–61.

Weinberg, Thomas, and G. W. Levi Kamel, eds. *S & M: Studies in Sadomasochism*. Buffalo, N.Y.: Prometheus Press, 1983.

Weldon, Fay. *The Life and Loves of a She-Devil*. New York: Random House/Ballantine, 1983.

Wharton, Edith. *The Ghost Stories of Edith Wharton*. New York: Charles Scribner's Sons, 1973.

——. "Kerfol." 1916. In *The Ghost Stories*. 79–102.

——. "The Lady's Maid's Bell." In *The Ghost Stories*. 5–26.

——. "Mr. Jones." In *The Ghost Stories*. 169–97.

——. "Pomegranate Seed." In *The Ghost Stories*. 199–230.

Wiesenfarth, Joseph. *Gothic Manners and the Classic English Novel*. Madison: University of Wisconsin Press, 1988.

Williams, Carolyn. "Closing the Book: The Intertextual End of *Jane Eyre*." In *Victorian Connections*. Ed. Jerome McGann. Charlottesville, Va.: University Press of Virginia, 1989. 60–87.

Wilt, Judith. *Ghosts of the Gothic: Austen, Eliot, Lawrence*. Princeton, N.J.: Princeton University Press, 1980.

Wolff, Cynthia Griffin. "The Radcliffean Gothic Model: A Form for Feminine Sexuality." In Fleenor, ed. 207–23.

Wollstonecraft, Mary. *Maria or the Wrongs of Women*. 1792. New York: W. W. Norton, 1975.

Woolf, Virginia. *A Room of One's Own*. 1929. New York: Harcourt Brace Jovanovich, 1957.

Young-Bruehl, Elisabeth. *Anna Freud: A Biography*. New York: Summit Books, 1988.

Index

Abraham, Karl, 57
Abuse
  as proof of existence/love, 84, 96, 99–106
  victim's replication of, 43, 47
  of women as "normal," 102–3
  See also Masochism; Oppression; Punishment; Sadism; Suffering; Trauma
Active drives
  and anal stage, 42, 77–83, 92
  assigned to other, 93n23
  in C. Brontë, 193, 195, 200–201
  in children, 96n27
  in du Maurier, 148–57, 163–77, 188–90
  education in uses of, 239–40
  girl's reversal and rechanneling of, 42, 74–85, 93–106
  and resisting the Gothic, 240–50
  use of self as object, 74–80, 84
  and will to mastery, 104
  See also Anal stage; Instincts; Repression; Sublimation; *entries for individual instincts*
Adams, Maurianne, 193n1, 225n16, 234n21, 236n22
Adler, Alfred, 58n22
Agency
  achieved through masochism, 44–45, 47–49
  in Gilman, 34
  and Gothic "script," 47
  See also Autonomy
Aggression
  in Atwood, 241, 256, 258, 260, 264
  in C. Brontë, 195, 196, 202–08, 227–31
  in Dinesen, 242–43, 270–73
  in Naylor, 244–50
  and resistance, 240–50

turned upon self, 74–83, 85n12
  See also Active drives; Instincts; Punishment; Sadism
Ainsworth, William, "The Spectre Bride," 23–25
Alcott, Louisa May, 266n15
  Behind a Mask: or, A Woman's Power, 251n7
  Jack and Jill, 252n8
  Little Women, 252n8
  The Marble Woman, 252, 265, 266n16
  Rose in Bloom, 252n8
  See also Barnard, A. M.
Allen, David, 53
Alternatives to the Gothic, 264–74, 265n14
  in C. Brontë, 232
  in Dinesen, 272
  in feminist detective fiction, 273
  in feminist science fiction, 273–74
  See also Genre; Gothic; Repetition compulsion, ending
Altruism, 42, 96–99
  and altruistic aggression, 243–44; in C. Brontë, 206, 235; in Dinesen, 270
  and altruistic surrender, 80n9, 96–99
  See also Sublimation
Anal stage, 74, 77–83
  cloaca theory, 79–80
  and eroticism, 78n4, 79n6
  father's role in, 65–66, 71–72
  and gift, 79–80
  girl's regression to, 86
  See also Active drives; Instincts; Masochism
Andersen, Hans Christian, 257
Anne of Swansea (a.k.a. Julia Anne Curtis), "The Unknown!" 23–25

Reading Women Writing

A SERIES EDITED BY
Shari Benstock and Celeste Schenck

Library of Congress Cataloging-in-Publication Data

Massé, Michelle A. (Michelle Annette), 1951–
   In the name of love : women, masochism, and the Gothic / Michelle A. Massé.
     p.   cm. — (Reading women writing)
   Includes bibliographical references and index.
   ISBN 0-8014-2616-2 (cloth : alk. paper). — ISBN 0-8014-9918-6 (paper : alk. paper)
    1. Gothic revival (Literature)   2. American fiction—Women authors—History and
criticism.   3. English fiction—Women authors—History and criticism.   4. Horror
tales, American—History and criticism.   5. Horror tales, English—History and
criticism.   6. Psychoanalysis and literature.   7. Women—Books and reading.
8. Masochism in literature.   9. Marriage in literature.   10. Women in literature.
11. Love in literature.   I. Title.   II. Series.
PS374.G68M37   1992
809.3'872909353—dc20

91-55552